ARABS IN THE JEWISH STATE

Modern Middle East Series, No. 6

*Sponsored by the Center for Middle Eastern Studies
The University of Texas at Austin*

Arabs in the Jewish State

Israel's Control of a National Minority

by Ian Lustick

UNIVERSITY OF TEXAS PRESS, AUSTIN AND LONDON

Requests for permission to reproduce material from this work should be sent
to Permissions, University of Texas Press, Box 7819, Austin, Texas 78712.

Grateful acknowledgment is made to the following for permission to reprint
previously published material:

Croom Helm Ltd, Publishers, for portions of "The Quiescent Palestinians:
The System of Control over Arabs in Israel," from *Sociology of the
Palestinians*, edited by K. Nakhleh and E. Zureik (1979).

The London School of Economics and Political Science, for "Zionism and the
State of Israel: Regime Goals and the Arab Minority in the First Years of
Statehood," *Middle Eastern Studies* (1980) (reprinted, with modifications, as
Chapter 2 of this book).

University Press of America, for portions of "Political Mobilization among
Israeli Arabs," from *The Mobilization of Collective Identity: Comparative
Perspectives*, edited by Ann Cottrell, Jeffrey Ross, and Robert St.-Cyr (1980).

World Politics, for portions of "Stability in Deeply Divided Societies:
Consociationalism versus Control," *World Politics* 31, no. 3 (April 1979).

Library of Congress Cataloging in Publication Data
Lustick, Ian, 1949–
    Arabs in the Jewish State.

    (Modern Middle East series; no. 6)
    Based on the author's thesis, University of California, Berkeley.
    Bibliography: p.
    Includes index.
    1. Palestinian Arabs—Israel.   2. Israel—Politics and government.
3. Minorities—Israel.   I. Title.   II. Series: Modern Middle East series
(Austin, Tex.); no. 6.
DS113.7.L87   1980   323.1'19'2705694   79-22311
ISBN 0-292-70347-3 (cloth)
ISBN 0-292-70348-1 (paper)

לכל המשפחה

Contents

MAPS

FIGURES

TABLES

Preface

I am deeply aware of the sensitive nature of the matters analyzed in this book. All my life I have been involved, as a participant, leader, and resource person, in Jewish and Zionist organizations. Because of my upbringing, my emotional commitments, and my involvement in Jewish affairs, I know from the inside—from inside myself and from inside the Jewish community—the painful issues which serious consideration of Jewish-Arab relations in Israel raises. Study of this problem and public discussion of it are difficult for those who love Israel and who are deeply concerned for the country's future.

However, harmonious relations between Jewish and Arab Israelis and the long-run security of the Jewish state require a thorough understanding of the problem of the Arab minority and a rejection of taboos on its discussion. Published material can always be misused and quoted out of context. This book may indeed provide ammunition for groups with which I strongly disagree. But this should not deprive those genuinely concerned for the welfare of Jews and Arabs in Israel of analysis which clarifies the basic issues, provides the facts necessary to clear the air of myth, and sets the stage for constructive proposals for the future of majority-minority relations. These are among the purposes of this book.

Field research for this study was carried out from July 1973 to June 1974 and in the summer of 1977. The project was made possible by a grant from the University Consortium for World Order Studies. Financial support for the preparation of the manuscript from the Danforth Foundation and from Dartmouth College is gratefully acknowledged. I would also like to express my appreciation to the Hebrew University in Jerusalem for use of library facilities; to the Institute for the Documentation of Israeli Society, also in Jerusalem, for the use of its files; to the *Jerusalem Post* for access to the newspaper's morgue; and to the Institute of International Studies at the University of California, Berkeley, for important administrative assistance. I would like to extend a special thanks to Mrs. Sylvia Landress, director of the Jewish Agency Library and Zionist Archives in New York, and to her staff, for their courtesy, their efficiency, and their good cheer.

A large number of people provided useful comments on preliminary drafts of the manuscript. In this regard I am especially appreciative of the encouragement and the guidance afforded me by Professors Robert Price, Ernst Haas, Don Peretz, and David Laitin. I would also like to thank Donna Norvell, Roxie Roberts, Barbara Pryce, and Janet Allen for typing the final draft. Most of all I would like to express my deepest appreciation to Hasan Dgheim, Michael Cantos, Jalal Abu-Tama, and the hundreds of Jewish and Arab Israelis who opened their homes and their offices to me. Their hospitality was generous, their patience inexhaustible, and their kindness sufficient to convince anyone that Israel and Israelis are worth worrying about.

I.L.
March 1979

ARABS IN THE JEWISH STATE

I.

The Quiescence of Israeli Arabs: Explaining Stability in a Deeply Divided Society

The rise of communal assertiveness in scores of "national" political arenas must certainly be seen as one of the broadest, strongest, and most interesting sociopolitical trends to have developed since World War II. Regardless of what elements—racial, linguistic, religious, ethnic, or otherwise—are used in the formulation of group identity, the restless discontent of many such groups with the conditions of their existence has led to powerful demands for change.[1] Variations on the theme of communal strife are abundant and are to be found in "transitional" as well as industrialized societies. In some countries, such as Iraq, Nigeria, Pakistan, Cyprus, and Lebanon, ethnic discontent has erupted into full-scale armed conflict. Elsewhere, as in Sri Lanka (Ceylon), Northern Ireland, and Malaysia, bitter rivalries between communal groups have led to recurrent waves of rioting and terrorism. In Spain, Canada, Belgium, Great Britain, and the United States, ethnic groups have attracted world-wide attention to their struggles for greater cultural expression, economic development, and/or political autonomy.

Common to political life in all these countries has been the central place occupied by communally based conflict. In nearly every case cited above, fights between communally organized groups have been highly visible and have produced the society's most fiercely contested issues. Communally based confrontation in these countries has generated more serious threats to internal order and political stability than any other type of domestic discontent.

Such turbulence has not gone unnoticed by social scientists. The extreme divisiveness of these conflicts and their seeming intractability clash with long-cherished notions of pluralist harmony through crosscutting cleavages.[2] In the last fifteen years political scientists as well as sociologists and anthropologists have shown particular interest in the etiology of ethnic discontent, the dynamics of ethnic conflict, and the implications of communal assertiveness for problems of "national integration" and the development and maintenance of democratic institutions. The persistence of politically significant communal cleavages and their intensification, in the context of economic development, social mobilization, and other components of "modernization," have led many to reconsider the long-run viability of the nation-state as an acceptable political formula for multinational or multiethnic societies.[3] Indeed, by the early 1970's the assumption of the politicization of communal identities in modern and modernizing societies had all but supplanted previous assumptions that such "primitive" emotional ties would be surrendered relatively quickly and easily as a result of urbanization, rational norms of economic development, and various movements of "national integration."[4] Thus Samuel Huntington, for example, argued that "Ethnic or religious groups which had lived side by side in traditional society become aroused to violent conflict as a result of the interaction, the tension, the inequalities generated by social and economic modernization."[5] Robert Melson and Harold Wolpe have offered several propositions, based on a study of Nigeria, that directly link increasing communal antagonisms to social mobilization, modernization, and political development. For example: "In a culturally plural society, the competition engendered by social mobilization will tend to be defined in communal terms." "Differential rates of mobilization among communal groups exacerbate communal conflict by multiplying coincident social cleavages." "Political institutions which encourage the participation of the masses in the recruitment of leaders tend to further politicize and intensify communal conflict."[6]

Enloe has suggested that the resurgence of ethnicity in the industrialized West is to be understood as a natural response to the alienating complexity and abstractness of modern society.[7] Alvin Rabushka and Kenneth Shepsle predict that in the absence of important crosscutting cleavages, culturally diverse and democratic nation-states will inevitably develop intense communal conflicts which will dominate the political arena and result in chronic instability.[8]

In light of such arguments regarding the likelihood of aggravated ethnic conflict in modernizing as well as modernized societies, concern has increasingly been directed toward the problem of "managing" or "regulating" conflict in "plural" or "deeply divided" societies. For if intense conflicts are to be expected in communally segmented societies, then political systems operating within such units and demonstrating stability and effectiveness require analysis and explanation. Accordingly, several authors have undertaken to explain the stability and effectiveness of political systems in certain segmented societies, such as Austria, Switzerland, and the Netherlands, by focusing on the cooperative behavior of subculture elites. The "consociational" approach to ethnic politics, as put forward most notably by Arend Lijphart, stresses the crucial role of these elites, through whose deliberate efforts vituperative competition is avoided, accommodation achieved, and the integrity of the political system as a whole preserved.[9] Similarly, Donald Rothchild has argued against those who see conflict and instability as inherent in plural societies by drawing attention to the ameliorative potential of interethnic bargaining in the context of an overall "spirit of reciprocity."[10] In *Conflict Regulation in Divided Societies*, Eric Nordlinger suggests six "conflict-regulating practices." The six are stable coalition, the proportionality principle, depoliticization, the mutual veto, compromise, and concessions.[11] Nordlinger's major thesis is that in the absence of one or more of these practices an "open" but deeply divided society will experience intense conflict among its segments.[12] Sidney Verba has observed that intense conflict among plural subcultures in various European democracies has been avoided by means of a protective compartmentalization of those subcultures. Such policies, he writes, may work best "where governmental aspirations are low . . . if politics involves the resolution of grievances." But he cautions that "when elites see their task as the transformation of a society in fundamental ways" pluralist protection is likely to give way to "the next stage . . . repression."[13]

The Case of Israel

Now Israel would seem to be fated for just the sort of severe ethnic disturbances which are anticipated by these analysts and which have developed in scores of countries around the world. Israel is deeply divided along congruent ethnic, religious, linguistic, and cultural lines between a Jewish majority and an Arab minority of approximately 14 percent.[14] Israel is, officially, an open and democratic society whose citizens are equal before the law and whose laws do not discriminate with regard to religion or nationality.[15] There is universal adult suffrage and, in fact, Israeli Arabs vote in higher proportions than do Jewish Israelis. In addition there are a multitude of active political parties which vie intensely for both Arab and Jewish votes during regularly held elections to the Knesset.

Yet in thirty years of the state's existence Israeli Arabs have not succeeded in forming an independent Arab political party which could appeal to the communal sentiments of the minority and exert itself on behalf of Arab rights and Arab opinion in Israel. Not only has no Arab political party developed, but no significant independent Arab social, economic, cultural, or professional organizations have been formed; there are no independent Arab newspapers; no Arab leaders of national stature have emerged; no Israeli-Arab terrorist organizations have crystallized; and there have been only scattered instances of protests or demonstrations. The communist-organized general strike on March 30, 1976, in which approximately 20–25 percent of the Arab work force participated, was by far the largest "mass action" of Arab citizens in Israel's history.[16] Indeed, far from being an issue which has dominated the political arena and resulted in chronic instability, the communal segmentation of Israeli society has been of almost no serious political consequence. Seldom have issues directly concerning Israel's Arab community attracted more than the passing interest of the Israeli media or the Jewish public. The wide gaps between Jews and Arabs in standards of living, occupational distributions, educational standards, and social status have failed to emerge as significant, let alone central, concerns of the Israeli political system.[17] Writing in 1975 in *Davar*, the official organ of the Labor Party–controlled Histadrut (General Federation of Israeli Workers), one Israeli journalist observed that "during the last decade there has been no discussion in the Cabinet on the subject of the Israeli Arabs."[18] A major text concerning the Arab-Israeli conflict, published in 1972, included a lengthy section in which Israel's domestic political structure and problems were discussed. The piece, written by one of the foremost scholars in the field, contained no mention whatsoever of Israel's Arab minority.[19]

In light of the contemporary experience of many other countries, the fact that the deep communal division of Israeli society has not emerged as a salient political issue is quite remarkable. How, indeed, is the striking political quiescence of Israel's Arab minority to be explained? Certainly not according to "traditional" pluralist theory. For historical reasons which I shall discuss in subsequent chapters, there are few if any crosscutting cleavages which might encourage Arabs and Jews to see each other as allies on specific instrumental issues. Nor is the consociational approach of assistance in the Israeli case. There simply does not exist an elite cartel within which leaders of the Jewish and Arab communal groups engage in quiet ethnic bargaining and careful apportionment of social, political, and economic resources. Neither can the absence of ethnic strife be ascribed to the implementation of one or more of Nordlinger's six "conflict-regulating practices." Though almost every aspect of Jewish-Arab relations in Israel has been politicized, no "stable governing coalition" of Jewish and Arab political parties has ever formed "with the avowed aim of conflict regulation." Arabs have not been given a veto over policies affecting their affairs. The "principle of proportionality" has never been used to distribute appointive positions to Jews and Arabs involving mutual adjustment on a single issue, nor have trade-offs on several issues taken place. Nor, finally, have "concessions" been made by the stronger Jewish communal group to the Arab minority.[20]

What makes this case especially puzzling is that there are powerful reasons for one to expect that, in Israel, the politics of ethnicity would be particularly salient and particularly difficult to "regulate." Strong irredentism on the part of Israel's neighbors, constant propaganda from Arab capitals, and strong bonds of kinship and national identity between Israeli Arabs and Arabs (including Palestinian refugees) across the border encourage feelings of alienation among the Arab minority in Israel and militate against its integration.[21] In addition, contact between Jews and Arabs, at least in the economic sphere, has been heavy and the rate of social mobilization, as measured by literacy and growth in the urban work force, has been high in both the Jewish and Arab sectors. Furthermore, politics in Israel has *not* been characterized, in Verba's terms, by the "resolution of grievances —satisfying the demands of a few groups here and there as social conditions demand."[22] While introducing the program of his government to the First Knesset in March 1949, Prime Minister David Ben-Gurion declared: "The establishment of the State of Israel was merely the first stage in the fulfillment of our historic vision. The ingathering of the exiles is a prerequisite to its full realization." [23] In pursuit of that vision, the prime minister continued: "The Government of Israel must be positive and dynamic. It must initiate, control, encourage, plan, direct, and push forward in every sphere of economic, cultural, and social life."[24] Indeed, under the leadership of such stalwart Zionists as David Ben-Gurion, Moshe Sharett, Levi Eshkol, Golda Meir, Yitzhak Rabin, and Menachem Begin, the Israeli regime has very definitely sought what Verba refers to as the "transformation of the society in fundamental ways."[25] From the very establishment of the state in 1948, Israeli leaders embarked upon an explicit and systematic implementation of the basic tenets of Zionist ideology—mass Jewish immigration or "the ingathering of the exiles" (*kibbutz galuiot*), "redemption of the land" through intensive Jewish agricultural settlement (*geulat haaretz*), the "Judaization of the Galilee" (*Yehud ha-Galil*), the consolidation of a Jewish proletariat (*avoda ivrit*), and so forth. According to Verba such dynamic regime objections are very likely to lead to violation of the positions of minority subcultures and their active resistance.

Finally, the expropriation of land owned by Israeli Arabs[26] and the wide, generally stable gaps between Arab and Jewish standards of living would seem to provide strong social, economic, and emotional incentives for the politicization of the Arab minority. The following statistics are intended to provide some indication of the objective socioeconomic gaps that have prevailed between Jews and Arabs in Israel. Table 1 compares the average gross annual income of families of Jewish and non-Jewish (i.e., Arab) urban employees.[27] Since the figures provided reflect the total income of an urban family it is important to note

Table 1. Average Gross Annual Income per Urban Employee's
Family (in Israeli Lira)

Year	Jews	Non-Jews
1967	9,400	7,000
1968	9,600	7,000
1969	10,500	8,400
1970	11,900	8,100
1971	12,900	8,600
1972	15,500	11,200
1973	17,600	14,900
1974	26,600	23,200
1975	31,500	29,300
1976	49,100	42,400

that an average urban Arab family during this period was approximately 45 percent larger than an average urban Jewish family. Official statistics available for 1975/1976 reveal that the average per capita income among Arabs living in urban areas was I£ 572, while per capita Jewish income in these same areas was I£ 1,687.[28] Figures are not readily available which compare non-urban incomes over time. This is particularly unfortunate in view of the fact that the large majority of the Arab population lives in areas classified as rural (compared to a small minority of the Jewish population). However, a survey sponsored by the Histadrut in thirty villages during 1969 revealed an average annual income per family of only I£ 3,910.[29] According to a 1971 study by an Israeli scholar concerning ethnic aspects of income inequality in Israel, the average income of Jewish families was found to be I£ 12,900, while that of Arab families was I£ 8,600.[30]

However, although the presence of objective deprivation may provide a rationale for political action, and although various circumstances—such as the irredentism of Israel's Arab neighbors, rapid socioeconomic change, and a dynamic self-actualizing regime—may reinforce one's expectation of ethnic conflict, in and of themselves they do not imply, even in the context of an open, democratic political system, that members of a subordinate group will see themselves as deprived or decide to take political action in order to improve their lot. The absence of ethnic strife in Israel, the lack of independent Arab political organization and activity, and the overall low visibility of the ethnicity issue appear anomalous only if, and to the extent that, Arabs have been dissatisfied with their place in the society and antagonisms between Jews and Arabs have been intense.

To pose effectively the problem of the political quiescence of communal relations in Israel it is therefore especially important to demonstrate that Arabs in Israel have been greatly dissatisfied with the conditions of their existence. Now, since part of what I wish to explain is the absence of an accepted Arab leadership of national stature—one that could be expected to articulate and represent the grievances of Israeli Arabs—I perforce cannot rely on the pronouncements of various leaders in order to prove that Israeli Arabs have felt dissatisfied.[31] Rather, information concerning the intensity of discontent experienced by Arabs in Israel over the last thirty years must of necessity come from diverse sources.

Arab Discontent in Israel

Unfortunately, there have been very few systematic surveys of Arab public opinion in Israel. The Israel Institute for Applied Social Research, for instance, which conducts sophisticated and continuous surveys of Israeli public opinion, has directed its attention primarily to Israel's Jewish population. Important studies of Israeli Arab attitudes were undertaken by Yochanan Peres and his associates in 1966 and 1967. In one of their surveys 57 percent of the Israeli Arabs interviewed responded that they would feel better living in an Arab state rather than in Israel.[32] Only 31 percent were willing, unreservedly, to grant the state of Israel a right to exist.[33] When asked what they would like the future to be for Israeli Arabs, 53 percent wanted to be a separate but equal people in the state of Israel, 17 percent preferred a separate state of their own, and 19 percent hoped that an Arab state would arise in all of Palestine.[34] A more recent study, conducted in the summer of 1976, found that Arab discontent in Israel had, if anything, increased. With regard to their future, only 37 percent of those Arabs interviewed in 1976 preferred a "separate-but-equal status in Israel," while 26 percent wanted to be included in a Palestinian state alongside of Israel, and 37 percent hoped for a "democratic secular state in which Arabs and Jews would have equal rights."[35]

Newspapers are another source for appraising Arab public opinion in Israel: *al-Ittihad*—the Arabic organ of the Communist Party (estimated circulation 6,000–8,000); *al-Mirsad*—published by Mapam, a small left-wing Zionist party that has shown substantial concern for the problems of the Arab minority (estimated circulation 4,000); and *al-Yaum* (now *al-Anba*), sponsored by the government and the Histadrut (estimated circulation 5,000–6,000).[36] Ellen Geffner, who made a thorough study of editorials and columns written by Arabs in these newspapers between 1948 and 1967, observed that although the Arabs who wrote in these newspapers "had to contend with the limitations of writing for newspapers which were supported by political parties that clearly had a vested interest in the publications. . . . [they—the writers] tried to present themselves as voices of the Arabs in Israel . . ."[37] Geffner wrote that the Arab columnists of *al-Ittihad* and *al-Mirsad* "protested constantly against such phenomena as military rule and the defense regulations, expropriation of Arab lands, displacement of the Arabs, a denial of their national affiliation, etc. The tenor of their writings was consistently critical; they were alienated from the state because they believed that it denied them some of their basic rights simply because they were Arabs. They saw themselves as a repressed minority in the state—not accepted by it and in turn, not accepting it."[38]

Geffner indicated as well that the Arab writers in *al-Yaum*, whose positions were generally formulated in terms that called for cooperation between Arabs and the Israeli establishment, nonetheless demanded equal rights for Arabs, criticized the government for failing to live up to its democratic principles, and were deeply disturbed at the failure of Israel to make significant progress toward the full integration of Arabs into the state. Geffner argued that these writers did not accept the legitimacy of Israel as an inherently Jewish-Zionist state. Rather they had as their goal the thorough "Israelization" of Israel—to make of Israel a liberal, secular democratic state with full equality of

Arabs and Jews. This, noted Geffner, was in direct conflict "with prevailing Zionist ideology concerning the equal civil rights to which the Arab minority was entitled."[39]

The content of Arabic literature in Israel also casts light upon the political sentiments of the Arab population. Before 1967 Israeli Arabs were cut off from the main sources of Arab culture and Arabic literature, except for radio and television broadcasts from Cairo and Amman. Nevertheless, they have succeeded in producing a substantial amount of both poetry and prose which constitutes an important vehicle for the expression of discontent and political commitment. "The Arab author in Israel sees himself as a 'writer in arms.' His mission as an artist is, first and foremost, a social and national struggle while at the same time it is, itself, a weapon in the struggle."[40] In scores of poems and stories written by young Israeli Arabs the main themes are the tragic loss of the homeland, the plight of the refugees, the expropriation of Arab land, the economic and social discrimination practiced against Arabs, and the emotions of revolt.

Thus, Samih al-Kassem, one of the most popular Arab poets in Israel, dedicates his poem "The Imprisoned Poet" to all those "who are chained and thrown into prison's darkness for struggling for freedom and peace."

You were imprisoned,
But is it possible to imprison the spirit of defiance?
Cry unto the arrogant jailer!
Torture my body with your whips,
Paint my ribs, and my uplifted brow with my own blood,
Smash my arm and my breast you son of dogs!
For my spirit continues to march for freedom,
The rivers of rebellion wash out the walls of the conqueror.[41]

In another poem, entitled "A Speech from the Market of Unemployment," Kassem urges Israeli Arabs to follow his example, not to yield to economic intimidation or to despair in the struggle for their rights.

I may lose my salary if you wish;
I may lose my clothes and bedding;
I may work in a quarry,

As a porter or a street cleaner!
I may collapse of hunger
But no, enemy of the sun, I shall never bargain.
I shall resist until the last pulse of my veins.

You may rob me of my land;
You may waste my youth in chains;
You may burn my poems and books;
You may make my village a nightmare of terror;
But no, enemy of the sun, I shall never bargain.
I shall resist until the last pulse of my veins.[42]

The intense skepticism of Israeli Arabs toward the government is expressed in a short story by Tawfiq Muammar in which "Waterworks and electricity, the laying of roads, social welfare, sickness and old age insurance, unionization of the workers—all these are compared to the last meal served to a man condemned to death. If the government lays a highway to a distant and isolated village, in the name of progress and development, its real intent is that its officials will be able to get to the village in order to collect taxes and expropriate lands."[43]

The tone of Israeli Arab literature has grown "steadily more acrimonious."[44] In a well-known poem entitled "Identity Card" Mahmud Darwish addresses Jewish Israelis as follows:

Write down, I am an Arab!
Fifty thousand is my number,
Eight children, the ninth will come next summer.
Angry? Write down, I am an Arab!

I work with my comrades in a quarry,
Bread, clothes, and notebooks I earn
    for my eight from the rock.
I beg no alms at your door,
Nor do I feel small before you.
Angry? Write down, I am an Arab!

You stole the vineyards of my parents,
The lands I used to plough,
And left us nothing but these rocks—
Will your government take them too,
    as has been said?

Then write at the top of the page—
I hate none, attack none, but
When I hunger I'll eat the flesh of my exploiter.
Beware of my hunger,
Beware of my anger.[45]

Rashid Hussein used to be described as "moderate."[46] In a poem entitled "The Executioner" he expressed his contempt for those Israeli Arabs who collaborate with the authorities for their own personal gain.

Give me a rope, a hammer, a steel bar,
For I shall build a gallows.
Among my people a group still lingers,
That feeds on shame and walks with downcast heads.
Let's stretch their necks!
How can we keep in our midst
One who licks every palm he meets?[47]

Thus, both Arabic newspapers and Arabic literature, in addition to the limited public opinion survey data available, provide evidence of the intense discontent experienced by Israel's Arab minority. But to illustrate more concretely the deprivation felt by Israeli Arabs I shall draw upon a variety of speeches, articles, and essays, as well as published and personal interviews. On the basis of such material it is possible to gain a clearer understanding of the specific issues that have been most salient for Arabs in their confrontation with Israeli society. For purposes of illustration I shall focus on three important issues: expropriation of land, economic discrimination, and the problem facing educated Arab youth. By choosing these particular issues for illustration I do not wish to belittle the significance of other sources of Arab dissatisfaction, such as the restrictions of the Military Administration (1948–1966), social prejudice and discrimination, or the state of Arab education. An examination of these issues would only reinforce the point I wish to make concerning the breadth and intensity of Arab discontent in Israel.

Without a doubt the extensive and continuous expropriation of Arab lands has aroused the passionate antagonism of Israeli Arabs to a greater degree than any other single issue. The extreme bitterness of Arab peasants toward the government following the confiscation of agricultural land is well reflected in the text of a letter addressed to "The People of Israel and the Authorities of the State." It was written in 1950 by Arabs from a village in the northern Galilee.

In spite of the fact that many inhabitants of our village fled—we decided to remain under the protection of a righteous and democratic state which bears the standard of freedom and equality. But suddenly members of Kibbutz Shachan came and seized our level and productive lands, the lands from which our community supports itself. All that remains to us are mountainous lands from which even weeds have difficulty growing. We begged and pleaded but to no avail, and we now ask this question: We are lawful Israeli citizens—why do you deny us our rights to our lands that have now been declared abandoned lands? Is this equality, is this democracy?[48]

In 1958 a noted Arab agriculturalist in Israel characterized the land problem as follows:

The Government introduced a number of laws which did injustice to the Arab villagers and deprived them of about 1,000,000 dunams of land from which they with their families had made, though often with much difficulty, a bare living. Those laws, such as the law of uncultivated land, of closed regions, of security regions, of possession of land, and so on can have but one aim: to deprive the Arab population of land which is then transferred to Jewish ownership and use. The Arab peasant clings to his land which he considers to be his soul. He regards, therefore, the laws depriving him of his land as the bitterest injustice done to him.[49]

In the words of one Bedouin sheik, "The land expropriation and the forced expulsions without compensation or the right to return have brought the Bedouin to a situation which is difficult both psychologically and materially, and to a lack of security unlike anything they have previously known."[50]

When the lands of several villages in western Galilee were threatened with confiscation in 1963 (indeed they soon were confiscated), the village elders, with assistance from leftist Jewish groups, traveled to Tel Aviv to hold a news conference. "We are a people," they declared,

who love our earth and our country; we have remained here because we loved our land and we hoped for a friendly attitude on the part of the state's authorities. We found the opposite to be true. . . . The expropriation of 500 hectares of our farm land and our quarries, which contain the country's best stone, is a blow at our very subsistence. We see this policy as directed at taking our livelihood away from us . . .

We are not nationalists, Communists, or Nasserists, and we do not want to organize demonstrations or rebellions .. [but] why should we give our land to others? If the authorities do take away the 500 hectares our three villages will be left with but a dunam per person, and our laborers, now employed in the quarries, will have to seek daily work in Haifa and Acre instead of working in their villages and on their land . . .[51]

The expropriation of land has been particularly galling to Arabs in view of the generous allocation of land to Jews:

Arab farmers [roam] about idly in the villages, jobless and landless, although their own lands lie within a few meters from their eyes. They are debarred from ploughing and cultivating their lands. They see the Jewish kibbutzim enjoy the fruits and blessings of their land when they, the rightful owners, long to fill their empty stomachs.[52]

There is no balance between obligations and rights . . . [e.g.,] the expropriation of lands and the setting up of Jewish settlements in place of Arab settlements, all this under the heading of abandoned property, development, etc. Of course for everything there is an explanation; in this case it is that lands are expropriated for reasons of security or development. But I have not yet found an answer to the question which needles me: just why is it necessary that all this take place precisely at the expense of the property and lands of the Arab?[53]

In 1975 and 1976 an intensification of land expropriations from Arabs in the Galilee triggered a flood of protests in affected villages. In February 1976, for example, an appeal was published in a leading Hebrew newspaper by inhabitants of the Galilean villages of Sakhnin, Arrabe, Deir-Hana, and Arb el-Sawaad. "We call upon persons of conscience, and those in Israel who possess a feeling of human justice, to act with us to foil the danger hanging over us, to prevent the injustice, to revoke the decree closing Area 9 [where lands of these villages are located], and to foil the danger of our lands being expropriated—so that we are permitted to live on our lands and make our livelihood from them."[54] Even more recently expropriations have focused on the lands of the Negev Bedouin. On May 17, 1978, one Bedouin returned from work to find his home demolished and his lands threatened with expropriation.

I returned at 5:30 P.M. . . . and found my children crying. I have three children. They had left us with nothing, like wild animals. There is an apple orchard here, figs, and almonds. There was a cottage here. The court ordered me to take down the cottage. Six days ago I did, but I was not told I would have to move from here. Never has anything like this happened to us. We have lived in this area for 300 years. Now they are removing us, illegally. At least they might come with orders in writing, but not with the army and the police. I shall stay here, even if I must die here![55]

For certain categories of expropriated land the government has offered compensation in an effort to legitimize the transfers. However, these offers have been severely criticized by Israeli Arabs as being absurdly low. Moreover, as is often pointed out, once an Arab farmer accepts cash compensation for his land, even if he considers the amount of the payment to have been fair,

there is no way for him to invest his compensation payment in a productive manner guaranteeing him a livelihood. For the Arabs of Israel have no non-agricultural means of livelihood to speak of except hired labor—mainly among the Jewish population.

This means that the Arab farmer's compensation represents a non-recurrent source of income that he can use only to get himself housing or consumption goods and leaves him without means of livelihood and dependent on hired labor. There is no need to stress that among the Jews the situation is entirely different . . .[56]

In addition to the confiscation of land, economic deprivation and discrimination have been another important source of discontent among the minority population. Wage discrimination, monopolistic marketing of Arab agricultural produce by Jewish firms, heavy restrictions on Arab labor mobility until the early 1960's, poor conditions for Arab workers, refusal to allow Arabs to become members of the Histadrut until 1958, and different rates of publicly sponsored economic development for the Jewish and Arab sectors have all featured as important economic grievances of Israeli Arabs.

Elias N. Koussa was a noted Arab attorney from Haifa who kept up a steady stream of letters to the press presenting the complaints of the Arab minority until his death in 1971. In 1952 he spoke out against economic discrimination.

The policy forbidding the employment of non-Jewish labour in Jewish concerns which was persistently followed during the mandatory regime by the Jewish Agency and by other Jewish bodies contributing, to a large extent, towards the creation of a feeling of mistrust and antagonism among the Arab people of Palestine, is now being resuscitated. Arab workers in Haifa and throughout Lower Galilee are being forcibly removed from their places of work in Jewish factories and establishments to provide employment for Jewish unemployed. These and many other hardships disturb the Israeli Arabs, and go to convince them that the Government does not harbour any good intentions.[57]

Describing the mood in the Arab community, he blamed the "spread of communism, unrest, discontent, and indeed, hate" on the "inimical policy" of the authorities.[58]

The cynicism of the Arab population toward the government's economic policies in the Arab sector is well reflected in a letter from Koussa to the editor of the *Jerusalem Post* in which he comments on a Cabinet decision to equalize wages for Arabs employed by public institutions and prices for Arab agricultural products. Koussa found the statement issued to this effect by the prime minister's adviser on Arab affairs

partly unconvincing because it is difficult to believe the Adviser's assertion that "the principle of economic equality had been decided as far back as two years ago, and that it was necessary to carry this out by stages so as to avoid dislocations in the economic life of the Arab population." This is a queer and unpalatable explanation. It amounts, in effect, to the ridiculous contention that it is unjust to do justice, for while the Adviser disclosed, on the one hand, that the Government had realized, two years ago, that Arab workmen and farmers were suffering flagrant grievances from which they complained time and again, and that it had felt that these grievances should be remedied, he justified, on the other hand, the deliberate withholding of the remedy on the childish pretense that the elimination of the grievances and the improvement of the lot of these Arabs would put the economic life of the Arab community into jeopardy. . . . Perhaps, the Government and its Adviser on Arab Affairs, endowed, as they are, with a high degree of intelligence and wisdom, would enlighten them on this amazing principle of political economy . . .[59]

In the same letter Koussa addresses himself to the adviser's contention that Arabs do not pay their fair share of the tax burden, and complains that the economic inequality between Jews and Arabs could be at least partially alleviated were it not that

the Government has taken control of all Moslem wakfs, and disburses the income amounting to some I£ 180,000 in conformity with its unfettered choice and desire. The revenue of these charitable institutions which could be doubled and tripled when administered by a Moslem body, is more than sufficient to provide the Arab villagers, the over-whelming majority of whom are Moslems, with better health, educa-tion and social services than are now offered. The Government has not only failed to constitute such a body, but has actually refused to allow the Moslems to set it up. If these charitable endowments were returned to the Arabs, the lawful beneficiaries, the villagers would be provided with these services without becoming a burden, if at all, on the Jewish taxpayer.[60]

Indeed Arab desire for rapid economic development has been strong. When Ze'ev Zur, deputy minister of agriculture, made a tour of Arab villages in 1957 he found dissatisfaction with the failure of the government to aid significantly in the de-velopment of Arab villages in Israel.

Wherever Mr. Zur called, at Shfar-Am, Ibelin, Tamra, Kaboul, Rama and elsewhere, local notables presented him with long lists of requests. The Minister's party had to make up with fast driving for the long speeches at the various stops. Problems raised concerned lack of arable lands; income tax assessments; long-term loans and rates of repay-ment; olive prices; water shortages; farm training and schooling; elec-tricity; sewerage and school buildings.[61]

Most Arab villagers find work by commuting on a daily or weekly basis from their villages to Jewish metropolitan areas. This has been the trend from 1949 to the present though the flow of workers has varied according to the labor requirements of the Jewish economy. The sometimes appalling living condi-tions of Arab commuters who remain overnight in the localities where they work have served as breeding grounds of Arab dis-content. In 1961 a group of reporters visited Arab workers' liv-ing quarters in Tel Aviv to hear their complaints.

Some 3,000 Arab workers are employed in the vicinity. They go back to their villages in the "Little Triangle"—Umm al-Fahm, Arara, Jatt and others—only for the weekend.

These labourers, some of whom are 14 and 15 years old, are put up for the night in tin huts and cowsheds. . . . They are housed 50 to a cowshed, for which each of them pays I£ 10 a month, or a day's wages or more. In the tin huts, which leak in the winter rain, the "rent" is I£ 4 to I£ 10. The crowding is intense, the sanitary conditions appalling. There are no toilets, and the workers prepare their meals on the spot. In the winter they make fires of wood debris indoors to keep them-selves warm.

The workers complained that they are often wakened from their sleep at night by the police, who come to investigate whether everyone is equipped with a travel permit from the military governor of his area.[62]

In 1957 one Jewish journalist found that hundreds of unregistered Arab youngsters from villages in the Galilee worked in Haifa to help support their families.

Many are the children of peasant families that do not have enough land to feed every mouth. Others are the sons of landless refugees. With their weekly pay of I£ 12–20 they must not only maintain themselves but help support their parents and their younger brothers and sisters.

In the summertime, the boys find themselves places to sleep in uncompleted houses under construction; in the winter you will find them in niches and dilapidated shacks in the Arab quarters of Haifa. Some sleep at their place of work: in the evening the owner pulls down the shutters and locks them up inside, releasing them in the morning when he comes to work.[63]

One of these boys led the reporter to his "hotel." During a nighttime visit the journalist found that inside the small shack "a dozen boys lined the walls, pressed to each other in their sleep. They sleep in their clothes, covered with old, tattered blankets. There was no latrine, not to speak of a washing sink. The shack and the ruins around it overflowed with filth." Under such conditions, in close proximity to Jews, feelings of intense deprivation naturally developed.

Muhamad Salmi [one of the young workers] had been afraid to talk to a newspaperman. He unfroze a bit only owing to the presence of an Arab friend that was with us. We found out that he had completed seven years of schooling and knew enough to follow what went on around him. He was familiar with Haifa and he knew what life in it was like for other, Jewish boys. Protected by the law, they were learning trades, they led their social life within a certain framework, they belonged to clubs. . . . He too dreamed of mastering a trade, of finding a place to spend his free hours. But where was he to turn? All the doors were closed to him; his very presence was only tolerated because he worked for less.[64]

When the reporter questioned a Labor Party leader in Haifa whose responsibility it was to work among the Arabs, he replied that, indeed, "We have brought up a whole anti-Israel generation. . . . When you tell them [higher government officials] about the boys' condition, you always get the same answer; they weren't better off under the Mandate; boys in Arab countries are just as neglected."[65] Seven years later, in 1964, another Jewish journalist interviewed a young Arab from Nazareth arrested for stealing jewels in Haifa.

"Look at the soft life those Jews lead on the Carmel," he told me. "They have got everything, and plenty of it. Every day I had to serve them in the restaurant and to see to their smallest whims—me, exploited, discriminated against, leading a dog's life. One night I couldn't stand it any more and I decided to take from them something of what they owed me. Why do the Jews have so much and I nothing? I wanted to do justice and to take something that belonged to me. It's a pity they caught me."[66]

Of those Arabs who do not commute to work but have remained in agriculture, many have become dependent on crops such as olives and tobacco, for which mechanized methods of cultivation have not been developed, which require intensive care, but which do not require level, fertile, or irrigated land. In 1971/1972 Arab farmers contributed 67 percent of Israel's olive production and 90 percent of Israel's tobacco.[67] The relative dependence of Arab farmers on these crops has been made more onerous by the operation of monopolisitic Jewish marketing concerns during the 1950's and the Jewish Agency practice of granting subsidies to Jewish tobacco farmers.

Those products grown only by the Arab farmers [e.g., olives] are not protected against the price of imported products whereas the products of Jewish farmers are protected against such competition. In the case of subsidies a 2-I£-per-kilo subsidy is given to Jewish growers of tobacco, but the Arab growers receive no subsidy even though the produce is the same. Because of the confiscation of lands the Arabs no longer have pasture land for cows, goats, sheep, etc. In addition since they have no capital to enter the business of breeding animals on a large scale, they are now gradually leaving an occupation in which they have been well known for centuries.[68]

And as a native of the Arab village of Rama wrote in 1957:

Olives are sold in Tel Aviv and Jerusalem at I£ 1.500 per kilo, whereas they are bought in Rama at 30–40 piastres per kilo. This absurd situation has been brought about by the fact that one or two large companies monopolize the marketing of olives in the three big cities.

The Rama villager feels embittered when he sees the government subsidizing the growers of tomatoes and other vegetables, without giving him a helping hand. He would even desire to imitate his Jewish neighbor by uprooting the olive trees and planting the land with vegetables. But how can he do this without irrigation water? . . . I have to buy drinking water at 17 piastres per can—which amounts to I£ 8,500 per cubic metre. I can't take a good shower, and I would not dream of having a little garden. So the Rama villager feels a certain resentment when he sees that water is brought to the new settlement of Shazor beside him from tens of miles away, he feels envious when he sees electric light brightening many a Jewish home, whereas he has to be satisfied with a kerosene lamp. He feels very skeptical about the statements made in the press concerning the improvement of the lot of the Arabs in this country.[69]

Thus the lack of economic development in the Arab sector, as compared to the rapid economic growth characteristic of the Jewish economy[70] and the lavish assistance given to newly established Jewish villages, has engendered deep resentment throughout the Arab community.

There are no equal rights for Arabs in Israel. When a new Jewish settlement is established the settlers are immediately provided with roads, electricity, piped water, etc. Arabs must wait for these services and pay a tremendous amount of money. . . . Even the turkeys in Jewish kibbutzim, who have electricity, are better off than many Arab villages![71]

While Jewish citizens and immigrants are offered financial concessions in order to establish themselves in business, such concessions are not offered to the Arabs and conditions are such as to discourage such business enterprises; for example—exaggerated taxes, lack of ready marketing facilities, no subsidies, etc.[72]

And so, while government spokesmen compare the economic situation of Israeli Arabs to their standard of living before 1948 or to that of Arabs in the surrounding countries, most Israeli Arabs vehemently reject the appropriateness of such a comparison.

One should not compare the situation of the Arabs of this country to the situation of Arabs in surrounding countries. No Arab compares his condition to the condition of Arabs outside the country but rather he makes the comparison with the condition of the Jew who lives here. That is the proper comparison for the Arabs are citizens of this state and not citizens of the Arab states.[73]

Nor do Israeli Arabs perceive the situation as improving significantly. "Every year the Jewish-Arab economic gap becomes

wider. Jews get money from the Jewish Agency and Jewish contributions. We're not Jews so we can't get money from the Jewish Agency, but we're Israelis so we can't get money from Kuwait
. . . during the last four years we haven't advanced one step."[74]

A source of very great dissatisfaction among Israeli Arabs
today is the absence of any appreciable industry in the Arab sector which could offer employment to Arab workers in their own
villages, supply profitable investment opportunities, and provide
managerial and technical positions for trained Arabs who are refused entrance into such occupations in the Jewish economy.

We compare ourselves to the Jewish sector. Why should we have to
commute every day to Jewish cities to work? We want industry in the
Arab sector very badly because as a result of expropriations there is no
longer enough land. It is said we lack initiative with regard to investment in industry. That is partially true, but without an infrastructure
such as high tension power lines there can be no industry. Unfortunately government policy is decided by the needs of Jews and for absorption of *aliyah*. Thus our local council receives an average of I£ 10
per capita in government aid while Jewish municipalities receive over
I£ 50 per capita.[75]

Arab villages are not included in Development Area "A" [highest priority area]. Nazareth is a good example. The boundary between Development Area "A" and Area "B" runs right between the Upper
[Jewish] and Lower [Arab] cities. This reflects official government policy. . . . The Histadrut owns 25 percent of Israel's industry. There are
65,000 Arab members of the Histadrut but there is not one Histadrut
industry located in the Arab sector.[76]

The inability of educated Arabs to find appropriate employment, commensurate in status and income with their training, is
a source of sharp discontent. Most Arab high school graduates
who succeed in finding jobs do so as school teachers in Arab villages. In a poll taken in 1963, for example, it was found that of
457 Arab high school graduates interviewed, 89 were unemployed and 112 were continuing their studies in Israel or abroad.
Of those who were employed, 29 worked as laborers, 76 as
clerks, and 142 as teachers.[77] In a government-sponsored survey
of Arab university graduates who received their degrees between
1961 and 1971 it was found that 47.3 percent of those employed in "white collar occupations" worked as teachers.[78] Because of their complete economic dependence on the Ministry of
Education Arab school teachers maintain an "uncomfortable

passivity." As a result "it is doubtful if today they command the same respect as the teachers did in the days of the Mandate. Because of this, an ambivalent relation has developed among them vis-à-vis the Israeli government. On the one hand, there is a positive but superficial rapport with the government; on the other hand, deep down there exists a kind of hatred and opposition to the government which they feel has forced its will upon them in the eyes of the Arab population."[79] In fact I was told by one school teacher in a large Arab village in the Galilee that there is a saying now among the villagers: "Throw a stone in an Arab village and you hit either a dog or a teacher."

Various government agencies, especially the Office of the Adviser to the Prime Minister on Arab Affairs, have expressed their concern over the employment problems of young educated Arabs, but efforts to locate jobs on a case-by-case basis have not succeeded in alleviating the problem. In 1962 the Adviser on Arab Affairs was Uri Lubrani. In a published interview he explained that finding suitable employment for Arab intellectuals, especially university graduates, was "no simple matter. If you only knew what difficulties we face trying to get them jobs! . . . It is virtually impossible to convince economic enterprises, be they public or private or even belonging to the Histadrut, to take on young Arabs."[80] In 1977 the number of Arab university graduates unable to find employment was large and still growing.[81] For educated Arabs the contrast between their life chances and those of their fellow Jewish students becomes exceedingly painful.

. . . the Arab student begins to compare himself not with his companion in the village who has had no chance to study, but with his Jewish contemporary who he is convinced really succeeds in fulfilling his ambitions and expectations in accordance with what he has achieved. Thus, the Arab intellectual attempts to explain his problems and his situation according to his national background, which only contributes, among other things, to an increased feeling of estrangement and strengthens all the more his national consciousness and identity.[82]

For the young Arab, the criterion is the Jewish township because whether consciously or unconsciously he considers himself an Israeli for all intents and purposes . . . just as no one justifies the situation of Yemenite immigrants, for example, by reference to what the situation of *his* parents was, so one cannot explain away the feelings of discrimination harboured by a young Arab by alleging that, as compared to his parents, he is living in Paradise.[83]

My brother is an architect. But no Jew employs him to build anything. Once when a motion picture theater was to be built near Haifa my brother submitted a bid which was better and lower than that submitted by five other Jewish architects. But he was turned down by the Jewish owners. "How can we be sure you won't build the cinema so that it would fall down on our heads one day and kill all the Jews inside?"[84]

In addition to generating bitter resentment and an intensification of a national "Arab" consciousness, these circumstances induce large numbers of young Arabs to leave the country.[85]

We are graduating as engineers from the Technion [an engineering and technical institute] but there is no work available for us in this country because Jewish firms refuse to hire Arab engineers. We need industry in the Arab sector in order to employ technically trained Arabs, but that does not exist. All that is open to us is teaching. I, for one, do not want to teach so I am planning to go to the United States to find work. In fact of the twenty-one Arabs in our graduating class at the Technion only seven are still in the country.[86]

The leader of a large hamula (an Arab patrilineal kinship association) in a central Galilean village put it this way:

Arab students are not allowed to study the subjects they choose, especially medicine and engineering. They are only allowed into the humanities. While Jewish young people can achieve whatever they desire, no Arabs are allowed to enter important positions. These conditions result in extremist tendencies and make it necessary for many educated young people to leave the country for further training and employment. One of my sons, for example, is studying medicine in Texas.[87]

In the words of an eighteen-year-old Arab from Nazareth, who in 1964 convinced his parents to emigrate,

Look, I'm a last-grade student and in another year I'll be graduating from secondary school. . . . Did you know that in the past five years more than 90 percent of the Arab students in Israel have failed the matriculation examinations? Do you think it's an accident? We Arabs know it isn't: they make the examinations hard for us on purpose, so as to have as few Arab intellectuals as possible in Israel. The authorities find it more convenient that we should be hewers of wood and drawers of water in this state . . . [but] let's say I'd passed the exam and got a matriculation certificate. Will that do me any good in Israel? Say I go to the university in Jerusalem and graduate in economics or in law. Will I find employment after that? Will they take me on as an economist at the Ministry of Finance or as an attorney in some public agency? You know very well all the doors are closed to us!

. . . I confess: I hate the state of Israel. I'm a stepchild here. I have no future. I want to get out. The choice is to get out or to become an enemy of Israel, be it as an Arab communist or an Arab nationalist, and to combat the authorities. I haven't the strength to do this.[88]

Explaining the Political Quiescence of Israeli Arabs

What explains the overall position of Arabs in Israel as an isolated and peripheral group, whose demands for a greater share of the country's resources are seldom if ever registered in the national political arena? What explains the existence, within Israel, of a substantial community with virtually no independently operated industrial, commercial, or financial institutions, no independent political parties, and almost no command over the attention or interest of the mainstream of Israeli society? On the basis of the above sampling of Arab opinion in three crucial issue areas it is possible to appreciate the frustrations and the intense sense of injustice which Israeli Arabs have experienced. Why, then, have Israeli Arabs failed to organize on a mass basis and act along communal lines in order to improve their status and safeguard their rights?[89] What, for instance, explains the fact that in every parliamentary election, except that held in 1977, the Labor Party and its coalition partners have received a majority of the votes cast by Arabs? The seeming docility of Israeli Arabs in a "vibrant democracy" such as Israel was something Bishop James Pike of the United States could not understand. After participating in a symposium in Israel on the problems of the Arab minority he did realize the magnitude of Arab grievances, but he was still puzzled: ". . . the problem I have not understood yet, is why the Arabs in Israel do not organize politically more than they do. It would seem that with this many voters something could be done."[90] The political quiescence of Israeli Arabs as a communal group is indeed perplexing, not only based on a comparison with ethnic relations in other countries, and not only in the context of a burgeoning theoretical literature on the instability of communally segmented societies. The stability of ethnic politics in Israel would also seem to clash with that country's image as a Middle Eastern version of American liberal democracy, where every minority has "the right to organize itself in order to insist through legal means on the abrogation of the injustice done it, be this a real or even imaginary injustice."[91]

In the face of this anomalous state of affairs, what I wish to argue is that *the failure of Israel's Arab minority to "organize itself" and the minimal significance, to date, of the communal segmentation of Israeli society for the operation and stability of the Israeli political system are due to the presence of a highly effective system of control which, since 1948, has operated over Israeli Arabs.* As I later indicate, severe challenges to the efficiency of this system of control emerged in the mid-1970's. These challenges are raising the costs of control over the Arab minority and, as is discussed in Chapter 7, they may result in certain changes in the techniques of control employed by the regime. However, they are not nearly strong enough to threaten the fundamental relationship of control analyzed in this study.

Unlike apartheid, for example, the system of control over Arabs in Israel is not explicitly recognized in the legal framework of the state. Quite the reverse; in the words of Israel's Proclamation of Independence, "[The state of Israel] will maintain complete equality of social and political rights for all citizens, without distinction of creed, race or sex. It will guarantee freedom of religion and conscience, of language, education and culture." Although the proclamation, in a formal sense, is not legally binding in Israel,

... it guides judicial interpretation of the statutes of Israel in such matters as freedom of the individual, freedom of expression, and equality of privileges, and this applies, no less, to Israel's Arabs, whether as individuals or, collectively, as a national minority.

Thus there can be no gainsaying that Israel's Arabs are accorded absolute parity with other citizens before the law. This is an indivisible part of the State's jurisprudence in concept, principle and performance. Discrimination against an Arab citizen on grounds of race or creed is anathema in the courts of Israel.[92]

Nevertheless, thanks to a sophisticated system of control, it has been possible for the Israeli regime and the Jewish majority which it represents to manipulate the Arab minority, to prevent it from organizing on an independent basis, and to extract from it resources required for the development of the Jewish sector—all this at very low cost to the regime in terms of resources expended, overt violent repression, and unfavorable international publicity.

This explanation for the political quiescence of Israeli Arabs stands in opposition to arguments put forward by government officials. Ori Stendel, formerly an official in the Office of the Adviser to the Prime Minister on Arab Affairs, has ascribed the absence of independent Arab leaders or organizations to the disrepute and ineptitude of the traditionalist leaders of the Arab community.[93] Perhaps the most widely accepted explanation for the phenomenon is that put forward by Micah Nino: "For the Government of Israel, the safety and well-being of minority life and property are not one iota less primary, not one iota less demanding on its resources and responsibilities, than are the protection and defense of its Jews: it is to this set and central policy . . . that the orderliness and pacific inter-relations of Israel's disparate communities may be ascribed."[94] Jacob Landau, a professor of political science at the Hebrew University in Jerusalem, in his well-known book on the Arab minority in Israel, rejects the notion that "The Arabs in Israel are prevented from forming their own political parties," but he does note that the policy of the government has been "to discourage the establishment of an Arab party."[95]

In treating the Arab minority question, Arab propagandists, such as Sami Hadawi, have generally stressed the overall and relatively abstract "political suppression" of Israeli Arabs. Graphic illustration of particular cases of such suppression are provided by Sabri Jiryis, an Israeli-trained Arab lawyer who left the country in 1966, and by Fouzi el-Asmar, in his personal account, *To Be an Arab in Israel.*[96]

Scholarly attempts to analyze Jewish-Arab relations in Israel according to one or another model of control or domination include *How Israel Lost Its Soul*, by Maxim Ghilan, in which the "instruments of control over Arabic-speaking minorities" are briefly discussed.[97] Elia Zureik, a sociologist, has argued that the concept of "internal colonialism," as developed by certain

Marxist writers, is applicable to the position of Arabs in Israel.[98] Sammy Smooha has also used a domination model for Jewish-Arab relations in his comparison of Sephardic-Ashkenazic, religious-nonreligious, and Arab-Jewish pluralism in Israel.[99]

The central purpose of this study, however, is not to assert that Arabs are controlled in Israel, but to analyze the system by which control has been achieved and maintained, i.e., to *describe* exactly how it has operated to serve important regime objectives, to *explain* why its operation has been so successful, and to *predict* the possibilities for future transformation, breakdown, or consolidation of the system. Chapter 2 begins with a prior examination of what the Zionist movement anticipated as the role and status of the non-Jewish population in the future Zionist entity. This provides a historical context for a detailed assessment of the relationship between the objectives of the Israeli regime, as they emerged in the first years of statehood, and the existence of a relatively small though substantial Arab minority. Chapter 3 describes the regime's general orientation toward the minority as one of "control" and examines political science literature relevant to the use of "control" as an explanation for stability in multiethnic societies. Chapter 3 concludes with an outline of the conceptual framework to be employed in the balance of the study. Chapters 4–6 are devoted to a systematic, multilevel analysis of how control is achieved on the basis of three "components"—segmentation, dependence, and cooptation. The final chapter includes an evaluation of the system of control as a whole, an examination of the impact of certain long-term trends on its present and future operation, and a discussion of important approaches to the system's adaptation now under consideration by the regime.

2.
Zionism and the Idea of an Arab Minority: Regime Objectives and Israeli Arabs in the First Years of Statehood

Prestate Zionism and the Problem of a Future Arab Minority

In 1948 when Chaim Weizmann learned of the mass Arab evacuation of Israeli territory, the senior statesman of the Zionist movement declared it "a miraculous simplification of Israel's tasks."[1] Out of a prewar population of more than 900,000 Arabs, approximately 750,000 fled or were expelled from Israeli-held territory during the fighting. Weizmann's exhilaration and relief must be understood in the context of Zionism's failure to solve the problem of what the role and status of the Arab population would be in the Jewish state which had now been established. Appreciation of the failure of Zionist ideology to solve this problem in the prestate era is essential to understanding Jewish policies toward the Arab minority after 1948.

The overall objective of the Zionist movement during the mandate period had been to build the organizational, territorial, and demographic infrastructure of a future Jewish state. When the state of Israel emerged in May 1948, it had at its disposal established representative political institutions, an army, several Jewish-run educational systems, a police force, a social welfare bureaucracy, and a variety of industrial, agricultural, and financial institutions. Moreover, although political rivalries among Jewish parties were intense, Zionist ideology provided fairly coherent formulas according to which the major economic, social, and political issues facing the new state could be addressed to the satisfaction of the Yishuv.

However, neither Zionist ideology nor the programs of the various organizations of the Zionist movement provided explicit guidance for dealing with the small though substantial (12 percent) Arab minority that continued to reside within the borders of the Jewish state after its creation in 1948. Serious, explicit attempts by important Zionist groups to address the problem of what the future role and status of a non-Jewish minority would be in a Jewish state were rare in the prestate era. It is necessary to provide a brief survey of such attempts before describing Israel's confrontation with its non-Jewish citizens in the early years of the state's existence. Throughout, the *tactical* nature of these formulations is emphasized in order to provide a backdrop for decisions which had to be made by the Israeli regime once Jewish sovereignty was attained. For, as a result of ideological orientation and Arab intransigence, long before 1948 the Zionist leadership had become accustomed to thinking of the internal "Arab problem" as a peripheral issue, to be dealt with in whatever fashion would most effectively serve the central objectives of Zionism. It was this general predisposition to ad hoc solution, rather than any set of fundamental policy decisions, which governed the initial attitude of the regime toward the Arab citizens of the Jewish state.

When the World Zionist Organization held its first meeting in Basel in 1897, the resolution adopted called for a Jewish "*Heimstätte*," a term suggestive of Jewish territorial sovereignty but containing enough ambiguity to provide wide room for diplomatic maneuver. In his diary Theodore Herzl, who convened and presided over the conference, was more explicit. "At Basle," he wrote, at the conclusion of the meeting, "I founded the Jewish State."[2] There were several important reasons why, in the early stages of its development, the Zionist movement was vague as to its final aims. Many, perhaps most, Jews were uncomfortable with the idea of a Jewish state, with its implication that "Jew" was a national-political category and with the latent danger that the existence of a "Jewish state" would precipitate expulsions of Jews from the countries in which they were citizens. Nor could Zionist leaders hope to convince the Ottoman sultan to grant a charter to Jews for colonization in Palestine if an independent Jewish state were the declared aim of the movement. But during the negotiations between Zionist leaders and the British government over the wording of the Balfour Declaration of 1917, and certainly in the course of the subsequent struggle between Arabs and Jews in British mandatory Palestine, it became clear that the numerical preponderance of Arabs to Jews in Palestine and the intensity of Arab opposition to Jewish political ambitions were the decisive factors inhibiting the Zionist movement from making its desire for a Jewish state explicit.

In the Balfour Declaration the British government announced that it viewed "with favor the establishment *in* Palestine of *a national home* for Jewish people . . . it being clearly understood that nothing shall be done which may prejudice the civil and religious rights of existing non-Jewish communities in Palestine . . ." The phraseology of the declaration was substantially and meaningfully different from that used in a draft which had been submitted by the Zionist leadership. The Zionist draft had contained the declaration that the reconstitution of Palestine as a Jewish state was one of the British government's essential war aims. Moreover, the Zionist draft had contained no reference whatsoever to "existing non-Jewish communities in Palestine."[3]

Many Zionists were disappointed with the vagueness of the Balfour Declaration, but Weizmann reassured them: "What did the Declaration mean? It did not mean a Jewish State. Not because you or I did not want a Jewish State. I trust to God that a Jewish State will come about, but it will come about not through political declarations, but through the sweat and blood of the Jewish people, that is the only way of building up a state . . . what I say is that it is the golden key which unlocks the doors of Palestine . . ."[4]

In 1921 Arab riots against Jews broke out in cities all over the country. The Arabs demanded a halt to Jewish immigration, prohibition of land sales to Jews, abrogation of the Balfour Declaration, and immediate independence for an Arab Palestinian state. However, in spite of fierce Arab opposition, the mainstream of the Zionist movement never abandoned its commitment to unlimited Jewish immigration, a Jewish majority, and eventual Jewish statehood.[5]

Nevertheless, throughout the 1920's the Zionist leadership, and Weizmann in particular, resisted the insistent demands of right-wing (revisionist) Zionists to declare openly the movement's ultimate objectives—Jewish statehood for all of Palestine. It must be remembered that in 1917 Jews constituted only 10 percent of the population of Palestine and by 1930 no more than 17 percent. Arab opposition to Zionism was intense and the political weight of the Arabs in the world political arena was increasing. In the 1920's even minimal British support for Zionist objectives was conditioned upon a Zionist attempt to appease the Arabs, in part by abstaining from declaring Jewish statehood as the movement's ultimate objective and by restraining maximalist elements within the Zionist movement. Weizmann's reliance on the notion of "organic Zionism"—the course of which would be determined not by official declarations, charters, or covenants but by day-to-day immigration, land settlement, and hard work—reflected his desire to maintain the integrity of the maximum objectives of the Zionist movement without explicitly denying the acceptability of other scenarios such as binationalism, a permanent Jewish minority, cantonization, parity, etc.

In an address delivered at the organizing convention of Mapai (the Palestine Labor Party) following the Arab riots of 1929, David Ben-Gurion denounced both maximalists and minimalists in the Zionist movement. According to Ben-Gurion the position of Mapai in support of "organic Zionism" was justified in light of the tactical realism on which it was based and the long-run commitment to Jewish statehood which it contained.

Our movement, the Socialist-Zionist Workers Movement, always carried the banner of the Great Zionism. . . . [but] It fully estimated the political factors that condition the realization of Zionism, and it knew how to activate the social forces necessary for political success. If we are now unalterably opposed to Revisionism, it is not only because of its Fascist and chauvinist tendencies, which imperil the welfare of the Yishuv, but also because Revisionism perverts and distorts the political content of Zionism. It substitutes for political activity the glitter of diplomacy with impotent mock-military bluffs; it indulges in farcical play, in confusing slogans and theatrical gestures where carefully planned political action and efforts are needed. Revisionism seeks to undermine whatever beginnings of statehood we have . . . and encourages all the forces of destruction, anarchy and irresponsibility that are now concentrating around the most reactionary elements of the Palestinian bourgeois . . .

We oppose the Brit Shalom [a small group of Jews who favored conciliation and a binational approach] not because of its desire for peace with the Arabs, but because of its attempt to obliterate the Jewish truth and to hide the Jewish flag as a price for peace. We do not believe in a peace that has no truth. Is our sole objective, here in Palestine, only peace with the Arabs? Should a free Jewish people not be established here, then the Arab question has no meaning for us. We have no wish to be in Palestine as the Schutz-Juden [protected Jews] of the Mufti. . . . We are struggling with the Arab question because of our conception of a Great Zionism, because of the historic necessity that the Jewish masses must root themselves in this land, and become a self-ruling nation.[6]

In the late 1920's and early and mid-1930's the notion of parity between Arabs and Jews was regularly advanced by the Zionist leadership in response to the political challenge of Arab opposition to Zionism. According to the doctrine of parity, neither the Jewish nation nor the Arab nation in Palestine "was to dominate or be dominated by the other in the self-governing institutions of the country. The principle was to apply under the mandate, while Arabs were in the majority, and it was to apply in independent Palestine when it was hoped that Jews would be the majority."[7] Again, this formula and others were tactically conceived as ways to bridge what was perceived as a temporary gap between Jewish aspirations in Palestine and the power of Jews to fulfill them. In 1933 Eliezer Liebenstein (Livne), one of the foremost ideologues of the Zionist movement, candidly expressed the role which ideas such as parity, cantonization, and federation were meant to play in relation to the ultimate quest for Jewish Statehood.

Politics is the art of the possible. . . . Political possibilities and political power are the results of actual economic and cultural facts. It is therefore necessary to change the actual facts of Palestine. Our most important political action is under all circumstances: Immigration and Colonization . . .

There are many political thoughts which are not ripe enough to serve as a basis for negotiations, but which are ripe enough to serve as a basis for discussion and expresson of opinion. The conception of an Arab-Jewish federation is an example. . . . Aliveness to the narrowness of our sphere of political potentialities which lie in the materialization of the upbuilding of Palestine, should be the guiding lines of our Zionist policies.[8]

Parity, binationalism, federation, nondomination, and other slogans used in the late 1920's and early and mid-1930's to characterize what Jewish-Arab relations would be like in the future Zionist entity were meant to appeal to liberal opinion in Great Britain and to mollify Arab opinion while not denying the ultimate aims of "Great Zionism" regarding Jewish sovereignty in Palestine. In particular, parity *regardless of relative population* was designed as a fair-sounding doctrine which could serve to justify Jewish opposition both to immediate independence for Palestine and to proposals for a proportionally elected legislature. What must be stressed is that these ideas, insofar as they were put forward by leaders of the Zionist movement, were not based on any careful analysis of Jewish-Arab relations in Palestine or upon any serious attempt to anticipate what sorts of relations might emerge between a Jewish majority and an Arab minority in the context of different constitutional arrangements.[9]

The tactical nature of Zionist proposals regarding the status of Arabs in the future Jewish homeland can easily be appreciated if one compares Zionist explanations of the concept of parity offered in the early 1930's to those offered after 1935. Parity was originally put forward as a constitutional scheme and political principle which would protect the right of the Jewish Yishuv to grow, develop, and absorb immigrants while it was still a minority in Palestine. Parity meant preventing the Arab majority from "democratically" putting an end to the development of the Jewish national home. The doctrine also held out the promise to Arabs that even if and when a Jewish majority emerged in Palestine the Arab community would nevertheless remain as an *equal* partner in the affairs of the country. As Chaim Weizmann said in his opening address to the Zionist Congress in Basel in 1931, "The Arabs must be made to feel, must be convinced, by deed as well as by word, that, whatever the future numerical relationship of the two nation's in Palestine, we, on our part, contemplate no political domination. But they must also remember that we, on our side, shall never submit to any political domination. Provided that the Mandate is both recognized and respected, we would welcome an agreement between the two kindred races on the basis of political parity."[10] One of the last pronouncements of a major Zionist leader in favor of a solution based on some form of parity came from Ben-Gurion in a speech to the Mapai Party Council in 1934.

I see the future of Palestine in the political constitutional sense as a federal state of cantons. We must take this approach not because of political tactics but because this is the political reality of our Zionism: non-domination of the Jews over the Arabs and non-domination of the Arabs over the Jews . . . we will demand change by bringing Jews and Arabs in equal numbers into the government of the country, who will participate also in the legislative power and the executive power. . . . In my opinion we must find Arab circles of value, who out of a realistic approach, out of the knowledge that what they want they cannot obtain and that they might as well take what can be had, will agree to an Arab-Jewish agreement on this basis.[11]

However, as refugees from Hitler's Germany streamed into Palestine the Jewish proportion of the population increased from 17 percent in 1931 to 33 percent in 1940. With a Jewish majority taking shape, at least in the minds of Zionist leaders, parity was abandoned as a long-range political program. As Ben-Gurion suggested at a meeting of the Zionist Actions Committee in the autumn of 1936,

The question of parity is one of public opinion, a political matter and we shall not introduce into it religious matters. We are not discussing here the final aim (we would not have found a uniform interpretation). We find ourselves in the midst of the situation in the country, the situation has no connection with the final aim . . . we wish to introduce in the area of the mandate the question of parity, and only as long as the British mandate lasts. What does parity mean? Parity means joint Jewish-Arab government, cooperation between representatives. . . . If I were to formulate it I would not say "two nations," I have said that the Jewish nation is not in the country and I do not recognize the Arabs [of Palestine] as a nation.[12]

Ben-Gurion's last comment, concerning the absence of a separate "Palestinian Arab nation," foreshadowed the complete rejection of parity or any other form of binationalism by mainstream Zionism. Unless two nations *in* Palestine, one Arab and one Jewish, were recognized, they could not each be accorded equal rights as "nationalities." In his testimony before the Peel Commission in 1937 Ben-Gurion expanded on his belief that the Jews had emerged as the only truly "national" group within the borders of Palestine. Aside from the Jews, who as a nation had full historic rights to Palestine, ". . . there is no other nation —I do not say population, I do not say sections of a people— there is no other race or nation as a whole which regards this country as their only homeland. All the inhabitants of Palestine are children of this country, not only as citizens but as children of this country. We have it as Jews, as children of the Jewish people, whether we are here already or whether we are not here yet."[13]

By this time the Nazi terror in Europe and the failure of Western nations to open their doors to Jewish immigration seemed to provide ample evidence, as Zionists had been saying for decades, not only that Europe was unfit for Jewish habitation but that only a Jewish-ruled Palestine could provide a secure future for the Jewish people as a whole. Finally, as the staggering dimensions of the Holocaust in Europe were becoming known, in 1942 the World Zionist Organization made its support for Jewish statehood explicit by approving what was called the Biltmore Platform (after the Biltmore Hotel in New York, where it was adopted). The Biltmore Platform contained a declaration that Palestine should be established as a "Jewish Commonwealth."

By 1942 Ben-Gurion was defending the Biltmore Platform and ridiculing proposed solutions involving parity and/or the continued presence of an outside arbiter or "third force."

. . . And so during X years a few million Jews will come but there will remain a regime of parity with a third force. Let us say that after a certain period there will be 3–4 million Jews and 1½ million Arabs . . . you consider the Jewish problem to be solved and there is parity in the country. There is no such thing in the world. In Egypt there will be Egyptians and a democratic government and no third force. In Syria there will be also a minority and a majority, and there will be a democratic regime without a third force. . . . Why will Palestine have an extraordinary regime, not democratic, not independent, but some peculiar arrangement? Nobody will understand it . . .[14]

Some factions of the Zionist movement (including Ihud, a small group of prominent Jewish personalities, mostly of central European origin, and Hashomer Hatzair, a left-wing kibbutz movement) still opposed this explicit call for Jewish sovereignty and preferred instead some sort of binational solution. The activities of these groups and of such individuals as Judah Magnes, former president of the Hebrew University, show that there were elements within the Yishuv concerned about Jewish-Arab relations in a multinational Palestine. But their proposals for various binational schemes, some of which included temporary restrictions on the growth of the Jewish national home, fell on deaf ears. Palestinian Arabs consistently refused to defer consideration of ultimate issues such as control over immigration, while Zionists, including Hashomer Hatzair, insisted that a future Jewish majority not be precluded.[15] Indeed, it had become clear to the overwhelming majority of Zionists that the overtures which had been made concerning parity, federation, cantons, etc.—whether sincere or not—had never found and would never elicit a satisfactory response from the Arabs of Palestine.

In 1946 there were 1,303,887 Arabs in Palestine and 583,327 Jews. Even in the dimunitive Jewish state whose borders were drawn by the United Nations in 1947 an initial Arab population of 49 percent was projected. Yet up until 1947 the official objective of the Zionist movement was a Jewish state in *all* of Palestine. Moreover, Ben-Gurion and others spoke of the Jewish state as a stage in and as an instrument for the further, continuous development of the Jewish national home.

We are building a Jewish State for two reasons. One is in order to enable us, those Jews who are already in this country, to live our own lives, and the other is to help the solution of their tragic problem, and great tragic historic problem of the Jewish people in the world. Because, Sir, only a Jewish State will be able to build a Jewish National Home without hindrance. We need a Jewish State in order to continue building the National Home for the Jewish people.[16]

What the relationship of non-Jewish citizens of the future state would be to the long-term enterprise of building and consolidating a Jewish national home was never specified. Even in the years immediately preceding the establishment of the state, the problem of what the *real* status of the Arab population would be was still ignored by Zionist planners. Only under close questioning by members of British and international investigatory commissions as to the ultimate aims of Zionism were the leaders of the movement willing to speculate about how Jewish-Arab relations would be ordered within the future Jewish state. But even in answer to such questions Zionist officials did not rely on a systematic analysis of the social structure, property relations, political power distribution, or demographic composition of the Arab community. Rather they tailored their responses to suit the lib-

eral predispositions of their (mostly) British and American inter-
locutors.

The profuse assurances offered by the Zionist leadership
that there would be strict equality of all citizens in the Jewish
state and nondomination of Jews over Arabs must be understood in light of Zionist arguments of earlier years that an Arab
state (and, as they argued at times, even a Jewish state) would,
by definition, entail domination of one group over another.[17]
Since the support of the liberal democracies was necessary for a
Jewish state to emerge and since, in theory at least, civil equality
for non-Jews contradicted no basic tenet of Zionism, Weizmann,
Ben-Gurion, and the rest were unrestrained in the promises
which they made regarding the status of Arabs in the Jewish
state-to-be. The following is a quotation from the testimony of
Moshe Sharett (foreign affairs director for the Jewish Agency
and later prime minister of Israel) before the Anglo-American
Committee of Inquiry on Palestine (1946):

Let me again assure the Committee: Palestine as a Jewish State implies
no superior status for the Jews save in one respect: the right of entry.
Inside the State there will be complete equality of rights for all inhabitants regardless of race or creed, complete eligibility of all for all offices, up to the highest. A Jewish majority is inevitable and indispensable. Inevitable because it is impossible to settle Jews in large numbers
in this country without their becoming a majority.

. . . It is indispensable because no other arrangement will serve as
an effective guarantee of the freedom of entry of Jews who might in the
future be in need of a home. Otherwise, I repeat, no privileges, no su-
periority of status, no special rights for the Jews of Palestine or for the
Jewish religion or for any Jewish institution.[18]

Testifying before the same Committee of Inquiry David Ben-
Gurion commented that the future Jewish state would have two
functions:

. . . one, the function to care for the welfare of the people of this country, all of them, without any difference between Jews, Arabs or others,
to care for their security, to work for their welfare and to raise them
higher and higher economically, socially, and intellectually. The other
function is to continue building a National Home.

We will have to treat our Arabs and other non-Jewish neighbors
on the basis of absolute equality as if they were Jews, but make every
effort that they should preserve their Arab characteristics, their lan-

guage, their Arab culture, their Arab religion, their Arab way of life, while making every effort to make all the citizens of the country equal civilly, socially, economically, politically, intellectually, and gradually raise the standard of life of everyone, Jews and others.[19]

In a memorandum to the United Nations Special Committee on Palestine in 1947, the Jewish Agency repeated these assurances:

What will be the character of this State? It will be an independent self-governing Palestinian State with a Jewish majority, in which all citizens regardless of race or creed will enjoy equal rights, and all communities will control their internal affairs. The State will not be Jewish in the sense that its Jewish citizens will have more rights than their non-Jewish fellows, or that the Jewish community will be superior in status to other communities, or that other religions will have an inferior rank to the Jewish religion.
. . . For the State to achieve these ends it is essential that it should have a Jewish majority. . . . A Jewish majority in Palestine necessarily implies that non-Jews will form a minority of the population. It does not imply that they will be reduced to what is commonly known as "minority status." . . . the individual non-Jewish citizen . . . will enjoy in full measure the rights which his Jewish fellow is entitled to exercise in the political, civic, religious and national domains. This means that he will have the franchise on the same terms as the Jew in elections to central and local representative bodies. He will be eligible to such bodies, he will be capable of being elected to every executive office, high or low, he will not be at a disadvantage because of his race or religion in the matter of employment in public office or in public works. He will enjoy full freedom of religious worship and practice.[20]

In response to questioning, the representatives of the Jewish Agency who appeared before these investigatory commissions outlined several "guarantees" for the future well-being of Arabs in a Jewish State.

The number of Arabs in this country is less than 3 percent of the number of Arabs who have gained their political independence. The Arabs in Palestine, even if they were a minority, would still be part of that large Arab majority in the Middle East. The existence of Arab States to the north, east and south of Palestine is an automatic guarantee, not only of the civil, religious and political rights of the Arabs in Palestine, but also of their national aspirations.[21]

Indeed, the role of neighboring Arab states as guarantors of the position and welfare of the Arab minority in the Jewish state was heavily stressed. On another occasion Ben-Gurion went so far as to predict that the Arab minority would enjoy a privileged position in the Jewish state.

When things in Palestine change, the Arabs would be a minority and we would become the majority, but the Arabs here would still be in a privileged position. They would have nothing to fear because they are surrounded by Arab countries that are independent. . . . Imagine that in the neighborhood of Poland there were a big State like Russia, with 180 million Jews, then the Jewish minority in Poland would not be persecuted; they would be perhaps in a privileged position. I am sure the Arabs will be in such a privileged position here.[22]

The Jewish Agency suggested as well that the economic self-interest of the Jewish community as a whole would guarantee the rights of Arab citizens and make internationally supervised safeguards unnecessary.

Mere self-interest, if nothing else, will compel the Jewish State studiously to safeguard the rights and concerns of its Arab citizens. On the economic side, it will . . . be a matter of self-interest for the Jews to raise the Arabs up to their own level. This will expand the market for Jewish industrial produce, discourage unfair competition in the labour market and make the Arabs themselves interested in preventing the influx of cheaper labour from neighbouring lands.[23]

In sum, the testimony of Zionist officials concerning a future Arab minority in the Jewish state emphasized the constitutional equality of Arabs and Jews, the eligibility of Arabs for all political offices in the state, the role of the Arab states as guarantors of the rights and welfare of Arab citizens, the strenuous efforts that would be made to equalize Jewish and Arab standards of living, and the opportunities for communal autonomy which would be afforded to the non-Jewish population. The complete failure of the Zionist leadership to come to grips with the Arab minority problem is reflected in the irrelevance of these factors and policy objectives for the actual ordering of relations between Arabs and Jews in Israel. The issues which did prove crucial in this regard, including the disposition of Arab-owned land, the relationship of Jewish Agency development activities to non-Jewish citizens of the state, and the question of the loyalty of the Arab population from a security point of view, were in essence ignored by the leaders of the Zionist movement. Thus, when a Jewish state *was* established in 1948, the stage was set for the Arab minority to be dealt with purely on the basis of what was expedient for the specific objectives of the regime in the early years of statehood.

Accordingly, it is now necessary to examine the interface between (1) the specific objectives of the regime in the early years of statehood and (2) the particular characteristics of the Arab community that remained in Israel after the 1948 war. In this regard there are five major policy spheres to be discussed: security, territorial consolidation, immigrant absorption, economic growth, and political stability. Within these spheres of activity the challenges which faced the young regime were enormous. The imperatives which the Israeli leadership accepted in connection with those challenges defined its policies toward the Arab minority.

Regime Objectives in the First Years of Statehood

Although the armistice agreements were not signed by Israel and Egypt, Jordan, and Syria until well into 1949, the fighting ceased on January 7. With the end of the fighting the new state of Israel confronted many problems of staggering dimensions relative to its resources. First and foremost in the eyes of Israel's leadership was the security problem. The Arab states, even after signing the armistice agreements, remained in a state of war with Israel. Though the Arab countries were still reeling from the shock of their defeat, there were already calls throughout the Arab world for a "second round" in which the "Zionist entity" would be liquidated. Infiltration across the border by refugees bent on return, theft, murder, or destruction was heavy and was seen by the Israeli army as a serious menace to security. Indeed it is estimated that "from 1949 to the middle of 1954 there was an average of 1,000 cases of infiltration per month along various frontiers."[24]

There had been almost constant fighting in Palestine between Jews and Arabs ever since the passage of the United Nations partition resolution on November 29, 1947. In the fourteen months of fighting, over six thousand of the Jewish Yishuv (of approximately 600,000) had been killed and something of a siege mentality had developed. The hypersensitive mood in Israel regarding the question of security in the first few years of the state's existence is well reflected in an address delivered by the minister of education to a conference of Israeli school teachers at the beginning of 1950. He called upon Israelis to recognize that Jews needed to become "a nation of soldiers" rather than the traditional "nation of priests." "Military training must become an inseparable part of education. 'All Israel—soldiers!'—this must be [our] slogan. . . . The school must impart to the child all the characteristics that go into making a soldier, so that when our youth finish their schooling they will have only to practice in order to become full-fledged soldiers."[25]

Besides achieving security, another major task facing Israel was the consolidation of its hold over territories acquired during the fighting which had not been allotted to the Jewish state by the United Nations. Most important among these were the western and central Galilee, large portions of the northern Negev, a corridor to Jerusalem, and the "Little Triangle" (a narrow strip of land ceded to Israel under the terms of the armistice with Jordan).[26] Since these areas were very sparsely settled by Jews, Ben-Gurion, for one, stressed the vital necessity of establishing in them substantial numbers of new Jewish settlements. "Our territorial conquests and redemptions will not be assured if we do not succeed in erecting a great and closely linked chain of settlements, especially settlements of soldiers, on the borders, in the Negev, on the coast, in the Jerusalem corridor, around Safed, and in all other areas of strategic importance."[27]

By means of such settlements Ben-Gurion and the Israeli leadership hoped to preclude the return of Arab refugees, to establish *faits accomplis* in opposition to demands made by the Arab states that Israel evacuate immediately those areas outside the borders drawn by the United Nations, to avoid a dangerous concentration of the Jewish population along the central coastal plain, and "to constitute a human wall against the dangers of invasion."[28] Beyond the desire for intensive Jewish colonization of these territories the government and the Jewish National Fund (JNF) also undertook to fulfill "the Zionist aim of placing all the lands in the homeland in the hands of the people by having most of the real estate in Israel become the property of the State and the Zionist Movement."[29]

Map 1. The U.N. Partition Plan, 1947.

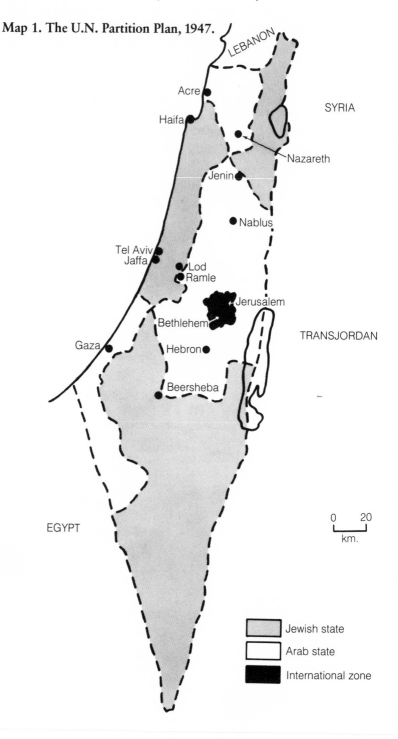

Map 2. Israel: 1949 Armistice Lines.

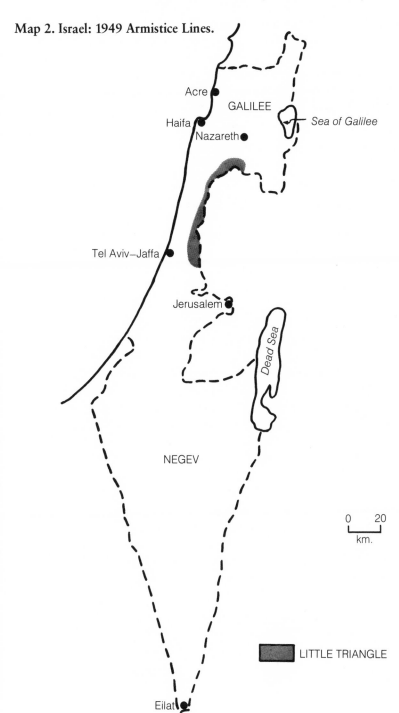

Acre

GALILEE

Sea of Galilee

Haifa

Nazareth

Tel Aviv–Jaffa

Jerusalem

Dead Sea

NEGEV

0   20
km.

LITTLE TRIANGLE

Eilat

The *raison d'être* of the state of Israel in Zionist ideology is the "ingathering of the exiles" (*kibbutz galluiot*), to make it possible for most if not all the Jews of the diaspora to settle in the "Land of Israel." The first act of the Provisional State Council on May 14, 1948, was to abolish all restrictions on Jewish immigration and land sales to Jews. The Law of Return, passed by the Knesset in 1950, and the Citizenship Law of 1952 granted every Jew the right to immediate citizenship upon arrival in Israel. Between May 1948 and December 1951, over 684,000 Jews entered the country as new immigrants, thereby more than doubling the Jewish population in two and a half years. While the arrival of this mass of Jews was in itself fulfillment of an important Zionist objective, it also presented enormous problems of absorption and settlement. Of these immigrants approximately 50 percent were from Europe (including 100,000 Jews from displaced-persons camps in Germany, Austria, Italy, and Cyprus) and 50 percent from countries in Asia and Africa—Iraq, Yemen, Turkey, Iran, Morocco, Tunisia, and Algeria.[30] Most of these immigrants were indigent, and nearly all required food, shelter, medical attention, and language training. These problems were compounded by a clash of cultures which ensued with the influx of large numbers of "Oriental Jews" who lacked the Zionist elan and European outlook of the primarily Ashkenazic Yishuv. The absorption of the immigrants was set forth as a national goal, and it strained the capacities of the society to the breaking point.

The development of a sound economy was also a primary objective of the state. The war and the mass immigration which followed brought Israel to the brink of economic disaster. From 1949 to 1952, agricultural production declined as a result of the prolonged total mobilization of the army, the depredations of the war, and the flight of tens of thousands of Arab agriculturalists. Serious food and raw material shortages developed and a Ministry of Supply and Rationing was established to administer a strict system of controls over food, clothing, and imports. By 1949 a severe shortage of workers had been replaced by large-scale unemployment. Inflation intensified, aggravated by an enormous defense budget and wasteful make-work projects for new immigrants.

Besides these problems of security, territory, immigration

absorption, and economic development the state also faced substantial political problems. In the words of Count Folke Bernadotte, the U.N. Mediator on Palestine, "The most pressing need of the Jewish State since its inception has been the opportunity to consolidate its position, both internally and externally, and to perfect its administrative and political organization."[31] Internally a government apparatus was in the process of emerging from the Jewish Agency. Difficult problems remained concerning the future relationship between the Jewish Agency and other "national institutions" (nonstate organizations, such as the JNF, the Basic Fund, and the World Zionist Organization) and the government of Israel. The role of the army—whether it would serve as a pioneering people's army with a socialistic political thrust or develop as a politically neutral tool of the state—was another sensitive issue. A lack of administrative structures and legal procedures for supervising the use and disposition of abandoned Arab property resulted in a chaotic scramble by new immigrants, established settlements of demobilized soldiers, the Histadrut, the JNF, and the government's own "Custodian of Absentee Property." Attempts to formulate a constitution failed, mainly as a result of profound disagreements between clericalists and sectarians concerning the implications of "Jewish statehood." When the first elections to the Knesset were held in January 1949, a continuation of the Zionist movement's proportional representation system resulted in fierce competition for votes. Of the twenty-one different "lists" or slates of candidates, twelve were represented in the First Knesset and a fragile coalition government emerged. (Under Israel's proportional-representation electoral system, the entire country is treated as one district. Each voter casts a ballot for one list of candidates. Political parties may organize more than one list. Each list is awarded a number of seats in the Knesset roughly equal to the proportion of the popular vote it receives.)

Nor was Israel secure on the international scene from serious political threats to its legitimacy as a sovereign state and to its territorial and demographic integrity. The Arab states continued to call for the elimination of the Jewish state, undertook an economic boycott against Israel, and deprived it of the use of the Suez Canal. Count Folke Bernadotte submitted a plan to the

United Nations which called on Israel to relinquish control over the southern Negev in return for retention of western and central Galilee. The "Bernadotte Plan" envisioned the assimilation of southern and eastern Palestine by Transjordan and vested ultimate control over Jewish immigration in the United Nations. The count's assassination on the outskirts of Jerusalem by Jewish terrorists in September 1948 generated a wave of support for the plan at the United Nations. Great Britain worked on its behalf with particular energy, primarily because of the strategic advantages that would accrue to Britain from Transjordan's control of the southern Negev and the opening of the Haifa port and Lydda airport.[32]

At the conferences sponsored by the United Nations Conciliation Commission for Palestine in Lausanne, New York, and Paris from 1949 through 1951, the Arab states continuously demanded the return of the Arab refugees and immediate Israeli withdrawal from territories outside the U.N. partition boundaries for the Jewish state. In addition to U.N. resolutions calling for the return of the refugees who chose to do so "at the earliest practicable date," Israel was pressed by the United States in the summer of 1949 to admit between 200,000 and 250,000 refugees and to withdraw from the southern part of the Negev.[33]

The United States was also in the forefront of worldwide opposition to Israel's decision to make Jerusalem the state's capital. The transfer of Israeli government ministries from Tel Aviv to Jerusalem was contrary to a U.N. resolution of December 1949, which called for an international regime in the Holy City. The Israeli move also called down the wrath of the Vatican and focused the attention of the Christian world on Jewish governance over Christian holy places and over Christian inhabitants of the Holy Land.

The external political factor was of additional significance in regard to the state's rapid utilization of abandoned Arab property. Immediate exploitation of abandoned Arab land was seen as highly desirable from a political point of view. The Israeli leadership anticipated that the buildings and lands of the refugees, if left deserted, would reinforce pressures for the return of their owners. At the same time procedures had to be formulated which would not "be interpreted as confiscation of the abandoned property . . . [which] would have been unfavorably regarded abroad, and, no doubt, opposed."[34]

Thus Israel, in its early years, faced seemingly overwhelming military, social, economic, and political problems. The regime also entertained certain powerful ideological goals. Furthermore, as has been suggested, Zionism had not succeeded in formulating a coherent vision of what the role and status of an Arab minority would be in the new Jewish society. Nor did the crisis conditions under which that society emerged as a sovereign political entity encourage serious and explicit consideration of the internal Arab problem. But the Jewish leadership, in its efforts to cope with those problems which it did perceive as major, did adopt specific policies regarding Israeli Arabs, policies designed to put Arab resources at the disposal of the Jewish authorities.

However, before considering the interface between the government's efforts to meet the major challenges that it faced and the existence of a substantial Arab minority, it is first necessary to provide a brief description of the Arab community that found itself under Israeli control after the war and after the mass Arab exodus.

The Instant Minority

For the Arabs who remained in the territory controlled by Israel the war and the flight of the refugees were events of cataclysmic dimensions. Four-fifths of the Arab population had fled—overnight, it seemed, the Arabs had become a minority in a Jewish state. The Arab economy had disintegrated. There was mass unemployment in Arab areas as well as severe shortages of food. Thousands of families were divided during the fighting. Contacts with friends, relatives, and property across the armistice lines were severed. Conscious of the savagery of the fighting and Arab plans for the Jews in the event of an Arab victory, Israeli Arabs were fearful of the treatment they might receive at the hands of the Jews. Many were unconvinced of the permanence of the Israeli state and all were uncertain as to their status within it.

Moreover, these Arabs now lacked leadership of any national stature. Practically the entire political, social, economic, religious, and intellectual elite had participated in the near total evacuation of Arab urban centers. The struggle of Palestinian Arabs against Zionism and against the British mandate had been dominated, since the late 1920's, by a small number of large, powerful families located in the largest cities of Palestine (not including Tel Aviv, which was wholly Jewish)—Jerusalem, Nablus, Haifa, and Jaffa. The political strengths of the Palestinian national movement were based on the feudalistic links between these families and networks of smaller clans and extended families in villages throughout the country, as well as on the active support of a substantial urban professional and merchant class, largely Christian and highly nationalistic.[35] When these families disappeared along with the urban bourgeoisie from Israeli-controlled territory in 1948, there was no Arab political elite to replace them.

Consider the (approximate) non-Jewish population figures for the major Arab cities in Israel-Palestine given in Table 2.

The armistice lines separated Israeli Arabs from the remaining Palestinian Arab population centers on the West Bank and the Gaza Strip. In the words of the first Israeli adviser to the prime minister on Arab affairs, Yehoshua Palmon, "the people [Arabs] who remained were like a headless body . . . the social, commercial, and religious elite had gone."[36]

Nor did the Arabs who remained in Israel any longer constitute a base of support for a "national" political leadership. The economic infrastructure of Arab Palestine (at least that part under Israeli control) had been shattered. There were no longer any Arab marketing concerns or Arab-owned industries; there were no Arab newspapers or publishing houses and no Arab political parties or labor unions.[37] In addition to the cities, most Arab villages had also been evacuated. Out of over 550 Arab villages in the territory controlled by Israel, only 121 (including northern Bedouin encampments) remained intact.[38] The "center" had fled; the Arabs who stayed were, in effect, the remnants of what had been the "periphery" of the Arab community.

The first census in November 1948 counted only 69,000 Arabs in Israel, compared to approximately 860,000 in the same area before the war. However, the best estimate of the Arab pop-

Table 2. Arab Population in Major Cities, 1947–1949

City	Before the War	After the War [a]
Jerusalem	75,000	3,500
Jaffa	70,000	3,600
Haifa	71,200	2,900
Lydda-Ramle	34,920	2,000
Nazareth	15,540	16,800
Acre	15,000	3,500
Tiberias	5,310	———
Safed	9,530	———

[a]The figures, especially those for Acre and Nazareth, include substantial numbers of internal refugees. The statistics for Jerusalem refer to the Western Zone, which remained under Israeli control after 1948.

ulation in Israel at the end of 1949 is 160,000, or about 12.5 percent of Israel's population. This increase was due to three factors: (1) under the conditions of war prevailing in November 1948, not all Arabs were counted; (2) under the terms of the armistice signed with Jordan in March 1949, the Little Triangle, which contained approximately 31,000 Arab villagers, was ceded to Israel; and (3) there had been a steady flow of Arab refugees back into the country, both clandestinely and under the terms of the reunion-of-families program.

Most Israeli Arabs lived in the northern part of the country, with 90,000 in central and western Galilee. Other substantial concentrations of Arabs included 31,000 in the Little Triangle in the central sector and 13,000, mostly Bedouin, in the Negev desert in the south. The rest were scattered primarily among the "mixed" cities of Haifa, Tel Aviv–Jaffa, Jerusalem, Acre, and Ramle—all having overwhelming Jewish majorities. Except for the city of Nazareth and the large villages of Shfar Am (4,000) and Um el Fahm (5,000), the 121 Arab settlements in Israel were small or very small villages.

The minority was fragmented along religious as well as geographical lines. Moslems constituted 70 percent of the population, several Christian sects accounted for 21 percent and Druse, Circassians, and others made up 9 percent. (The Circassians are a small—2,400 in Israel in 1976—Sunni-Moslem community, concentrated in two Galilean villages. Like the Druse, they must serve in the armed forces.)

No matter what the religion of the inhabitants, the traditional Arab villages were dominated by hamulas, groups of extended families associated with one another on a kinship basis. Traditionally hamulas acted as mutual protection societies and accepted collective responsibility for the deeds of their men and the honor of their women. Rivalry between hamulas was intense and blood feuds were common. Village politics tended to polarize around the two strongest hamulas, with smaller or less unified hamulas allying themselves with the more powerful ones.

By encouraging intra-hamula marriages and strategic inter-hamula marriages, clan elders strove to increase the solidarity and size of their hamulas. Contacts established by these elders with other larger clans outside the village or with the central authorities were designed to strengthen the political position of their hamula vis-à-vis others in the village. Many of these hamulas relied on their links with the British authorities and the important Arab families of Palestine to maintain their political supremacy on the village level. With the departure of the British and the flight of the major Arab families of Palestine, local politics in many Arab villages were thrown into turmoil. The previously unassailable positions of the largest hamulas came under attack, new hamula coalitions formed, and smaller clans emerged seeking power for themselves.

The economic situation was equally chaotic. Before the war over 50 percent of employed Israeli Arabs had worked in agriculture, either as small farmers, as sharecroppers, or as agricultural laborers. Most agriculture in the Arab sector, aside from citriculture (Arab-owned citrus groves were almost entirely destroyed or confiscated as a result of the 1948 fighting), consisted of subsistence farming. Yet few Arab families owned enough land, given their primitive agricultural techniques, to subsist in any acceptable form. Thus during the mandate large numbers of Arabs had hired themselves out as laborers to the British army, the British mandatory authorities, and those Jewish enterprises, especially citrus plantations, which would accept them. These Arabs remained in their villages, commuting on a daily or weekly basis to work in the ports, urban areas, and Jewish fields and groves. Farming on small family plots, usually undertaken by women and old men, served to supplement their wages.

But the peasantry, especially in the Moslem hill country,

was rarely out of debt and almost never financially secure. The departure of the British and the disruptions of the war deprived the Arab villages of a market for their surplus labor. No crafts or small industries which might have absorbed that surplus had developed in the villages, and high levels of Jewish immigration and unemployment, as well as the security situation, resulted in severe restrictions against Arabs entering the Jewish labor market. Consequently Arab villagers were forced back into almost complete reliance on farming at a time when much of their land was being confiscated by the Jewish authorities.

Much of the Arab land acquired by the Custodian of Absentee Property, by the JNF, or directly by Jewish agricultural settlements and municipalities in the first years of the state's existence consisted of property owned by Palestinian Arabs who fled from one part of Israeli-controlled territory to another, or who for some other reason were assigned the status of "internal refugee" or "present absentee." In other words, although these Arabs were Israeli citizens, they were forcibly prevented from reasserting possession over property declared to have been "abandoned." In 1949 approximately 75,000 of Israel's 160,000 Arabs were in this category.[39] One of the primary concerns of Israeli Arabs at this juncture was that the government allow "internal refugees" to return to their homes and/or reclaim their property.

To summarize, the Arab minority in the new state of Israel was in complete disarray. Fragmented along geographic, religious, and familial lines, it was entirely devoid of leadership above the municipal level. Dumbfounded by the defeat of the Arab armies, Israeli Arabs were as yet unconvinced of the permanence of the new state of affairs and hopeful, at least, that the refugees would be allowed to return. Their economic situation was desperate; their immediate concerns were the integrity of their property and the safety and unification of their families.

Regime Goals and the Arab Minority

As noted earlier, Zionist ideology provided no clear guidance for the manner in which Jewish-Arab relations would be regulated once independence was achieved. Nor, in the crisis atmosphere that followed the 1948 war, did the leadership of the new state have time or energy for issues which did not press directly upon vital concerns or present problems in need of dynamic action for their immediate solution. Perceiving the internal Arab problem as incidental and even trivial when compared to the awesome and urgent tasks before them in the first years of statehood, Jewish leaders left the establishment of government policy and procedure in Arab areas to lower-echelon officials.

The ad hoc, contingent nature of policy formation and implementation in the Arab sector during this period can be seen most clearly with regard to the crystallization of the "Military Administration" (or "military government") (*Memshal Tzvai*) in the last stages of the 1948 war. Military administration over Arab areas in Israel (which was gradually reformed and eventually abolished in 1966) was formally established on October 21, 1948. On that date five military governors were named in predominantly Arab districts conquered by Jewish forces in the course of the fighting. This measure, signed by Brigadier General Elimelech Avner, gave official recognition to the de facto role which Jewish units had been fulfilling in those areas since their capture—that of an occupation army.[40] Treatment of the Arab inhabitants of these areas—Nazareth, western Galilee, Ramle-Lod, Jaffa, and the Negev—varied widely according to the inclination of the local military governor.[41]

In fact neither Avner, who assumed overall responsibility for the military administration, nor Emanuel Mor, who succeeded him in this capacity in 1949, received any important guidance from higher military or political echelons.[42] Ben-Gurion set an example of indifference to the internal Arab problem by refusing to finance the salaries of Arab policemen in Nazareth hired by the Military Administration and, according to one military governor, "by treating this problem as one for which he had no time." Taking his cue from the attitude of the political leadership, Yakov Dori, chief of staff until November 1949, told Mor: ". . . the military administration is none of my concern, Ben-Gurion dumped it on me. I could not refuse, but I did not want it; I have no interest in it. In other words, don't bother me about it—do what you want." The attitude of Yigal Yadin, who succeeded Dori as chief of staff, was no different. Soon after his appointment, he told Mor: "Listen Emanuel, you should know that I am not going to help you with anything, the military administration is no business of the army . . . I am telling you now, you won't get one good officer, so don't wait for any help from me."[43]

Even after the end of the fighting in 1949 the Jewish leadership continued to believe that the minority problem had been all but eliminated by the mass Arab exodus—that the number of Arabs left in the state was insignificant.[44] This point of view is documented in an official Israeli government booklet (published in 1950) regarding the inconceivability of the return of the Arab refugees. "As a result of the war and the flight of the Arabs, Israel has become a State with an ethnically almost homogeneous population. The whole economic and social life of the State is centered on the problem of absorbing new immigrants. The culture of the State is Jewish, the government administration, the army and all its important institutions are almost exclusively Jewish. It would be folly to resurrect artificially a minority problem which has been almost eliminated by the war."[45] However, the Arab minority which did materialize, although nothing near the 49 percent envisioned under the terms of the U.N. partition plan,[46] was nevertheless quite substantial, especially in the context of a Jewish state struggling with all its meager means to meet overwhelming problems. It was as an incidental result of dealing with the large questions with which it was preoccupied—questions of security, immigration, territorial consolidation, economic development, and political survival—that the new government was forced to develop specific policies toward the Arab minority.

In the context of efforts to provide for the security of Israel against a second invasion by the Arab states, civilian officials as well as the military administration confronted the Arab minority as a potential fifth column.[47] Thus Behor Shitreet, the head the short-lived Ministry of Minorities (May 1948–July 1949), was at the same time minister of police. Indeed, for government departments that dealt with the Arab minority, "considerations of security" had priority over all others.[48] "[C]onsiderations of security and self-preservation inevitably dominated the Israel approach to the Arab problem. It was clearly not safe to lift security restrictions on Arab movement in the border areas or extend facilities for the return of Arab emigres while the danger of a resumption of war was ever-present and real . . ."[49]

Persistent tensions in the area reinforced the fears of the Israeli leadership. Arab propaganda encouraging Israeli Arabs to aid in the struggle for the elimination of Israel was relentless, and the Jewish leadership was certain that it found a responsive audience. After all, for forty years the vast majority of Arabs in what had become the state of Israel had been unrelenting and periodically violent in their opposition to the establishment of a Jewish national home in Palestine. The military authorities also emphasized the close family ties that existed between the Arabs of Israel and those Arabs, including the refugees, who lived across the armistice lines. To make matters worse, Israeli Arabs were concentrated in the sparsely settled Galilee and along the Jordanian border. The government worried that with the onset of a "second round," Arab villages in these areas would serve as convenient way-stations for the invaders. In fact the dominant attitude of the Jewish leadership was that the Arabs living in Israel were but an extension of the Arab world as a whole—an intrusion by the enemy into Israeli territory. Accordingly, the army regarded its relationship with the Arab minority as a "continuation of the historic Arab-Jewish national struggle."[50]

Besides the image of Israeli Arabs as a fifth column there was a more specific way in which they were considered a threat to security. That involved the question of infiltration:

. . . the acute problem of Arab marauders and robber gangs constantly infiltrating across Israel's frontiers. . . . Many of them were armed. . . . They have left a trail of blood and pillage in almost every frontier region. According to official statistics, up to June 1951, eighty-six inhabitants of Israel—apart from Israel military personnel—were murdered by these gangs, and a large number wounded. . . . It is clear that these large and continual incursions could not have been carried out without the active aid of Arabs in Israel.[51]

During the fighting, Arab areas conquered by Jewish units were immediately put under the control of the Israel Defense Forces. Once Jewish control was established over an area, every effort was made to prevent Arabs who had fled or been evacuated from entering the area and reestablishing residence there. In the cities the remainder of the Arab population was relocated so as to form compact Arab quarters which could easily be cordoned off.[52] Periodically the army swept through these Arab quarters in Haifa, Jaffa, and Acre searching for infiltrators. Searches were also conducted on a regular basis in Arab villages and in the single remaining Arab city of Nazareth. Tens of thousands of such infiltrators were found in the first years of the state's existence and expelled into the neighboring Arab countries. Many individuals were expelled two or three times after successive attempts to reenter the country. For the army did not think it "feasible to differentiate between infiltrees and guerrillas,"[53] i.e., between those Arab infiltrators who were actually intending to commit acts of sabotage and those who merely yearned to return to their homes and families. Nevertheless, approximately thirty thousand Arabs succeeded in establishing their residence in Israel after illegally crossing the border.[54]

Because they were used as underground-railroad stations by Arab refugees attempting to return to Israeli-controlled territory, Arab border villages in Israel were regarded by military authorities as "bases for infiltration, spying, and smuggling."[55] The military emphasized that the borders of Israel would not be respected and that security would be endangered as long as Arab villages remained along the armistice lines with Lebanon in the north, Jordan in the central sector, and Egypt in the Gaza Strip area. The problem was seen as particularly acute in the central sector, where a continuous line of Arab villages, ceded by Jordan under the armistice agreement, lay adjacent to the border along Israel's "narrow waist." Israel's military demanded that "Israel's long frontier be dotted with a string of fortress settlements . . . physically cordoning off the Israeli Arabs from the Arabs across the frontier."[56] In the army's view the struggle against infiltration justified such measures as the destruction of houses, the declaration of Arab lands as closed security areas, and the expulsion of Arabs from their villages along the borders.

The desire by military authorities to establish fortified Jewish settlements in place of Arab villages along the borders and especially to destroy the compactness of Arab settlement in the Little Triangle and the central Galilee accorded well with the efforts of Ben-Gurion and his colleagues in the Jewish Agency and the JNF to consolidate Israel's control over the lands acquired during the 1948 fighting through the rapid establishment of scores of new Jewish settlements. As indicated above, political pressure at the United Nations concerning Israeli withdrawal from the Negev and/or western and central Galilee was intense in late 1948 and early 1949. Ben-Gurion reports that in November 1948, representatives of the Israeli Ministry of Foreign Affairs participating in United Nations discussions

told us it was necessary to establish new settlements in the Negev in order to prove that Israel really controlled the area. On November 6, the Prime Minister [Ben-Gurion] met with Yosef Weitz [director of the Land and Afforestation Division of the JNF] and Levi Eshkol [director of the Land Settlement Department of the Jewish Agency] to discuss the settlement of the first 300 Jews in Beersheba (until that time there had not been a single Jewish civilian in the town), as well as the establishment of settlements in the vicinity. They also discussed the setting up of new villages in Upper Galilee, along the Lebanese border in the north. The establishment of settlements in the Negev and the Galilee [Israel did not yet have control over the Little Triangle] was no less important than the military conquest of those areas.[57]

The objective of rapid, diffuse Jewish settlement had enormous significance not only for the lands abandoned by Arab refugees who had fled into neighboring countries but also for the property of those Arabs who had remained in Israeli territory, whether classified as "internal refugees" or not. Speaking for the moment only of lands north of the Negev desert, it may be estimated that the Arabs who remained in Israel, including those classified as "internal refugees" or "technical absentees," formally owned over 11 percent of the land in Israel, including over 29 percent of the land under cultivation in 1949.[58] A very high proportion of these lands lay in border areas. Altogether they constituted a majority of privately owned real estate in Israel.[59] Consequently, Arab land holdings were a major obstacle to the concentration of land ownership in "public" (i.e., government and JNF hands).

Thus if the objectives of territorial consolidation, close settlement of Jews on the land, and a thorough extension of "public" ownership of land were to be attained, Arab-owned land would have to be put at the disposal of the Israeli government and the Jewish settlement institutions. In the words of Abraham Granott: "The former lands of the Jewish National Fund were practically all utilized for settlement and housing and it no longer had any vacant land for disposal by the settlement institutions. The Jewish Agency Settlement Department planned the erection of hundreds of new villages, the implementation of which called for fertile areas."[60] In fact, during the fighting and in the months following the end of the war Jewish individuals (both new immigrants and veteran settlers), Jewish municipalities and collective settlements, the Histadrut, the army, the Jewish Agency, the JNF, various government ministries, and newly formed administrative agencies all participated in a chaotic scramble for Arab lands which had been "abandoned" (or which were thought to have been abandoned).[61] Between 1948 and 1953, 370 new Jewish settlements were established—350 on land classified as abandoned.[62] At least 250,000 dunams of the land so classified were in fact owned by Arab residents of Israel who had been assigned "absentee" status by the government under the Absentee Property Act of 1950.[63]

The development plans of the Israeli government and the "national institutions" and the desire to consolidate sovereignty over politically contested areas also conflicted with the Bedouin's customary rights over, if not their ownership of, large tracts of land in the Negev. Over sixty thousand Bedouin inhabited the Negev before 1948. They were accustomed to wandering back and forth over the desert area, ranging from the Sinai Peninsula into the Judean wilderness and even into Transjordan. Economically, the Bedouin relied on smuggling and tending their flocks of sheep and goats in addition to extensive and rather haphazard farming on plots scattered throughout the desert. It is estimated that prior to 1948 the Bedouin cultivated over 2,200,000 dunams in the Negev.[64] Although at the end of the fighting less than fifteen thousand Bedouin remained in the Negev, their nomadic lifestyle and their claims to large tracts of land were incompatible with the systematic settlement and development of the area as envisioned by Israeli leaders. Indeed, the Israeli government preferred to classify those lands as "crown lands" which reverted to the sovereign government of Israel upon the termination of the British mandate. In addition sovereignty over the el-Auja area on the border with Egypt was in dispute, and attempts by Bedouin tribes which had sided with Egypt during the war to resume their use of the area were seen as hostile acts designed to interfere with the exercise of Jewish rights in the district.[65]

The interface between Israeli objectives concerning security and territorial consolidation and the Arabs minority's existence and resources has thus far been examined. Security and land have been, in fact, the most important issues in connection with Israel's policy toward the Arab minority. However, it is also necessary to trace the intersection of Israeli attempts to achieve three other goals—immigrant absorption, economic development, and political support and legitimacy—and the existence and resources of the Arab population. For in pursuit of these objectives, as well, it has been necessary to elicit Arab compliance and make available Arab resources.

In the first massive wave of immigration, nearly 200,000 Jews were able to obtain housing by moving into abandoned Arab towns and villages.[66] "In 1954, more than one third of Israel's Jewish population lived on absentee property and nearly a third of the new immigrants (250,000 people) settled in urban areas abandoned by the Arabs."[67] Most of this property was of course that of Arab refugees who had fled across the armistice lines, but a substantial percentage was the property of those Israeli Arabs who, as explained above, had been classified as "internal refugees" or "present absentees." In order to preserve the houses, shops, and businesses of those Israeli Arabs for occupation and use by Jewish immigrants it was necessary to prevent them from moving back to their empty villages and neighborhoods. It was also seen as necessary to prevent any form of political organization among Israeli Arabs that might lead to Arab residents "squatting" in their former villages. In the case of Arab villages such as Ghabasiyeh, "internal refugees" who had managed clandestinely to resume residence in their still-vacant villages were forcibly expelled.[68] More houses were made available for Jewish habitation as a result of the removal of Arabs from their homes in the large "mixed cities" and their concentration in specified Arab quarters.

Besides the private property of Israeli Arabs used to accommodate new Jewish immigrants, there were in addition the considerable resources of the Moslem Waqf. The Waqf was a religious endowment to which the faithful could donate their wealth for the benefit of the Moslem community, to avoid taxation by the secular authorities, and/or to maintain the integrity of their estates. Property could be donated in various ways, including the donation of annual tithes without an effective transfer of ownership. After the war the Moslem community remaining in Israel claimed the right to control and administer these properties. However, in 1950 the government imposed the Law of Abandoned Property upon the assets of the Waqf, thereby putting hundreds of thousands of dunams of agricultural land, large tracts of urban real estate, and thousands of houses, businesses, and shops under the control of the Custodian of Absentee Property and ultimately at the disposal of new Jewish immigrants.[69]

In addition to being substantial contributions to the settlement and absorption of new immigrants, the properties under the control of the Custodian of Absentee Property, including Waqf properties, were in sheer economic terms enormously important to the new state. The United Nations estimated the value of abandoned Arab immovable property as £P 100,383,784 while the value of abandoned movable property was put at £P 19,100,000.[70] These properties included extensive stone quarries, forty thousand dunams of vineyards, 95 percent of Israel's olive groves, nearly one hundred thousand dunams of citrus groves, and ten thousand shops, businesses, and stores.[71] The abandoned olive and citrus groves were instrumental in alleviating the serious balance-of-payments problem which Israel suffered from 1948 to 1953.

Again, most of this property, both movable and immovable, was that of the Arabs who had fled to neighboring countries, but a substantial amount had been the property of "present absentees" within Israel. All in all, approximately one-half the Arab population of Israel was subject to categorization as "absentees" under the terms of the Absentee Property Law of 1950. Although no official breakdown of abandoned property has been released which would indicate what proportion of property classified as abandoned had previously been owned by Arabs who

remained within Israel's borders, Don Peretz has estimated that
"40% of the land owned by legal residents of Israel was confiscated by the authorities as part of the absentee property policy."[72]

The material resources of the Israeli Arab population as a
whole—land, labor, and agricultural produce—were also important factors in Israel's early struggle for economic viability.
Comprehensive restrictions on the movement of Arabs from
place to place eliminated Arab labor mobility and protected new
Jewish immigrants, workers, and merchants from Arab economic competition.[73] Initial shortages of workers were in part alleviated by channeling unemployed Arab villagers to the areas in
Israel most in need of labor. When the influx of Jewish immigration reached mammoth proportions and severe unemployment developed, Arab villagers could be removed from the labor
market to provide jobs for as many Jews as possible.[74] The value
of Arab labor to the Israeli economy was increased by the substantially lower wages paid Arab workers.[75] Similarly, in the
early years of acute food shortages, Arabs were forced to sell
their produce to Jewish marketing concerns at much lower
prices than were paid to Jewish farmers.[76] With the financial resources of the state under severe strain, the new regime found it
convenient not to have to expend scarce resources on the integration of the Arab community into the Jewish economy and society or on efforts to raise the Arab standard of living to that of
Israel's Jewish citizens. Food rations allotted to Arab citizens
were, for example, markedly lower than those provided to Israel's Jewish population.[77]

The goals of the Israeli leadership, to summarize, were centered around the development of a strong Jewish state, society,
and economy. These goals did not include the integration of
Arabs into the Zionist framework. Nevertheless, in one sphere,
the electoral, vigorous attempts were made to integrate the Arab
minority into the affairs of the Jewish community, though even
here the "integration" was on a formal level only.[78]

The Arab minority, in addition to the new immigrants, constituted one of the few large blocs of free-floating votes in the
new Israeli polity. In the hotly contested elections to the First
Knesset in 1949 many Jewish parties made extraordinary efforts

to woo these new voters. Competition for votes was conditioned and, indeed, made somewhat easier, by the social structure of the Arab population. If the elders of a hamula could be persuaded to support a given political party, they were almost certain to be able to deliver the votes of all the members of their clan, both male and female. Several Zionist parties, particularly Mapai (the predominant Labor Party), Mapam, the General Zionists, the National Religious Party, and the Sephardic list used the various agencies and institutions under their control (the Histadrut, the Military Government, the Ministries of Religion, of the Interior, and of Minorities, the Custodian of Absentee Property, etc.) to develop electoral support in the Arab sector. As a result, the difficult problem of developing administrative structures and procedures for the Arab sector amidst the economic and political chaos prevailing in the villages was made even more complicated. This intense partisan activity further confused the Arabs of Israel, who were, as yet, quite unfamiliar with the electoral process and uncertain as to the wisdom of their participation.

The political activities of Israeli Arabs were also of significance to the Jewish leadership insofar as they might result in protests concerning the treatment of the minority which could have international ramifications. For one of the charges leveled at Israel by the Arab delegations at the United Nations was that there was a "complete absence of security for the Arabs in areas under Israel control, in violation of guarantees provided for minorities under the partition plan . . ."[79] As a result of the complaints of the Arab delegations the United Nations Conciliation Commission for Palestine (UNCCP) undertook a study of several issues involving Israeli Arabs, among them the Arab demand for the abrogation of the Absentee Property Act, the requisition and proscription of Arab houses and lands, the reunion of families, and the freezing of Waqf property.[80]

In December 1948 Israel was refused admission to the United Nations, and in May 1949 it tried again. In his address before the United Nations Ad Hoc Political Committee, which was evaluating this second application, Abba Eban declared: "The Government of Israel reaffirms its obligation to protect the persons and property of all communities living within its borders. It will discountenance any discrimination or interference with the rights and liberties of individuals or groups forming such minorities. The Government of Israel looks forward to the restoration of peaceful conditions which might enable relaxation of any restrictions on the liberty of persons or property."[81]

In the final analysis Israeli leaders were worried lest Israeli Arabs, in the context of negotiations over permanent borders, raise the demand for political self-determination in areas, such as central Galilee and the Little Triangle, where their proportion of the population was overwhelming.[82] Accordingly the Israeli leadership endeavored to lower the visibility of the Arab minority in order to prevent the question of self-determination from developing into an important international issue. In order to divert international attention from the problem of Arab refugees within Israel, the government requested that the United Nations Relief and Works Agency (UNRWA) aid to these refugees be discontinued.[83] Government ministers worked assiduously in the Knesset to prevent open and prolonged debate on issues related to the Arab minority.[84] In the semiofficial press scant attention was paid to Israeli Arabs except to demonstrate how great was their material progress and how happy were their relations with their fellow Jewish citizens. Such coverage was generally limited to showcases such as the Haifa Arab community and rather explicitly put forward for the appreciation of "the gentlemen of the United Nations General Assembly and Security Council."[85]

Another specific factor was quite important with regard to Israel's treatment of its Arab minority and world opinion. In 1948 it was as yet unclear whether or not the large Jewish communities in Arab countries such as Iraq, Yemen, Morocco, and Libya would be allowed to emigrate freely to Israel and whether or not they would be allowed to transfer their possessions. Israeli treatment of its Arab minority was seen by some as "a powerful card in Jewish hands" which would, incidentally, be lost if the government adopted the suggestions of certain right-wing elements and resorted to the expulsion of Israeli Arabs.[86] The government, for international consumption, contrasted its treatment of Israeli Arabs with the harassment of Jews in Arab countries and the confiscation of the property of Jewish emigrants.[87] It was disturbed by critics of government policy who pointed out the similarity between the provisions of the Absentee Property Act and the measures taken by the Iraqi government regarding the confiscation of Jewish property.[88]

But at any rate the government did not want to paint too rosy a picture of Arab life in Israel, since it was interested in convincing the international community of the unworkability of a large-scale return of Arab refugees and the refugees themselves of its undesirability. Such a delicate propaganda posture could not be maintained if Arab dissatisfaction inside Israel were allowed free expression.

By 1948 Zionism had long been dedicated to the establishment of a Jewish state in Palestine. With the creation of Israel, however, the Zionist movement did not see its mission as having come to an end. The state existed, but only precariously. Its territorial and demographic integrity were under attack; it contained only a small percentage of world Jewry; and its internal structure reflected neither the socialist utopia of the labor Zionist movement nor the hierocratic ambitions of the religious Zionists. Slogans such as "redeeming the land," "Judaizing the Galilee," "ingathering of the exiles," and "building the Jewish state" still had real motive power.

In this context the relationship between the Jewish-Zionist community in Israel and the Arab minority was defined in strict accordance with the goals of the dominant group. The leadership of the new state wanted to prevent the Arab minority from serving as a fifth column or abetting large-scale infiltration; to acquire from Israeli Arabs a large percentage of their land-holdings; to take advantage of Arab resources for the absorption of new immigrants; to harness Arab economic power for the rapid development of the Jewish-controlled Israeli economy; to aggregate political support among Israeli Arabs for partisan advantage; and to prevent the Arab minority from becoming a burden in the arena of international politics. The regime did not want, nor did it strive to achieve, the integration or absorption of the Arab population into the Jewish community. Neither did it entertain seriously the possibility of wholesale expulsion, though various schemes of population transfer were discussed. Rather it set out to maintain the social segregation of Arabs and Jews, to extract certain important resources from the Arab population, and to regulate and direct the behavior of the Arab minority to serve the interests of the Jewish majority. Thus Israeli policy toward the Arab minority was determined by an overriding objective—to control the Arab community in Israel rather than to eliminate, integrate, absorb, or develop it.

The following chapters establish a frame of reference for the analysis of such a policy and then describe the manner in which effective control over Israeli Arabs has been achieved and maintained.

3.
Control of Arabs in Israel:
An Analytic Framework

The Perceptions of the Central Authorities

From a historical point of view the regime's approach to the Arab minority has been heavily conditioned by Zionism's interpretation of the experience of Jewish minorities in the diaspora. This was well illustrated in a *Jerusalem Post* editorial published in June 1976. The editorial was addressed to a group of Arab mayors who had suggested that Israel be conceived of as a "binational state" rather than a "Jewish state."

> It may . . . be essential to reiterate to Israel's Arab citizens that while they have an inalienable right to fight for greater equality and more opportunities—a fight in which many Jews will enlist on their side—Israel is, and will remain, irrevocably Jewish.
>
> As a millennia-old minority par excellence, experience taught the Jewish people a major lesson: that a minority must develop a finely tuned sensitivity to the majority's sensibilities, and must be eternally alive to the invisible boundaries that dare not be crossed in the area of majority-minority relations. These truths hold all the more in the tension-laden atmosphere which accompanies the continuing threat to Israel's existence from its Arab neighbors.[1]

A decade and a half earlier Yigal Allon wrote that "Jews should understand the situation of Israeli Arabs because they have been living historically as a national minority." He continued:

> It is necessary to declare it openly: Israel is a single-nationality Jewish state. The fact that an Arab minority lives within the country does not make it a multinational state. It only requires that the state grant equal citizenship to every citizen of the state, with no differences based on religion, race, or nationality. The Arabs have many states, the Jews have one state only. The Arabs of this country must understand that they also must make a substantial contribution toward the alleviation of Jewish suspicion regarding most of the Arab population.[2]

Gideon Spiegel commented in a similar vein in a theoretical article on Zionist ideology and the Arab minority. Writing in 1967 in *Ramzor*, a publication of the central committee of Mapai, Spiegel explicitly rejected American-style liberalism as a model for Jewish-Arab relations in Israel, but admitted that both Jews and Arabs were hesitant to discuss the ultimate solution for Arabs in Israel. Spiegel concluded his discussion of the political role of the Arab population by observing, "In truth, it is not pleasant to be a national minority."[3]

The regime's fundamental distrust of the Arab minority has been reflected in the fact that five of the six men who have served as Adviser to the Prime Minister on Arab Affairs—Yehoshua Palmon, Uri Lubrani, Shmuel Divon, Rehavam Amir, and Shmuel Toledano—were recruited for their post from the secret service.[4] From the official biography of Shmuel Toledano, for example, who served as Arab affairs adviser from 1966 to 1976, one can deduce the type of expertise which the prime minister's office has sought in connection with the management of "the Arab problem" (*habaayah haAravit*): "He joined the army in 1948 and served in the Intelligence Corps with the rank of Major. He was responsible for Arab affairs. In 1952 he left the army and was appointed to a high-ranking position in the Central Intelligence and Defence Institution where he stayed until 1966 undertaking special assignments (abroad and at home) and which for obvious reasons cannot yet be publicized."[5]

However, there is no need to rely only on what can be inferred from Zionist theory or administrative recruitment patterns. Officials in charge of implementing policy in the Arab sector have, from time to time, made their own conception of their task quite clear. Ben-Gurion's basic attitude toward the Arab sector was described by Shmuel Divon, the prime minister's second Arab affairs adviser, as follows: "Ben-Gurion always reminds us that we cannot be guided by subversion which the Arab minority has *not* engaged in. We must be guided by what they *might* have done if they had been given the chance."[6]

In 1958 the military governor of the Little Triangle described his assignment quite explicitly. "My job is not defense. That is the task of the frontier police and the Jewish farming villages along the border. My job is controlling the Arab population of the area as long as there is no peace. We know that the great part of the population is loyal. But we also know that another part is not loyal, and they must be checked, patrolled, and supervised."[7]

Yigal Allon, perhaps more than any other senior Israeli government official, has been involved in the formulation and implementation of policy in the Arab sector. In 1959 he catalogued the arguments put forward *within* the Israeli establishment in support of continuance of the Military Administration.

(A) Efficient control over the Arab population and its movements in order to prevent organization and hostile military activity by Arab citizens of the State.

(B) To prevent the unwanted movement of Arabs into certain delicate areas such as divided Jerusalem, the Negev, and especially Eilat.

(C) So that there will exist a legal basis for actions taken against treasonous assemblies and so that traitors can be punished.

(D) So that there will be a basis to prevent and deter hostile political actions and organizations.

(E) A separation between the Arab population and new settlements; mainly between those Jews who came as immigrants from revolutionary Arab countries, who harbor hatred and feelings of revenge regarding their brothers who were oppressed by the Arabs in the past.[8]

Allon proceeded to call for the abolition of the military government (which underwent major reforms in the early 1960's and was abolished in 1966) essentially on the basis that, given the talents of Israel's various security services, given the possibility of additional legislation regulating movement into "sensitive areas," given the bad publicity which the Military Administration attracted in the international arena, and in light of the resentment which the Military Administration engendered among local Arabs, control over the minority could be achieved more efficiently without the Military Administration than with it.[9]

In 1962 Shimon Peres, later minister of defense and leader of the Labor Party, divided Israel's Arab minority into three categories: "the indifferent resigned; the actively hostile; the hostile resigned." For Peres, control over "which of these elements will dominate the Arab community" was *the* vital concern of the government vis-à-vis the Arab population.[10]

Uri Lubrani, who served as Arab affairs adviser from 1960 to 1963, was typically more blunt in the expression of his opins than the other men who served in that capacity. In a lecture ivered to a Jewish audience in Tel Aviv in April 1961, Lubrani allenged anyone to contradict his belief that Israeli Arabs were u.e "sworn and everlasting enemies" of the state. Lubrani acknowledged that Arabs had grievances: "With one hand we take what we give them with the other. We give them tractors, electricity, and progress, but we take land and restrict their free movement. We give them high schools, but we prevent their graduates from entering honorable occupations . . ."[11] According to Lubrani, given Arab discontent and because "we do not want Algeria to happen here," it was the task of the government to "maintain a low temperature." For Lubrani "maintaining a low temperature" meant, in particular, forestalling the development of country-wide Arab leaders or the crystallization of purely Arab parties. "Were there no Arab students perhaps it would be better. If they would remain hewers of wood perhaps it would be easier to control them. But there are things which do not depend on our wish. There is then no escape from this issue, so we must be careful to understand the nature of the problems involved and to devise appropriate strategies."[12]

In February 1975, Dani Rubinstein, Arab affairs correspondent for *Davar*, wrote, "The official policy towards the Israeli Arabs was and is not to allow them any activity within a political, social, or economic framework which is independent and Arab."[13] One and a half years later a confidential memorandum on the Arab problem, entitled "Handling the Arabs of Israel" and written by the Ministry of the Interior's senior Arabist, Israel Koenig, was published in full by the leftist Zionist Party newspaper *al-Hamishmar*. Koenig, a member of the National Religious Party, which has traditionally controlled the Ministry of the Interior, was district commissioner for the Galilee. Though publicly the government condemned the report and its recommendations, many rabbis and prominent Jewish politicians from the Galilee endorsed Koenig's proposals.[14] Israel Koenig was allowed to remain at his post and Prime Minister Rabin subsequently chose Zvi Aldoraty, a coauthor of the memorandum, as his candidate for appointment as director of the Labor Party's Arab Department.[15]

Specific points made in the Koenig memorandum are considered in a later chapter, but the document as a whole reflects more clearly and comprehensively than any other published source the overall orientation toward the Arab minority of those officials with responsibility for the affairs of the non-Jewish population. In the memorandum, Koenig identifies a number of worrisome demographic, political, and economic trends within the Arab sector. His specific suggestions for coping with these trends appeal to and accurately reflect the government's commitment to control the Arab minority. Among his proposals are the creation of a new political force in the Arab sector which the government would "control" by means of a "covert presence." He also advocates the adoption of "tough measures at all levels against various agitators among college and university students" and the intensification of economic discrimination against Arabs in order to deprive them of the "social and economic security that relieves the individual and the family of day-to-day pressures, [and] grants them, consciously and subconsciously, leisure for 'social-nationalist' thought." [16]

Theories of Control in Deeply Divided Societies

In Chapter 1 it was pointed out that much of the literature which has dealt with the politics of multiethnic or communally divided societies has been concerned with either predicting instability for such societies or explaining its anomalous absence. Traditional theories of crosscutting pluralist cleavages, notions of consociationalism, and other concepts related to the idea of subelite cartels have been wisely used as analytical approaches for those cases in which communal turmoil and severe political instability have not gone hand in hand with the continued existence of a multiplicity of primordial identities. It was further suggested that these ideas can be of little assistance in explaining the stability of Jewish-Arab relations in Israel and the absence of Arab political organization. Rather, the stability of Jewish-Arab relations in Israel can be explained only in terms of an approach which focuses on the *control* of the Arab minority.

In general, "control" as an analytical formula for explaining the anomaly of political stability in deeply divided societies has attracted much less attention than the pluralist and subelite cartel approaches. Nevertheless, though conceptually underdeveloped, a "literature" of sorts does exist. In 1958 Manning Nash, as a result of his investigation of Guatemala's "multiple society," counseled students of comparative ethnic relations to analyze systematically and in detail "how the multiple society operates, the mechanisms of political control, and the social and cultural circumstances which are amenable to, or inimical to, the perpetuation and continuity of such a political structure."[17] In 1966 Leo Kuper, discussing the prospects for system change in plural societies, speculated that "the system of domination" may be "the crucial factor affecting the possibility of evolutionary change. Different types of domination may have their own somewhat specific laws of change, with varying potentialities for evolutionary transformation."[18]

A significant number of writers have included control or domination categories within typologies describing the integration of segmented societies. M. G. Smith has written of "structural pluralism" or "differential incorporation" as one "mode of collective accommodation." Such societies, according to Smith, "owe their maintenance to a central regulative organization which is prescriptively reserved for the dominant corporate group."[19] But Smith's primary concern is in relating the "mode of collective accommodation" (equivalent, universalistic, differential) to the depth and extent of diversity within societies. The category of "differential incorporation" is itself left undeveloped.[20] Concerning the emergence, operation, and variable impact of different types of control systems or mechanisms, all we are told is that "however variable the system may be in its specific conditions and properties, the collective character, and the scope of its substantive differentiations, must be sufficiently rigorous and pervasive to establish an effective order of corporate inequalities and subordination by the differential distribution of civil and political rights and the economic, social, and other opportunities that these permit or enjoin."[21]

Pierre Van den Berghe, using a four-box matrix that crosses a homogeneous-heterogeneous variable with a democratic-despotic variable, generates a category (Type III) of "Pluralistic-Despotic" societies in which stability and equilibrium are explained by "a combination of political coercion and economic interdependence. . . . Debt peonage, slavery, contract labor, indenture, and other forms of economic dependence serve at once to reinforce political subjection, to make the latter profitable, and to sustain the ruling group and its repressive apparatus." However, Van den Berghe's analysis does not go beyond this list of typical economic techniques of control, except to offer the subcategory of "Herrenvolk democracies," i.e., those Type III societies "wherein power is relatively diffusely and equally distributed among the members of an ascriptively defined group which, in turn, rules despotically over other such groups."[22]

The general argument made by Alvin Rabushka and Kenneth Shepsle is that plural (deeply divided) societies cannot develop as stable democracies. One way the tension between the plural character of a society and a democratic political ethos can be resolved is according to what they call "the dominant majority configuration." This is characterized by "infrequent ethnic cooperation, immoderate ethnic politics at the expense of minority groups at the constitutional as well as the policy level, and eventual repression of minority political activity. Majoritarianism is the cause of the dominant community and electoral machination is its method of preserving its dominance. Violence is often fostered. . . . The symbols of democracy remain; the substance atrophies."[23]

Similarly, Milton Esman has suggested "institutionalized dominance" as one of four paths to the "management of communal conflict." (The other three are "induced assimilation, syncretic integration, and balanced pluralism.") Esman asserts that regimes committed to the dominance of one communal group at the expense of another or others will "always use three methods of conflict management":

(1) proscribe or closely control the political expression of collective interest among dominated groups, (2) prohibit entry by members of dominated groups into the dominant community, and (3) provide monopoly or preferential access for members of the dominant group to political participation, advanced education, economic opportunities, and symbols of status such as official language, the flag, national heroes, and holidays, which reinforce the political, economic and psychic control of the dominant group.[24]

Esman emphasizes that though "basically coercive . . . a network of controls for maintaining hegemony is often highly sophisticated and deeply institutionalized."[25] Although he provides several historical and contemporary examples of the variation which this category contains, he—like Smith, Rabushka and Shepsle, and Van den Berghe—does not go beyond the generation of a "control" category and provision of historical and praxeological illustration.

Leo Kuper, however, does go beyond the listing of "typical" methods of subordination by employing the concept of a "system of domination"—a system which may or may not be "self-sustaining" and which, accordingly, may depend to a greater or lesser degree on "force and repression."[26] In his analysis of white settler regimes in Africa, Kuper uses this concept to focus on domination resulting from the calculated re-creation and strengthening of diversity among subordinate groups (divide and rule) combined with the establishment of "intercalary structures, functioning between dominant and subordinate sections, and serving both to maintain separation and to provide contact and control."[27] For Kuper it is the exploitation of existing social structural and cultural circumstances by a battery of complementary regime policies which gives domination its systemic character in white settler societies. Kuper goes on to argue that, in fact, the system of control sponsored by the white settler regime in South Africa "is far from self-sustaining; on the contrary it is increasingly sustained by force and repression."[28] To be able to see the overt use of coercion as a sign of the breakdown of domination or control and not merely as evidence of its presence is an important insight occasioned by Kuper's conceptual advance.

Heribert Adam, in his study of South Africa, uses an approach quite similar to that of Kuper but comes to a different conclusion. Like Kuper, Adam is interested in investigating the question "What apart from naked coercion enables a society ridden with such deep-seated conflicts to continue to function?" Adam's answer to this central question is contained in his analysis of apartheid as a "pragmatic race oligarchy" and as "an increasingly streamlined and expanding system of sophisticated dominance."[29] He goes on to discuss a variety of mechanisms which the regime has adopted to maintain white supremacy in South Africa and effective control over the nonwhite population. These mechanisms have included exclusion of nonwhites from

even a qualified franchise, elaborate legislation erecting and enforcing social barriers between whites and nonwhites, government-sponsored programs to rejuvenate and maintain tribal
identities and traditional social structures, energetic propagation
of the concept of separate development, use of local and regional
nonwhite self-governing bodies to deflect mass dissatisfaction
among nonwhites, and explicit state intervention in the private
sector of the economy on behalf of the white minority. Adam
uses his framework to highlight the adaptiveness and success of
South African apartheid as new policies are designed and implemented by a regime anxious to maintain effective control, at
bearable cost, while faced with gradual social and economic
change.

Unfortunately Adam's treatment is somewhat haphazard.
For example, he fails to establish systematic linkages among
these policies of a sort that would perhaps justify his characterization of domination in South Africa as a "system." Nevertheless, there is immense value in Adam's study. It is especially instructive in regard to (1) the fundamental way in which he poses
and answers the central question of the stability of the South African political system; (2) his emphasis on the *peculiar* characteristics of the South African system of domination; (3) the sensitivity which he demonstrates for the manner in which specific
techniques of domination were tailored to suit particular social
and historical circumstances; and (4) his willingness to formulate conceptual categories appropriate for the South African case
without insisting that they fit into a generally applicable and/or
preconceived category, e.g., "fascism."

In the development of any new analytical approach there is
the possibility of borrowing frameworks and models from cog-
nate fields. The value of such theoretical poaching is dependent
on the coherence of the "borrowed" models themselves, and the
extent of isomorphism or "fit" between the problem at hand
and the problem toward which the borrowed models apply.
"Control" is a concept which plays a central role in the study of
many political phenomena, but the only body of theory and empirical evidence which has significantly influenced the study of
control relations in deeply divided societies is that associated
with the study of overseas European imperialism.

As many scholars have observed, the geographical separation of metropolis and colony is difficult to justify as a necessary condition for the emergence of "imperialist" or "colonialist" patterns of relations. As a result of this insight, the concept of "internal colonialism" and the vocabulary associated especially with the study of nineteenth-century European imperialism have been used to describe superordinate-subordinate group relations within "national" political units. Those who have taken this approach and applied it to specific societies have generally succeeded in matching patterns in the development of superordinate-subordinate group interaction within societies with those commonly thought of as characteristic of nineteenth-century imperialism. The economic dependence of colonies on the imperial mother country, the erection of jurisdictional and administrative barriers between colonists and natives, the systematic extraction of primary products from the colony and their transfer to the metropolis, the emergence of "comprador" groups within the colony, the limitations placed on free political activity by natives, the attempts to impose the values and doctrines of the metropolis on the colonial populations, the development of a "slave mentality" by colonized peoples, and the conservation of traditional forms of social organization in close association with the limited introduction of modern means of production and administration—all these have their counterparts in the relations between superordinate and subordinate groups *within* various societies.[30]

The problem with "internal colonialism" as an approach to the study of control in deeply divided societies is, then, not a lack of "fit" between the phenomena under consideration and those that served as the empirical referents for classical theories of imperialism. Rather, the study of internal colonialism has been obstructed by a failure to elicit, from the rich diversity of European imperial expansion and from the full range of theories describing it, a set of defining characteristics.[31] It soon becomes tedious rather than interesting to notice again and again that superordinate-subordinate relationships within societies have some features which resemble development patterns, social formations, psychological reactions, or motivations characteristic of one or another example or theory of European overseas colonialism. If Wales, Scotland, Ireland, Blacks in the pre–World War II American South, Chicanos in the barrios of large American cities in the 1970's, and Indian populations in rural Brazil are all accepted as examples of internal colonies, then what has in fact happened is that the category of "internal colonialism" has become coextensive with that of "inequality." One could conceivably go on to differentiate various forms of internal colonialism. However, "internal colonialism" is a term so weighted down with historical and rhetorical freight that such an analytical process is likely to be more impeded than assisted by its use in such a highly abstract fashion.

Harold Wolpe has adopted another approach to the use of the concept of internal colonialism for studying deeply divided societies. By drawing explicitly on Marx and Lenin for what he deems to be a coherent theory of imperialism, Wolpe attempts to distinguish internal colonialism from other superordinate-subordinate relations. Regardless of whether Marxist-Leninist theories of European overseas imperialism are correct, and regardless of the success of Wolpe's attempt to use these theories to analyze white-nonwhite relations in South Africa, this approach (i.e., the explicit elaboration of internal colonialism according to a particular and well-developed theory of overseas imperialism) is legitimate and promising.[32]

Though unimpressive when compared with the amount of research devoted to alternative methods of explaining stability in deeply divided societies, studies of control have yielded results. Primarily they have demonstrated that effective control can be based on a wide range of political and economic mechanisms, institutional arrangements, legal frameworks, and sociocultural circumstances in addition to coercion or the threat of coercion. A number of authors have attempted to introduce a measure of coherence into the field by differentiating among various syndromic mixes of control techniques. The notion of internal colonialism, even if used only as a suggestive metaphor, has helped develop sensitivity to circumstantial factors which permit the systematic and sustained subordination of one group by another.

However, such efforts have not provided an analytic framework within which certain crucial questions, questions with particular relevance to the Israeli case, might be posed and answered. These questions include the following:

   1. In what ways do particular social, cultural, or economic

circumstances support certain types of control techniques but make others more difficult or costly to implement?

2. In what ways might the content of superordinate group ideology or the organizing principles of superordinate group institutions affect the type of control techniques adopted or rejected?

3. Do different mixes of control techniques contain different possibilities for evolutionary or revolutionary change?

4. Specifically, do different mixes of control techniques contain different strategic opportunities to subordinate group members desirous of breaking the control relationship, and, if so, what can analysis of these opportunities reveal about the costs and benefits associated with different modes of resistance in the context of different types of control relationships?

If these and other such questions are to be addressed effectively, an analytic framework is necessary within which the great variety of control techniques employed in deeply divided societies can be meaningfully plotted. To accomplish this task such a framework should, for any control relationship, (1) specify the kinds of factors requiring investigation; and (2) specify the functional requisites for achieving effective control in any deeply divided society. The satisfaction of the first condition requires a multilevel analysis which systematically distinguishes pertinent cultural, geographical, ecological, or social structural "givens" from institutional or ideological factors and from the calculated policies which superordinate groups design and implement in order to achieve control or reinforce the conditions which make its maintenance possible. The satisfaction of the second condition involves focus on (1) how subordinate group members are deprived of facilities for united political action, (2) how the subordinate group is denied access to independent sources of economic support, and (3) how (for purposes of surveillance and resource extraction) effective superordinate penetration of the subordinate group is achieved.

In the Israeli case, the second condition can be fulfilled by analyzing control over Arabs as a "system" made up of three "components" and the network of relationships among them. Each component fulfills one of the three functional requisites mentioned above, so that although separately no one component results in control, operating in conjunction the three components form a "system" which does result in control.

These three components are segmentation, dependence, and cooptation. "Segmentation" refers to the isolation of the Arab minority from the Jewish population and the Arab minority's internal fragmentation. "Dependence" refers to the enforced reliance of Arabs on the Jewish majority for important economic and political resources. "Cooptation" refers to the use of side payments to Arab elites or potential elites for purposes of surveillance and resource extraction.[33] In a consideration of these three components of control, analysis cannot be limited to a discussion of how specific policies of the Israeli regime have been designed to fragment the Arab minority, to isolate it from the Jewish majority, to make Arabs dependent on Jews, or to coopt potential leaders of the Arab community. Such policies are of crucial importance and are discussed at length. But also important are those cultural habits, primordial identities, historical patterns of ecological and economic development, etc., which have contributed to making the Arab minority *susceptible* to control based on techniques of segmentation, dependence, and cooptation. Moreover, aside from these basic kinds of circumstances which have conduced toward control, and aside from policies designed and implemented by the regime to achieve and maintain control, it is necessary to appreciate how the normal operation of Israel's major institutions has contributed to the isolation of the Arab minority, to its internal fragmentation, to its dependence on the Jewish majority, and to the cooptation of Arab elites.

Consonant with the first analytical condition specified above, each component of control—segmentation, dependence, and cooptation—will be examined on each of three levels of analysis: the structural (basic historical, cultural, ecological, and economic circumstances); the institutional (pertaining to the normal pattern of operation of Israel's major institutions); and the programmatic (concerning those specific policies designed and implemented by the regime for the purpose of controlling the Arab minority). The network of mutually reinforcing relations which has emerged from these structural, institutional, and programmatic patterns makes it necessary to understand control

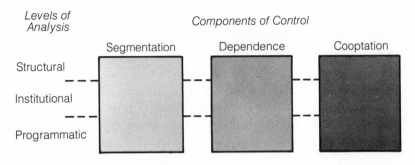

Figure 1. The System of Control.

over Israeli Arabs in systemic terms. Figure 1 may serve as a helpful mnemonic.

As suggested at the beginning of this chapter and as described in the programmatic sections of the following chapters, the authorities have consciously devised and implemented various techniques and mechanisms in order to maintain control over Israeli Arabs. That is not to say, however, that the overall effectiveness of the control which has been exerted over Israeli Arabs and the low cost at which it has been achieved have been due to a massive and brilliant conspiracy on the part of Jewish officials responsible for Arab affairs. Such a hypothesis, which I do not entertain, would be based on an assumption that these officials could and did engineer primordial attachments, traditional social structures, cultural habits, and overarching institutional frameworks for the purpose of better controlling the Arab minority. What I argue is that in order to understand the implications and efficacy of regime policies in the Arab sector, one must understand the structural and institutional contexts within which they have been implemented. The systemic framework of analysis used in this study is designed to highlight reciprocal interdependencies among structural and institutional circumstances that have conduced toward control, and policies tailored to exploit and reinforce them. The system metaphor also helps avoid the suggestion of comprehensive conspiracy by permitting analysis of how specific policies, because of the structural and institutional contexts within which they are adopted, tend to have *unanticipated* consequences which also reinforce one or another component of control. Thus the "system of control" described and analyzed in this study is offered as an analytical construct for interpreting a complex social, economic, and political reality. It is not offered as a description of a comprehensive image held by Israeli bureaucrats (though on the programmatic level of analysis individual Israeli officials have tended to see the policies which they have implemented in the Arab sector in "segmentalist," "dependency," or "cooptive" terms).

From an analytical standpoint, then, the systemic character of control in Israel derives from the synergistic relationships that exist among the three components of control—segmentation, dependence, and cooptation—and that exist within each component among structural conditions, institutional arrangements, and implemented policies. For instance, the fact that the Arab sector is fragmented among religious groups, clans, villages, etc., means that Arab groups and individuals are more easily made dependent on the Jewish authorities; the fact that Arabs are dependent in so many ways on the Jewish sector makes the cooptation of Arab elites easier because those elites lack alternative "Arab" sources of support; the fact that Arab elites are so easily cooptable makes it relatively easy to maintain the fragmentation of the Arab community by playing off different Arab elites against one another. As indicated, mutually reinforcing relationships also exist within each component among factors examined on different levels of analysis. With regard to dependence, for example, wide gaps in the levels of economic development which characterized the Jewish and Arab sectors in 1948 (structural level) would have made it difficult in the best of circumstances for infant Arab industrial or financial enterprises to compete with Jewish firms. The Jewish Agency, by funneling massive amounts of foreign capital into the Jewish sector of the Israeli economy (institutional level), has had the effect of institutionalizing these gaps in economic development and has increased the number of Arab workers dependent on Jewish industry for employment. Moreover, specific policies of the regime (programmatic level) have included discrimination against Arab communities as regards loans and grants for economic development. Such actions by the authorities have helped to block Arab attempts to overcome their economic dependence on the Jewish sector.

In the following four chapters the system of control is analyzed. Each of the next three chapters involves an examination of a different component of control. For each component of control patterns of structural conditions, institutional arrangements, and implemented policies which conduce toward, which support, or which are designed to achieve and maintain that component are described. For each of the three components, factors examined on different levels of analysis are of greater or lesser consequence, and require more or less attention. However, before all three components can be discussed as a system of control, each component must first be examined in terms of programmatic, institutional, and structural patterns and in terms of the particular functions which it fulfills in regard to control. From this description of the segmentation of the Arab minority, its dependence on the Jewish majority, and the cooptation of its potential leadership, the *effectiveness* of the system of control is demonstrated. From the description of the appropriate ways in which policies have been designed and adapted to harness, exploit, and reinforce convenient institutional and structural conditions and from the discussion of the mutually reinforcing relationships which exist among the components, the low cost of effective control is explained.

A danger associated with any systemic or, more broadly speaking, structural functional analysis is not only that certain aspects of social-political-economic reality will be overinterpreted to "fit" the analytical molds but also that the sets of mutually reinforcing causal connections which are illuminated will suggest a permanence and/or a perfection which the system lacks. Though (as is emphasized in subsequent chapters) social, cultural, and economic conditions as well as institutional arrangements have proved to be enormously convenient for the achievement of effective control, the system of control is not, and has never been, coterminous with the social fabric. There have existed certain structural conditions, certain institutionalized norms, and even some aspects of official policy in the Arab sector which have interfered with the exertion of effective control over the Arab population and which have provided

Arabs with opportunities for limited resistance to the regime. These factors are referred to as structural, institutional, or programmatic "aberrations" and are discussed most fully in Chapter 7. It is in this context that the long-run effects of the gradual modernization of the Arab sector, and the impact of political constellations and developments outside of Israel's borders, are linked to an analysis of the regime's "reconsideration" of its policies in the Arab sector and to predictions concerning the eventual instability, transformation, and/or breakdown of the system of control.

4.
Segmentation
as a Component of Control:
The Isolation and Fragmentation
of the Arab Minority

The concept of segmentation is intended to capture the fact that on each of three levels of analysis—structural, institutional, and programmatic—there are important elements which favor the isolation of the Arab minority from the Jewish majority and/or its internal fragmentation. This chapter describes these three patterns of segmentation and suggests the kinds of mutually reinforcing relationships which obtain among them.

The Structural Pattern of Segmentation

On the structural level of analysis, attention is focused on basic ecological, social structural, religious, cultural, and historical circumstances, as well as on deep-seated attitudes which themselves constitute divisions within the Arab sector and between the Arab and Jewish sectors. These factors are significant for the way in which they have made the Arab population susceptible to effective control (1) by inhibiting the formation of political alliances within the Arab population or between Arabs and dissident Jewish groups and (2) by providing the regime with an array of primordial identities and divisions which can be reinforced and exploited by appropriate "segmentalist" policies.

STRUCTURAL FRAGMENTATION

The internal fragmentation of the Arab population has been a common theme among observers of Israeli society. As Abner Cohen, an anthropologist, wrote in 1965:

The Arabs in Israel do not constitute a united, integrated community. They are divided on many lines which tend to overlap, rather than cut across each other. There is the broad division into bedouin, village dwellers, and townsmen, with hardly any links between these divisions. Furthermore, each of these divisions is divided internally. The village dwellers live in villages which are scattered over the central and northern parts of the country and are interspersed by Jewish settlements. Because of the nature of their economy their external economic interaction is mostly with Jews and they have hardly any economic relations among themselves. The Arab urban population are similarly scattered. About 20,000 of them live in Nazareth, about 7,000 in Shfar'am and the rest are dispersed among Jews in the three main Jewish towns (Jerusalem, Haifa, and Tel Aviv) and in three smaller towns (Lod, Ramle, and Acre).[1]

The Arab minority is fragmented along religious lines as well. Of the present non-Jewish population approximately 77 percent is Moslem, five Christian sects represent 15 percent, and 8 percent is Druse.[2] Most of Israel's minority population is found in nearly 150 villages and Bedouin encampments located in the Galilee to the north, in the Little Triangle in the center, and in a large reservation for Bedouin in the Negev to the south. While the Negev Arab population is almost entirely Bedouin, the Bedouin themselves are divided into forty-one tribal factions. Moreover, as discussed in Chapter 2, the Arab village population is splintered into hundreds of clans or hamulas which constitute the primary units of political competition and social life in almost every Arab community.

Whereas the village dweller-Bedouin, Christian-Moslem-Druse, and clan-to-clan fragmentations of Arab society have longstanding cultural, religious, and social structural foundations, the absence of major Arab urban centers is largely a historical consequence of the 1948 war. As indicated in Chapter 2, between the outbreak of guerrilla warfare in late 1947 and the end of fighting in early 1949, fully four-fifths of the Arab population in what became the state of Israel left the country. Included in this mass exodus were the social, political, economic, and intellectual elites who, though wracked with dissension, had provided a national leadership for the Arabs of Palestine during the British mandate. Their departure explains the absence of any established unifying urban elite among Israeli Arabs which could have served as an initial focus for Arab political action on a countrywide basis.

Chapter 7 discusses the gradual attenuation of kinship and sectarian divisions among Israeli Arabs as a factor which has contributed to higher levels of Arab political activity in the mid-1970's. Nevertheless, the continued significance of parochial identities is reflected in both the hamula-sponsored violence in Nazareth in May 1978 and the increased tensions between Israeli Christians and Moslems generated by the civil war in Lebanon.[3] The structural pattern of fragmentation along kinship, geographical, cultural, and religious lines, including the absence of an established urban elite, continues to inhibit the development of a coherent Arab political movement. To be sure, the Jewish regime has worked vigorously to reinforce this pattern of structural fragmentation, but serious structural obstacles to united political action on the part of Israeli Arabs would have existed independent of such efforts.

STRUCTURAL ISOLATION

As I have suggested, the structural pattern of segmentation which has characterized the Arab population of Israel refers not only to various divisions within the Arab collectivity, but also to the division of Israeli society into Jewish and Arab segments. Since 1948 the social and ecological segregation of Jewish and Arab citizens has been a characteristic feature of Israeli society. In 1951 the five "mixed cities" of Tel Aviv–Jaffa, Lod, Ramle, Acre, and Haifa had a combined Arab population of 20, 170, or approximately 12 percent of the total Israeli Arab population. In 1976 the combined Arab population of these same cities was 40,000, or less than 9 percent of the total Israeli Arab population.[4] Thus, if anything, the proportion of Israeli Arabs living in mixed cities has decreased over time. But even within these localities it is nearly impossible to find mixed Arab-Jewish residential districts.[5] Indeed, social contacts of any kind between Arabs and Jews are very limited. Arab-Jewish intermarriage rates are negligible. In a study of Israeli high school students conducted in 1975 only 16 percent of the Jewish students interviewed said they had opportunities for contact with Arabs.[6] Although there are instances of Arab students attending Jewish schools, there is no expectation that in the foreseeable future this will develop beyond the experimental stage, not only because of the opposition of Jewish parents but also because of the language-of-instruction problem.

It is in the context of this de facto but nonetheless systematic segregation of Jews and Arabs in Israel, as well as in the context of the continuing state of belligerency between Israel and the Arab states, that one must understand the stereotypical attitudes toward Arab citizens that have prevailed in the Jewish sector. For deep-seated attitudes of distaste toward Arabs constitute additional barriers to the development of social, cultural, and political links between Jewish and Arab citizens. These attitudes, encouraged by a security situation in which Jews have felt constrained to treat every Arab as a potential terrorist, combine with differences in language, religion, lifestyle, and historical experience to produce a feeling among Jews that Arabs are strange, alien, somewhat primitive, and rarely to be trusted.

Thus, based on a survey conducted in 1968, it was reported that 91 percent of all Israeli Jews believed that "it would be better if there were fewer Arabs." Eighty percent believed that "every Arab hates Jews." Seventy-six percent maintained that Arabs would "not reach the level of progress of Jews." Eighty-six percent said they would refuse to rent a room to an Arab, and 67 percent indicated that they would not agree "to have an Arab as a neighbor."[7] According to a similar survey in 1976, "71 percent of the respondents [Jews] declared that Arabs will not reach the level of progress of Jews, 97 percent thought that it would be better if there were fewer Arabs in Israel, 83 percent believed that it is impossible to trust Arabs, 87 percent agreed that surveillance of Arabs should be expanded, and 76 percent rejected the possibility of having an Arab superior at work."[8] Ordinary language in Israel includes the use of "Arab" as an adjective to denote faulty work, undependable performance, etc. Epithets such as "Araboosh" and "dirty Arab" are widely used. It is also common to hear Arabs referred to as "dogs," especially among working-class Jews.

In a recent survey of Israeli children's literature, Tamar Meroz noted that one theme predominates in adventure books popular among Israeli children: "The Arabs slaughter Jews for pleasure and the pure Jewish child defeats the cowardly pigs."[9] One of the most popular series of adventure stories for children, "Oz-Ya'oz," is written under the pseudonym of "Ido Seter." The following passage from one of his stories, entitled "The Young Detectives in the Sinai Campaign," is quoted by Meroz as typical.

"Min Hada?" ("who's there?"—in Arabic) shouted the Egyptian sentry. From the darkness Eli approached. The Egyptian, a character with a thick black mustache and cruel eyes, stared at the boy the way a cat stares at a mouse who has fallen prey to its claws. "What's your name?" he asked . . . revealing beneath his mustache the teeth of a carnivorous wolf. "If you won't tell me your name right away, I shall order ten soldiers to stick ten bayonets in your eyes."

"If you do (that), the Commander of the Egyptian army in Sinai will hang you on the nearest electricity pole," Eli answered him calmly.

The Egyptian officer was frightened. "What are you standing there like a dummy for? May your house be mined!" (curse) he yelled at the sentry who guarded Eli. "Bring a car and I'll take him to the Commander of the Egyptian army." Throughout their whole ride he did not cease to threaten Eli that [he'd] crush his fingers, scorch his ears, cut off his nose, pull out his teeth, blind his eyes, and spill out his brains.[10]

The general antipathy of Israeli Jews toward Arabs, including Israeli Arabs, and the identification of Israeli Arabs with the "Arab enemy" as a whole are made manifest in the spontaneous attacks made by Jews in Israel on Arabs, usually as a reaction to terrorist incidents. The Israeli population, both Jewish and Arab, has been subject to bloody acts of terror ever since the state was created in 1948. The overwhelming majority of these acts have been perpetrated by Arabs from across Israel's borders. Yet the intense hatreds which they generate in a Jewish population extremely sensitive to the loss of life are let loose regularly on the Arab population of Israel.[11] Of all such incidents none compares, in its searing impact on Jewish-Arab relations in Israel, to the massacre in the village of Kfar Kassem on the eve of the Suez War, October 29, 1956. Enforcing a 6 P.M. curfew which had been imposed on the village while most of its inhabitants were away at their places of work, an Israeli Army unit summarily executed forty-three Israeli Arab citizens, including many women and children. Besides firmly establishing in Arab minds the Jewish capacity for brutality, the incident reflects the deep segmentation of Israeli society—a society in which Jews tend to see themselves as "Jews" over and against "Arabs" whom they see not as "Israelis" but as aliens.[12]

Co-existence, a well-known play written by an Israeli Arab in 1970, reflects the impact which the Kfar Kassem massacre and other incidents have had on Arab expectations regarding their relations with Israel's Jewish citizens. Upon securing work in Tel Aviv, an Arab character in the play relates:

. . . friends told me to pick a Jewish name. It's more convenient they said. I agreed. I thought and thought and finally chose the name Max. I think it suits me. I have blue eyes and blond hair. A Yemenite fellow who is a regular customer discovered somehow that I'm an Arab. I remember the day of the hand-grenades in the central bus station. At noon the grenades began to explode very close to us. I saw people running and yelling. Suddenly they began to attack the restaurant. They broke window panes. I was afraid. I didn't know what to do with myself. While I was standing next to the espresso machine, I saw Chaim, the Yemenite. He looked at me and I looked at him. I don't remember much after that. I think I trembled. And suddenly, without thinking, I impulsively attacked him and began to yell: "Arab; he's an Arab, grab him!" The people assaulted him. I ran. I wanted to laugh. Maybe I actually did laugh. That's the first time I ever saw Jews beating up a fellow Jew while thinking that they were beating an Arab.[13]

This passage also reflects the near-complete psychological isolation of Israeli Arabs from Jewish society—a theme which has been elaborated by another Israeli Arab writer, Fouzi el-Asmar, in *To Be an Arab in Israel*. "It became apparent to me that not only newspaper advertisements but also most other things in this country, apart from laws and taxes, were not for Arabs. When the problem of youth was presented on the radio, television or in the newspapers, we were not mentioned. If there was a symposium about some social problem in Israeli society, again we were not mentioned. It was as though we did not exist."[14]

That Arabs have been so completely cut off—socially, culturally, linguistically, psychologically, etc.—from the Jewish population has substantially reduced their political potential. Jewish understanding of and sympathy for the problems of the Arab community, except among certain select groups in the Jewish sector, has rarely been forthcoming. On the structural level, a clear pattern of Arab isolation from the Jewish sector continues to prevail in Israel. However, there have been two important breaks in the overall isolation of Israeli arabs. First, Israeli Arabs have had, through the Israeli Communist Party (Rakah), access to the political and economic resources of the Soviet bloc and to Jews active in Communist Party politics in Israel. Second, as a result of being employed in Jewish metropolitan areas and on

Jewish agricultural settlements, Arab workers have had regular exposure to modern Jewish lifestyles and living standards. (The implications of such aberrations, apparent on both the structural and institutional levels of analysis, are examined in some detail in Chapter 7 in consideration of the current and future stability of the system of control.)

The Institutional Pattern of Segmentation

As suggested in Chapter 3, the overall structural pattern of seg-mentation (including both fragmentation and isolation) has been maintained, reinforced, and exploited by institutional and programmatic factors. Analysis of these relationships first re-quires a systematic and rather lengthy examination of the major institutions of Israeli society. Such an analysis shows how their standard operating procedures have, in effect, institutionalized the isolation of the Arab minority from the Jewish sector. On the institutional level of analysis it is this *isolation* of the Arab mi-nority which is of major significance, though certain aspects of the system of local council government in Arab villages, which help to institutionalize the social and political *fragmentation* of the Arab community, must also be examined.

THE ISOLATION OF THE ARAB MINORITY

Israel has defined itself as a Jewish state: "a state that embodies Jewish nationalism and serves the national interest of the Jewish people."[15] Indeed the Jewish character of Israel is manifest in all the trappings of its official existence, from its national anthem to its seals, emblems, calendar, and postage stamps. But no one has described the idea of a Jewish state more succinctly than did David Ben-Gurion in his testimony before the Anglo-American Committee of Inquiry on Palestine in 1947. "When we say 'Jew-ish independence' or a 'Jewish State' we mean Jewish country, Jewish soil, we mean Jewish labour, we mean Jewish economy, Jewish agriculture, Jewish industry, Jewish sea. We mean Jewish safety, security, independence, complete independence, as for any other free people."[16] Yet besides being a Jewish state Israel has also conceived of itself as a "Zionist state"; a state that contrary to other states, must regard itself as the State of a people the majority of which is not concentrated within its borders. As a Zionist state, it must bear the responsibility for the security, well-being, unity, and continuous cultural identity of the Jewish people ... [a] State whose political, economic, social, and cultural image is that of an immigrant-absorbing state ...

... a State which was established in order to solve the problems of the Jewish people's existence ... problems [which] have not yet been solved.[17]

These overarching ideological commitments and the overall "project" character of Israel are embodied in a set of institutions that have been fighting, for over fifty years, for Jewish independence in Palestine (Eretz-Yisrael), for mass Jewish immigration, for the expansion of Jewish land ownership, and for other Zionist objectives. Together these institutions represent the organizational apparatus of the Zionist movement, which, seeing itself as the agent of the Jewish people as a whole, has basically conceived of its task as the liberation of the Jewish nation and its unification in the ancient homeland. Before 1948 the institutions of the movement—including the Jewish Agency, the Histadrut, the Haganah (underground army), the JNF, the Basic Fund (Keren Hayesod), and the various political parties and their associated school systems and kibbutz (agricultural collective) movements—constituted, administratively and substantively, a kind of protostate.

After 1948 these institutions continued to function, and their commitment to the basic tenets of Zionist ideology remained intact, but with the emergence of Israel as a sovereign state the division of labor among them was somewhat rearranged. Though the Jewish Agency retained primary responsibility for encouraging Jewish immigration and for the absorption of new immigrants into Israeli society, almost all its administrative functions in the Yishuv as well as its role as the Zionist movement's diplomatic representative were taken over by the new state. The JNF continued to acquire land and lease it to Jewish settlements, but after 1948 it did so in close coordination with agencies of the Israeli government such as the Ministry of Agriculture and the Custodian of Absentee Property. The various Zionist political parties and kibbutz movements continued to compete for resources and political power, but, in the governmental arena at least, subject to the parliamentary ground rules of the Knesset. The Histadrut, having grown into the second largest employer in the country (after the government) as well as the official representative of Israeli workers, has continued its efforts to consolidate the position of the Jewish working class and maintains a wide-ranging program of educational and economic projects designed to enhance the realization of Zionist objectives; again, in close cooperation with various agencies of the Israeli government and the Jewish Agency. Finally, the army continues to serve as a vehicle for the transmission of Zionist values, though no longer is it the explicit instrument of a particular political party or trend.

When considering the position of the Arab minority in Israeli society, one must remember that the organizational ideologies of these institutions and the personal commitments of the individuals who control them are rooted in bitter struggles with Palestinian Arabs for Jewish land ownership, Jewish immigration, Jewish labor, and Jewish political rights. The men and women who filled the bureaus and agencies of the new Israeli government, as well as those who remained at the helm of the "national institutions," experienced this struggle as the determining fact of their sociopolitical existence. Spurred then by individual commitment and endowed finally with the sanction and encouragement of the government, these institutions in large measure continued after 1948 the struggle with Israel's Arab minority that they had waged in the decades before with the Arab majority of Palestine.

The point is that Israel *is* both a Jewish state and a Zionist state, the character of the state having been determined by the ideological commitments that its major institutions have been designed to serve. Segmented from the Jewish community on the institutional as well as the structural level, Israeli Arabs are cut off from the mainstream of public power and purpose in Israeli society. But such an assertion requires a systematic examination of the institutions, mentioned above, which have dominated that society and defined its purposes.

Public Institutions   Examination of Israeli institutions should begin with the government itself. One indication of the absence of Arab participation in the workings of the Israeli government is the fact that of 1,860 officials listed in Israeli government ministries and independent agencies in 1976 only 26 were Arabs. In twenty-one of the thirty departments described in the official government yearbook there were no Arabs at all. Eleven of the 26 Arab officials listed were functionaries in the Moslem and Druse religious court systems, while all the rest were assigned to specific minority localities or worked in special departments that deal only with the Arab sector.[18] This reflects the fact that government ministries, such as those of Education, Labor, the Interior, and Housing, are organized and oriented to serve the needs of the Jewish sector.[19] Arab citizens establish contact with these and other ministries through special "Arab Departments" which operate on a case-by-case basis without established budgets or long-range programs.

The explicit character of the Israeli government's commitment to the Jewish-Zionist mission of the state was clearly reflected in a document entitled "Basic Principles of the Government's Programme," submitted to the Knesset in March 1974 by the newly elected Labor Party coalition.[20] First on the list of the "Central Objectives of the Cabinet" was "Perseverance in the establishment of the social, economic and spiritual conditions for realizing the central aim of the State of Israel: the ingathering of the dispersion of the Jewish people in its Homeland; stepping up immigration from all countries and from all strata of the people; encouragement of immigration from the affluent countries; stimulation of pioneering immigration."[21] Elsewhere in this same document it is declared that

The Government will assist, as always, in the strengthening and expansion of the Zionist Movement and the fulfillment of its tasks: mounting immigration to Israel, the study of Hebrew by the Jewish masses, the cultivation of pioneering movements and the promotion of child and youth immigration, expansion of settlement on the land, and the attraction of Diaspora youth to schooling and training in Israel. The Government will encourage the Zionist Movement in its educational work in the Diaspora, in enhancing attachment to the nation's cultural heritage, in the ideological struggle against every manifestation of national alienation, assimilation or contamination, and in support of Israel in its fight for peace within defensible borders.[22]

The commitment of the government to the Jewish-Zionist mission of the state was, if anything, intensified following the election of Menachem Begin as prime minister in May 1977 at the head of a right-wing clericalist coalition. The first four points of the new administration's "Basic Policy Guidelines" read as follows:

1. Recognition of the unity of the destiny and the common struggle for existence of the Jewish People in the Land of Israel and in Diaspora.
2. The Jewish People has an eternal, historic right to the Land of Israel, the inalienable inheritance of its forefathers.
3. The Government will plan, establish and encourage urban and rural settlement on the soil of the homeland.
4. The Government will make the encouragement of aliyah [immigration] a chief national task.[23]

Although the regime has consistently maintained that its policy "will be aimed at the complete integration of the minorities in Israel into all spheres of life in the State,"[24] the affairs of the Arab community continue, in effect, to be governed separately by the Office of the Adviser to the Prime Minister on Arab Affairs. The task of this department has been to coordinate the activities of the various governmental and nongovernmental agencies that operate in the Arab sector, to provide them with information concerning individual Arabs and current developments, and to represent the government among the Arab population. Thus government institutions relate to the Jewish and Arab sectors in a highly segregated fashion. Arab clerks do not work in offices which serve the Jewish population. Nor, as a general rule, do Arab citizens mix with Jewish citizens in the public offices of the government bureaucracy. The agencies that operate in the Arab sector and the officials who have responsibilities there are practically unknown to the Jewish public at large.

If you listen carefully, during conversations with [Israeli Arabs], you will hear the names of people about whose very existence Jewish citizens of this country are unaware . . . officials of the Jewish National Fund, representatives of the Development Authority, or officers of the Military Administration. They are the "Authorities" in the eyes of the Arabs and they constitute a barrier between the Arabs and the Government. It is to these officials that Arabs must complain, to them that Arabs must present their various applications. Moreover these are the individuals who either grant or refuse these requests. . . . Nor is there any opportunity [for Arabs] to appeal their decisions . . .[25]

Although the names of some of the agencies responsible for the affairs of the Arab minority have changed, the bureaucratic segregation of the government in its dealings with the Jewish and Arab sectors is as prevalent today as it was in December 1954, when the above passage was written.[26]

The pattern of Jewish-Arab segmentation that has characterized the civilian arm of the government has extended in an even more rigid fashion to the military sphere. The armed services, known as Tzahal (the Israel Defense Forces) constitute by far the single largest and most important organization in the Israeli government. Military expenditure has been more than 40 percent of the government's budget and represents approximately one-third of the country's GNP. Regular service, three years for men and two years for unmarried women, is mandatory for most Jews.[27] From the time of their release from regular service, Jewish citizens are required to serve annually in the reserves (thirty to sixty days for men, two weeks for women). Thus, participation in the military becomes a regular part of the average Israeli Jew's annual schedule. For Israeli society as a whole, army service has been a dominant factor in the gradual integration of Sephardic and Ashkenazic Jews, in the creation of a strong sense of Jewish-Israeli solidarity, and in the transmission of a wide assortment of mechanical and technical skills. It has also served as a training ground for traditional Zionist values, including communal devotion, strong identification of Israel with the historical struggles of the Jewish people, and commitment to a pioneering ethos.[28] One branch of Tzahal—Nahal (Pioneering and Fighting Youth)—encompasses military training as well as agricultural work in mixed units of men and women. Its purpose is to produce cohesive groups of Jews who will seek to join or establish kibbutzim upon the completion of their regular military obligation.

Again, the relationship of Israel's Arab citizens to the military is quite different from that of Israel's Jewish population. Most Moslem Arabs, who constitute the overwhelming majority of Israeli Arab citizens, do not serve in the armed forces—they are not conscripted, nor are they permitted to volunteer for service. Christians and Bedouin (who are Moslems) may volunteer for duty, and some do, the Bedouin serving mainly as scouts.

The men of the small Druse and Circassian communities (Druse and Circassians represent approximately 9 percent of the total non-Jewish population in Israel) have been subject to conscription, the Druse since 1956, the Circassians from a somewhat later date. However, although there are "mixed units" of Jews and non-Jews in the border police, most non-Jewish recruits serve in a separate "minorities unit" commanded, but not entirely officered, by Jews. There are no mixed units outside the border police. Bedouin scouts, for example, do not participate as regular members of army units but are instead assigned to particular sectors, serving whatever regular Jewish units are stationed there.

The fact that the army is not an integrated Jewish-Arab institution is of enormous significance for Arab citizens. The possession of veteran status is a prerequisite to a wide variety of jobs and public assistance programs.[29] The personal associations, as well as the rank and service records, a soldier establishes in the course of regular service and reserve duty are among the most important elements in the determination of a future career in Israeli society—the officer corps being, perhaps, the primary conduit for administrative and managerial personnel in all branches of Israeli industry, commerce, and government.

It has been correctly said that participation in the army "defines the extent to which an individual is 'in' the social-evaluative system of Israel—a system whose boundaries are not identified with those of the formal political system. . . . Thus Israeli Arabs are 'in' in relation to the formal system and 'out' in relation to the informal system which is clearly oriented to Jewish nationalism."[30] Excluded from the ranks of Tzahal, most Israeli Arabs are thus cut off from the major dynamic processes of social integration and mobility which exist in Israel.

But the army and the government of which it is a part are not the only institutional arenas in which such processes occur or within which access to economic resources and political power is available. Any analysis of the institutional make-up of Israeli society must concern itself as well with the General Federation of Workers of the Land of Israel, better known as the Histadrut. This sprawling institution is first and foremost a general union of workers, representing in collective bargaining over two-thirds of all the wage and salary earners in the country. In addition the Histadrut's membership includes "self-employed" workers such as those organized in collective and cooperative agricultural settlements as well as housewives. But the Histadrut is much more than a union. It is also a welfare organization. It provides the primary health insurance program in Israel and backs it up by an entire Histadrut-owned and -operated network of hospitals, dispensaries, and rest homes. It sponsors vocational training programs, evening educational courses, social and cultural clubs, and sports leagues. It publishes books and periodicals, sponsors group tours abroad, and conducts a host of educational, technical, and propaganda activities. Furthermore it is a dominant force in the Israeli economy, controlling through its industrial holding company Hevrat Ovdim approximately 21 percent of Israel's industry. The enterprises owned by the Histadrut operate in all spheres of economic activity— wholesale and retail marketing, construction, commerce and banking, insurance, shipping, and manufacturing.

The Histadrut played a crucial role in the pre-1948 Zionist struggle in Palestine. Founded in 1920, it set out to organize Jewish workers along socialist-Zionist principles and carried on a tireless struggle for "Jewish labor"—a principle according to which Jewish firms would hire only Jewish workers as part of an effort to "normalize" the "inverted" occupational pyramid of the Jewish people. In support of this principle the Histadrut conducted extensive and sometimes violent picketing of Jewish firms and farms that employed Arabs. In 1935 the Histadrut representatives on the Zionist Executive Council "promoted a motion (which was unanimously adopted) emphasizing the duty of all members of the Zionist Organization to employ only Jewish labor. Defiance of this resolution would entail expulsion from the Zionist Organization."[31] The Histadrut also created and maintained the Haganah, the underground army which fought against the Arabs and the British and became, in 1948, the foundation of the Israel Defense Forces. From 1920 until the present day it has served as the economic and institutional backbone of the Labor Zionist Movement in Israel, i.e., that trend in the Zionist movement as a whole which has dominated Zionist and Israeli politics since the mid-1930s.

The achievement of Jewish statehood in 1948 changed but did not transform the character of the Histadrut and its relationship to the objectives of Labor Zionism. In cooperation with the Ministry of Labor and other government agencies the Histadrut has continued its efforts to consolidate and strengthen a Jewish working class. Especially in the early and mid-1950s, when massive waves of Jewish immigration combined with very difficult economic circumstances, the Histadrut did all in its power to preserve available jobs for Jewish workers and new immigrants. The success of its efforts in this regard was due in part to the fact that until the late 1950's the Histadrut controlled all Israel's labor exchanges, while Arabs were not permitted full membership in the organization until 1959. The Histadrut also exercised a veto during this period over the assignment of work permits to Arab villagers wishing to work in metropolitan areas.[32]

Eventually, the clash between the working-class, socialist-internationalist aspects of the Histadrut's ideology and the blatant fact that it excluded Arab workers from membership led the organization, in 1959, officially to open its ranks to Arabs. In 1965 Arabs were permitted to participate actively in the elections to the Histadrut convention, and subsequently the official name of the Histadrut, which had been the General Federation of Jewish Workers of the Land of Israel was changed by omitting the work "Jewish." In 1978 there were 130,000 Arab members of the Histadrut, or somewhat less than 10 percent of its total membership. The single most important factor involved in the growth of Arab membership has been the desire by Arabs to become eligible for Kupat Holim, the Histadrut's reasonably priced, comprehensive health insurance program. The Histadrut has also sponsored many different kinds of activities in the Arab sector, including cooperative societies, vocational training courses, social clubs, Arabic publishing houses, and youth groups.

Yet one should not infer from such activities that the Histadrut has made an important contribution toward the integration of Jews and Arabs in Israel. Of the thousands of Histadrut-owned firms and factories, not one was located in an Arab village in 1977. After sixteen years of full membership there were, in 1975, only 5 Arabs on the 168-member Histadrut

Executive (Vaad Hapoel) and no Arab members of the 18-member Central Committee of the Histadrut. Nor were there any Arabs among the over 600 managers and directors-general of Hevrat Ovdim industries. Actually the Histadrut per se does not involve itself with the Arab population—rather there exists a special Histadrut "Arab Department" that has responsibility for the Arab sector.

In sum, the Histadrut has not provided an institutional arena in which Jews and Arabs establish important economic, political, or social interdependencies. Although it has served as a channel for Arab access to certain resources—especially health care—and although it sponsors certain cosmetic programs, such as the Israel Society for Friendship and Understanding,[33] the continued concentration of the Histadrut's whole panoply of industrial and agricultural resources in the Jewish sector, the maintenance of a separate Arab Department (long after the Arab population has learned to speak Hebrew, language being the original justification for the department's existence), and its refusal to allow Arabs entrance into positions of authority reflect the fundamental character of the Histadrut as a Jewish-Zionist institution and a contributing factor in the segmentation of Israeli society between Jews and Arabs.[34]

National Institutions   So far attention has been directed to institutions—government ministries and departments, the armed forces, and the Histadrut—which officially, though to varying degrees, serve the interests of and are open to the Arab population. But the Jewish Agency (known in Israel simply as the "Sochnut" or "Agency"), the JNF (Keren Kayemet L'Yisrael), the World Zionist Organization,[35] etc., are institutions which in theory as well as in practice are part of the international Zionist movement. As such they legally operate in Israel as communal-ideological organizations serving and involving only the Jewish population. Together they are known as the "national institutions."

Since its establishment in 1901 as "the first instrument for the practical implementation of the idea of Jewish renaissance," the JNF has been dedicated to the acquisition and development of land in Eretz Yisrael as the "inalienable property of the Jewish people."[36] Under no circumstances is the JNF allowed to transfer ownership of land once acquired. Its mission has been to care for the land on behalf of its "real" owner, engage in reclamation, afforestation, and other land development projects, and *lease* parcels of land for whatever specific purpose and to whosoever it judges would serve the best interests of the Jewish people and the Zionist movement.

Since 1948 the overall objectives of the JNF, including its efforts toward the "Judaization of the Galilee" (Yehud ha-Galil),[37] correspond to the fundamental goals of the prestate Zionist struggle: Jewish settlement on the land, Jewish labor, and the expansion of Jewish land ownership. Thus in the prestate period it was forbidden for Arabs to work on lands controlled by the JNF or in businesses established on those lands. Before and during the British Mandate in Palestine the leadership of the JNF was dedicated to the acquisition of as much land as possible. Yet throughout this period the JNF was plagued by a British colonial administration which, in response to fierce Arab opposition to Zionism, placed restriction after restriction on Jewish land purchases—making the extension of Jewish land ownership a stealthy, difficult, and expensive process. These problems were swept away by the establishment of the state in 1948. Since then the JNF, continuing to operate under the direction of the World Zionist Organization[38] and maintaining its own international fund-raising apparatus, has taken full advantage, to say the least, of a highly sympathetic and cooperative regime. The Development Authority Law, passed in 1950 in order to facilitate the transfer to Jewish possession of lands abandoned by Arab refugees, is an excellent example of how this relationship has worked. In the words of Abraham Granott, chairman of the board of directors of the JNF from 1945 to 1960, this law

expressly states that the Authority shall not be able to sell or alienate land . . . in any manner excepting the following four bodies: the State of Israel; the Jewish National Fund; Local Authorities; and the institutions for settling landless Arabs.

In practice only two of these bodies are of concern—the State and the JNF, since the body for settling landless Arabs has never been established. Thus a great rule was laid down, which has a decisive and basic significance—that the property of absentees cannot be transferred in ownership to anyone but [the] national public institutions above, either the State itself, or the original Land Institution of the Zionist Movement.[39]

As a matter of fact the law gave priority to the requirements of the JNF. Again, in Granott's words: "Every area must first be offered to the JNF and only if it gives notice in writing that it is not interested, may it be transferred to others, whether by sale or lease."[40]

In 1961 a "land covenant" was signed between the JNF and the government "vesting the Fund with the exclusive responsibility for land development in Israel. This task, performed by the Fund's Land Development Authority, comprises land reclamation, drainage, afforestation and the opening of new border areas for settlement on all public lands."[41] The JNF shares responsibility for another body, the Israel Land Administration, with the Ministry of Agriculture. In this context it participates in the exercise of administrative control over all state lands, which combined with JNF holdings equal 92 percent of Israel's land area.[42]

Indeed, as a result of these elaborate legal arrangements and thirty years of intensive activity,[43] the land holdings of the JNF have grown enormously (see Chapter 5). Considering "that JNF holdings, unlike State lands, are for the greater part either under cultivation, in other economic use, or in various stages of the process of reclamation, the weight of these lands in the country's economy is larger than the absolute figures would lead one to assume."[44]

It does not necessarily follow that the existence of such a huge and powerful institution as the JNF, working as it does in close cooperation with the government, undertaking tasks which the government prefers to avoid,[45] and having responsibility for so vital a resource as land, would because of these characteristics contribute to the segmentation of Israeli society. However, it should be stressed that the JNF does not concern itself directly with the problem of the Arab minority. JNF officials do not consider the implications of the accomplishment of their organizational objectives for the economic and political position of the Arab community; and during interviews conducted in 1974 they tended to express puzzlement that their ac-

tivities would be of interest to someone concerned with the situation of Arabs in Israel.[46] Nonetheless, for Israeli Arabs, the
continued existence of the JNF since 1948 has been of enormous
significance: The very *raison d'être* of the institution is its Zionist mission; its leadership is appointed by the World Zionist Organization; its personnel are recruited from the ranks of the
Zionist movement. It is then, as an institution, dedicated to serving the interests of the Jewish people according to the tenets of
Zionist ideology. It is in this sense, in the sense that it constitutes
both an institutional lobby and a convenient instrument for an
acquisitive, exclusivist land policy, that the JNF contributes to
the segmentation of Israeli society between Jews and Arabs.

As with the JNF, so too with the Jewish Agency, but on a
larger scale and in a different realm. The organizational mission
of the JNF concerns land and its development. The Jewish Agency has, since 1948, been primarily responsible for Jewish immigrants and their "absorption" into Israeli society. During the
early 1950's there were many spheres of governmental activity
in which departments of the Jewish Agency acted as substitutes
for nonexistent government agencies. Then, as an elaborate and
articulated state bureaucracy developed, the tasks allotted to the
Jewish Agency were subsumed more and more under the head-
ings of immigration and immigrant absorption. The official relationship between Israel's government and the Jewish Agency was
set forth in the World Zionist Organization–Jewish Agency Status Law of 1952. Under the terms of this law: "The World Zionist Organization, represented by the Jewish Agency, was . . .
charged to encourage and organize immigration and assist in the
absorption of the immigrants in close cooperation with the Government of Israel."[47]

Notwithstanding intense periodic criticism in Zionist-Israeli
circles of the notoriously inefficient bureaucracy of the Jewish
Agency, the Sochnut has generally performed its assigned tasks.
From the establishment of the state until the end of 1972, the
Jewish Agency supervised the immigration, settlement, and
absorption of 1,400,000 Jews—equaling more than twice
the Jewish population of Palestine at the end of the mandate.
The first massive waves of immigration in 1948–1951 presented
the greatest problems. Mostly poverty-stricken and desperate—

many from the backward countries of Asia Minor and North Africa and many others survivors of the European holocaust—these immigrants had to be fed, clothed, housed, medically cared for, and employed. Subsequent, smaller waves of immigration came in the mid-1950's, the early 1960's, and the early 1970's. In order to achieve the absorption and settlement of these masses of immigrants, the Land Settlement Department of the Jewish Agency (which under the mandate had been the Palestine Office of the Jewish Agency) took over responsibility for directing large numbers of these Jews into rural agricultural settlements. It launched

vast agricultural settlement projects . . . The department was responsible for the planning, execution, and supervision of the work, including the siting of the villages; the planning of buildings, water supply, and irrigation networks; the provision of equipment, seeds, and livestock; and expert guidance in farming methods and the problems involved in the establishment of self-reliant, socially integrated rural communities . . .

At first the settlers were employed largely in building or (in the case of abandoned Arab villages) repairing houses, paving roads, and laying pipelines; they were usually provided with outside employment in afforestation and the like until they could live on the produce of their farms. The department's central and regional offices, with their expert agronomists, engineers, and architects, supervised the work of the men in the field and, in conjunction with the Ministry of Agriculture, coordinated the choice of crops and the methods of cultivation in accordance with the climate and soil conditions in various parts of the country.[48]

By the end of August 1973, the Land Settlement Department of the Jewish Agency had established 564 settlements of all types, including over 500 agricultural settlements.[49] In 1971 "the total area cultivated by settlements established after 1948 reached 1.5 million dunams, out of a total of 4.2 million dunams . . . the total agricultural output in the new settlements amounts to forty percent of the total agricultural output in Israel."[50]

But the Jewish Agency's assistance to new immigrants has not been directed solely to those living in agricultural settlements. Indeed the great majority of immigrants have settled in the three metropolitan areas—Jerusalem, Tel Aviv, and Haifa—

and in nonagricultural "development towns." The Jewish Agency has built sprawling housing projects for these immigrants and provided them with essential services, including schools, health centers, social services, labor exchanges, and relief payments. In addition, the Jewish Agency has funded and built industrial plants in development towns as well as in many kibbutzim (collective settlements) and moshavim (cooperative settlements). The expenditures of the Jewish Agency from 1948 to the end of 1973 totaled more than $3.3 billion. Included in this figure are $1.2 billion spent on the absorption and housing of new immigrants and $977 million spent on agricultural settlements.[51] The massive scale of the Jewish Agency's activities can be appreciated if one considers for example that the budget of the Jewish Agency in 1972–1973 was $465 million as compared to a total Israeli government development budget for the same fiscal year of $604 million.[52] Indeed, at times the Jewish Agency budget has been larger than the development budget of the government.

It is worthwhile examining briefly some of the specific ways in which the Jewish Agency carries out its multiple mission of bringing in immigrants, absorbing them into Israeli society, and dispersing the population or "Judaizing" outlying areas. First in regard to agricultural settlement: In close cooperation with the government, the Land Settlement Department of the Jewish Agency decides where a new settlement is to be established and what the economic base of the settlement will be. If the land is not already in the possession of the JNF or the state, the JNF or the state acquires it, whereupon the Land Development Administration of the JNF lays approach roads and transmission lines, clears the land of rocks or scrub, etc. The Land Settlement Department of the Jewish Agency then

allocates means of production to the settlers, purchasing for them livestock, farm equipment, seeds, water rights, and necessary permits. The Ministry of Housing does the construction work, paid for by the Land Settlement Department in the form of long-term loans to the settlers at 2 percent interest. But the settlers do not begin repaying these loans until after the settlement has been officially "consolidated," which often takes ten to fifteen years or longer. Even when settlers do begin to repay the loans they do so at the rate of sixty to one hundred I£ per month for the whole settlement—in other words these "loans" are in reality grants.[53]

The failure of many rural settlements to become self-reliant and their continued dependence on Jewish Agency grants and subsidies is reflected in the fact that three hundred, or 55 percent, of the agricultural settlements established between 1948 and 1971 had failed, by that later date, to reach the stage of "consolidation."[54] In order to rescue many such settlements the Jewish Agency has engaged in an intensive program of industrialization in previously established "agricultural villages." The growing commitment of the Jewish Agency to new types of Jewish settlement on the land is revealed in the following statement by Yosef Lichtman, coordinator of the board of directors of the Land Settlement Department of the Jewish Agency:

We have a plan now which we will bring before the Interministerial Committee on Land Settlement in connection with the fact that the Galilee is not yet Jewish. We are planning to bring Jews there as well as very important new forms of settlement which will not necessarily involve more land acquisition. We are planning to establish industrial villages using the same types of loans, grants, and subsidies that were used to establish agricultural settlements. Again these industrial villages would be for Jews only. The establishment and consolidation of such industrial villages is much more expensive, however, than previous agricultural settlements because the plant is much larger.[55]

But, as indicated above, the Jewish Agency also concerns itself with absorbing Jewish immigrants in nonrural settings. In order to do this it has provided a wide variety of facilities, concessions, and subsidies to Jewish immigrants. They include

interest-free loans to cover passage and part of shipping costs; exemption from purchase tax and reduction in customs on automobiles; on purchasing house or business premises; preferential treatment in obtaining employment; partial exemption from income tax and capital gains tax; the right to hold foreign currency for ten years and to redeem State of Israel bonds; accommodation in absorption centers, hostels, and *ulpanim*; housing on easy terms or assistance through a sick fund for six months; various concessions in national insurance benefits; free secondary schooling and university education; exemption from travel tax.[56]

Jewish immigrants and, indeed, the Jewish sector as a whole benefit from the fact that the Jewish Agency controls a good portion of the Israeli economy. For the activities of the Jewish Agency in the corporate sphere have sprung from its commitment to the development of a strong Jewish economy and the establishment of facilities which can directly serve, in construction, insurance, real-estate management, etc., in the absorption of Jewish immigration. Investments which the Jewish Agency has made in financially unsound firms represent explicit attempts to support and protect infant Jewish industries and subsidize infrastructural growth in the Jewish sector. Companies in which the Jewish Agency owns a majority of shares include Rassco and the Israel Land Development Company Ltd. The former is a gigantic company, in Israeli terms:

active in all fields of construction as general contractor as well as for its own account, [it] has a long record in developing real-estate schemes, ranging from self-contained suburbs, through urban apartment house centers and shopping centers to hotels and industrial parks, and it takes its share in Government sponsored building programs for new immigrants, young couples and slum clearing. Rassco is also building a great number of public buildings and Government offices and it takes part in building operations for the Ministry of Defence.[57]

The Jewish Agency shares with the JNF ownership of the Israel Land Development Company, which has fixed assets, including large tracts of urban land, industrial buildings, and hotels and resorts, worth over I£ 100 million. The Jewish Agency, along with the government and the Histadrut, is a one-third owner of Mekorot, a company which has a virtual monopoly over water supply in Israel and includes among its assets waterworks representing over $1 billion of investment. The Jewish Agency also owns 25 percent of Amidar, a company which administers and maintains hundreds of thousands of mostly government-owned housing units. The Agency has important holdings in Zim, Israel's national shipping lines; the *Jerusalem Post*, Israel's only English-language newspaper; and many other companies. All in all the Jewish Agency, through its Companies Bureau, supervises "some sixty companies in Israel, which are wholly or partially owned by the Agency. . . . The Bureau appoints Jewish Agency representatives to the directorial boards, formulates and reviews business policies, calls for regular reports on activities and finances, [and] offers—when necessary—managerial guidance."[58]

Consideration of how the Jewish Agency has financed its vast operation helps explain why it has been allowed to maintain its autonomous existence and underscores the significance of its character as an independent institution for the Jewish-Arab segmentation of Israeli society. According to Minister of Finance Simcha Erlich in 1977, from 1948 to 1976 world Jewry had contributed $5,000,000,000 to Israel, 65 percent of this money coming from American Jews.[59] The Jewish Agency has been the chief instrument through which these enormous sums have been expended. From 1948 through mid-1977 the total income of the Jewish Agency was $5,092,500,000.[60] This figure includes German reparations (minus those paid to private individuals) and loans and grants from the Israeli government. It does *not* include the funds collected and disbursed by the JNF or the monies donated to the World Zionist Organization since 1971 through the Basic Fund (Keren Hayesod). The official nongovernmental status of all these institutions is of crucial importance for two reasons. First, the contributions of American Jewry (and those of Jewish communities in some other countries) are tax exempt; but their tax-exempt status would be invalidated if the funds were directed to and disbursed by a foreign government. The fact that the Jewish Agency and the JNF are classified as philanthropies by the American Internal Revenue Service has, in fact, protected them from attempts by the Israeli government to take over several of their administrative and substantive tasks.

In June of 1968 the Government [also] decided on the creation of a new Ministry of Immigrant Absorption (Klitah) with which the Agency would henceforth have to share its central function. The *modus operandi* provided for continued Jewish Agency responsibility for the staging of immigration abroad, while the new Ministry was to deal with most areas of reception and integration within the country. The first incumbent was Yigal Allon, and it was anticipated that his Ministry would eventually unite under one roof the "absorption" functions not only of the Jewish Agency but also of the various Government Ministries . . . but this was not to be . . . the Agency was able to marshall a potent argument in support of its continued independent existence: the fact that contributions of American Jewry (and some other communities, as well) must be disbursed by a non-Governmental, voluntary organization in order to enjoy exemption from income taxes.

. . . Their reasoning proved convincing, above all to Minister of Finance Pinhas Sapir, and the integrity of the Agency was maintained.[61]

There is a second factor of even greater importance in appreciating the significance of the autonomous existence of these institutions. Because they are not formally part of the Israeli government apparatus they do not serve a constituency of "Israeli citizens." Rather they are communal Jewish-Zionist organizations which serve a transnational constituency—the Jewish people. That is, although the government of Israel is bound according to its own democratic norms to address itself, in the laws it promulgates, in the programs it sponsors, and in the services it provides, to Jewish and Arab citizens alike, the Jewish Agency and the JNF are mandated to operate only in regard to Israel's Jewish population. They therefore constitute efficient conduits for channeling resources to the *Jewish* population only, resources which are converted into capital-intensive economic development projects, educational vocational training, social services, land acquisition, etc. In the implementation of such programs, officials of these institutions see themselves ideologically as well as legally justified in ignoring the needs of Arab Israelis and the impact of their activities on the Arab sector. Consider the following statements by JNF and Jewish Agency officials.

The economic impact of our land purchases and our activities on Arabs is not considered. . . . The government would have to look after all citizens if they owned the land; since the JNF owns the land, let's be frank, we can serve just the Jewish people.[62]

Arab villages are of course ineligible [for our economic assistance] because this is a *Jewish* Agency.[63]

The activities of the Jewish Agency in subsidizing economic development in the Jewish sector may create problems—gaps—between Arabs and Jews in Israel, but the mission of the Jewish Agency is a Jewish one. There is no role for the Jewish Agency in solving such problems.[64]

The Jewish Agency and the JNF, then, serve as convenient instruments for accomplishing Zionist tasks which the state itself is unable to undertake. One of the best examples of such a task, undertaken primarily by the JNF, is the protection of "national" or "redeemed" land and its preservation for use by Jews. Between 1948 and 1970 the government of Israel transferred 1,330 square kilometers (1,330,000 dunams) of land to the JNF.

Another 500 square kilometers of waste land was placed at the disposal of the JNF without being registered as JNF property.[65] Most of the land transferred to the JNF was that of Arab refugees; much, however, was land expropriated from Arabs who remained to become citizens of Israel.[66] Israeli government circles desired that these tracts and the evacuated villages which they contained be used for the accomplishment of such Zionist objectives as the close settlement of Jews on the land, the dispersal of Jews throughout the country, the development of a "Jewish peasantry," and so forth. By transferring these lands to the control of the JNF, which of course works closely with the Land Settlement Department of the Jewish Agency, the government was able to insure that decisions about the use of the land would be made strictly on the basis of Jewish-Zionist considerations. As indicated earlier, all "state" lands were placed at the disposal of the JNF by the creation of the Israel Land Administration and the Land Development Authority. The latter operates wholly within the JNF framework, with eight JNF representatives and seven representatives of the government on its council; the former has seven JNF members and eight representatives of the government. As noted, these two bodies develop, lease, and administer 92 percent of Israel's land area. Furthermore, the Zionist-JNF principle of "inalienability" has been applied to all the holdings which are, *in toto*, referred to as "national" (*leumi*) or "Israel" lands.

But these terms, although used interchangeably, mean quite different things and their interchangeable usage has great significance. "National land," i.e., land of the Jewish nation, is properly speaking only that registered as owned by the JNF. But the term "Israel lands" also includes lands registered as state domain or as the property of the state-appointed Development Authority.[67] These holdings, lumped together under the jurisdiction of the Israel Land Administration, are in fact referred to and treated as both "Israel" or "state" lands and as "national" or "redeemed" lands.[68] Thus, because of the availability of Zionist institutions embodying and engaged in the task of implementing Zionist ideology, "state" lands can become "national" lands placed at the disposal of the Jewish community and the Zionist movement. Since the JNF, as an institution, does not and cannot address itself to the Arab sector, Arab access to JNF-controlled lands for purposes of long-term leasing or development is effectively denied.

The extent to which these "public" lands are in fact thought of and treated as Jewish "national lands" is reflected in periodic uproars in Israel over the "protection" of national land or "irregularities" in the use of "the property of the nation and the state." These problems derive from the practice of many Jews or Jewish settlements of leasing, at nominal rates, more land than they can profitably use or even work by themselves, then subletting the land to Arabs (pocketing the difference) or hiring Arabs to work the land.[69] One such uproar occurred in 1966. In a typical article published in *Haaretz* in October of that year, entitled "Ishmael's National Fund" (a pun on the Hebrew name of the JNF—Keren Kayemet L'Yisrael), the author quoted the director general of the JNF as labeling the "irregularities" in the use of public land a "national sin." The author went on to write, "If this trend is not stopped and if the practice of subletting land to Arab laborers is not completely eradicated—then the development plan for the Northern region will prove to be an empty dream." Referring to the growth in the early 1960's of a large Arab majority in the northern Galilee, the author urged that action be taken immediately to deal with the situation and quoted the deputy director of the Israel Land Administration to the effect that "Only a clearly formulated law will solve the problem."[70] Two weeks later the Agricultural Settlement Law was introduced in the Knesset. Under the terms of this law any individual or settlement engaged in the "irregular" practices mentioned above would be subject to the expropriation of the land involved. The land would then revert to the JNF or the Israel Land Administration, whereupon these bodies would make arrangements for the use of the land in a more suitable fashion.[71]

Of course the Jewish Agency is also available to pursue Zionist objectives, objectives which the state, because of its "citizen" rather than "Jewish" constituency, would find awkward to pursue. For example, consider David Ben-Gurion's discussion of how to cope with the problem of the gap between Jewish and Arab rates of natural increase:

Since the problem of the birthrate does not affect all the inhabitants but only the Jewish community, it cannot be solved by the Government. Israel provides equal rights for all its citizens without distinction of race and nationality. . . . Consequently if the Government plans to increase the birthrate by providing special assistance to large families, the main beneficiaries will be Arab families, which are generally larger than Jewish families.

Since it is only the Jews who need such incentives, the Government is unable to deal with the problem, and the matter should be transferred to the Jewish Agency or some special Jewish organization. If the Jewish birthrate is not increased, it is doubtful that the Jewish State will survive.[72]

The role of the JNF, the Jewish Agency, and other institutional components of the world Zionist movement in the distribution of resources in Israel and the concentrated development of the Jewish sector is augmented by common statutory provisions which assure these institutions representation on various public regulatory agencies, marketing boards, and planning authorities.[73] In addition, during the early and mid-1960's, when financial contributions from world Jewry were at a low ebb, the Israeli government effected unilateral transfers of public monies into the treasuries of the national institutions. Between 1959 and 1967, for example, the Israeli government donated over $100 million to the Jewish Agency.[74]

What should be emphasized is that the existence of separate, *Jewish* institutions such as the JNF and the Jewish Agency, controlling as they do vast resources and not including Arabs in the purview of their activities, enables the government to use the legal system to transfer resources from the public domain to the Jewish sector. It does this without discriminating in the law between Jews and Arabs, but by assigning responsibility for the disposition of those resources (especially land and funds from abroad) to institutions which are historical creations of the Zionist movement with personnel imbued with the desire to consolidate and strengthen the *Jewish* community in Eretz Yisrael.

Political Parties   Thus far two types of institutions have been discussed. The first type includes government ministries and agencies, the army, and the Histadrut, which to greater or lesser degrees are open to and officially serve the interests of Jewish and Arab Israelis. Despite their official functions, these institutions do not provide arenas for Jewish and Arab integration. Indeed, several ways in which they act to institutionalize the segmentation of Jews and Arabs have been pointed out. Second, institutions operating in Israel which are explicitly and officially communal-ideological have been discussed. The Jewish Agency and the JNF were the examples chosen, and they are the most significant.

However, as the attentive reader may have already perceived, this distinction is difficult to warrant. For yet another set of institutions—the Zionist political parties—through their control of the government, the Histadrut, and the organs of the Zionist movement, make of all these institutions a more or less coordinated network in which the channels for recruitment, demands, and effective participation are open almost solely to Jews.

Few would argue with the proposition that in Israel political power is concentrated in the governing bodies (the central committees, the secretariats, the nomination committees, etc.) of the Zionist political parties. These are the arenas in which party policy is hammered out and slates of candidates for the Knesset, for the Executive Council and the Central Committee of the Histadrut, and for the governing bodies of the Jewish Agency and the World Zionist Organization are drawn up. In each of these institutions the same set of six or seven Zionist political parties compete for control. From 1948 to mid-1977 the same party—the Labor Party—played the preeminent role in the formation of governing coalitions. In May 1977 Likud, an alignment of right-wing Zionist parties, defeated the Labor Party in the ninth Knesset elections. Allied with the religious parties, it took control of the government with Menachem Begin, leader of Herut (its best-organized and most extreme constituent party), as prime minister. Likud soon formed governing coalitions as well in the World Zionist Organization and the Jewish Agency. The Labor Party, thanks to a victory in the June 1977 Histadrut elections, maintained its dominance in the Histadrut. Although the implications of the Likud victory for future relations among these institutions are not yet entirely clear, Likud's ability to translate its control of the government into a dominant position in at least two of the national institutions would seem to indicate that roughly the same pattern of party supremacy that prevailed until 1977 will continue. This pattern, whereby the central and executive committees of the dominant Zionist political parties determined the directors of the Histadrut and of the national institutions and the policies which they followed, is well reflected in the careers of the following individuals.

David Ben-Gurion, a cofounder of the Histadrut and its first secretary-general in 1921, also presided over the formation in 1930 of Mapai (the Israel Workers' Party, or Labor Party, which combined with other parties in 1968 to form the present Israel Labor Party). From 1935 to 1948 he served as chairman of the Jewish Agency and for most of Israel's first fifteen years as a state was both prime minister and defense minister.

Moshe Sharet, a founding member of Ahdut Avoda, one of the factions which went into the formation of Mapai, was head of the Jewish Agency's Political Department from 1933 to 1948. Foreign minister from 1948 to 1956, he served as prime minister during Ben-Gurion's brief retirement in 1954. In 1960 he became the chairman of the Jewish Agency and served in that capacity until his death in 1965.

Levi Eshkol was Israel's prime minister from 1964 to 1969 and its defense minister from 1964 to 1967. He had been very active in the 1920's and 1930's in the financial affairs of both the Histadrut and the Labor Party. Selected as the director of the Land Settlement Department of the Jewish Agency in 1948, he continued to serve in that capacity while also holding, until 1963, the post of minister of finance.

In the late 1930's and the 1940's Golda Meir worked as head of the Political Department of the Histadrut. In 1946 she took over as director of the Political Department of the Jewish Agency while Moshe Sharett was under British arrest. Elected as a Mapai member of Knesset in 1949, she was appointed minister of labor and later foreign minister, a post which she held from 1956 to 1965. In 1965 she became secretary-general of the Labor Party. After Eshkol's death in 1969 she became prime minister and held that post until 1974.

Before his immigration to Israel in 1948 Louis Pincus had been chairman of the South African wing of the Labor Party and vice-chairman of the South African Zionist Federation. Shortly after his arrival in Israel he was appointed general secretary of the Ministry of Transportation and soon became active in the central governing bodies of the Labor Party, the Histadrut, and the Labor Zionist Movement. In 1961 he was selected as the treasurer of the Jewish Agency and from 1966 to 1974 served as the chairman of the Jewish Agency.[75]

Partially reflected in these brief career sketches of prominent Labor Party leaders is the fact that, in spite of innumerable inter- and intra-party splits, unions, agreements, dissolutions, etc., and despite the Likud victory in the 1977 Knesset elections, Israel's political spectrum today is hardly more than an extrapolation, characterized by a trend toward the right, of the political spectrum of the World Zionist Organization in the mid-1930's. The endurance and the continuing vigor of these parties is rooted in the struggles they waged, the institutions they nurtured, the ideologies they developed, and the cadre they recruited during the struggle of the Zionist movement for Jewish independence in Palestine. Most continue to maintain their own interpretations of the imperatives of Zionism, their own youth organizations, banks, insurance firms, schools, social clubs, newspapers, and agricultural settlement associations. After 1948 these political parties or "movements" (*tnuot*), constituting highly articulated subcultural communities more than anything else, remained as almost the only relevant political units in the society.[76]

The relationship of these political parties to Israeli Arabs, and in particular to Arab voters in the new state, was of course powerfully affected by their historically antagonistic development vis-à-vis the Arabs of Palestine. Arabs had not been members of the party clubs or agricultural settlements; they did not subscribe to party newspapers, send their children to party schools, or put their money in party banks. For these subcultures were thoroughly Jewish-Zionist in character, and not only were Arabs not Jewish but the Arab population as a whole had been consistently, intensely, and even violently anti-Zionist.

However, after 1948 the Arabs comprised one of the largest blocs of uncommitted votes in the new state. The Zionist parties competed for these votes in Knesset elections and later in Histadrut elections, but not by opening up their ranks to Arab members and their associated institutions to Arab participation. Rather they sponsored "affiliated lists" of Arabs, lists supported and funded by the various Zionist parties and committed to their sponsors—the General Zionists, Herut, the Labor Party, etc. Nor have these lists maintained an independent institutional existence between campaigns. Some parties, such as the short-lived Sephardic Party, the Progressive Party, and the National Religious Party, chose to solicit Arab votes to their own lists by appealing to personal relationships or religious interest. Although formal membership in a few Zionist parties (Mapam, Herut, and, since 1973, the Labor Party) has been possible for Arabs, only Mapam has made strong efforts to recruit Arab members. At present, although more than 40 percent of the adult Jewish population are card-carrying, dues-paying party members, the total Arab membership in Zionist parties is no more than 6 to 7 thousand. Of these only a few in Mapam participate in serious internal party debates.[77]

The Israel Communist Party—since its split in 1965, the New Israel Communist Party or Rakah—is the one political party to which Arabs have had effective access and in which their participation has been relatively heavy. Widespread desire by Arabs to cast protest votes has resulted in substantial increases in the number of Arab votes cast for Rakah in recent Knesset elections.[78] But the source of Rakah's appeal to Arabs and the explanation for the relatively extensive participation of Israeli Arabs in Rakah affairs—the party's anti-Zionist stance—also explains why Arab access to and participation in the Communist Party apparatus has had almost no consequences as far as introducing Arabs into positions of status and power in Israeli society.

Especially since the departure from its ranks in 1965 of several leading Jewish communists, the Communist Party has been almost totally cut off from the mainstream of Israeli political life. In the 1973 Knesset elections Rakah received only 3.4 percent of the total vote.[79] On the other hand, the political ostracism of Rakah has not been complete. Since 1965 Rakah has had three to five seats in the Knesset (about half of them held by Arab communists); in 1974 Rakah received 2.41 percent of the vote in the Histadrut elections, on the basis of which two Arab Rakah members were seated on the Histadrut's 168-member Vaad Hapoel. In the 1977 Histadrut elections Rakah's percentage of the vote rose to 3.03 percent. However, Rakah has never participated in a governing coalition, either in the Knesset or in the

Histadrut. Nor have Rakah members been allowed to participate in the work of the substantive Knesset committees or been
appointed to the Central Committee of the Histadrut or its various administrative organs. Of course, since it is anti-Zionist,
Rakah has had nothing whatsoever to do with the Jewish Agency or any other of the "national institutions."

Not surprisingly Rakah has always given strong support to
Soviet foreign policy, which since 1949 has been hostile to Israel.
This has helped to make the party automatically suspect in the
eyes of almost all Jewish Israelis. Indeed Jews who are active
Rakah members are commonly thought of in Israel as "traitors."[80] Furthermore, Rakah's doctrinaire political line has
made it difficult for the party to adapt its position on instrumental issues in order to broaden its base of support. Its anti-Zionist
posture, for example, has made it all but impossible for Rakah
to penetrate into the slum neighborhoods populated by poor
Sephardic Jews.[81]

Indeed, the separation of Rakah from the rest of the society
is so complete and its illegitimacy so widely accepted that its existence serves basically to reinforce the institutional isolation of
Arabs from the Jewish sector. For instance, as Arab support for
Rakah has visibly increased, the efforts to establish closer Jewish-Arab links by Mapam and other Zionist groups sympathetic
to Israeli Arabs have been undercut and all but eliminated. Partly
as a consequence, Jewish perceptions of Israeli Arabs as fundamentally outside the pale of Israeli society and as potentially
traitorous have been strengthened. This means that Jewish
groups that publicly solicit Arab political support risk losing
Jewish votes as a result. After the Yom Kippur War, several sociopolitical protest movements developed in Israel calling for
thorough-going reforms and a fundamental re-examination of
government policy in all sectors of the society. However, these
groups were uniformly silent on the internal "Arab problem,"
and attempts by noncommunist Arabs to join these organizations were rebuffed out of fear by their organizers that they
would thereby lose legitimacy and support in the Jewish sector.[82]

Institutional Isolation and Arab Vulnerability   The absence of
effective Arab access to the Jewish sector and to the institutions

of power and legitimacy which it contains is enormously significant in explaining Arab vulnerability to repression and exploitation. In a highly interesting article published in 1954, Moshe Keren (Arab-affairs editor for *Haaretz*) described the Arab minority in Israel as "the opposite of a pressure group." He went on to explain and exemplify his characterization:

The Government and the Jewish Agency, the Histadrut and the Army, the executive class and middle echelon officials as well, the institutions and all the other factors that together form the character of our State; they are all purely Jewish and they strive, of course, first and foremost, for the achievement of the goals of Zionism.

A corollary to this is that the Arabs who live in our State are the opposite of a pressure group; they constitute a group which has at its disposal almost no means of exerting pressure. Anyone who is aware of the decisive importance, in a system such as ours, of having access to means of exerting pressure in order to obtain some favor or satisfy some demand, will easily understand how not having access to such means of pressure influences the status of such a group and the likelihood that its needs will be met.

Compare, for example, the demonstrations of the Neturei Karta [an ultra-orthodox Jewish sect whose members do not recognize the state of Israel] in Jerusalem against the opening of nightclubs with the demonstration of the inhabitants of Kfar Manda against the surveys conducted by the Israel Water Authority, and you will understand the fundamental difference. The same police force stood before each demonstration. But powerful champions of the cause of the Neturei Karta exist in the Jewish community, both outside and inside Israel, they are supported by some newspapers and important political parties stand at their side. Their struggle becomes an issue in domestic politics. The police are urged to act with great caution. They are not able to make mass arrests and are thus not able to completely suppress the demonstrations. The clashes are repeated and no one knows what the outcome of the affair will be. However, when the Arabs of Manda demonstrate and interrupt the activities of the Israel Water Authority they feel the strong hand of the authorities. The police appear in full strength. Most of the men of the village are put under arrest and taken to the police station in Shfar-Am. The newspapers adopt a negative stand toward the demonstration. The Knesset proceeds with business as usual. Their opposition [to the activities of the Water Authority] is broken easily. Nor do any of us come forward to argue that the police acted incorrectly or that they behaved with undue severity. Rather the police force is urged to prove to the Arabs that breaking the law will not be tolerated.

Thus a comparison of these two cases teaches the value of being a member of a group that has access to means of pressure that are legitimate in our State, and from this comparison it is clear that Arabs have almost no access to circles influential with the authorities.[83]

In other words, although by law Arab citizens of Israel are equal to Jewish Israelis, their Israeli citizenship does not provide them with effective access to those institutions and organizations that dominate the life of the state—this, in spite of the fact that the institutional organization of the Jewish sector is by no means monolithic. For in addition to often vitriolic competition among the Zionist political parties, there are important rivalries: between the Jewish Agency and the government, for example, over immigrant absorption, between the JNF and the Ministry of Agriculture over the administration of lands, and between the Histadrut and the government over economic policy and jurisdictional issues. No matter how bitter these differences, however, they have not provided Arabs with opportunities to penetrate the Jewish sector, lending their support to one institution or party against another in return for a more sympathetic treatment of Arab demands.

One of the most important reasons for this is that Arabs are precluded from drawing upon Zionist ideology in order to legitimize their demands. Appeals to the welfare of the Jewish people, its security, pride, and independence, the speedy in-gathering of the exiles, the "Judaization of the Galilee," and so forth, are the common currency of Israeli political debate. Arabs cannot use these slogans. They are forced to frame their demands in the context of an image of Israel as a democratic liberal society where citizenship and not nationality is of paramount importance. But these very doctrines, although promulgated officially by the state, are from a Zionist point of view not only unconvincing but potentially dangerous, since they do not incorporate the notion of Israel as "the Jewish State," endowed with a specifically Jewish character as well as a transcendent Jewish mission. Arab articulation of such liberal-democratic doctrines has thus tended to be regarded with great suspicion.

Perhaps the best-known attempt by Israeli Arabs to articulate a nationalist "Israeli" ideology was the formation of the Arab-Jewish Committee for Israel. The leader of the group, Rustum Bastuni, rejected the notion that there even existed an "Arab nation" with which Israeli Arabs should or could be identified. The committee called for recognition of an *Israeli* identity which would unite both Jewish and Arab citizens and on the basis of which Israeli Arabs could give their wholehearted support to the state. The committee's efforts, however, met with severe government disapproval. The committee soon collapsed, and Bastuni himself emigrated to North America. However, although Bastuni and various Jewish personalities and groups who have spoken in terms of a "Canaanite" or "Semitic" nation (a meld of Israeli Jews and Arabs) have met with little success in the political arena, the very existence of a civic realm in which Arabs and Jews, if only on a formal level, are treated as equal *Israeli* citizens is of great significance.[84] For it represents an aberration in the pattern of institutional segmentation and, most importantly, has opened the doors of Israeli universities to several thousand Israeli Arabs.

THE FRAGMENTATION OF ARAB VILLAGES

In this examination of segmentation as a component of the system of control, the division of Israeli society between Jews and Arabs has been examined at some length on the institutional level of analysis. For on this level of analysis and regarding this component of control, it is the Jewish-Arab bifurcation which primarily engages interest and attracts analytical attention. Arab "institutions" have not been discussed—for the compelling reason that they do not exist. But the absence of country-wide Arab organizations is part of a pattern of institutional segmentation that extends beyond the Jewish-Arab bifurcation to the fragmentation of the Arab collectivity itself. Moreover, aspects of this pattern of fragmentation are reinforced in ways best analyzed on the institutional level: specifically, the impact of the "local council" system of municipal government on the fragmentation of Arab villages into clans, or hamulas.

A hamula is a patrilineal kinship association whose members are theoretically descendants of one ancestor. All members of one hamula bear the same name, but rarely can the particular blood ties that link all the members to the supposed common ancestor be specified accurately. In other words, the constitution of any given hamula is not fixed. In the traditional Arab village, family quarrels, political and economic convenience, or new theories of patrilineage could result in the unification of smaller hamulas or extended families into a larger hamula or the separation of extended families or groups of extended families from an established hamula to form a new, smaller hamula.

One of the most significant trends in Israeli Arab villages since 1948 has been the reinvigoration of hamula rivalries. This has involved both the resurgence of small hamulas and the secession of groups of extended families from large hamulas to form smaller ones. This trend was identified in separate monographs concerning Israeli Arab villages (both written as Ph.D. dissertations, one in anthropology and the other in political science). In *Arab Border Villages in Israel* (the research for which was done in 1959) Abner Cohen argued that during the 1930's and 1940's the hamula in the average Arab village had "ceased to be a political group or it was in the process of ceasing to be so."[85] Country-wide networks of clans, led by powerful families in the cities, and a British colonial administration that typically appointed the head of the largest clan in the village as mukhtar had resulted in the emergence, in most villages, of two large hamulas or hamula blocs—one siding, on the national level, with the Husseini clan and the other with the Nashishibi clan; one comprising, on the local level, the supporters of the muhktar and the other constituting the opposition. But after 1948, Cohen contended, with the destruction of country-wide networks of clans and of the Arab political parties molded in the image of these networks, hamulas on the village level re-emerged as the crucial form of political participation, their numbers greatly increased, and inter-hamula rivalries intensified. Some years later Subhi Abu-Ghosh, in his study "The Politics of an Arab Village in Israel," noted as well the intensification of inter-hamula politics, the increasing solidarity of previously small and disunited hamulas, and the disintegration of previously large hamulas into several smaller clans.[86]

In both of these monographs the organization of Arab municipal affairs by the Israeli regime according to a proportionally representative local council system was identified as a crucial factor in explaining the pattern of increasing hamula fragmentation and the intensification of political competition among hamulas. Abner Cohen, in his study of a village he called "Bint el-Hudud," described with what enthusiasm previously weak hamulas welcomed the introduction of the local council system. For in the context of a local council these traditionally "downtrodden" clans hoped to form a governing village coalition with which to take revenge on the dominant village clan. In the midst of bitter hamula feuding over seats on the local council and control of the chairmanship, Cohen reported, "Some villagers genuinely believed (in 1959) that the Israeli authorities were setting up these councils in order to sow the seeds of dissension and bloodshed among the Arabs by reviving the old hamula fanaticism. They asserted, with much bitterness, that peace and quiet reigned in the villages until (the so-called) Israeli democracy came."[87] Inhabitants of "Qabila," the name given the village studied by Abu-Ghosh, had a similar complaint concerning the local council system. "The new system which has been introduced into the village is [seen as] 'an ingenious creation' of the Israeli Government to keep the village in a constant state of furor by its insistence upon elections as the only legitimate means whereby the various leaders may gain confirmation for their relative positions in the formal village power-structure. They [the villagers] point to the prevailing cold inter-hamula relations at Qabila and insist that it is a by-product of the elective system."[88] Abu-Ghosh observes that the introduction of the local council system, per se, resulted in the revival and intensification of hamula politics.

The introduction of the elective local administration system into the villages has changed the status of the relatively weak hamulas; their needed votes have made them partners rather than client hamulas.[89]

Since the introduction into Qabila of the elective local council system, hamula-ism and solidarity within the hamula have become intensified. In the era of the Mukhtarship, the largest single hamula in the village was the most likely to hold the position of headman. Today, the largest hamula may not necessarily continue to be the most powerful hamula; coalitions among hamulas can change the old power structure.[90]

On this institutional level of analysis my concern is not with the particular policies of the authorities or their specific efforts to enliven hamula politics in order to maintain or increase the political segmentation of any given Arab village. Rather, I wish to point out, without imputing to the authorities intent or design, how the proportional system of local government, used in both the Jewish and Arab sectors to organize and administer municipal affairs, had by itself the effect of reinforcing hamula rivalry and further fragmenting Arab villages along clan lines.

Many "development towns" in the Jewish sector were populated by Jewish immigrants from Arab countries. Among these Jews the hamula form of social organization was also prevalent. But the proportional system of representation in municipal affairs and regular elections in those communities did not result in the reinforcement of this mode of social organization or in an intensification of interclan rivalry. For in these development towns the national Zionist parties were present and were extremely energetic in organizing the immigrants and absorbing them into their own subcultural institutions.[91] Although it was common for immigrants from particular countries to side with particular parties in a given town, the point is that political competition tended to weaken traditional family associations, as nontraditional routes to local power and prestige became available through membership and participation in the national political parties.

In Arab communities these parties, although often active in seeking the support of hamula leaders in national elections, did not strive to organize the Arab population as party members. The difference can be seen clearly in the selection process for first local councils in Arab and Jewish villages. Rules inherited from the British mandate and laid down by the Ministry of the Interior required that the first council in any village be appointed. Its members were to be chosen on the basis of an evaluation of the proportional balance of political power in the village. In the Jewish sector this translated into an estimate of the relative strength of the Labor Party, the National Religious Party, Herut, etc., in a particular town and an appropriate allotment of seats on the council. However, in the Arab sector the systematic use of this procedure has had important, and quite different, political consequences. The knowledge that seats would be allotted on the basis of hamula strength has encouraged previously weak or disunited hamulas to form themselves into more cohesive units. On the other hand, since the number of seats on the council is determined by the population of the village as a whole, and since, more often than not, the number of hamulas in the village is exceeded by the number of seats projected for the first council, large extended families or close-knit groups of families inside hamulas have sought a seat or seats of their own by breaking away from the large hamulas with which they had been associated.

Once the local council has been set in motion in an Arab village, participation in the governing coalition and especially control of the chairmanship become issues of crucial social, economic, and political importance. For the council collects taxes, decides where approach roads will be built or electrical transmission lines connected, countersigns various kinds of permits, appoints school administrators, and otherwise controls all sorts of petty but, in the local context, vitally important sources of remuneration, influence, and prestige. A frenetic pattern of hamula politics results, characterized by a never-ending chain of hamula splits, defections, realignments, and personal recrimination. Hamula leaders concentrate on building the internal cohesiveness of their hamulas by arranging that as many marriages as possible take place within their hamulas (i.e., between cousins).[92] Meanwhile the leaders of extended families within hamulas monitor the shifting coalitions of village politics closely to determine if and when they might secure a seat on the council, or even its chairmanship, by a precisely timed separation or defection. The trend toward the fragmentation of large hamulas has continued from the introduction of local councils in several Arab villages in the early 1950's at least up until 1973. In 1969, for example, thirty-two Arab local councils held elections and in those thirty-two villages 157 different hamula lists participated. In 1973, in those same thirty-two villages, 174 hamula lists vied for local council representation.[93]

In many of these villages "reformist" (i.e., officially non-hamula) lists have participated, organized by younger people who resent the traditionalist bickering of the clans and claim to represent the interests of the village as a whole. But reformist lists have had a notable lack of success in Arab village politics, and in recent years there has been a sharp decline in the number of such lists. Basically they suffer from the fact that united hamulas, with strong familial bonds, hierarchical organization, and the total control which they can exercise over their female members, are ideal instruments for engaging in local electoral competition. They are also usually the only indigenous organizational units capable of financing an election campaign. Those reformist slates that have enjoyed some measure of success are largely those that have depended on the hamula of the lists' organizers for the bulk of their electoral support.[94] Even the Communist Party, whose Arab cadres condemn hamulaism and the tendency of hamula leaders to ally themselves with ruling Jewish parties, has often found it necessary to join coalitions formed by hamulas in order to participate significantly in local affairs.

The Programmatic Level of Segmentation

The preceding discussion has documented the institutionalization of the Arab minority's social and political isolation, as well as its internal fragmentation (at least on the village level). In light of those factors discussed on the structural level of analysis, some of the enormous obstacles to effective political action on the part of Israeli Arabs can be appreciated. Yet these institutional and structural factors remain only the "raw material" available to the regime in its efforts to achieve and maintain control. Had the regime entertained objectives other than control with regard to the Arab population, and, in accordance with those objectives, had it preferred not to maintain the patterns of structural and institutional segmentation that have been discussed, it might well have implemented policies designed to reduce the isolation of the Arab community and/or its internal fragmentation.

The purpose of this section is to show how regime policies were specifically designed to preserve and strengthen just those structural circumstances and institutional arrangements which contributed to the segmentation of the Arab community, both internally and in its relations with the Jewish sector. Concurrently the authorities have acted to break apart nascent attempts at independent Arab organization and to discourage the emergence of identities, leaders, and associational frameworks that might have led to country-wide Arab political action or meaningful alliances between Arab and Jewish Israelis. What follows is an examination of a third pattern of segmentation, this time on the programmatic level of analysis. It involves a systematic discussion of how the regime has acted in particular ways to achieve the isolation of the Arab minority and its internal fragmentation.

THE FRAGMENTATION OF THE ARAB MINORITY: PROGRAMMATIC LEVEL

The Role of the Military Government During its eighteen-year existence (1948–1966) the "Military Administration" or "Military Government" (Memshal Tzvai) was the most important instrument used by the regime to control the Arab minority. One of the central objectives of the Military Administration was to reinforce the patterns of segmentation described previously on the structural and institutional levels. In addition it undertook to destroy any organized attempt by Arabs to overcome either the internal fragmentation of their community or their isolation from Jewish society.

The Military Administration was divided into three regional commands corresponding to the geographical concentrations of Israel's Arab inhabitants—the Northern Command, encompassing the Galilee and the Haifa area; the Central Command, with responsibility for the Little Triangle; and the Southern Command, responsible for the Bedouin of the Negev. In 1949 these areas contained over 90 percent of Israel's Arab population, and still in 1958 fully 85 percent of all Israeli Arabs lived in areas assigned to the Military Administration. Military governors, appointed directly by the defense minister, exercised their authority on the basis of what are known as the Emergency Regulations or the Defense Laws. These statutes, consisting of 170 articles divided into fifteen sections, were inherited from the British mandate. The British had originally enacted them in order to subdue the Palestinian Arab revolt of 1936–1939. Later they were used by the British against the Jewish underground when, in the late 1940's, Jewish forces launched military efforts to bring an end to the mandate. The regulations can become operative only after an "emergency situation" has been declared. In Israel an "emergency situation" was declared immediately following the establishment of the state and that declaration is still in force.

These regulations give appointed military governors almost dictatorial powers in the districts to which they are assigned. Of particular interest here are their powers with regard to the restriction of travel. The Arab villages which remained intact after 1948 were, as I have said, only the scattered remnants of a much larger network of Arab towns and villages which had existed in pre-1948 Palestine. By requiring Arabs to obtain military permits for travel outside their own villages the Military Administration effectively reinforced the geographical fragmentation of the Arab community which had resulted from the upheavals of 1948. The Galilee, for example, in the early years of the Military Administration, was divided into over fifty districts. Every Arab in the Galilee needed a permit from the military authorities in order to pass from one district to another or, in effect, from one village to another. These travel permits specified not only the date on which they were valid, but also the destination, the route that was to be taken, and the time of return. Permits for inhabitants of one village to visit friends or relatives in other villages were not commonly issued. Statistics are nearly impossible to obtain, but the government did report that in 1953–1954 80 percent of all travel permits "were issued in connection with employment, the rest being for medical treatment, contact with courts and legal advisers, and contact with Government departments."[95] Since essentially all Arabs who worked outside their villages worked as unskilled laborers in Jewish cities or agricultural settlements, and since government departments and medical facilities were also located in Jewish metropolitan areas, it is clear that contacts among Arab villages were severely limited.

Besides regulating interaction among Arab villages, the Military Administration's system of travel restrictions also barred Arabs living in the mixed cities of Haifa, Jaffa, Acre, Ramle-Lod, and Jerusalem from visiting, without permits, Arab settlements in the Galilee, the Little Triangle, or the Negev. Nor could Arabs travel from the Galilee to the Little Triangle or the Negev (or vice versa) without the written permission of the Military Administration. Arabs found on roads or in towns or villages without appropriate permits were subject to fines and imprisonment.

As the years passed, travel restrictions were gradually relaxed. Yet in 1958 only one out of three Arabs in the military zones, at any given time, held travel permits, and only half of these permits were granted for "long periods."[96] In 1964 Arabs in northern and eastern Galilee still needed permission from the Military Administration to leave their villages, and all Arabs were still required to carry permits in order to travel from one Military Administration district to another or from the mixed urban areas to one of the military districts.[97]

Officially, travel restrictions were implemented for "security reasons," but as time went on and travel restrictions remained in force, it became clear to many, including several leading military figures, that the maintenance of the restrictions derived from political and economic as well as security considerations.[98] Indeed, the regime greatly feared that freedom of movement for Arabs could result in assemblies of politically minded Arabs and the formation of regional or even countrywide political associations. In particular it was feared that "internal refugees," scattered after 1948 among various Arab villages, would return to their abandoned villages and attempt to reclaim their lands and rebuild their houses.

Consider what would happen if we abolished the restrictions. The Arabs who used to live in the empty villages, egged on and organized by the communists, would go back and squat on their ruins, demanding their lands back. What good would that do? Their lands are in use. And then, when they have made as much trouble as possible about their own lands, they will start clamouring for the return of the refugees. They will form organizations, parties, fronts, anything to make trouble.[99]

The pattern of structural segmentation described at the beginning of this chapter—including the Arab community's lack of large urban centers, its division along sectarian lines among Moslems, Druse, and several Christian sects, and the fragmentation of Arab villages into antagonistic kinship groups—made the task of the Military Administration considerably easier, for these structural conditions all militated against the formation of united independent Arab political groups. Yet, until its abolition in 1966, the Military Administration was continually faced with attempts, especially by the Communist Party, to mobilize and unite Arabs in connection with issues such as economic discrimination, the expropriation of Arab lands, and the existence of the Military Administration itself. There were also repeated attempts by Arab village leaders, and later by younger Arab intellectuals, to overcome the fragmentation of the Arab community by joining together on issues of mutual concern—most commonly the continuing expropriation of land.

Officially the Military Administration served no political purpose, and government spokesmen claimed that Israeli Arabs within its jurisdiction were "no whit less free than the rest of the inhabitants [of Israel]."[100] Yet privately government officials responsible for the Arab sector justified the political mission of the Military Administration. In a series of articles published by *Davar* in 1958 the results of interviews with highly placed but unnamed officers of the Military Administration were set forth. The military authorities, observed the author, had nothing against Arab notables speaking out *separately*.

For instance, a certain Arab notable may be well known for his extreme nationalist activities, yet is allowed to live peacefully in his house in such and such a village. A certain Moslem religious leader with a large congregation preaches subversive sermons every Friday but he has no need to go into hiding or conceal his views. A clergyman from a neighboring town may hold similar views. The views they openly express, and their negative attitude towards the military regime and the State of Israel as a whole do not differ in principle from the views of the Communist Party as expressed within the military government area and outside it. Nevertheless if these three were to organize gatherings in an attempt to form an Arab Nationalist Party or movement, the military authorities would take the necessary preventive measures. Their travel permits may be confiscated, or one of them may receive an expulsion order. . . . It is a principle of the military authorities not to tolerate nationalistic organizing within the area under its control.[101]

Indeed, the Military Administration strove to prevent or eliminate any form of autonomous Arab organization. "[In] the process of preventing hostile activity, any sort of public association becomes prohibited. The military authorities are afraid that in the course of time it will be difficult to know what really goes on within such organizations which appear outwardly to be perfectly in order. . . . Thus even the establishment of a central organization representing Arab municipalities was prevented."[102] In the late 1950's and early 1960's, there were many attempts by communist and noncommunist Arabs to assemble and organize in protest of the expropriation of Arab lands and the continuation of the Military Administration. These attempts were nearly all suppressed by the direct action of the Military Administration. In June 1959 the military governor of the Galilee, by authority given him under the Emergency Regulations, banished thirteen communists and communist "sympathizers" to various Jewish towns for four days in order to prevent them from assembling to plan a "Conference of Refugees and Displaced Landowners."[103] In October 1959, the deputy military governor of the Galilee threatened one member of an "Independent Arab List" with a similar fate if he would not withdraw his candidacy for the Knesset.[104] Closing the roads to Binah, a western Galilee Arab village, the Military Administration forced the cancellation of a meeting that had been called in April 1962 by "the Communist Party and Arab nationalist circles" to protest the expropriation of Arab lands. Restraining orders were issued against organizers of the rally; arrests were also made.[105] Again in September 1962 the Military Administration issued restraining orders against the Arab organizers of a Communist Party rally in Haifa to protest land expropriations. By requiring that these activists report twice daily to the police stations nearest their villages, the authorities made it impossible for them to attend the rally.[106] Three months later the Military Administration confined nine Arab communists to their homes in order to prevent them from attending a convention of the Popular Front, a short-lived communist-inspired Arab nationalist organization.[107] In August 1963 the Military Administration declared Taiybe, an Arab village in the Little Triangle, a "closed area." This step was taken after the authorities learned that a meeting of Arabs from various villages was to be held there to discuss joint protests against the continuation of the Military Administration. Eighteen Arabs were arrested for attempting to enter what had been declared—without their having been informed—

a closed area.[108] In 1964, Arab university students attempted to organize an Association of Arab Sports Club to include Arab youth from both the Galilee and the Little Triangle. In April of that year the students called a meeting in Kfar Kara, an Arab village in the Little Triangle, inviting representatives of Arab sports clubs from many Arab villages. The response of the Military Administration was to arrest five organizers of the conference the night before it was to convene. When the others decided to go ahead with the meeting as planned, the military authorities declared the village a closed area and arrested forty Arabs who attempted to enter. A spokesman for the Military Administration indicated that he was not opposed to the establishment of sports clubs in different Arab villages, but that it was feared a country-wide association would serve as an organizational framework for nationalist political activity.[109] In 1965 the "el-Ard Group," a small number of Arab intellectuals best known for the strongly nationalist tone of a magazine which they intermittently published, presented a list of candidates for the Knesset elections to be called the Arab Socialist List. In response to the attempt of this group to present itself in country-wide elections as the representative of the Arab minority, the Military Administration moved hard and fast. Permission for the Arab Socialist List to appear on the ballot was refused, el-Ard's leaders were separated and banished to remote Jewish towns, many members were put under administrative detention, and the organization itself was finally declared illegal. Subsequently several of its leaders were offered a choice of imprisonment or exile from the country.[110]

The role of the Military Administration in preventing the emergence of a united Arab political party was fully appreciated by Israeli Arabs. One anonymous young Arab in 1959 asked himself: "Why have we not got an independent Arab party, unconnected with the Jewish parties? Why do we not elect our own representatives as a united Arab block? Why should we be divided into Mapai, Mapam, Communists, Ahdut Ha-Avoda, and even General Zionists, National Religious Party, and Herut? . . . Why should there not be a united and independent Arab party, which by reason of its numbers could become an important factor in the Knesset and compel everyone, including the Government, to reckon with it?" For the author the answer to these questions was the resolute opposition of the military governor "to every sign of organized Arab nationalism. He will try by all possible means to prevent the establishment of a United Arab Party for the Knesset elections. He will use every weapon at his disposal, such as expulsions, removals, cancelling of travel permits and work permits . . ."[111] Elias Koussa, in 1962, anticipated that if the Military Administration were to be abolished, the Arab community would indeed "form a political party that would present its own list of candidates."[112]

The Reinforcement of Fragmentation   Elias Koussa was wrong. The Military Administration was abolished in 1966; yet no Arab political parties, indeed no mass-based independent Arab organizations of any kind, have emerged. The explanation for this failure involves an appreciation of the effective manner by which the regime, through various instrumentalities and techniques (including the Military Administration), has fostered the cultural, religious, ecological, and kinship divisions already present in the Arab sector. These divisions (which have been considered on the structural and institutional levels) have been preserved and elaborated by the policies of the regime in order to reinforce the internal fragmentation of the Arab population and its isolation from the Jewish majority.

The Military Administration, by its own divisions into three separate commands and through the imposition of severe restrictions on travel and migration within the districts governed by these commands, reinforced the isolation of Arab villages from one another and the segmentation of the Arab population as a whole into three geographically separate rural areas. In addition, substantial effort has been directed toward breaking up the "compactness" of Arab settlement—in the central Galilee, in the Little Triangle, and in the cities of Acre and Nazareth. This policy has been aimed at hindering the emergence either of important metropolitan centers in the Arab sector or of territorially contiguous Arab "cantons."

The "Judaization of the Galilee" (Yehud ha-Galil) has been an ongoing program of the regime undertaken by various governmental and nongovernmental agencies. Strenuous efforts have been made to channel Jewish settlers to isolated settlements in the upper Galilee. Large tracts of Arab land have been expropriated and new towns, such as Maalot and Carmiel, established as urban Jewish centers in an otherwise almost totally Arab area. In addition, various economic and social benefits have been extended as incentives to Jewish families willing to settle in outlying districts of the Galilee. Yet the regime has had a great deal of difficulty in persuading Jews to settle in these towns and villages and to remain there once having settled. Many settlements have had to be abandoned, and neither Maalot nor Carmiel nor Upper Nazareth has grown to anything near the proportions that had been projected. The continued presence of something close to an Arab majority in the Galilee has been a source of worry and embarrassment to the authorities. As one official in charge of the Arab Department of the Ministry of Education observed, "Our big problem in Israel with the Arabs is their concentration in the Galilee . . . even Ben-Gurion said that with the concentration of Arabs in Galilee they have the right to ask to be annexed to Lebanon."[113]

Recent increases in the rate of Jewish out-migration from the Galilee have led to an intensification, since 1975, of the Yehud ha-Galil program. This has included additional expropriations of land, ideological exhortations directed toward Jewish residents and potential settlers, and stepped-up programs for the economic development of Jewish settlements in the Galilee.[114]

In the Little Triangle the government moved quickly to break up the territorial continuity of Arab settlements. Eighty percent of the land of the inhabitants of Um el Fahm, the largest village in the Little Triangle, was expropriated (see Chapter 5). There were also several cases of Arab village populations being deported *en masse* across the border into Jordan.[115] These expropriations and population transfers, in the words of one military governor, "were generally associated with the establishment of Jewish settlements so that there wouldn't be, at the very least, a continuous strip of Arab settlements along the border, but that there would also be some Jewish points."[116] From 1949 to 1955 over thirty Jewish agricultural settlements were established in this previously homogeneously Arab area.[117]

Nazareth was the only Arab city that experienced an increase in population as a result of the 1948 war—from 15,540 to 16,880. This was the result of an influx from towns and villages throughout the Galilee of Arab refugees who were not allowed to return to their places of origin. Although before 1948 its significance was minimal in the affairs of the Arabs of Palestine, today Nazareth is the only city in Israel where Arabs constitute a majority of the population. The regime's concern with the existence of this Arab urban center led to a decision to found a Jewish city—Upper Nazareth (Nazaret Illit)—on the hills overlooking the town. In 1973 the population of Jewish Upper Nazareth was 18,000 while the population of Arab Nazareth was 35,400. However, the land area allotted for the expansion of Upper Nazareth was three times that allotted to lower Nazareth.[118]

The only other Arab urban concentration of potential political significance is in Acre. Of 15,000 Arabs in Acre before 1948, only 3,500 remained after the war—many of these refugees from other areas in Israel. The city's Jewish population had grown from a few hundred in 1948 to 27,400 in 1974. After 1948 the Arabs have been concentrated in the "Old Town." Generally speaking, economic conditions have not been good in Acre, and government attempts to consolidate a large Jewish majority in the city have been set back by a constant out-migration of discouraged Jewish residents. By the early 1970's, however, severe overcrowding problems had developed among the 9,000 Arab inhabitants of the Old Town, where many houses were on the point of collapse. The response of the authorities to this serious housing problem in the Arab section of Acre is reflective of the regime's general opposition to large urban concentrations of Arabs.

The Arab community has repeatedly stressed its desire for Arab housing projects to be constructed outside the walls of the Old Town, but adjacent to it, on empty lots within Acre itself. However, although thousands of housing units have been built in Acre, up to 1973 the government had allotted only forty of its new units to Arab residents. The main concern of the authorities as regards the issue of Arab housing in Acre is the relative political seclusion and autonomy that the Arabs of the city enjoy. The densely populated Arab Old Town continues to be seen as a hothouse for hostile Arab political activity.[119] The instability of the Jewish population of Acre and the high rate of natural increase among Arab residents are seen to pose a threat to the continued "Jewish character" of the city. The response of the authorities to these concerns was contained in a master plan for the city of Acre drawn up in 1971 and now in the process of implementation. The document proposes

> to establish an Arab quarter, which will reach an eventual population of 11,500 by 1985, on an as yet unspecified site in the Arab rural area *beyond the boundaries of the city.* . . . The net effect of the whole maneuver would be a considerable reduction in the number of Arabs in the city of Acre. The proposal for the new master plan indeed foresees merely 4,000 Arabs within the present boundaries of the city in 1985, when the population of Acre is expected to reach 68,000 inhabitants. The Arab population would thus be reduced from more than a quarter in 1971 to about 6 percent in 1985.[120]

Under the terms of the government proposal the Arab section of Acre will be converted from an Arab urban district to a "living museum city" serving almost exclusively as a Jewish-owned and -operated tourist attraction.[121] The plan is typical of a consistent government policy toward the Arabs of Acre—a policy which has included "attempts by the local authorities to limit Arab migration into Acre, to put obstacles in the way of those Arabs who sought to move from the Old Town into the once-Arab houses in the New Town, and to induce Arabs living in substandard housing to accept loans for the construction of new houses in one of the surrounding villages instead of being given substitute housing in the city."[122] The resettlement of some Acre Arabs in a new village eight kilometers east of Acre began in 1976. Population statistics for 1976 indicate that the number of Arabs living in Acre fell from 9,100 in 1973 to 8,600 in 1976.[123]

In the first section of this chapter, concerning structural segmentation, the religious division of Israeli Arabs into Christians, Moslems, and Druse was suggested as a circumstance contributing to the fragmentation of the Arab sector. However, there is nothing inevitable about the political implications of these religious identities, either in Israel or in any other Middle Eastern country. What I wish to argue here, in line with my discussion of other government policies and their relationship to existing structural conditions, is that the particular programs implemented by the regime with respect to the religious segmentation of the Arab population were designed to preserve these identities and encourage their use as meaningful political categories. These efforts must be understood as part of a general desire to inhibit the emergence of "Arab" as the most meaningful category of political identity and association for Israel's non-Jewish population.

Thus the Arab population is generally not referred to as such by government officials. The terms most commonly used include "the minorities," the "non-Jewish population," or "the Arabs and the Druse." Members of the Druse community who have expressed the desire to list Arab rather than Druse as their nationality on their identity cards have been refused permission. The religious, cultural, and political division of the Druse from Moslem and Christian Arabs has been quite explicitly encouraged, mainly by a policy of treating Druse more favorably than other Arabs and by emphasizing the significance of the Druse community out of all proportion to its size. In 1957 the Ministry of Religious Affairs recognized the Druse as an independent religious community (*millet*), a communal status which the Druse never experienced under Ottoman rule. One important implication of this action, given the absence of civil marriage in Israel, is that intermarriage, within Israel, between Druse, Christian, and Moslem Arabs is prohibited. In 1962 a special system of separate Druse courts was established. With government encouragement the Druse religious holiday of *Nebi Shueib* was transformed into a major annual national-religious festival including a mass gathering of Druse from all over Israel, speeches by government ministers, and widespread coverage in the national media. In 1956 conscription into the army, and thus veteran status, was extended to Druse men. In 1962, four years before the Military Administration was abolished, its application in Druse villages was formally brought to an end.[124] In addition, financial assistance to Druse villages has been substantially greater, per capita, than for Moslem and Christian villages.[125]

Besides the special treatment accorded the Druse population, the government has taken other measures to encourage the religious fragmentation of the Arab minority. These include the establishment of separate scouting organizations for Moslem and Druse youth and similar scouting movements for the youth of various Christian sects. Indeed special regard has been shown for the different Christian communities: the Greek Catholic, Greek Orthodox, Latin, and Maronite. The government has returned the consecrated property of absentee Christians to the control of the individual sects, unlike its treatment of the Moslem Waqf. Each Christian sect maintains its own religious court system, which under Israeli law has complete jurisdiction over matters of personal status regarding its members (marriage, divorce, adoption, etc.). The Israeli government has even recognized the small Protestant Arab community as an autonomous sect with an independent jurisdiction.

The regime's policies toward the Negev Bedouin have been designed to maintain the cultural and ecological isolation of that community from the rest of Israel's Arab population and to strengthen those kinship associations which fragment the Bedouin population internally. Out of 65,750 Bedouin who inhabited the Negev desert before 1948, only 11,000 remained to become Israeli citizens. The majority had either fled or been expelled to Egypt and Jordan. Of those who remained, almost all belonged to the Tiaha Confederation and were confined in their wanderings to a reservation in the northeastern corner of the Negev. Although Bedouin were set apart from other Moslem Arabs by the government's decision to allow Bedouin (but not other Moslem Arabs) to volunteer for service in the armed forces, the rule of the Military Administration in the southern region was particularly stringent. During the tenure of the Military Administration great care was taken to prevent the migration of Bedouin out of the reservation in the northeastern Negev to which they had been confined. Bedouin men who were given permits to work on Jewish citrus plantations during the harvest season were not allowed to bring their families with them, thus insuring their return to the reservation.[126] The regime also cultivated the internal fragmentation of the Bedouin and the break-up of the Tiaha Confederation. Bedouin were required to register with the Military Administration according to their *tribal* affiliation (tribes being quasi-kinship subgroups of confederations). Bedouin tribesmen were also obliged to obtain the permission of the military governor before crossing a boundary between one tribe and another.[127] By seeking out and supporting strong tribal chiefs the Military Administration had, by 1960, succeeded in substituting the tribe for the confederation as the widest form of political association among the Negev Bedouin.[128]

Moslem Arabs recognize and resent the segmentalist policies of the government, including the favoritism shown toward Christians, and especially toward the Druse. The distrust and suspicion which such policies engender hamper the ability of these groups to organize politically on an "all Arab" basis. On the village level, the overlap of religious identification and kinship group intensifies antagonisms among rival clans.

The government's preferences with regard to the maintenance of separate Druse, Christian, Moslem, Bedouin, and Circassian identities, as opposed to the emergence among the non-Jewish minority of an overarching Arab or Palestinian sentiment, are also reflected in the curriculum used in Arab secondary schools. The studious avoidance of themes, events, and personalities involved in the Arab and Palestinian nationalist movements contrasts sharply with the explicit attempts made in Jewish schools to instill loyalty and pride in the historical struggles of the Jewish nation.[129]

In 1956 Elias Dalal, principal of the Orthodox Community Secondary School in Haifa, submitted a lengthy memorandum to the minister of education and culture. With regard to the syllabus Dalal indicated that

Important contributions to national and patriotic literature have been expurgated in line with the policy of repression of Arab nationalism, spelling out an attempt to lower the prestige of his nation in the pupil's eyes. . . .
. . . Too little time has been allotted to Arab history. . . . Further, the section dealing with the Arab revolt against Ottoman rule has been eliminated from the books in the secondary classes.[130]

According to a study published in 1968, the time allotted for Jewish history in Jewish schools was more than twice that allotted for Arab history in Arab schools. Although Jewish students were required to spend forty hours studying Jewish history for every one and a half hours spent on Arab history, Arabs spent more time on the history of the Jews than on the history of the Arabs.[131]

More recently, Fouzi el-Asmar, an Arab poet and journalist, has written of his own education in Israel:

The material chosen from Arabic literature . . . lacked any patriotic feeling and had no national tone. Moreover, it was as if the Palestinian authors did not exist; they were ignored. Daily we experienced the close connection between the Hebrew literary works we were learning and the Arab-Israeli conflict: while the Jewish works gave expression to a live and aware people united in its feelings and actions, the Arab works that we were taught did not concern themselves at all with any nationalist ideals but were mostly works describing nature and lyrical moods.

. . . The names of a number of these poems will give a feeling of their content; "A Description of the Earthquake which hit the Italian village of Messina in 1908"; "An Evening on the Coast of Alexandria"; "A Description of the Poet's Room"; "Autumn"; "Spring"; "The Butterfly"; "A Description of a Long Face." I am not saying that these poems were not good. . . . But we felt deprived because of the total absence of national poems, patriotic poems, especially since the Hebrew curriculum was full of them. In addition to this, it hurt us to see the total absence of Palestinian authors from the studies of the poetry, and we could not see any reason for this except as a way of suppressing our national feelings.[132]

The regime's desire to preserve cultural, kinship, and religious divisions among the Arab population and to maintain local as opposed to country-wide political loyalties has been clearly reflected in the careful selection of candidates for "affiliated Arab Knesset lists." In every Knesset election the Labor Party, as well as other Zionist political parties, has financed separate "affiliated" lists of Arab candidates. In each of nine parliamentary elections a minimum of one and a maximum of five Arabs have been elected on labor-affiliated lists. Although no other Zionist party has sponsored a successful Arab affiliated list, many (including Likud) have tried, and have benefited by adding the votes obtained by such lists to their totals. As Jacob Landau has observed, the persons chosen as candidates on such lists "are important only in their local and familial framework, and they are supported . . . almost solely for vote-catching purposes. . . . Their significance is far from country-wide. This feature may be easily ascertained from the fact that in all Knesset elections the Arab lists allied with Jewish parties obtained practically the whole of their electoral support in certain areas [and only scattered votes elsewhere]."[133]

The use of "affiliated Arab lists" reinforces the parochial segmentation of the Arab population by rewarding those notables who succeed in maintaining the vitality of sectional, sectarian, or familial loyalties. Parochial antipathies are also fostered in the course of replacing, from election to election, representatives of one sect or geographical area with representatives of another. "Safe spots" on these lists are allotted on an irregular rotating basis to Arab personalities who represent various religious, geographical, or familial constituencies. In 1973 there was considerable resentment in the Greek Catholic community and in the Little Triangle toward the Bedouin as a result of the Labor Party's decision to drop Elias Nakhle (an eighteen-year Greek Catholic incumbent member of Knesset) and De'ib Obeid (a twelve-year incumbent member of Knesset from a village in the Little Triangle) in order to secure a seat for a Bedouin Sheik, Hamad Abu Rabiah.[134]

Labor Party support of two or three Arab lists, rather than one central one, has also been designed to provide local hamulas with opportunities to express their rivalry through competition in supporting *different* Labor Party–affiliated lists.[135] This coincides with what has been the sustained policy of the Military Administration, the Arab Department of the Histadrut, the Office of the Adviser to the Prime Minister on Arab Affairs, and the Labor Party's Arab Department: to encourage, maintain, and exploit the hamula fragmentation of Arab villages.

Implementation of such policies began in Arab villages even before the organization of local councils. Typically, an official of the Military Administration would visit a village to seek out the leaders of one of the largest hamulas. Very often the hamula chosen would be the one which had played second fiddle in the village during the British mandate, for the members of such a hamula would be likely to welcome any opportunity to reverse their subordinate position. But the very fact that such a visit took place with the leaders of any hamula would be enough to trigger a slew of rumors and whispered suspicions throughout the village. Members of other hamulas would hurriedly meet to discuss the implications of this development. Typically the Military Administration would offer favors of one sort or another to the leader of the chosen hamula: a book of travel permits to be issued at his discretion, the release of a relative from prison, speedy medical assistance provided for a member of the hamula taken ill, permission to lease additional land, supplementary water allocations, or an option and/or a loan for the purchase of a tractor. The son of the patriarch contacted might be named the representative of the Histadrut Labor Exchange in the village, a post which would secure fairly regular employment for the members of his hamula and constitute, as well, a source of great power over other villagers.

But whatever the mix of favors extended, the result would be the same. Frightened by the prospect that an unchallenged alliance between one hamula in the village and the Military Administration would result in the predominance of that hamula, the elders of other hamulas were forced to respond by seeking to establish their own connections with the authorities. Typically, the Military Administration would then encourage each hamula to compete for its favors. Such competition would include discouraging hamula members from associating with communists or engaging in any political activity; informing representatives of the Military Administration as to the activities of members of other hamulas—smuggling, harboring of refugees, association with communists, antigovernment sentiments, etc.; agreeing to the sale of hamula land; and delivering the votes of hamula members to the Labor Party or its affiliated Arab lists during Knesset elections. For this latter purpose the Military Administration, and after its abolition other agencies responsible for the affairs of the Arab sector, made it a practice to distribute differently printed ballots to different hamulas. Knowing that the results would be carefully tabulated and recorded, the leaders of hamulas would strive to ensure that hamula members voted strictly according to instructions (see Figure 2).

One of the most important resources of the military governor was his power to recommend the list of participants for the first village local council to the minister of the interior. Hamula elders had to seek the favor of the military governor or risk being left out of the local council or deprived of the number of seats proportional to the size of their hamulas. In villages where hamulas had weakened to the point that clan leaders could not

Figure 2. **Differently printed ballots for the same "Arab List for Bedouin and Villagers"—affiliated to the Labor Party.** Separate
packages of these ballots were distributed to two different
hamulas in the village of Baka el-Gharbiyeh prior to the
Knesset elections held in December 1973.

claim the support of most villagers, the Ministry of the Interior
and/or the Military Administration simply postponed indefi-
nitely the establishment of local councils. *Elections* for a *first*
council, which in the absence of strong hamulas might have led
to less traditional, nonfamilial forms of political organization,
have never been permitted. Thus there were villages (Deir Hana
for instance, in the central Galilee) where in 1974 local councils
had still not been established because the villagers refused to take
their hamulas seriously. In such villages, the economic hardship
resulting from the absence of a local council (ineligibility for government economic programs) serves as a constant source of support for villagers who favor a return to the more traditional
hamula form of social and political organization.

The implementation of policies designed to reinforce the division among hamulas has continued despite the abolition of the
Military Administration. Yehoshua Palmon, Israel's first adviser
to the prime minister on Arab affairs, was quoted in 1972,
characterizing Israel's overall policy with regard to the internal

affairs of Arab villages and their local councils: "to arouse the Israeli Arabs and to stir them to participate in the Knesset elections by placing them inside a political whirlpool."[136] One technique used for this purpose by the Arab Department of the Ministry of Education, in coordination on an ad hoc basis with other agencies responsible for the Arab sector, is to approve the dismissals and appointments of school administrators in Arab villages by newly formed local council coalitions. Administrative positions in village elementary and secondary schools are the choicest plums of local patronage. Typically, a new coalition of hamulas loses no time in replacing previous appointees with members of those clans who have, for the moment, attained power. In most cases the approval of the Arab Department of the Ministry of Education is necessary for such dismissals and replacements. By regularly granting such approval and, at times, by suggesting that such approval would be forthcoming in the event of the dismissal of one administrator from hamula X and his replacement with a member of hamula Y, the Arab Department of the ministry can precipitate defections from governing coalitions and help other government agencies orchestrate the emergence of a new coalition.[137]

Maintaining Arab village life in a state of permanent political flux is only one technique among many at the disposal of government agencies. Besides keeping the political pot boiling and mobilizing traditional kinship associations for the electoral advantage of the Labor Party, the Likud, or the National Religious Party, the agencies that have inherited the tasks of the Military Administration—the Office of the Adviser to the Prime Minister on Arab Affairs, the Arab Department of the Histadrut, the Arab Department of the Labor Party, and the Arab Departments of the Ministries of the Interior and of Education— have acted energetically and systematically to preserve the sociopolitical fragmentation of Arab village life by striving to prevent nontraditional political associations from achieving prominence in Arab villages and/or power on local councils. These efforts have included opposition, on the local level, to almost any group that has made appeals across hamula lines. Specifically they have been directed against the participation of non-hamula reformist lists and, more importantly, of local Rakah lists on governing local council coalitions. The object has been to prevent local councils from developing into public frameworks for the expressions of Arab nationalist sentiment or the development of leadership cadre with the potential to appeal to Arabs on a country-wide basis.

In an interview with *Maariv* in 1969 Shmuel Toledano observed that "the public officials who deal with the formation of local councils in the Arab sector have made it clear and explicit that they will not tolerate nationalist representatives on one local council! We want to arrive at the situation where nationalist Arabs will be isolated in the village; simply closed off from the society."[138] In accordance with this policy, representatives of various agencies responsible for the Arab sector have striven mightily to prevent communists and "independents" from gaining significant representation on local councils. Indeed, the political preeminence of the clans on the village level has made it very difficult for Rakah to succeed in local elections. Although Rakah received 37 percent of the Arab vote in the 1973 Knesset election it was rare to find more than one communist local council member in any given Arab village in 1974. Despite the election of a communist mayor of Nazareth in December 1975, and although the Rakah-sponsored Democratic Front for Peace and Equality received 49 percent of the Arab vote in the 1977 Knesset election, the overwhelming majority of heads of Arab local councils in 1977 were elected as hamula-sponsored candidates.

If the balance of power among local clans in a particular village is such that a communist representative threatens to emerge as a coalition member upon whom the hamula leaders will be dependent, one or another of the agencies which deal with the Arab sector takes the initiative in patching up hamula quarrels and organizing an alternative coalition, excluding the communists. A variety of techniques have been used to discourage "wall-to-wall coalitions" or other political arrangements which would include the representatives of nonkinship-based political associations. The villagers may be given to understand that a council governed by a coalition involving communists will have trouble securing Interior Ministry loans for school or road construction. Construction schedules regarding electrical transmission lines to Arab villages are also subject to drastic change. Hamulas that fail to cooperate with government representatives to exclude undesirable elements may be punished by sudden adjustments in property tax assessments or by the assignment of responsibility for tax assessment to members of rival hamulas. Coalitions without communist members are rewarded by official visits and public congratulations from Jewish dignitaries. But often it is necessary to provide recalcitrant hamula leaders with bribes—usually in the form of jobs (or promises of jobs) for relatives; junkets within Israel, to Europe, or to the United States; a gas station or taxi cab franchise, etc.

In one case with which I am personally familiar, the village of Arrabe (central Galilee) in 1973–1974, the government failed in its efforts to prevent a communist-run coalition from taking control of the local council. Much to the chagrin of the Office of the Adviser to the Prime Minister on Arab Affairs, the Arab Department of the Ministry of the Interior, and the Labor Party Arab Department, the local council of Arrabe began to issue political statements condemning the continued occupation of the West Bank and the Gaza Strip and various forms of national discrimination against Arabs in Israel. It also issued appeals and complaints to the United Nations concerning land expropriations, and in general interested itself in issues of national and international as well as local concern. The initial response of the authorities was to withhold from the village various permits as well as financial assistance in regard to school and road construction projects already underway. When the villagers of Arrabe managed to overcome these difficulties, in part by contributing their labor on a voluntary basis, the Office of the Adviser to the Prime Minister on Arab Affairs took stronger measures. Early in March 1974, the Arrabe local council was disbanded and replaced by a committee of three Jews, representing the Labor, Education, and Interior ministries. Meanwhile the adviser's office worked behind the scenes to engineer a coalition of hamula elders which would exclude the representatives elected on the communist-sponsored "Democratic List."[139]

The dissolution of the Arrabe local council, although unusual, was not a singular occurrence. Abu Ghosh reported in 1965 that dissolution of Arab local councils by the Ministry of the Interior's Arab Department, merely on the basis of a district officer's dissatisfaction with a particular council member, was a common phenomenon.[140] In 1976 the ministry disbanded the

Galilean village of Tamra's local council, and in 1977 it threatened Um el Fahm, the largest Arab village in Israel, with the dissolution of its local council because of a communist-sponsored no-confidence vote against the village's progovernment mayor.[141] The prerogative held by the authorities to disband a local council is an ever-present threat. Because some form of municipal government is necessary if a village is to qualify for most government loans, grants, and permits, such a threat constitutes a powerful constraint against using the local council in ways which the authorities are likely to find unpleasant.

The Emergence of Arab Student Organizations The political fragmentation of the Arab minority on the national level, as opposed to the local level, is in large measure the result of there being few arenas within which Arabs from all over the country and from different religious backgrounds can meet to talk and associate freely. University campuses are an exception, however. As mentioned previously, due to the existence—if primarily on a formal level—of a "civic realm," in the context of which Arabs and Jews can apply on a relatively equal basis for admission to institutions of higher learning, a substantial Arab student population has emerged on Israeli campuses. In 1950 there were only ten Arab students in Israeli universities, but by 1977 there were approximately 2,100, mostly concentrated at the Hebrew University in Jerusalem and at the University of Haifa. Although Arabs comprise only 4 percent of the students enrolled at Israeli universities, college campuses have emerged as the only places where sizable numbers of Arabs from various localities and religions have a regular opportunity to congregate. Moreover, serious difficulties in finding housing and part-time jobs in Jewish cities, the distrust of the Jewish student body, and the overall strangeness of the academic environment encourage Arab students to band together as "Arabs," regardless of kinship affiliations, religion, or place of origin.

The first Arab Students Committee was founded in 1958 at the Hebrew University. Its protests against various forms of discrimination against Arabs in Israel and after 1967 against the continued occupation of the West Bank and Gaza by Israel have been vigorous. It has participated in demonstrations against the Military Administration (before 1966), the expropriation of

Arab land, and the use of administrative detention. It has also declared its strong support of the Palestinian and Arab nationalist movements and has voiced its opinions as well with regard to issues of international concern. In the early 1970's Arab Students Committees formed at Haifa University, Bar Ilan University, the Technion, and Tel Aviv University. Like the Arab Students Committee at the Hebrew University these groups have offered aid to Arab students in their adjustment to university life, including—especially—assistance in securing accommodations and part-time employment. Rakah's support for these groups has been strong and its influence among them has grown, but the students have so far resisted attempts by communist members to take full control.

Harassment of Arab university student organizations has been an important element in the government's overall campaign to prevent the emergence of Arab political groups or leaders that could effectively appeal to the minority on a countrywide basis. In line with this policy, no Arab Students Committee has ever been accorded official recognition by university administrators or government authorities. Denied official recognition, Arab students are quite often refused permission to use university facilities to publicize or to hold meetings and symposia. In 1968 the chairman of the Arab Students Committee at the Hebrew University, Khalil Tuma, was arrested and sentenced to nine months in jail. In 1971 another chairman of the group, Walid Fahoum, was arrested but was soon released.[142] In 1975 and 1976 police harassment of the Tel Aviv Students Committee was intensified. In 1977 Isam Mahoul, secretary-general of the National Association of Arab Students, was arrested, as was Azmi Bishara, secretary of the Haifa University Arab student committee.[143] Middle-of-the-night raids, searches, and interrogations have formed part of an overall effort to intimidate Arab students and encourage them to dissolve their organizations or leave the universities. The Office of the Adviser to the Prime Minister on Arab Affairs has also been engaged in attempts to break up these committees, by suggesting to university authorities that such organizations constitute threats to the security of the state which ought not be encouraged, by infiltrating student groups with informants and provocateurs, and by bribing individual committee members to give up their participation and accept instead paid positions with Jewish-Arab student groups set up by the Histadrut and/or the Arab Department of the Information Center (a branch of the Secret Service which works closely with the adviser's office).[144] The Secret Service itself (known in Israel by its Hebrew initials, Shin Bet) plays an active role in advising university officials as to the degree of political hostility or cooperativeness individual Arab students have displayed.[145]

In a study of Arab university graduates that was partially funded by the government, one question dealt with the topic of political interference by the government in the private lives and careers of the Arab graduates. According to Eli Rehkess, the author of the study, "The resulting picture [was] . . . chilling. Some of them asserted that as professional men, their political activities were subject to restrictions and pressures, the freedom of expression which they enjoyed was limited, and political considerations decided the future of any minorities graduate in Israel.[146] In conversations with Arab university students one is, in fact, repeatedly told that in order to hope for a decent job upon graduation an Arab student must be careful to be a *yeled tov* (good boy), i.e., to avoid involvement with the Arab Students Committee or any other sort of political activity not directly supportive of the government.

THE ISOLATION OF THE ARAB MINORITY: PROGRAMMATIC LEVEL

In the analysis of institutional segmentation, attention was primarily directed toward factors which have contributed to the isolation of the Arab minority. On the other hand, the sole concern thus far in examining segmentation on the programmatic level has been with policies implemented to maintain and reinforce the internal fragmentation of the minority population. That analysis on the programmatic level focuses mainly upon "fragmentation" rather than upon "isolation" should not be surprising, in view of the weight of factors which operate on the structural and institutional levels to isolate the Arab minority and keep it isolated from the Jewish majority. Nevertheless it is important to appreciate how the regime, in spite of official commitments to "integrate the minorities in all the paths of the life of the State,"[147] has acted to preserve and reinforce the barriers which separate Jewish and Arab Israelis.

Again attention must be directed to the Military Administration. As suggested in Chapter 2, the objectives of the regime in the early years of Israeli independence required that the Arab minority not be integrated or assimilated into Jewish-Israeli society. ". . . the authorities did not even try to think, after the establishment of the State, about the possibility of 'Israelizing' the Arab minority. Instead they preferred to go the way that seemed, on the fact of it, to be easier and more convenient, and that was the segregation of the minority and its limitation by means of declaring the areas in which [the Arabs] live to be closed areas and by the establishment of a Military Administration in those areas."[148] The Military Administration itself rejected "any plan to integrate [educated Israeli Arabs] into the economy of the State or the Civil Service . . ."[149] As one military governor put it: "The function, a positive function, which the Military Administration fulfilled was that of a barrier that separated the Jewish and Arab societies and prevented both a sharp clash and the shock which would have resulted from such a clash."[150]

Although Jews living in areas officially under the jurisdiction of the Military Administration could dispense with travel permits, it was often the case that Jewish citizens sympathetic to the complaints of the Arab minority and active on their behalf were not only required to abide by the travel restrictions but were often denied permits for visits to Arab villages.[151] According to the director of the Arab Department of Mapam from 1954 to 1965, Jewish members of Mapam who were active politically on behalf of Israeli Arabs were harassed by the Military Administration and often denied travel permits to visit Arab areas.[152] A particularly significant aspect of the Military Administration was the practice of trying Arabs before military tribunals. The substantive decisions of these tribunals, in regard to infringement of travel restrictions, curfews, land ownership, or legal status, could not be appealed to the civilian court system. Nor could a military court judge be required to explain the use of the term "security considerations" as a justification for suspicion, punishment, or procedure.

The regime's characterization of the Arab minority as, first and foremost, a threat to the security of the state and a potential fifth column has served to compound the Jewish majority's fear and mistrust of Arab Israelis. It is a common complaint among Israeli Arabs that the government and the media, over which it maintains a strong influence, distort events in the Arab sector to make them seem dangerous to Jewish citizens and potentially or actually subversive.[153] Officials responsible for the Arab sector commonly refer to the non-Jewish population as constituting "a national minority which is unique throughout the world. For which no parallel case, of a national minority living in a country at war with its people, is known . . ."[154] Under such conditions, say government spokesmen, Arab Israelis cannot be expected and should not be required to act as fully loyal and trustworthy citizens.

In the discussion of institutional segmentation, reference was made to the isolation of Rakah (the New Israel Communist Party) in Israeli politics and the way that Arab support for and identification with it contaminates Arabs further in the eyes of the Jewish public. On the programmatic level of analysis, what is of interest is that the regime has itself acted to maintain the political ostracism of Rakah. Indeed there have been many indications that government toleration of the communists is in no small measure due to recognition of the fact that Rakah's existence militates against the emergence of moderate but independent Arab political groups, whose greater flexibility would give them more effective access to the Jewish sector.[155] In 1975, after a series of occasions during which noted left-wing Zionists shared platforms or otherwise cooperated with Rakah representatives, several articles appeared condemning the trend toward the "legitimization of Rakah." In one such article, published in *Davar*, Daniel Bloch wrote of "distressing signs" that the "wall of isolation surrounding Rakah" might be breaking down. Bloch also reported that senior officials were quick to express their shock and anger when, for the first time in Israel's twenty-seven-year history, a representative of the Communist Party was given the opportunity of a lengthy appearance in a national broadcasting service talk show.[156] Official support for and cultivation of the ostracism of Rakah were also reflected in an address delivered by Shmuel Toledano to a conference on the problems of the Arab sector in February 1974. Toledano expressed his opinion that there were two and only two categories of Israeli Arabs—those who voted for Rakah and those who voted for a Jewish party. Those in the first category he termed "Russian agents" and "enemies of the state"; he expressed unconcern at whether those in the second category voted for Meir Pa'il (leader of Moked, a small leftist-Zionist party) or Meir Kahane (leader of the right-wing Jewish Defense League).[157]

Before the conclusion of this discussion of segmentation, a short digression is in order. As has been suggested, the segmentation of the Arab minority has manifested itself in a variety of ways. Overall, the fragmentation of the Arab sector, its segregation from the Jewish population, and especially its isolation from the institutions of power and social and economic mobility in Israeli society have been fairly rigidly preserved. But it must be remembered that these patterns represent abstractions from a complicated and fluid reality—a reality which includes a variety of conditions, interpersonal relationships, events, and processes involving contact between groups of Arabs and between Arabs and Jews. A number of small private organizations, some of which receive assistance from the government and/or the Histadrut, have been formed with the expressly nonpolitical purpose of increasing cultural exchange and interpersonal ties between Arabs and Jews. The Communist Party certainly has provided a framework within which a crosscutting ideology has been promulgated and within which Arabs from various cultural backgrounds form all sorts of interdependencies. The potential importance of Arab student organizations on university campuses as incubators for a noncommunist Arab leadership of national stature should not be underestimated. Nor should the growing sentiment among Israeli Arabs toward a specifically Palestinian identity which would cut across kinship, cultural, and religious divisions be ignored.[158]

Segmentation as a Component of Control

Reference, then, to segmentation as one component of a system of control is a self-conscious abstraction. However, the insights which that abstraction allows with regard to the question at hand—namely, how to explain the relative absence of independent political organization among the Arab minority and the minimum impact the existence of a discontented Arab minority has had on the stability and operation of the Israeli political system—justifies the distortions which such a conceptualization risks.

Segmentation itself does not necessarily result in control. For example, one could argue that the isolation of the Arab minority from the Jewish population might, in and of itself, make it more difficult for effective control to be exerted over Arabs. It is, rather, in combination with the structural conditions, institutional arrangements, and programmatic elements of the other two components—dependence and cooptation—that segmentation contributes so powerfully to the effective control of the Arab minority.

Specifically, in terms of the *system* of control, the function of the segmentation component has been to deprive Arabs in Israel of facilities for united political action, whether involving alliances among Arabs on a country-wide basis or between groups of Arabs and politically significant groups of Jews. But segmentation does not imply the atomization of the Arab population and thus it cannot insure that relatively isolated groups of Arabs —Moslems, Bedouin tribes, large clans, churches, or villages— will not act in a sustained way to sponsor political activities which the regime would find unpleasant. Segmentation itself can not enable the regime to extract certain highly valued resources from the minority population, such as land, cheap and dependable labor, and electoral support. Nor can segmentation provide the regime with a surveillance capacity over the Israeli Arab population with which to monitor developments in the Arab sector and to notice if and how policies need to be adapted to changing circumstances at any given time and place. It is only in combination with the *dependence* of the Arab community on the Jewish population and the *cooptation* of traditional and other potential Arab elites that the overall control of the minority has been achieved.

5.
Dependence
as a Component of Control:
The Economics of Arab Subordination

As a component in the system of control, "dependence" has two aspects. First, and of central importance, has been the overall reliance of Israeli Arabs on the Jewish sector for jobs, permits, status, and other economic, social, and political resources. The bulk of this chapter is devoted to structural, institutional, and programmatic analysis of this aspect of dependence. The second aspect of dependence concerns those ties which have bound the great mass of Arabs to traditional patriarchs, religious figures, and other Arab notables with whom the Jewish authorities have maintained close relations. These ties have not been institutionalized, but attention is directed to this aspect of the dependence component on the structural and programmatic levels of analysis.

Dependence: The Structural Level

On the structural level of analysis the questions are: What historical circumstances and what fundamental characteristics of Jewish and Arab life in Palestine and Israel have conduced toward and/or reinforced the dependence of Arabs on Jews in Israel? And how have such factors contributed to the dependence of the Arab population as a whole on those elements within the Arab sector that have enjoyed close relations with the Jewish authorities?

THE HISTORICAL GAP IN LEVELS OF DEVELOPMENT
With regard to dependence, the most important structural factor has been the tremendous gap in levels of economic, social, and political development which emerged between the Jewish

and Arab communities in British-ruled Palestine. During World War II all sectors of Palestine's economy experienced a surge of activity, primarily because of the presence of large numbers of British troops and the market for agricultural and industrial goods provided by the British Middle East Supply Center. In the Arab sector this had the important effect of encouraging more and more Arab villagers to seek employment outside their places of residence, leaving their fields to lie fallow or to be tended by other members of their families. In one Galileean Arab village anthropologist Henry Rosenfeld found that during World War II up to 42 percent of village workingmen were employed outside the village.[1]

Yet in spite of the wartime boom, the Arab economy of Palestine had only barely emerged from its feudalist past. In 1944 69 percent of Palestinian Arabs lived in villages with fewer than three thousand inhabitants.[2] Farming techniques were rudimentary and centered primarily around extensive cultivation of cereals. The vast majority of Arab villagers still lived on a subsistence basis; in 1942 only 35 percent of Arab agricultural produce was sold in the marketplace.[3] Large numbers of Arab agriculturalists labored as sharecroppers, most of these suffering under a crushing burden of debt. Although by the end of the war the beginnings of Arab industrial development could be seen in the urban centers of Palestine—small workshops, a few sizable manufacturing companies (cigarettes, textiles, and soap), brokerage houses, some marketing and import-export firms, and two banks—neither workshops, nor power facilities, nor all-weather roads had been introduced into Arab villages during this period. Moreover, as opportunities for wage labor disappeared with the dissolution of the Middle East Supply Center at the end of the war, many Arabs returned to the land.

In Arab Palestine as a whole there were no vocational schools, no commercial or agricultural training centers, no substantial agricultural organizations, and no coordinating bodies for the supervision of Arab economic development. The Arab labor movement, though gaining strength in the mid-1940's, was still in its infancy and relied heavily on the support of the mandatory authorities.[4] Although there were four Arab daily newspapers in postwar Palestine their circulation was mainly confined to the urban areas. Literacy rates in Arab villages were very low. Notwithstanding facilities provided by various religious denominations, the Arabs of Palestine were essentially dependent on the British mandatory authorities for schools, health care, development projects, and social services. The major political institutions of Arab Palestine—the Supreme Moslem Council, political parties based for the most part on clan loyalties, and the Christian churches—were all hierarchically organized and controlled by notables living in the urban districts. Political organization, participation, and leadership at the village level were nonexistent except in association with kinship affiliation. Such was the character of Arab society in Palestine at the close of the British mandate.[5]

"It is of fundamental importance," noted a British government statistician in 1944, "that for all important economic purposes, Palestine contains two distinct economies . . . Branches of economic activities called by the same name have yet such profound differences as between the two communities that it is necessary to carry into the economic field the distinction between the two races which, in the past, has been avoided as an apparent denial of the common citizenship of Jew and Arab."[6] There were, indeed, enormous differences in the levels of economic, social, educational, and organizational development which had been attained by the Arab and Jewish communities of Palestine by the end of World War II. These differences—these gaps in levels of development—must be fully appreciated if the position of Arabs in the Jewish state which emerged in 1948 is to be understood.

As noted in Chapter 2, the central objective of the Zionist movement in the prestate era was the creation of the economic, social, and political infrastructure of a Jewish state. Of decisive importance was the creation of an autonomous Jewish economy with the capacity for sustained growth and large-scale immigrant absorption. Such an economy, with a solid agricultural and industrial foundation, was to be built with Jewish capital, by Jewish labor, using Jewish expertise, and for a Jewish market. In this way it would be secure from Arab boycotts, strikes, or other sanctions. By 1947 this objective had been largely achieved.

In 1947 the Jewish Yishuv had over £P 75 million (one Palestinian pound was equal to one pound sterling) in fixed reproducible capital of £P 124.1 of capital stock per person.[7] The national income of the Jewish economy in 1944 was £P 73.4 million as compared to an income of £P 49.6 million in the Arab sector. Income per capita in the Jewish sector was nearly twice that in the Arab sector.[8] Whereas the Arab economy was basically agricultural with some infant industries, the Jewish economy was industrial with a well-organized agricultural branch. Although in 1942 the Arab population of Palestine was twice that of the Jewish population, Jewish industrial output was five times that in the Arab sector.[9]

Between 1923 and 1943 electric power consumption in Jewish factories and workshops had risen from 1,400 HP to 58,300 HP.[10] Moreover, the Palestine Electric Corporation, which supplied almost all the electric power in Palestine, was owned by the Jewish Agency. The demands of the Middle East Supply Center for foodstuffs, durable goods, and construction gave real impetus to the expansion of Jewish industry in Palestine during World War II, as did the demand generated by the hundreds of thousands of immigrants who had arrived during the 1930's. Over nine hundred Jewish-owned firms emerged, based on both private investment and capital supplied by the Jewish Agency, the JNF, the Histadrut, and other of the national institutions of the Zionist movement.[11] Solel Boneh, for example, a construction company founded by the Histadrut in 1920, trained thousands of Jews for skilled work in construction trades. It soon became the largest building contracting firm in the Middle East. Between 1940 and 1945 Solel Boneh executed £P 10 million worth of construction.[12] Substantial Jewish industrial enterprises also emerged in the fields of diamond cutting, metal working, chemicals, food processing, and textiles.

Furthermore, in the Jewish sector the capital market was highly organized and great efforts were made to coordinate various aspects of economic development and to avoid duplication. Almost all Jewish firms were organized within the Manufacturers' Association of Palestine, which maintained close ties with the Jewish Agency. The association sponsored vocational and commercial schools, engaged in mediation of labor disputes, and formulated and enforced various forms of regulation within the Jewish economy. It also founded an industrial bank—one of many Jewish financial institutions in Palestine—

and was vigorous and sophisticated in its promotion of Palestinian Jewish exports.

From an economic and technological standpoint Jewish agriculture was much more highly developed than Arab agriculture. Augmented by privately owned citrus plantations, Jewish agriculture was based on hundreds of cooperative and collective settlements founded by the various Zionist settlement movements in cooperation with the JNF, the Jewish Agency, and the Histadrut. In the mid-1940's, Jewish farmers, cultivating 8.3 percent of the land in Palestine, produced 29.8 percent of agricultural gross production.[13] Depending on the agricultural unit involved, 60 to 90 percent of Jewish produce was sold in the marketplace.[14] An assured market for almost all Jewish agricultural produce was provided by Tnuva, the Histadrut's giant marketing, processing, and distribution facility. Hamashbir Hamerkazi, another arm of the Histadrut, acted as a central marketing and purchasing cooperative for grains and dry goods going to or coming from Jewish cooperative and collective settlements.

Overall supervision of the economic and social development of the Jewish Yishuv was undertaken by the JNF, the Histadrut, and various departments within the Jewish Agency such as Trade and Industry, Colonization, Labor, Technology, etc. Jewish Palestinians, in addition to whatever direct political affiliation they maintained with the Zionist movement, also participated in the elections to the Assembly of Deputies (Asefat Nevcharim) of the Jewish Yishuv. The assembly chose a National Council (Vaad Leumi) which collected taxes and maintained and supervised community and social services, schools, police forces, etc. The vitality of this very elaborate network of institutions in the Jewish sector and the dramatic growth of the Jewish economy were made possible by the capital which flowed into the Jewish sector from world Jewry, the effective mobilization of Jewish manpower, the administrative skills of European immigrants, and the wholehearted commitment of the Jewish population to the development process.

Of particular satisfaction to the Zionist leadership was the relative political and economic autonomy which, by the late 1940's, the Jewish population had achieved vis-à-vis the Arabs of Palestine and the British mandatory authorities. In contrast, the Arab population, as noted above, had come to rely very heavily on the British colonial regime for jobs as well as social, educational, and medical services. With the evacuation of Palestine by British forces in the spring of 1948, thousands of Arabs whose employment had been connected with the British presence were thrown out of work. The surplus of labor in Arab villages was intensified by the effective expropriation of large tracts of Arab-owned agricultural land during the course of the fighting in 1948, and by the absence of any industrial capacity whatsoever in the Arab sector which could have absorbed unemployed workers. For with the flight of the Arab urban population (see Chapter 2) the fledgling industrial base of the Arab community in Palestine had been eliminated. The swollen ranks of unemployed Arab villagers found themselves almost completely dependent on the Jewish economy for jobs. In addition, Arab villagers were unprepared to assume responsibility for vital public functions. As the military situation stabilized, Arab village leaders were forced to turn to the Jewish authorities in order to maintain schools and social services and install and repair public utilities.

Given the well-known tendency of capital investments to flow to those areas in a developing country in which electrical transmission lines, roads, railroads, telephone lines, skilled manpower, piped water, and an industrial base already exist, and given the near total absence of such facilities and resources in Arab areas in 1948–1949, there were strong *structural* constraints against the industrialization or rapid economic development of the Arab sector in Israel.[15] Thus, as a result of the differing levels of development achieved by the Arab and Jewish communities in Palestine before the creation of Israel, and as a result of the historical consequences of the 1948 war, the structural position of the Arab population was from the very outset one which made the Arab minority's economic dependence upon the Jewish majority very likely.

DEPENDENCE AND THE PRESERVATION OF TRADITIONAL ARAB SOCIAL STRUCTURE

This overall dependence of Arabs on the Jewish sector, which developed for institutional and programmatic as well as structural reasons, had important implications for the conservation

of traditional forms of social organization within the Arab sector itself—forms of social organization which involve the dependence of the great majority of the Arab population on a relatively small number of patriarchal leaders.

As Henry Rosenfeld has pointed out, the traditional
hamula social structure which has prevailed in Arab Palestine
for several centuries has suffered from a variety of serious internal contradictions. These have centered around disruptive inheritance practices, which pit every son against his brothers, and
the exercise of total authority over family resources by the patriarch until his death.[16] Yet, as Rosenfeld himself noted in
1968, among Israeli Arabs

traditional village patterns of behavior remain in force: the internal
struggle for political position and recognition by the Government is a
function of the alignments constructed by male lineage heads; bride
price is demanded for all marriages; women are not free to move
about; and so on. These are not simply deeply rooted residues . . . they
are sign posts of the preservation of the status quo ante.[17]

As Rosenfeld frames the question: in light of the acute stresses
and strains to which the hamula system has been subject, what
explains the persistence of the traditional hamula social structure and the continued dependence of Arab villagers on clan elders?

One factor which Rosenfeld identifies as crucial in his analysis of this problem is the economic dependence of Arab villagers on Jewish-owned sources of employment outside the village.
Because Arab wage laborers lack any form of meaningful economic security, they have been constrained to maintain allegiance to their hamulas and extended families. Not only does
the kinship unit serve as a relatively comfortable social refuge
from a hostile and alien Jewish society, but only if an Arab la-
borer preserves his good standing within his hamula can he expect succor and support from his kinsmen in the event that he is
discharged from work. In Rosenfeld's words,

the existing state of structural continuity is due not only to the fact
that economic and technical changes have not been radical enough but
also . . . to the fact that those working outside the village lack skills,
job permanence, and security. They are mainly in services, transport,
and the building trades and simple manual and agricultural labor;

they are totally dependent on prosperity in the general Israeli economy for full or partial employment. What we emphasize here is that for the overwhelming majority *the condition of insecurity in work outside the village does not free the Arab worker from ongoing dependence on this underdeveloped village. Outside wage labor is not, as yet, an alternative to the village economy and to the village social structure.*[18]

As has been observed, this phenomenon—a mass lumpen-proletariat, maintaining rural residence, still tied to a traditional social structure, but dependent on outside wage labor for its sustenance—had been slowly developing among Palestinian Arab villagers during the Mandate. In order to reverse this trend toward the creation within Israel of a "residual peasantry,"[19] large-scale investment and development programs in the Arab sector would have been required. In fact, as is argued in the following sections, the Zionist character of those institutions which have sponsored economic development in Israel, as well as specific policies implemented by the government, have contributed very importantly to the continuing *underdevelopment* of the Arab sector and to the *increased dependence* of Arabs on the Jewish population.

Dependence: The Institutional Level

Although the structural factors discussed above are suggestive of why a dual economy and Arab dependence on the Jewish sector might have been expected to develop in Israel under any political circumstances, structural factors cannot be used to explain the rapid economic development of outlying Jewish areas, areas as isolated from previously existing infrastructural facilities as most Arab localities. Nor can structural factors provide a satisfactory explanation for the near total absence, thirty years after the establishment of the state, of any substantial industrial, commercial, or financial enterprises in the Arab sector.

In this section the institutionalization of Arab dependence on the Jewish sector is discussed. Primarily, this involves an examination of various ways in which the normal patterns of operation of Israel's major institutions have contributed to the retardation of Arab economic development, relative to the development of the Jewish sector, and, in turn, to the dependence of the Arab population on the Jewish majority. Attention is also directed to the significance of the cooperatization of most of Jewish agriculture and the relative absence of cooperative organizational forms in the Arab sector. The third section of this chapter, that concerning programmatic dependence, explains how the economic inequalities generated between the Jewish and Arab sectors on the institutional and structural levels have favored regime attempts to enforce the dependence of Arabs on Jews.

A DUAL ECONOMY

The economic underdevelopment of the Arab sector has remained one of the most striking characteristics of Israel's economic structure. The Public Committee for the Investigation of Agriculture revealed that in 1960 the yearly income of an Arab employed in agriculture was 40 percent that of a Jew so employed.[20] The average yearly income of the Arab population in 1971 was 66 percent that of the general per capita income.[21] In 1974, 94.2 percent of all Jewish families owned electric refrigerators compared to 53.8 percent of non-Jewish families. In that same year 48.0 percent of all Israeli families owned private telephones, 79.7 percent owned television sets, and 26.1 percent owned private cars. For Arab families the respective statistics are 7.0 percent, 46.2 percent and 11.5 percent.[22] Part of the reason for this gap in the ownership of durable goods is that in 1973, although virtually every Jewish household in Israel was connected to the national power grid, 44 percent of the Arab village population was still without electricity.[23] Additional evidence for the sharp disparity in levels of economic development between the Jewish and Arab sectors is contained in Table 3, which shows that the infant mortality rate among Arabs in Israel has remained approximately twice that among Jews. Although data are not available to compare post-1974 infant mortality rates, official statistics do indicate that between 1973 and 1976 the death rate among Arab children ages 0–5 was more than twice that among Jewish children.[24]

As noted, the Arab sector as a whole (and especially Arab villages) still lacks any substantial nonagricultural means of pro-

Table 3. Comparison of Infant Deaths per Thousand among Jews
and Non-Jews

Year	Jews	Non-Jews
1960	27.2	48.0
1961	24.3	48.0
1962	28.3	47.5
1963	22.5	44.6
1964	24.0	42.6
1965	22.7	43.4
1966	21.7	41.8
1967	20.8	44.3
1968	20.3	42.4
1969	19.0	40.3
1970	18.9	39.1
1971	18.6	37.7
1972	18.8	40.2
1973	18.1	37.1
1974	19.2	37.0

Source: Statistical Abstract of Israel 26 (1975): 91.

duction. In 1971 Arab-owned industries employed 2,247 workers, or 0.9 percent of the total number of workers employed in
Israeli industry.[25] Industrial enterprises located in Arab villages
in 1974 were described as follows:

A marble plant in Ba'ana in the Galilee, a metal works in Yerka, three
plants of the "Gibor" Textile concern in Daliat-El-Karmel, Yerka and
Gish (*Gush Halav*). These enterprises employ about 200 workers
each, on the average. Apart from them there are about 30 small-scale
enterprises, mostly sewing shops with some workers. All told, there
are some 59 enterprises in minority villages. Lately, a diamond grind-
ing plant has been set up at Ussafiyeh and an electronics plant at
Daliat-El-Karmel. The approximate number of employed in the industrial enterprises is 4,000.[26]

Most male workers in Arab villages are employed in Jewish
metropolitan areas as unskilled or semiskilled laborers, especially in construction, and as porters, maintenance men, etc., in
hotels, restaurants, garages, and shops. The men typically commute to work on a daily basis, leaving their villages in the Little
Triangle or in the Galilee between 5 and 6 A.M. and returning

from work in the evening. More often than not their status is not permanent and job insecurity is high, especially during periods of economic strain. Table 4 provides a comparison of Jewish and Arab occupational distributions in selected categories. The figures represent percentages of the Jewish and Arab labor forces in Israel so employed. They illustrate the general point that a dual economy still exists in Israel and that the gaps between levels of economic development of the Jewish and Arab communities in Palestine in 1947 have not narrowed since the creation of the state.

A large proportion of Arabs employed in agriculture work as laborers on Jewish farms, though many Arabs still cultivate land which they own or have leased. Yet here, too, are serious disparities in levels of development. Indeed, in order to survive against competition from Jewish farmers, Arabs have been forced to rely on olives and table grapes, for whose cultivation no effective mechanical technologies have been developed; on livestock, such as sheep and goats, whose husbandry Jewish farmers have not found profitable; and, more recently, on strawberries, whose cultivation requires the intensive use of unskilled labor on very small plots of land.[27]

On the institutional level of analysis the most important element in the maintenance and expansion of these gaps in levels of economic development has been the historical momentum of the institutions of the Zionist movement. As described in Chapter 4, after the creation of the Jewish state in 1948 the Histadrut, the Jewish Agency, the JNF, and the Zionist political parties continued to operate. As a result, ideological commitments whose roots lay in the pre-1948 struggle for Jewish sovereignty in Palestine were institutionalized within the framework of the new society. Many of these commitments have been reflected in standard operating procedures which, regardless of government policies toward the economic development of the Arab sector, have tended to maintain inequalities between Arabs and Jews, reinforcing the economically peripheral position of Israeli Arabs and deepening the dependence of Arab Israelis on the Jewish population.

Table 4. Jewish and Arab Occupational Distributions in Selected Categories (by Occupation and Economic Branch)

Year	Jewish (%)	Arab (%)
A. Administrative, Executive, and Clerical Workers[a]		
1963	16.9	2.0
1964	17.2	2.7
1965	17.9	1.8
1966	17.4	2.6
1967	17.5	3.1
1968	17.8	3.3
1969	18.4	3.5
1970	18.8	3.2
B. Administrators and Managers[b]		
1972	3.3	0.9
1973	3.5	0.7
1974	3.6	0.4
1975	3.5	0.4
1976	4.3	0.4
1977	4.8	0.4
C. Clerical and Related Workers[b]		
1972	16.5	3.8
1973	17.2	8.2
1974	18.2	3.6
1975	18.7	3.8
1976	18.6	4.3
1977	19.4	4.0
D. Professional, Scientific, and Technical Workers[a]		
1963	12.8	5.3
1964	12.9	4.1
1965	13.7	5.0
1966	14.4	4.6
1967	15.0	4.5
1968	14.1	5.7
1969	14.6	5.1
1970	16.4	6.0

Table 4. Jewish and Arab Occupational Distributions in Selected Categories (by Occupation and Economic Branch) (con't.)

Year	Jewish (%)	Arab (%)

E. Scientific and Academic Workers[b]

Year	Jewish (%)	Arab (%)
1972	6.2	0.6
1973	6.2	0.7
1974	6.8	1.2
1975	7.3	1.0
1976	7.5	1.2
1977	7.7	0.9

F. Other Professional, Technical and Related Workers[b]

Year	Jewish (%)	Arab (%)
1972	11.2	6.2
1973	11.7	7.6
1974	12.6	9.1
1975	13.2	7.5
1976	13.4	7.5
1977	13.6	8.2

G. Construction (Building and Public Works)[c]

Year	Jewish (%)	Arab (%)
1970	7.1	20.2
1971	7.4	23.3
1972	7.7	26.6
1973	7.1	25.0
1974	6.6	22.6
1975	6.5	24.2
1976	6.2	22.1
1977	5.7	22.9

H. Financing and Business Services[c]

Year	Jewish (%)	Arab (%)
1970	5.6	1.2
1971	6.2	.7
1972	6.3	.8
1973	6.8	1.4
1974	6.8	1.3
1975	7.2	1.8
1976	7.3	1.8
1977	7.8	1.7

Table 4. Jewish and Arab Occupational Distributions in Selected
Categories (by Occupation and Economic Branch) (con't.)

Year	Jewish (%)	Arab (%)

I. Agriculture, Forestry, and Fishing[c]

Year	Jewish (%)	Arab (%)
1970	7.4	22.8
1971	7.0	22.4
1972	6.8	19.1
1973	6.2	19.2
1974	5.8	13.8
1975	5.4	16.1
1976	5.5	15.7
1977	5.2	16.7

[a] Figures taken from the yearly *Labor Force Surveys* of the Israeli Government Central Bureau of Statistics.

[b] *Statistical Abstract of Israel* 28 (1977): 322–323, 326–327; 29 (1978): 351, 366–367. A change in the categories used to classify workers by occupation in 1972 makes perfectly congruent comparisons with occupational patterns prior to 1972 impossible.

[c] Ibid. 24 (1973): 317; 25 (1974): 321–323; 28 (1977): 313–315; 29 (1978): 351, 354–355.

THE STAGNATION OF THE ARAB ECONOMY: INSTITUTIONAL
FACTORS

There is no question that rapid economic development in Jewish areas, including Jewish rural communities and "development towns," has been due, largely, to a continuous flow of capital and expertise from the Jewish Agency and other of the national institutions. From 1948 through 1977 the Jewish Agency alone was able to pour more than $5 billion into the economic and social development of the Jewish sector. As explained in Chapter 4, these revenues have come from contributions of world Jewry, augmented by German reparations payments and donations from the Israeli government itself.[28] It is precisely because these funds have been controlled by the Jewish Agency and the JNF, which operate according to ideological norms and not according to the constraints of economic rationality, that Jewish settlements in outlying areas have enjoyed piped water, high-tension power lines, paved roads, and industrial growth, while Arab villages, located no more inconveniently with regard to previously existing infrastructure facilities, have been bypassed.

By the time Jewish settlers move into a newly constructed settlement, the JNF has already paved roads to the settlement, cleared the land, and readied it for cultivation. The Jewish Agency has already connected their homes, barns, and factories to the national power grid, paved the roads inside the village, and allocated whatever seeds, livestock, irrigation pipe, or other capital goods the village economy will require. Besides constructing transportation, communication, and energy systems the national institutions have also financed the introduction of highly sophisticated agricultural techniques and new types of crops and have undertaken the industrialization and reindustrialization of many formerly agricultural settlements.[29]

The continuing commitment of the Jewish Agency to the consolidation of a strong Jewish economy in Israel has found expression, as well, in the extension of subsidies to Jewish industries, bonus payments to wholesalers who buy Jewish crops, loans and guarantees for new Jewish enterprises, etc.[30] This is the institutional context within which Arab capitalists have refrained from investing their money in Arab-owned enterprises. They have tended to fear that competition with Jewish firms having access to subsidies, low interest loans, and so on would be impossible. The inability of the last large Arab-owned company in Israel, the Arab Cigarette and Tobacco Factory Ltd., in Nazareth, to secure loans on the same terms as its Jewish competitors was a major factor in the decision of its owners to liquidate their assets.[31] There are, in other words, institutional as well as structural reasons why there has been so little industrial development in the Arab sector, why the rapidly expanding Arab village labor force has had to depend on Jewish-owned industry within Jewish metropolitan areas for employment, and why the growing stratum of educated and ambitious young Arabs has had to depend on Jewish firms and organizations (including the government) in order to secure the white-collar jobs, promotions, status, and salaries which it desires.

The institutionalization of Arab economic insecurity has also resulted from the continued commitment of the Histadrut and the national institutions to the principle of "Jewish labor." Until 1960 the Histadrut was responsible for almost all labor exchanges in Israel. Accordingly, Arab villagers wishing to secure temporary or permanent jobs in Jewish metropolitan areas were often forced to rely on the Histadrut for assistance. But the struggle which the Histadrut waged throughout the Mandate period against cheap, unorganized Arab labor was not abandoned upon independence. After 1948 the Histadrut restricted entry of Arab villagers into the labor market by not opening employment offices in Arab areas and through the use of lobbying, picketing, and roadblocks. The network of labor exchanges which was eventually set up in Arab areas served only to regulate and distribute government relief work; "these exchanges played no role in actually finding work for Arabs in the Jewish sector."[32] Until the mid-1950's even in mixed cities Histadrut exchanges refused to deal with Arab workers.[33] Since membership in Histadrut-affiliated trade unions was not permitted for Arabs until 1957, and since Arab labor was not unionized on an independent basis, a law barring the use of "unorganized labor" gave Histadrut officials the legal machinery for demanding the dismissal of Arab workers when and where Jewish labor became available.[34]

The continued commitment of the JNF to the principle of Jewish labor was reflected in the continued enforcement, after 1948, of regulations requiring that only Jews be employed on JNF land.[35] Similarly, the Jewish Agency has continued to enforce regulations which give preference to the hiring of Jews in Jewish Agency—owned enterprises and the use of Jewish subcontractors on Jewish Agency—sponsored projects. Thus a large proportion of jobs in the public sector have been closed to Arab Israelis simply as a result of the standard operating procedures of Israel's major institutions. Consequently, members of the minority population have found themselves more dependent than they would have been otherwise on jobs which Jews have generally considered to be unsuitable and, during periods of economic strain, on government-provided relief work.

Many Arab villagers who have sought employment in Jewish urban centers have done so because they have found it increasingly difficult to earn a living in agriculture. Despite trends toward mechanization, the use of fertilizers, and irrigation, Arab agriculture in Israel has remained backward in comparison with agriculture in the Jewish sector.[36] Whereas in 1975–76

43.3 percent of the land cultivated by Jews was irrigated, only 7.6 percent of the land cultivated by Arabs was irrigated.[37] In 1952–1953 the gross productivity per worker in Arab agriculture was 30 percent of the gross productivity per worker in Jewish agriculture. By 1962–1963 this figure had dropped to 20 percent.[38] In 1975–1976 the gross productivity of Arab farmers was approximately 16 percent that of the gross productivity of Jewish farmers.[39] The low productivity of Arab agriculture has sent many would-be Arab farmers into the labor market, forcing them to depend on Jewish industry or on Jewish agriculture for employment.

On the institutional level at least two important factors have contributed to the stagnation of Arab agriculture. One of these factors has been the relative absence in Arab communities of cooperative or collective types of organizations. Whereas Jewish agricultural settlements are almost always organized on a cooperative basis (as in *moshavim*) or collectively (as in kibbutzim), attempts to develop farming cooperatives among Israeli Arabs have been largely unsuccessful.[40] The significance of this failure should not be considered primarily in terms of the increased efficiency that might result from the effective cooperatization of Arab farming. More important, Arab agriculturalists who are not members of cooperatives are automatically excluded from membership and participation in certain key organizations in Israel, organizations which serve the interests of the cooperative sector as a whole and cooperative agriculture in particular. Perhaps the most important of these are the kibbutz federations, which offer a wide variety of technical, advisory, and social services to member settlements. The kibbutz federations (and the federations of *moshavim* and *moshavim shituffyim*) also provide their members with cost-cutting central purchasing and marketing facilities. Of particular interest is the financial assistance which the federations can provide through their loan funds and the services which they render as lobbyists with the central organs of the government, the Histadrut, and the national institutions. In addition certain departments of the Histadrut itself which supervise and coordinate agricultural policy in Israel are open only to the participation of cooperatively or collectively organized farmers. These agencies provide subsidies for agricultural projects involving mechanization, intensification, and irrigation. They also act on behalf of their membership to put pressure on the Ministry of Agriculture concerning supplemental water allocations, export subsidies, land leasing, and other issues of crucial importance for Israeli farmers.[41] This, then, is the institutional context within which Arab farmers, who by and large are not organized cooperatively, find it consistently necessary to depend on the Arab Department of the Histadrut and other instruments of the regime to represent their interests. And thus it is also the institutional context within which Arab farmers, who cultivated over 20 percent of the crop area in 1974–1975, received only 2 percent of the water allocated for agriculture.[42]

The general backwardness of Arab agriculture and the relatively unprofitable branches of agricultural production to which Arab farmers have been relegated have been important factors in the willingness of Arab landowners to accept JNF offers to buy their lands.[43] Indeed, perhaps the most important single factor in the stagnation of Arab agriculture has been the transfer, since 1948, of a high proportion of Arab-owned agricultural land to Jewish ownership.[44] This transfer has been due in large measure to the ceaseless efforts of the JNF to expand the area of Jewish land ownership. As one Israeli scholar noted in 1962, "land acquisition officials who spent their best years implementing the philosophy of acquiring land at any cost during the Mandatory period have carried over this mentality into our own time."[45]

The postindependence vigor of the JNF's drive to increase the area of Jewish land ownership is reflected in the fact that from 1948 to 1977 land owned by the JNF increased from 942,000 dunams to 2,650,000 dunams.[46] Although the bulk of this land was acquired between 1948 and 1953, available statistics show that in 1973 there were 149,000 dunams less Arab-owned agricultural land than in 1953—a reduction of approximately 28 percent.[47] Included among the lands transferred to Jewish control have been almost all Arab agricultural lands in the valleys and the coastal plain.[48] More than half the land presently listed as cultivated by Israeli Arabs is located in the Negev desert.

On the programmatic level of analysis I shall describe how

the government itself has acted in a determined and systematic fashion to acquire Arab lands. Here, on the institutional level, what is important to understand is how the JNF's campaign for Jewish land acquisition, like the struggle for "Jewish labor," reflects the projection and institutionalization of ideological commitments developed during the Mandate period. Again, these patterns of institutional behavior do *not* spring from calculations concerning the necessity to deprive Arabs of economic security. Nor do they represent policies which the regime has fashioned in order to create a lumpenproletariat of Arab villagers dependent on the Jewish economy. Yet the restrictions placed upon the employment of non-Jews or the use of non-Jewish subcontractors on projects sponsored by the national institutions, as well as the substantial reduction in Arab land holdings attendant upon the JNF's campaign for increased Jewish land ownership, have contributed significantly to the growth of just such a class.[49]

The contraction of the Arab-owned land area and the absence of substantial corporate activity in the Arab sector also mean that the tax base of Arab localities is considerably smaller than that of Jewish towns and villages. Yet whereas Jewish settlements receive electricity, sewage systems, paved roads, waterworks, land development, etc. essentially free of charge, Arab villages must collect taxes from their inhabitants in order to make even a down payment on any *one* of these projects.[50] While Arab local councils must use their lower tax revenues for the installation of basic services and facilities, their Jewish counterparts are free to spend their tax monies on, among other things, better schools and university scholarships.

Indeed the economic underdevelopment of the Arab sector is a primary cause of the low educational standards which prevail in Arab schools. In 1975/1976, 62.5 percent of classes in Arab schools had thirty or more pupils compared to 39.9 percent of classes in Jewish schools.[51] According to a government comptoller's report in 1972 more than half of all teachers in Arab schools lacked appropriate training (compared to 16 percent of all teachers in Jewish schools).[52] In 13,320 Israeli students who passed the national high-school matriculation examination in 1975/1976, only 970 (7.3 percent) were Arabs, even though Arabs comprised 19.8 percent of all secondary school students.[53] According to a government study conducted in 1973, there was a shortage of 4,400 classrooms in the Arab sector.[54] The generally poor quality of public schools in Arab localities makes it that much more difficult for young Arabs to compete with Jews for places in technical or professional schools, or for well-paying, high-status jobs in the Israeli economy. And it makes it that much more difficult for the Arab minority as a whole to break out of its economic backwardness and its dependence on the Jewish sector.

Dependence: The Programmatic Level

The structural circumstances and the institutional factors discussed thus far provide strong reasons to suspect that, especially from an economic standpoint, the development of the Arab sector was bound to lag far behind that of the Jewish sector. Nor, in light of the material presented above, can the overall dependence of the Arab minority on the Jewish population be considered surprising. On the other hand, the government could have exerted itself to narrow the social and economic gaps between Arabs and Jews and thereby help to develop a balanced and integrated Israeli economy. The regime has acted rather vigorously to close the "social gap" between Oriental and Ashkenazic Jews, a gap measured in terms of occupational distribution, educational achievement, living standards, etc.[55] But, as is argued in the last section of this chapter, government policy has *not* been designed to close or even substantially narrow the gaps between Arabs and Jews. On the contrary, government policies with regard to the Arab minority have been characterized by economic discrimination, neglect, a studied attempt to prevent Arab-owned centers of economic power from emerging, and a conscious effort to create and sustain ties of dependence—dependence of Arabs on Jews and dependence of Arabs on Arabs serving the interests of Jews.

Concerning the continuing dependence of the Arab population on the Jewish sector, two aspects of government policy need to be examined. The first involves those policies, designed and implemented by the regime, which have inhibited the economic development of the Arab sector relative to the Jewish sector. These policies, including that of expropriating Arab land, have reinforced the structural and institutional factors discussed previously. To be discussed, then, are not only policies implemented explicitly for the purpose of discouraging rapid Arab economic development, but also policies which, undertaken in the context of the regime's overall commitments, have had as an unanticipated consequence just such an impact. The second aspect of government policy examined in this section concerns the techniques and instrumentalities which the regime has used to translate the backwardness of the Arab economy into the dependence of Arabs on the Jewish population in general and on the Jewish regime in particular.

GOVERNMENT LAND POLICIES

On the institutional level of analysis, as has been discussed, the JNF's continuing commitment to expanded Jewish land ownership has contributed to the institutionalization of the Arab population's economic dependence. As has been indicated, after 1948 real estate—agricultural land, pasture land, quarries, etc.—was, essentially, the only type of income-producing property in the Arab sector. The expropriation of land, by denying Arabs access to a great portion of their traditional means of production, has not only forced them and their families to rely more heavily than they otherwise would have on Jewish-owned means of production, but has also prevented them from translating that resource into other forms of economic wealth. Here I shall illustrate how *government policies* have also contributed to the dispossession of Arab landowners. For it must be remembered that the JNF and other of the national institutions, regardless of how convenient they may have been in the context of the policies which the regime did adopt, and however important they were as lobbyists for the adoption of activist Zionist policies, did not make the implementation of such policies inevitable. Not only did the Israeli government agree to the terms of the Land Covenant of 1961 (see Chapter 4) but, through various ministries and agencies, it has formulated, applied, and enforced the laws and regulations governing expropriation of land, land leasing, and compensation.

According to Yitzhak Oded, probably the foremost authority on land policies in Israel as they relate to the Arab minority, the regime's attitude toward the land of Arab villagers has been the opposite of that which prevailed during Ottoman and British rule over Palestine.

... under the Ottoman system ... subject to overriding needs such as afforestation, the lands surrounding a village were considered the patrimony of the local population and constituted a reserve for future development.

Since 1948 the opposite attitude has prevailed: all land is national patrimony except what the villagers can prove is theirs under the narrowest interpretation of the law.[56]

Oded goes on to point out that, in Israel, "national patrimony" has

consistently been taken to imply the Jewish population only. Land settlements and development on areas adjudicated to the State in all of its capacities—vacant land, public land, State domain, Arab absentee property, etc.—have been assigned exclusively to Jewish institutions, settlements and individuals (except for the small reserve maintained for compensating expropriated Arabs), and where Government agencies have handled the task, development planning has involved Jews only...

New legislation, administrative regulations and executive policies and procedures have been focused ... on restricting or altering the legal basis on which the villagers could claim land and on cutting down land already held by them.[57]

Writing in 1964, Oded characterized the government's policy as "consistent, systematic ... [t]olerant in all other respects, it seems to have one purpose: to strike at the tottering land base of the country's Arab population."[58]

A wide variety of government agencies have been involved in the implementation of its land policies. In 1950 the adviser to the prime minister for Arab affairs acted as chairman of an interministerial committee for Arab lands. In this capacity he provided information and assistance to the various governmental and nongovernmental agencies concerned with Jewish land acquisition and settlement. Also in the prime minister's office was the adviser on lands and boundaries, who offered

counsel to the Prime Minister's office and the Ministries of Finance and Foreign Affairs on matters relating to land policy and territorial and demographic problems . . . [and who was] charged with defining areas and boundaries for purposes of economic planning; transfer of State lands from abandoned properties to the JNF; participation in the regrouping of Arab populations and in their placement for purposes of housing and rehabilitation; . . . and study of problems of compensation to Arabs.[59]

As time went on the agencies responsible for land acquisition, supervision, and settlement underwent various reorganizations. In 1948 a Custodian for Enemy Property was appointed to supervise and administer abandoned Arab properties. His office was soon replaced by that of the Custodian for Absentee Property. Eventually most of the property under the control of the custodian was transferred to the Development Authority, which was empowered to sell the lands it acquired to the JNF or the state. In 1961 the Israel Lands Administration was formed, under the joint control of the Ministry of Agriculture and the JNF. It assumed many of the responsibilities which had previously been carried out by the Development Authority in connection with the acquisition and use of Arab lands. In 1971 the Interministerial Committee on Land Settlement was organized to oversee all matters pertaining to land acquisition and settlement. In addition to the representatives of various ministries who sit on this committee, the participants also include the adviser to the prime minister on Arab affairs and representatives of the Israel Lands Administration, the Jewish Agency Land Settlement Department, the JNF, and the Development Authority. It is this committee which is responsible for deciding what lands will be acquired and to what use they will be put. It works closely with the Expropriations Committee of the Ministry of Finance, whose chairman was, in 1976, also the director of the Israeli Lands Administration.

This complicated array of government agencies has had at its disposal an even more complicated array of laws and regulations, which have provided the legal machinery for the implementation of the government's land policies. The Emergency Articles for the Exploitation of Uncultivated Lands (also known as the Cultivation of Waste Lands Ordinance), passed in October 1948, empowers the minister of agriculture to take possession of uncultivated land or of any lands in cases where the minister "is not satisfied that the owner of the land has begun or is about to begin or will continue to cultivate the land."[60] The Emergency Land Requisition Law, passed in 1949, gives the government the right to expropriate land whenever a "competent authority" (appointed by the government) determines that the land "is required for the defense of the State, the security of the people, to safeguard essential provisions or essential services, or to absorb immigrants or settle retired soldiers or men disabled while on active service."[61] In addition, specific sections of the Emergency Regulations, which have been valid ever since the government declared a state of emergency on May 19, 1948, have been used to expel whole villages from "security zones," making possible the subsequent expropriation of their lands. On the basis of these laws, the inhabitants of Biram, Ikrit, Ghabasiyeh, and several other Arab villages were dispossessed.[62]

In 1950 the Knesset passed the Absentees Property Law in an attempt to regularize the rather haphazard rules and procedures used to define and administer abandoned Arab properties. This law defined the term "absentee" and provided for the transfer of property rights from anyone fitting that definition to the custodian of absentee property.[63] This law also enabled the custodian to sell abandoned property to the Development Authority, from which it could be transferred to Jewish settlements and institutions (kibbutzim, the JNF, the Israel Lands Authority, etc.).[64] Most of the property acquired by the custodian under the terms of this law was that of Arabs who left Israel entirely in 1948. But, as indicated in Chapter 2, a substantial portion of this property belonged to Arabs who became legal residents of the state. These "present absentees" (*nifkadim nochachim*) can roughly be divided into three categories: (1) Arabs in the Galilee or in the mixed cities who for one reason or another were not "at their usual place of residence" when Jewish forces took control; (2) Arabs of the Little Triangle who became Israeli residents when the area was ceded to Israel by Jordan in 1949, but whose lands on the Israeli side of the old cease-fire line had already been classified as absentee property; and (3) Arabs who became Israeli residents in the first years of Israel's existence either by infiltrating back across the borders or under the terms of the reunion-of-families program. There were approximately

15,000 persons in the first category, 31,000 in the second, and 35,000 in the third for a total of 81,000 out of the 160,000 non-Jews who lived in Israel in 1949. In other words, half of the Arab inhabitants of Israel could, at the discretion of the custodian, be declared absentees and their property thereby made subject to confiscation.[65]

The Absentee Property Law and to a lesser extent the other ordinances mentioned above were designed to provide, retroactively, a legal justification for seizures of Arab lands that had already taken place. Yet in the early years of Israeli statehood the scramble for Arab property—by Jewish settlements, by the national institutions, by the Histadrut, by government agencies, by the army, and by new immigrants—had been so chaotic that hundreds of thousands of dunams of land had been confiscated which, even under a very strict application of these laws, could no longer be kept from their former proprietors. Furthermore, the laws passed up until 1953 made it possible for the government only to "assume control"[66] over the lands, "take possession"[67] of the lands, or assign to the lands the status of being "vested in the Custodian."[68] In other words, under these laws and regulations the Arab landowners retained formal title to the land. These and other such considerations account for the passage, in 1953, of the Land Acquisition (Validation of Acts and Compensation) Law.

This law empowered the finance minister to make a list of lands that had been confiscated, in whatever manner, from the establishment of the state on May 14, 1948, to April 1, 1952. If the minister certified that these lands were "used or assigned for purposes of essential development, settlement or security" and were "still required for any of these purposes," then, as a result of this certification, these lands would automatically become the property of the Development Authority.[69] The Ministry of Finance was required to issue such certificates before March 1954. Compensation was to be paid to the former owners. But once land had been "gazetted" (i.e., the certificates had been published in the *Official Gazette*) the Development Authority assumed formal title and was free to sell the land to the JNF.[70]

In practical terms the law meant that the status quo of April 1952 would be preserved as far as the status of requisitioned

Arab lands was concerned and that, essentially, regardless of the stipulations made in the Cultivation of Waste Lands Ordinance or in the Emergency Land Requisition Law, and regardless of the violations of due process which had occurred, no land would be returned to Arabs. Not only would the land not be returned, but the Arab landowners were now also deprived of formal title to it. Aharon Liskovsky, a supporter of the government's land policies, explained the rationale behind the Land Acquisition Law of 1953 in the following way:

When the authorities began to consolidate absentee lands which had been confiscated for reasons of security or vital development, it was discovered that various lands, primarily agricultural in character, had been taken over as well. Rights of possession in regard to these lands was not at all clear, especially in the context of the many difficulties associated with any action pertaining to lands (difficulties which derive from lack of consensus concerning the ownership of large tracts of land in this country). Only gradually did it become clear that these lands were owned in part by persons who were not absentees. ... Meanwhile facts had been created on these lands that were impossible to erase; on some of these lands settlements had been constructed or were planned; elsewhere development projects had been built; other portions were required by *Tzahal* itself for security reasons. Therefore considerations of security and considerations bearing upon the implementation of vital development plans prevented the return of these lands to their owners ... [therefore] on March 10, 1953, the Knesset passed the law for the Acquisition of Lands (Validation of Acts and Compensation) whose goal was as follows: to provide a legal basis for the acquisition of these lands, and to grant the right of compensation to their owners.[71]

In short, the purpose of this law was to legitimize the massive land transfers that had taken place from 1948 to 1952 and to preclude legal attempts by Arab residents to take advantage of loopholes in the laws or the absence of due process in order to press their claims in the courts. Under the terms of this law fully 1,250,000 dunams were expropriated. If state-owned lands that were "gazetted" by mistake and Bedouin lands in the Negev are subtracted from this total, it appears that approximately 67,000 dunams of Arab land were confiscated in this fashion.[72] In 1955 Moshe Keren, then Arab-affairs editor for *Haaretz*, characterized the sweeping land acquisitions of the late 1940's and early 1950's as "wholesale robbery in legal guise. Hundreds of thou-

sands of dunams were taken away from the Arab minority . . .
The future student of history will never cease to be astonished at
how it happened . . ."[73]

Although the lands acquired under the laws discussed
above represent the vast majority of lands expropriated from
Arab citizens of Israel, the policy of acquiring Arab land did not
cease in 1953. In 1958 the Prescription Law was passed by the
Knesset. This law, in effect, amended the older Ottoman law so
that occupiers of unregistered land were required to demonstrate
unchallenged possession, not for ten years as had been the rule,
but for fifteen to twenty-five.[74] Under the terms of this law Arabs
were forced to produce records from the British Mandate period. As was well known to the government lawyers who drafted
this law, the British Mandatory authorities had undertaken

the systematic survey and settlement of title to land, aimed *inter alia* at
establishing the occupier's rights on more exact and secure foundations; *but* in view of the need to adjudicate first of all the area where
Arab and Jewish claims conflicted, *the all Arab parts of Palestine were
left till last, and the process of settlement of title only began in most of
Arab Galilee after Israel's establishment.*[75]

Furthermore, many of the records which did exist were lost
in the midst of the wartime conditions of 1947–1949. Thus, in
the many battles over documentation which have ensued since
the passage of the Prescription Law, Arab landowners, pitted
against batteries of lawyers hired by the land settlement and acquisition institutions of the government and the Zionist movement, have been at a distinct disadvantage. According to Oded,
in the context of its overall survey of land registration in Israel
the government has made a point of challenging every Arab
claim to land ownership, no matter how small the plot of land
involved. As a result the government has become a "major land-
holder in every village, . . . endowed with thousands of separate
plots, some of them tiny, with which it can do very little."[76] This
has had a direct effect in terms of the development of Arab
agriculture, since the interposition of government-owned or
-claimed plots among the holdings of Arab farmers discourages
investment and inhibits the implementation of modern agricultural techniques.

The agencies in charge of the government's land policies

have also made use of the Law for the Acquisition of Land in the Public Interest. In 1956 1,200 dunams of the best land in Nazareth were expropriated "in the public interest." The "public purpose" for which the land had been expropriated was designated as the construction of housing and privately owned factories for the nucleus of a new Jewish township, Upper Nazareth.[77] In 1965 this same law was used to confiscate some of the best farm land that remained in Arab hands. This confiscation occurred in connection with the Water Authority's decision to construct the national water carrier across the Batteuf plain. The authority had confronted the problem of transversing cultivated land before, but when the lands in question were cultivated by Jews it had found ways either to put a pipeline underground or to bypass the most fertile areas. In the Batteuf Plain the lands were cultivated by Arabs from the villages of Sakhnin and Arrabe. Here the Water Authority decided to build the carrier above ground, bisecting the plain. Although the carrier itself is only four meters wide, the strip of land expropriated was ninety-three meters wide. In all, 3,000 dunams were expropriated.[78]

However, the best known application of the Law for the Acquisition of Land in the Public Interest was the confiscation of 5,100 dunams from the Arab villages of Deir el-Assad, Binah, and Nahaf. In the early years of Israeli statehood, these villages lost 3,500 dunams of cultivated land. In 1962 the regime, as part of its continuing effort to "Judaize the Galilee," decided that more village lands were needed in order to build a new Jewish development town, Carmiel. The government's policy of encouraging Arabs to depend on the Jewish economy for their livelihood is quite evident in the details of this case. The lands expropriated included quarries and orchards from which the bulk of the villages' workers made their living. Although the inhabitants suggested that other of their lands in the area be used for the construction of the new town so that they would not be forced to travel to Jewish cities for employment, their requests were refused. Rather, the government indicated that the industries to be built in Carmiel would create jobs for those Arabs left unemployed as a result of the expropriations.[79]

Still another technique employed quite often to expropriate Arab land involves the use of Article 125 of the Emergency Regulations. As described in Chapter 4, Article 125 empowers the defense minister or his authorized representatives (including military governors) to prohibit entry of persons into designated "closed areas." In combination with the provisions of the Cultivation of Waste Lands Ordinance, Article 125 has been the vehicle for substantial expropriations of Arab agricultural land. Typically the process works in the following way: An area encompassing Arab-owned agricultural lands is declared a "closed area." The owners of the lands are then denied permission by the security authorities to enter the area for any purpose whatsoever, including cultivation. After three years pass, the Ministry of Agriculture issues certificates which classify the lands as uncultivated. The owners are notified that unless cultivation is renewed immediately the lands will be subject to expropriation. The owners, still barred by the security authorities from entering the "closed area" within which their lands are located, cannot resume cultivation. The lands are then expropriated and become part of the general land reserve for Jewish settlement. Eventually permission to enter the "closed area" is granted to Jewish farmers; alternatively the classification of the area as "closed" is lifted altogether. That this technique has been used, consciously, by the authorities in order to expand the area of Jewish land ownership and settlement is evident in a remark made in 1962 by Shimon Peres, then director general of the Ministry of Defense: "by making use of Article 125, on which the Military Government is to a great extent based, we can directly continue the struggle for Jewish settlement and Jewish immigration."[80]

There are no official government figures available for the total extent or percentage of Arab lands expropriated since 1948. This is in part due to disagreements over what lands the Arab community held before 1948 and what holdings now cultivated by Israeli Arabs are, in the opinion of the authorities, the property of the state or the JNF. Moreover, because government figures describing the land area under cultivation by Israeli Arabs include lands leased on a short-term basis, and because they exclude consideration of agricultural lands lost by "present absentees," statistics which are available, showing that the area cultivated by non-Jews has risen since 1949, are deceiving. The

Table 5. Expropriation of Arab Land since 1948 (Selected Villages)

Name of Village	Area Possessed in 1947 (Dunams)	Area Possessed after Expropriations (Dunams)
1. Jatt	12,000	9,000
2. Qalansawe	18,850	6,780
3. Jaljuliah	14,000	800
4. Tira	40,000	8,000
5. Taibeh	45,000	13,000
6. Ara-Arrara	26,000	7,000
7. Kfar Bara	4,000	2,000
8. Baka el-Gharbiyeh	22,000	7,000
9. Kfar Kassem	12,000	9,000
10. Um el-Fahm	125,000	25,000
11. Pekein	14,000	5,500
12. Deir-el-Assad, Binah, and Nahaf	16,000	7,000
13. Beit Jann	26,500	13,000
14. Yirka	55,000	18,000
15. Sakhnin	55,000	30,000
16. Arrabe	95,000	11,350
17. Deir Hana	16,000	9,500
18. Majd el-Krum	20,000	7,000

Sources: See note 81 for this chapter.

statistics in Table 5, collated from a variety of sources, indicate losses of land in a number of not unrepresentative Israeli Arab villages. The figures reflect the overall scale of the expropriations that have been carried out.[81]

Landowners whose property was expropriated under the Law for the Acquisition of Land in the Public Interest are, under the terms of this law, entitled to compensation. Adequate compensation, whether in the form of alternative lands or in the form of other capital resources, could conceivably have played an important role in the economic rehabilitation of Arab farmers. In fact, however, the government's compensation program has been of little consequence. Available statistics show that, in the twenty years following the passage of the Acquisition of Lands (Validation of Acts and Compensation) Law in 1953, compensation had been paid for 175,000 dunams of land, or approximately 25 percent of the land area acquired from Israeli Arabs under the terms of that law. This compensation included I£ 26,442,000 in cash and 44,907 dunams of alternate lands (whether through lease or transfer of ownership). Although rates for compensation have risen considerably since the mid-1950's, when payments were based on land values and the value of the Palestinian pound that prevailed in 1950, the average cash payment per dunam during this entire period was only I£ 209, a figure which bears little relationship to the free market value of the land.[82] On the other hand, even if Arab claimants were to receive realistic compensation payments from the Development Authority or the Israel Lands Administration, they still would be unable to buy land; their fellow villagers have none to spare and the government will not sell. Furthermore, for reasons discussed above, Arabs lack opportunities for investment in their communities, and such compensation payments, in practical terms, represent nonrecurrent cash bonuses which can be used for immediate consumption only. Consequently the issue of alternative land as a form of compensation has been of tremendous importance in the Arab sector.

Under the terms of the Acquisition of Lands (Validation of Acts and Compensation) Law, claimants may receive alternate land as compensation only by reaching agreement with the Development Authority or, later, with the Israel Lands Administration. A claimant who is not satisfied with the terms of compensation offered by the government may take the case to court. The court, however, is empowered only to grant cash compensation, not compensation in the form of additional land. Thus an Arab farmer who wants land rather than cash in exchange for confiscated property must get it directly from the government. But the government has placed very stringent rules on the allotment of land as compensation. According to Section 3, Article (b), of the 1953 law, a claimant may receive land as compensation only "where the acquired property was used for agriculture and was the main source of livelihood of its owner."[83] As interpreted by the government this provision has come to mean that in order to qualify for compensation in land "not only the owner who loses the land but also his family must have supported themselves mainly from agriculture."[84] This means that a farmer whose sons worked as hired laborers would not qualify for compensation in land. The government's operational definition of "family" as one *nuclear* family has caused further problems. The government's policy has been that no "family" can be awarded more than thirty dunams of land as compensation—this in spite of the fact that in the Arab community unmarried and also married sons and their families commonly remain in the father's household until his death.[85] As a result of the government's definition of "family," confiscated land which had supported a father and several sons and their families can be replaced only by what the government has determined to be enough land to support one *nuclear* family.

Moreover, the government's maximum allotment of thirty dunams, given the stony, hilly nature of land in most Arab areas, is not enough to support even one nuclear family. In a special report submitted to the Ministry of Agriculture by the Joint Agricultural Planning Center in 1963 it was recommended that farms of thirty dunams or less were too small to be considered anything but "auxiliary" and should therefore not be accorded eligibility for agricultural development programs.[86]

These are the reasons most potential Arab claimants have not stepped forward to accept compensation. Besides an emotional attachment to "ancestral lands" and a reluctance to accept as compensation lands formerly owned by Arab refugees, it is clearly recognized by Arab villagers that the capital resources lost as a result of the expropriations cannot be replaced by the kind of compensation the government has generally been willing to provide.

Arab farmers have attempted to make up for their expropriated property by subletting land from Jewish settlements or by leasing land directly from the Israel Lands Administration. As discussed in Chapter 4, the government and the national institutions have waged a vigorous campaign to bring a halt to the subletting of land by Jewish farmers. Although Arabs have been able to lease substantial amounts of land from the Israel Lands Administration, the government's policy has been to lease land to Arabs on a short-term (usually one-year) basis only.[87] Since they are not granted the forty-nine-year leases which are standard in connection with the lease of land to Jewish settlements, and since the rents which Arabs must pay correspond to the market value of the land as opposed to the nominal payments required from Jewish lessees, Arab farmers cannot and do not invest in the development of leased land through clearing operations, the installation of irrigation facilities, etc.[88]

The mass expropriation of Arab land has been the heaviest single blow which government policy has dealt to the economic integrity of the Arab sector. But the expropriations, the inadequacy of compensation programs, and discrimination against Arabs in regard to the leasing of land are even more significant as aspects of a general pattern of economic discrimination against Arabs in all matters pertaining to development—a pattern that corresponds to government policy and that contributes to the continued economic underdevelopment of the Arab sector.

GOVERNMENT POLICY AND ECONOMIC DEVELOPMENT OF THE ARAB SECTOR

When discussing the status of the Arab minority in Israel government spokesmen stress, more than anything else, the tremendous changes that have taken place in the living standards of Israeli Arabs since 1948. One government pamphlet reads as follows:

Antiquated and crowded dwellings have been ousted by new, spacious, stone homes equipped with modern sanitation, running water, refrigerators, television sets, and gas cookers.

Of the total Arab population of Israel, 85 percent have electric lighting, and of that proportion 65 percent belong to the peasantry. Most of the villages now have ready and smooth access to the national highway system, and, inside the villages, the narrow, dusty or muddy lanes are gone and proper interior communications exist. New schools, mosques and churches are being built and old ones reconditioned. Most villages have youth and cultural clubs, sports teams, clinics, and shopping centres.[89]

It may be fairly claimed that, by 1973, the members of Israel's minority groups have risen to a level of economic prosperity far and away superior to the conditions of 1948 and that progress so swift and so extensive would be hard to match in any other society.[90]

Such descriptions, though exaggerated and misleading,[91] are not far enough off the mark to warrant an elaborate critique. It is definitely the case that Israeli Arabs enjoy a much higher standard of living than they did in 1948 and that this living standard surpasses by a wide margin that of most of the inhabitants of the Arab states bordering upon Israel. It is also the case that the prosperity of the Arab sector is due, overwhelmingly, to the earnings of Arab workers in Jewish industry and agriculture. These earnings have been translated into higher levels of consumption and, in a more limited sense, into basic facilities such as roads, electricity, and water systems. But, as has been stated previously, when measured in terms of the establishment of workshops or industrial concerns, the formation of financial organizations, or the diversification of agriculture to include a substantial proportion of irrigated and/or industrial crops, Arab economic development has not taken place.

To the structural and institutional factors involved in the continued backwardness of the Arab sector must be added the neglect of the government and its discrimination in favor of the Jewish sector with respect to development projects of all kinds. In an analysis of the problems of Israel's Arab minority which appeared in *Maariv* in 1972, one Israeli journalist noted that "in spite of an intention to close the gap between Arabs and Jews—nothing serious was done until the first five-year plan in 1965."[92] During a personal interview, Aga Schwartz, an official of the (now defunct) Ministry of Development responsible for the ministry's programs in the Arab sector, commented in a similar vein. "Until 1967 essentially nothing was done by the government with regard to the development of electrical or other infrastructural facilities for Arabs."[93] Kemal Kassem, appointed in 1974 as an adviser to the minister of commerce and industry for problems associated with industry in the Arab sector, in an interview stated that "despite the decline in the importance of agriculture in the Arab economic sector, the availability of a significant amount of Arab capital, and an increase in the number of Arabs who have received technical training and education . . . government policy has so far not encouraged the industrial development of Arab areas."[94]

According to Yaacov Cohen, director of the Arab Department of the Histadrut, the Histadrut's leadership has rejected the industrialization of the Arab sector as a policy goal.[95] Indeed, although there are over 70,000 Arab members of the Histadrut and although the Histadrut owns more than one-fifth of all Israeli industry, in 1974 not one of its thousands of firms and factories was located in an Arab village or town.[96]

The decision of the government not to push hard for the economic development of the Arab sector was largely based on a desire to prevent the emergence of Arab-owned centers of economic power. The attitude of the Military Administration, for example, toward economic development was that it should be "carried out in such a way as not to create a self-contained Arab economy, for this would encourage hostile activity."[97] Although in recent years the government has taken steps to introduce certain types of light industry into Arab villages, these enterprises are *jointly* owned by Jews and Arabs. They have been designed, almost solely, to take advantage of what has in recent years been the only source of additional labor left in Israel—Arab village women.

The overall attitude of the government toward the industrialization of the Arab sector and the development of Arab-owned enterprises has been that these are, first and foremost, *political* rather than economic problems. "Given the political sensitivity of these issues," one official of the Ministry of Commerce and Industry told me, "no man in government will say what they really think [concerning them]."[98]

But despite the reticence of government officials, a clear pattern of systematic economic discrimination against Arabs can nonetheless be discerned in government programs and policies. In the early 1950's monopolistic marketing firms for Arab produce were established under the auspices of the Histadrut, the Military Administration, and the Office of the Adviser to the Prime Minister for Arab Affairs. During this period Arab farmers were not allowed to market their crops independently but were forced to accept the prices offered by these firms—prices which often represented only one-third of the market value.[99] Up until 1952 official government policy sanctioned the use of separate wage scales for Jewish and Arab workers, including employees of public utilities.[100] Not until the early 1960's were wage differentials between Jewish and Arab workers eliminated.[101] In 1961 government relief work was given to unemployed workers in the Arab sector at the rate of thirty-five work days per unemployed person. For Jews the rate used by the government was one hundred work days per unemployed person.[102]

Table 6. Housing Density: Percentages of Jewish and Non-Jewish
Families

			Persons per Room (1976)				
4.00+	3.00– 3.99	2.01– 2.99	2.00	1.50– 1.99	1.01– 1.49	1.00	−1.00
Jews 0.8	2.8	5.4	8.3	13.0	15.5	28.1	26.1
Non-Jews 22.5	19.6	15.4	12.9	11.6	4.6	9.3	4.0

Source: Statistical Abstract of Israel 28 (1977): 283. For additional in-
formation concerning the housing situation in the Arab sector, see *Zoo
Haderech*, February 17, 1974; October 16, 1974; November 19, 1975;
April 9, 1975; and Attalah Mansour, "A Wall of Strangeness between
Nazareth and Upper Nazareth," *Haaretz*, July 14, 1975.

Until 1971 government welfare payments to poverty-stricken
Arabs were considerably lower, as a matter of policy in the Ministry of Social Welfare, than payments made to Jewish poor. "In
the Arab villages, where the living standard is lower, the payments total about 60 percent of those in the Jewish sector. The
distinction . . . applies to all 'totally rural communities.' In practice, however, this classification applies only to the Arab villages."[103]

The Arab sector, which is faced by a severe housing shortage (see Table 6), continues to suffer from discrimination by the
Ministry of Housing. In 1962/1963 the government's allocation
for housing was I£336 million. Of this amount I£4 million (1.2
percent) was allocated for "Minorities and others."[104] According to the report to the Knesset issued by the minister of housing
in 1971, the ministry planned to erect 19,100 new dwelling
units in 1971/1972. Of these, 250 (1.4 percent) were to be built
in the Arab sector.[105] In an interview conducted in 1974, Akiva
Feinstein, director of the Arab Department of the Ministry of
Housing, stated that since his department came into existence in
1957 the ministry had constructed 2,000 housing units for
Arabs, an average of 118 per year.[106] In another interview the
official spokesman for Housing refused to provide statistics concerning funds allotted during the 1973/1974 fiscal year for Jewish and Arab housing. "A comparison of such figures," he explained, "would appear ridiculous."[107]

The government's desire to channel investment capital into

Jewish as opposed to Arab areas is reflected in the terms of the Law for the Encouragement of Capital Investments. Under the terms of this law Israel has been divided into three development zones. The development of Zone "A" has been considered to be of the highest priority, and incentives for investments there are very generous. The incentives are for "industrial projects" and include "reduced rent for industrial buildings, low-interest loans for the construction of their own buildings and for working capital, and grants for industrial site development, for on-the-job training of workers and for the transfer of existing enterprises.[108] In Zone "B" the same incentives are available but at lower rates, while in the "central zone" incentives are not offered. For example, in 1973 rent for industrial premises was I£ 28 per square meter in Zone "A" and I£ 36 per square meter in Zone "B," while in the central zone rents ranged from I£ 100 to I£ 150 per square meter.[109] The purpose of this system is to encourage industries to move to relatively underdeveloped areas outside the heavily populated coastal plain. What is particularly revealing is how certain Arab areas, more underdeveloped economically than any others in Israel, are excluded from the development zones. For example most of the Little Triangle, populated by over eighty thousand Arabs and almost completely devoid of industry, is not included in either Zone "A" or Zone "B." Especially striking is the manner in which the border between the central zone and Zone "B" actually bisects the city of Nazareth, including Upper (Jewish) Nazareth in Zone "B" while leaving lower (Arab) Nazareth in the central zone. The borders of Zones "A" and "B" in the Galilee are drawn so as to include Shelomi, Ma'alot, Carmiel, and Tiberias (all Jewish towns) in Zone "A" while leaving the clusters of Arab villages in central and western Galilee in Zone "B," and Shfar Am, the largest Arab town in Israel, and Kfar Yasif, a smaller Arab town east of Acre, in the central zone.[110] (See Map 3 for the development zones. It is significant that no Arab localities other than Nazareth are shown on this official Israeli government map.)

Since the early 1970's the Ministry of the Interior has come under strong criticism in the Arab sector concerning discrimination in the allotment of development loans and grants to Arab local councils. In 1972 the ministry appointed a commission

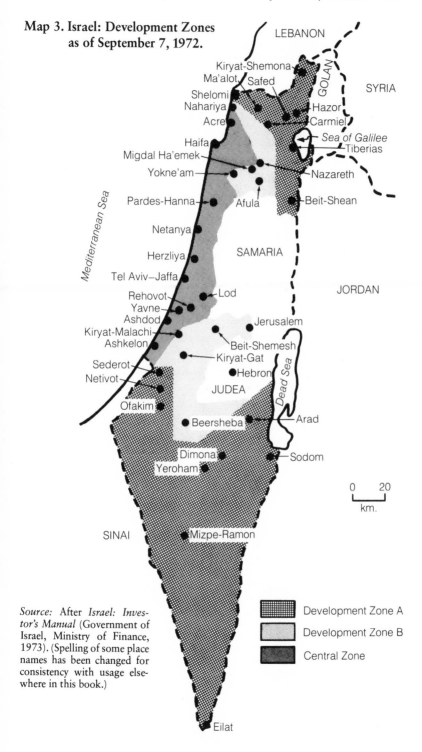

Map 3. Israel: Development Zones as of September 7, 1972.

Source: After *Israel: Investor's Manual* (Government of Israel, Ministry of Finance, 1973). (Spelling of some place names has been changed for consistency with usage elsewhere in this book.)

Development Zone A

Development Zone B

Central Zone

headed by a prominent Arab sociologist, Dr. Sami Jerisi, to study the problems of local councils in the Arab sector. The "Jerisi Report," submitted to the Ministry of the Interior in 1973, described these problems in great detail and gave particular attention to discrimination by Interior against Arab local councils. Although the ministry has refused to make the report public, the findings of the commission have nevertheless come to light. The data in Table 7, comparison of per capita allotments of grants and loans by the Ministry of the Interior to Jewish and Arab local councils, were contained in the Jerisi Report.[111]

In May 1974, the Ministry of the Interior held a conference in Jerusalem to discuss problems faced by local councils in Israel. In a lecture delivered during one of the sessions at the conference, Kamal Tibi, a member of the Jerisi Comission, confirmed the accuracy of published reports of the commission findings. He went on to say that the commission found there to be, overall, two distinct levels in the economic aid provided by the regime to the Jewish and Arab sectors. In response to Tibi's charges of discrimination, Interior officials emphasized the failure of Arabs to contribute tax revenues at the same rate as Jews.[112] However, according to government statistics, in 1972 Arab villagers paid I£ 8.5 million in municipal taxes, equaling 26 percent of the total ordinary budget of local councils in the Arab sector.[113] In 1971–1972 the proportion of the ordinary budget of all local councils in Israel covered by municipal taxes was 11 percent.[114] In 1975 Mahmud Bayadsi, mayor of a large Arab village in the Little Triangle, charged that government grants "constitute 30 percent of the total usual budgets of Jewish municipalities, but only 3 percent for Arab local authorities, [although] local tax constitutes 14 percent of the usual budgets of Jewish local councils and 30 percent of the usual budgets in Arab ones."[115]

On the other hand there is no question that in absolute terms taxes collected per capita in Arab villages are substantially lower than those raised in Jewish villages. Arab local councils are therefore less able than Jewish local councils to qualify for matching funds for various development projects. But, as indicated previously, the tax base of an average Jewish locality is very much larger than the tax base of an average Arab settlement. It is the Ministry of the Interior's policy of using *absolute*

Table 7. Ministry of the Interior Grants and Loans to Arab and
Jewish Local Councils, 1973

Arab Localities	Financial Aid per Capita (I£)	Jewish Localities	Financial Aid per Capita (I£)
Shfar Am	10	Acre	80
Abu-Sinan	20	Rosh Pina	100
Iksal	10	Kinnereth	80
Ibbilin	10	Yavniel	125
Bismat Tibon	10	Migdal	125
Sakhnin	10	Nazareth (Upper)	80
Arrabe	7	Migdal Haemek	125
Ein Mahul	7	Tzefat	80
Nahaf	7	Maalot-Tarshisha	125
Kfar Manda	7	Hatzor	125
Kfar Kana	7	Zichron Yaacov	80
Kfar Kama	20	Metulla	80
Ussifiyah	20	Kiryat Shmona	100
Daliyaat el-Carmel	20	Raksim	85
Taiybe	10	Tiberias	80
Qalansuwa	10	Tabor	60
Jaljulya	10	Menachemiyah	100
Baka el-Gharbiyeh	10	Beit-Shean	125
Um el-Fahm	10	Raanana	40
Arara	7	Hod HaSharon	60

levels of tax revenue to determine what grants and loans will be awarded that deprives the Arab population of a proportionate share of the ministry's development funds.

Among the policy decisions made by the regime which have interfered with the economic development and autonomy of the Arab sector, one of the most significant was its seizure of the assets of the Moslem Waqf (religious endowment) in 1950 (see Chapter 2). Today the great majority of Waqf properties, which in 1946 included approximately one-tenth of all the land in Palestine as well as 70 percent of all the shops in some Arab cities, have been sold or leased to private Jewish companies or individuals or to the national institutions.[116] Only 25 to 30 percent of the properties—specifically those actually dedicated for religious use, such as mosques, cemeteries, and other shrines—are still regarded by the regime as Waqf assets.[117] Formal control over these properties is exercised by boards of trustees appointed by the Ministry of Religion. But under the terms of a law passed in 1965, the government has the right to determine how properties leased by these trustees are to be used. For example, although the board of trustees in charge of the Waqf in Acre has attempted several times to use its resources for housing construction and other projects in the Arab slums of that city, its efforts have always been frustrated by government opposition.[118] On the other hand the Hilton Hotel in Tel Aviv, located on what was the Abed al-Nabi Moslem cemetery, was leased from the Jaffa Board of Trustees with full government approval.[119] In general the Waqf boards of trustees, having been carefully chosen by the government for their religious and traditionalist orientations, have not even tried to use what funds they have had at their disposal for the economic development of the Arab sector.[120]

In response to occasional charges of economic discrimination against the Arab sector the government has usually stressed its implementation of two "five-year plans" drawn up by the Office of the Adviser to the Prime Minister on Arab Affairs. As Shmuel Toledano himself has stated on several occasions, no such special expenditures for the development of a particular sector of Israeli society are to be found anywhere else in the government's budget.[121] As portrayed by the government, the purpose of the five-year plans, 1962–1967 and 1967–1972, was to install basic services such as electricity, water, approach roads, and schools; encourage the development of commerce and industry in the Arab sector; increase the employment of women; accelerate housing construction for Arabs; modernize Arab agricultural techniques; build health facilities; and raise Arab income levels. According to the government the plans attained the following objectives:

completion of a system of basic services; water supply, access and inner roads, electricity and telephone lines;

organized housing construction and aid in the private building of homes;

expansion and amelioration of health, educational and welfare services;

modernization and diversification of agriculture;

establishment of industries and trade centers.[122]

However, as has been indicated, industry is still practically nonexistent in the Arab sector; industrial crops do not comprise a significant percentage of Arab agriculture; Arab schools lack thousands of classrooms as well as libraries, lavatories, and other facilities; relatively high infant-mortality rates reflect the absence of adequate health care facilities in most Arab villages; the housing situation in Arab localities is desperate; only one of 104 Arab villages in 1976 had a sewer system; many Arab localities are still without electricity or paved roads; and higher and higher proportions of Arabs work in localities other than their places of residence.[123]

The basic reason for the failure of the development plans to have more than a marginal impact on the economic underdevelopment of the Arab sector was the lack of government funding. The first five-year plan included the expenditure of I£ 84 million, but government outlays, including loans and grants, amounted to only I£ 44 million. The balance was to be invested by commercial banks, private Arab citizens, and Arab municipalities. The second five-year plan involved the expenditure of I£ 114 million, including I£ 58.6 million in government loans to Arab local councils and I£ 39.3 million in government grants.[124] Although these expenditures were approximately seven times higher than those undertaken from 1957 to 1962 for similar purposes,[125] government investments have not come close to what several economists have estimated would be required for the modernization of the Arab economy. In 1966 Shaul Zarhi and A. Achiezra estimated that in order to increase the percentage of Arabs working in their places of residence to 60 percent of the total of Arabs employed and to construct adequate housing in Arab towns and villages, an average annual net investment (excluding depreciation) of I£ 129 million was required from 1963 to 1973.[126] In 1973 an American economist calculated that the modernization of the Arab sector would require the investment of approximately I£ 125 million per year for ten years.[127] Comparison of annual government expenditure for the development of the Arab sector with total annual expenditures for such projects, as shown in Table 8, can provide a reasonably accurate reflection of the government's true priorities with regard to economic development in the Arab sector.[128]

Table 8. Five-Year Annual Average for Government Development
Budget Expenditure

	Expenditure for Jews and Arabs (Selected Categories) (in Millions of I£)	Expenditure in Arab Sector (in Millions of I£)	Expenditure in Arab Sector as % of Total Development Budget Expenditure
1957/58–1961/62	350.34	0.71	0.2
1962/63–1966/67	579.06	8.80	1.5
1967/68–1971/72	894.26	11.72	1.3

Sources: See note 128 for this chapter.

THE ENFORCEMENT OF ARAB DEPENDENCE

The five-year plans, although they did not attain their stated objectives, did have the effect of centralizing control over government expenditures for Arabs in the Office of the Adviser to the Prime Minister on Arab Affairs. This was particularly important in view of the gradual abolition of the Military Administration, well underway in 1962 and completed by 1966. After the abolition of the Military Administration the Office of the Adviser to the Prime Minister on Arab Affairs emerged as the agency most directly responsible for the government's Arab policies. Translating the overall economic backwardness of the Arab sector into concrete relationships of Arab dependence on Jewish centers of power and wealth was one of the tasks which the adviser's office, and other departments responsible for Arab affairs, inherited from the Military Administration.[129]

Both the Military Administration and the adviser's office found that the underdevelopment of the Arab sector made blacklisting a very effective technique for keeping individual Arabs or individual Arab villages dependent on the good graces of the authorities. Neither before nor after the abolition of the Military Administration could blacklisted Arabs hope to receive government development loans or options to lease land or farm equipment. In some ways, however, the use of blacklists by the Military Administration differed from that of the adviser's office.

The blacklists circulated by military governors included the names of Arabs active in Mapam, the Communist Party, el-Ard, and communist-front organizations such as the Democratic Teachers List of the Histadrut, as well as the names of Arabs who incurred the displeasure of the authorities for not cooperating in the election of this or that local council chairman, for refusing to sell land, or for refusing to act as informers.[130]

During the tenure of the Military Administration being blacklisted also meant having serious difficulties in obtaining travel permits. Given the reliance of most Arabs on employment outside their economically backward villages, delays in the issuance of permits, additional restrictions in the routes of travel allowed, reductions in the length of a permit's validity, and especially refusal to grant a travel permit were likely to have severe and immediate economic implications. Although the Military Administration was abolished in 1966, the economic dependence of Arabs on the Jewish economy has remained; and occasional government threats, implicit and explicit, to reintroduce military government in Arab areas have always carried important economic overtones.[131]

Since the abolition of the Military Administration, blacklisting has primarily been used by the adviser's office in connection with the employment of young Arab intellectuals. On the basis of information gathered by the "Information Center—Arab Branch," i.e., the adviser's liaison with the security services, a list is maintained of Arab high school and college graduates suspected of "antigovernment activities." Individuals blacklisted by the adviser's office are able to obtain employment neither in government agencies nor in privately owned Jewish establishments (where the adviser's recommendation is also necessary).[132] For most Arabs with a secondary school education the question of whether or not they will be accepted for teaching positions in Arab village schools is crucial. Besides exercising a veto over admissions to the Arab teachers' seminary, the adviser's office also participates, in coordination with the Arab Department of the Ministry of Education and Culture, in hiring and firing Arab school teachers. A young educated Arab can expect to get and keep a job as a teacher only by staying off the government's blacklist.[133] Again, due to the nondevelopment of the Arab economy, the only opportunities for appropriate employment available to educated Arabs are located in the government or in the private Jewish sector. Hence, for educated Arabs seeking white-collar employment, the threat of being blacklisted is potent indeed.[134]

In another form blacklisting has been used by the adviser's office to punish entire villages where local communist representatives or other "extremist" elements have been permitted to participate in governing coalitions. It is not uncommon in such cases for village applications for school construction loans to be turned down or ignored, for connection of the village to the national power grid to be delayed, or for the Histadrut to close a sporting or cultural facility within the village.[135]

An additional technique used by the regime to enforce the dependence of individual Arabs on the Jewish authorities is the issuance or refusal of building permits. The vulnerability of Arab citizens to this type of manipulation stems from the overcrowding of Arab villages and their greatly reduced land area. Jewish officials in the Ministry of the Interior and in the Israel Lands Administration have taken advantage of this vulnerability, and of zoning regulations which apply equally to Jews as well as Arabs, in order to create and maintain relations of dependence with individual Arabs. According to Israeli zoning laws every village and town, Jewish and Arab, must submit a master plan for the ministry's approval. The plan must outline future growth and delineate areas to be used for residential buildings, public facilities, roads, agriculture, etc. In the absence of an approved master plan, any construction projects undertaken must be approved by Ministry of the Interior representatives before work is begun. This includes additions to private homes or construction of separate dwelling units by private individuals. Master plans have now been approved for almost every Jewish locality. It is also standard procedure in the Jewish sector for the ministry to recognize local councils as official zoning committees, empowered to issue permits for construction projects within their jurisdictions. In the Arab sector, however, up until 1979, the Ministry of the Interior had approved only six master plans. In other words more than 90 percent of Arab localities lacked master plans. Moreover, not one Arab local council had been accorded the status of a zoning committee.[136]

The most important reason for the refusal of the authorities to approve master plans submitted by Arab towns and villages is that, more often than not, lands surrounding these localities and designated for various purposes under the terms of the proposed plans are claimed by the regime as state domain, abandoned land, or unregistered land. In the absence of approved master plans or recognized local zoning authorities, and with an exploding rate of population increase, the building of new homes has become an issue of bitter contention in the Arab sector. In the context of severe overcrowding thousands of Arabs have built homes or made additions to older dwellings without the approval of the Ministry of the Interior. Many of these structures have been built on village lands claimed by the government or the JNF. Each year many unlicensed buildings are demolished by the government; heavy fines are levied on the owners of others. In 1976 the government agreed in principle to legitimize buildings constructed in many villages on land that would inevitably be zoned as residential.[137] However, the Likud government has delayed approving applications for such retroactive licensing and in 1977 began an intensified campaign against unauthorized Arab building on "national land."[138] In 1977 it was estimated that there were twenty-four thousand unlicensed Arab houses.[139] The enforcement of the licensing laws and of demolition orders is at the discretion of the Arab Department of the Ministry of the Interior, which works in close coordination with the Development Authority, the Israel Lands Administration and the adviser's office.

The knowledge that their homes may be destroyed at any time makes those Arabs who have built houses without permission from the Ministry of the Interior particularly dependent on the continuing good will of government officials. Moreover, any Arab contemplating a private construction project in a village that does not have an approved master plan must obtain a special license from the Ministry of the Interior. It is very often the case that building permits or revocations of demolition orders are traded by the authorities for agreements by Arab citizens to surrender claims to land confiscated by the regime, accept compensation, or even deliver the votes of kinship groups to a particular Zionist political party.[140]

Regime policy among the Negev Bedouin has been particularly successful in establishing relationships of dependence between Bedouin tribes and the authorities. As with Arab villages in Israel "the main income of the Negev Bedouin is from wage labor in the Jewish economy, mostly as unskilled agricultural and construction workers, tractorists, truck drivers, and hotel personnel."[141] Bedouin agriculture has been hampered by government land expropriations, which have been undertaken on an even more massive scale than in the north. Ever since 1948 the Bedouin of the Negev have pressed for government recognition of their claim to 2 million dunams of land in the southern part of the country. Substantial portions of this land had been cultivated successfully by the Bedouin for generations.[142] But in 1949 almost all of the Negev's Bedouin were confined to a reservation known as the Sayigh, whose 1.1 million dunams contain only 40,000 to 45,000 dunams of cultivable land. Furthermore, even within the Sayigh the government has refused to recognize land as privately owned by the Bedouin. As Yitzhak Oded wrote in 1964, "It is this refusal . . . which may be held primarily responsible for the tribesmen's woeful social and economic backwardness. For so long as these lands are not confirmed as their own there is no point in their building houses or planning a proper crop rotation."[143] Most land now cultivated by Bedouin farmers is leased from the government for eight months yearly. Crop rotation or investment in land reclamation or irrigation on these lands is therefore impossible. Bedouin agriculture has also suffered from discrimination in drought relief payments and water allotments.[144]

Complementing its refusal to encourage the development of Bedouin agriculture and its intensive campaign to acquire lands used and claimed by the Bedouin, the government has repeatedly implemented various "sedentarization programs." Villages are envisioned, and some have already been created, in which Bedouin would surrender claims to traditional holdings in return for housing and a small plot of land.[145] Economically, the inhabitants of such "villages" can expect to be completely dependent on wage labor. A 1972 study of one Bedouin tribe resettled by the government concluded that "sedentarization" had resulted in a greater dependence of the tribe and its elders on the government and a strengthening of those agnatic ties within the tribe which bound the tribe members to their patriarchal leaders.[146]

Dependence as a Component of Control

In terms of the function which it has fulfilled as a component in the system of control, "dependence" has, most importantly, meant that Arab Israelis have lacked autonomous bases of economic power which could have been used to support dissident political parties or movements. It has also meant that Arabs have generally been extremely vulnerable to noncoercive forms of pressure and reprisal. Overall, dependence has made it less likely that the disunited and isolated segments of the Arab population could, even individually, launch sustained drives for social, economic, or political change, and it has made it less necessary than otherwise would have been the case for the regime to employ coercive and more costly methods of control.

Nonetheless, segmentation and dependence, even in combination, have not provided and cannot provide the Israeli leadership with the kind of access to Arab resources, especially votes, which has been desired. Neither have these two components provided, nor can they provide, the regime with a comprehensive surveillance capability—that continuing and spontaneous flow of information which has made it possible, at relatively low cost, to identify dissidents, to locate centers of authority within individual Arab villages or clans, and to monitor emotional, social, and political trends within the Arab sector as a whole. To accomplish these tasks the regime has had to penetrate the Arab sector. "Cooptation," the third component in the system of control, has been the primary vehicle for this penetration.

6.
Cooptation
as a Component of Control:
The Capture of Arab Elites

Cooptation: The Structural Level of Analysis

It has thus far been shown how certain characteristics of the hamula-centered social structure of Arab society have contributed to the fragmentation of the Arab community and the enforcement of relations of dependence within it. There are, as well, very definite ways in which the hamula social structure has contributed to the success of cooptation as a strategy for penetrating Arab village society. As "segmented units," hamulas are large enough and contain hierarchical chains of dependence which are long enough—from sons through fathers through extended family patriarchs to hamula elders—that cooptation of a relatively small number of strategic individuals by the central authorities can provide the regime with effective access to very large numbers of Arabs. It is not surprising that the convenience of this form of social organization was fully recognized by the Military Administration. As Abu-Ghosh noted in his study of an Arab village in the Little Triangle, it was "in the interests of the Military Government to maintain hamula unity, and not only that, but to maintain it under the leadership of its traditional leaders and elders. From the point of view of the Military Government, it is far easier to control the political activity and behavior of the few thousand people of Qabila by using the cooperative services of the few leaders and elders."[1]

Nor is it surprising, in light of the convenient aspects of Arab social structure in Palestine, that central government control over Arab inhabitants through the cooptation of clan notables or tribal chieftains was well established as a historical tradition long before the creation of Israel. Describing the pattern of

Ottoman rule in the late nineteenth and early twentieth centuries, Henry Rosenfeld observed:

As long as a village maintained the agricultural, economic, political status quo, as long as it kept the order necessary for the collection of taxes, rents, the overlords would give recognition to a particular family which represented a particular lineage, or a segment of it, or in large villages allocate recognition to a number of lineages or lineage segments. Such recognition took the form of a title given to certain individuals (mukhtar, sheik), allowances for the use of internal authority within the village reflecting the connection of the privileged with the external power, tax preferences, land dispensation, etc.[2]

Assuming control over Palestine after World War I, the British Mandatory authorities continued to employ the same basic approach as the Ottomans. District officers representing the central government sought out the elders of the most powerful hamula in any given village. In return for his cooperation the leader of that hamula (or coalition) was recognized as Mukhtar; relations between the villagers and the central authorities were carried on with the mukhtar and the district officer serving as intermediaries. The recognized mukhtar, as a result of his contacts and official status, exercised wide personal discretion in the internal affairs of the village, and the dominant position of his hamula in village politics was more or less taken for granted.[3]

Besides convenient social structural features and historical traditions, longstanding cultural patterns of behavior and belief have also favored the adoption of cooptive techniques by an Israeli government committed to the control of the Arab population. The most important such cultural pattern is that known in colloquial Arabic as *wasta*, or "connection." The term refers to the function of a mediator representing the interest of one party in negotiations with neighbors, potential in-laws, or government officials. The practice of mediation in personal affairs is, in traditional Arab society, designed to prevent the loss of face and the outbreak of feuds liable to attend such matters. The traditional attitude among Arab villagers regarding business conducted with government officials was that favorable action simply could not or would not be taken on petitions, applications, or inquiries unless the matter were presented to the authorities by a sponsor with close informal ties to the government. Exploitation of such ties, sub-rosa payoffs, and failure to use formal channels and regulations were practices deemed both necessary and legitimate.[4] The ingrained desire to avoid face-to-face communication and conflict and the eagerness of Arab villagers to establish themselves as clients in relationship to a patron who could perform the function of *wasta* were easily exploited by the Israeli regime in the implementation of its cooptive policies.

The point is not that, given these social structural, historical, or cultural factors and wanting to control the Arab population, the government of Israel was bound to employ a strategy of cooptation in order to penetrate or gain access to Arab society, or that if implemented such a strategy was bound to succeed. Rather, the point is that other forms of traditional social organization, different historical traditions, or alternative cultural predilections would have been much less conducive to the success of such a strategy and would have made it more likely that the regime would have had to adopt more unwieldy, expensive methods of surveillance and resource extraction.[5]

Generally speaking, the penetration of Arab society by the Israeli regime has been accomplished by the cooptation of two types of opinion leaders and authority figures. Traditional patriarchs and other notables were the first and most important targets. The structural factors discussed above helped to ensure and continue to support the success of these efforts. However, the traditional social structure and traditional patterns of authority relations have been gradually eroding, and with the passage of time a substantial stratum of educated Arabs capable of interpreting political and economic issues for their fellow villagers according to modern criteria has developed. Although still closely tied to their hamulas in the context of village politics, these educated Arabs have represented a potential focus for nontraditional, dissident forms of political activity. At least one factor on the structural level has been crucial in encouraging the successful and relatively inexpensive cooptation of these elites— their near total dependence on the Jewish sector for white-collar jobs (described in some detail in Chapter 5). As a consequence of this economic dependence the younger, more educated elites have found themselves powerfully attracted to offers or promises of teaching positions with the Ministry of Education or of deputy posts in the various government and Histadrut agencies which operate in the Arab sector, regardless of the political strings inevitably attached to such jobs.

Cooptation: *The Institutional Level of Analysis*

Generally speaking, the cooptation of Arab elites has not been institutionalized. As is argued in the last section of this chapter, coopted Arabs—elders and sheiks, school administrators, scoutmasters, recently accredited Zionist party members, Waqf trustees, assistants in various departments and agencies responsible for Arab affairs, etc.—have been dealt with in a highly instrumental and summary fashion. These individuals have not, as a result of their connections with the government, participated in significant socialization processes leading to conformity with or commitment to any particular set of political norms. Nor has there emerged a coherent ideology which they have been expected to adopt and espouse.[6] Rather, cooptation has been rooted in the regime's belief that material inducements, threats of material deprivation, and individual self-interest are the keys to the successful manipulation of Arab elites.

However, before a discussion of the various types of payoffs which the regime has used to coopt Arab elites and the types of services which the coopted have been expected to perform, some attention needs to be directed to the role which the local council system of municipal government has played in verticalizing authority relationships within hamulas. As noted, the hierarchical authority structure of hamulas has been particularly conducive to the success of a strategy of cooptation. Some hamulas, of course, were more hierarchically ordered than others, depending in large measure upon the relative concentration of wealth in the hands of one or another extended family and/or the presence or absence of charismatic leaders. Traditionally, though, decisions were made for the hamula in collective fashion by a relatively small group of elder representatives of various extended families.

However, the establishment of a local council in "Qabila," the name given the Little Triangle village analyzed by Abu-Ghosh, subjected this relatively democratic feature of hamula social organization to serious strain. Since most hamulas were unlikely to be able to elect more than one or two members to the local council, the groups of elders in Qabila were constrained to choose formal leaders and representatives of their hamulas where none had previously existed. Thus, in Qabila at least, the local council system encouraged not only the proliferation of politically active hamulas (see Chapter 4) but also the verticalization of power within them.[7]

Cooptation: The Programmatic Level of Analysis

THE CAPTURE OF TRADITIONAL ELITES

Although most military governors were drawn directly from the ranks of the regular army, several of the officials responsible for the Arab sector in the years immediately following the establishment of the state, including Yehoshua Palmon (the first adviser to the prime minister on Arab affairs), had worked before 1948 in intelligence units associated with the Jewish Agency's Political Department.[8] These men were well acquainted with the social and political mores of Arab Palestine and had personal connections with a good many powerful clan leaders and religious dignitaries. In terms of the Arab minority problem per se, the view of these men was that, all things being equal, Israeli Arabs were likely to be enemies of the state, but that through appeals to the individual self-interest of traditional Arab elites the loyalty and good behavior of the Arab population could be assured—"loyalty" defined as abstinence from independent forms of political activity and "good behavior" made manifest by the delivery of votes to the ruling Labor Party.

In their efforts to bring order and control to the Arab sector in the first years of statehood, the Military Administration, the adviser's office, and other organs of the regime with responsibility for Arab affairs established contacts with traditionalist leaders in each of the various Arab towns, villages, and Bedouin encampments. Not to their surprise, those officials soon found that hamula elders, local notables, large landowners, mukhtars, Bedouin sheiks, religious functionaries, etc., were convenient and tractable allies. Each notable tended to hope that his connection with representatives of the regime would increase his influence and the standing of his kinship or religious group. Each feared that refusal to cooperate would result in the ascendance of antagonistic clans or personal enemies. Moreover, despite the nationalist character of the historical struggle between Arabs and Jews in Palestine, the type of political arrangements offered by the Israeli regime to notables on the local level were entirely consonant with their political culture and conformed to long-standing traditions concerning authority relations between villagers, local elites, and the central government.

The cooptation of Arab elites, both on the village and tribal level and on the level of country-wide religious denominations and national Knesset elections, was achieved by means of a careful distribution of favors, privileges, and special dispensations. These "side payments" were made not only to secure the loyalty and the services of individual patriarchs, *qadis* (religious judges), sheiks, or notables, but also as part of a general effort to strengthen the traditional social structural forms which made cooptation such a convenient, inexpensive, and effective technique for gaining access to the Arab population. The government, said Yosef Waschitz in 1950, "appears as a foreign regime, separated from the people and *supporting a class of intermediaries—a class which is concerned with personal favors and which has no sense of public responsibility. . . .* the old local leaders—those who did not flee—remain as the primary point of connection between the Government and the public."[9]

By the second Knesset election in 1951 a clear pattern of patron-client relationships between the regime and traditional Arab elites was visible. In 1953 one young Israeli political scientist and Mapai member was moved to take his party severely to task for failing to live up to its progressive traditions in the Arab sector. The party, he said, had chosen

to turn its back on precisely the small progressive and activist elements in the Arab sector . . . and addressed itself instead . . . to other groups from whose ranks it drew candidates for the minorities lists. So it happens that the representatives of the Arab minority who have supported the policies of Mapai in both the First and Second Knessets were not representatives of the working class, or of agricultural laborers, or of the fellahein. To a man they are representatives of the effendi class—

large landowners, Sheiks, heads of hamulas, notables, and religious leaders—Moslem, Christian, and Druze.

. . . It is ironic that our support in the Arab sector derives from precisely the most reactionary circles . . .[10]

As one former military governor put it: "In the 1950's we accepted the existing social institutions as given and we acted to preserve them. The policy of preserving the hamula social structure remained more or less the same throughout the existence of the Military Government."[11]

Nor did the regime's desire to preserve these traditional social forms disappear with the Military Administration's abolition in 1966. Although officially the government has been "neutral" with respect to the intergenerational conflict,[12] Henry Rosenfeld, writing in 1968 and 1969, observed that

Politically, the government often continues to support patriarchal leadership, to generate and manipulate hamula factionalism, or to promote young men who are prepared to support "traditional" relations between it and the village, even while the conditions that initially produced and perpetuated these forces have practically disappeared.[13]

The authorities exert pressure on the villagers to maintain the existing order, they support the traditional hamulas and grant favors to their representatives; manipulation from outside of patriarchal groups and factions assures their continuance on the inside.[14]

The distribution of special favors by the Military Administration, both as a reward for cooperative behavior and as a means of strengthening the traditional social structure, took many varied forms, from seats in the Knesset to the most trivial sorts of political patronage. In return for services rendered, officials of the Military Administration might, for example, promise to remove "rumors" accumulating in files kept on certain hamula members,[15] to make farm machinery available for purchase at half the market price,[16] to arrange for the speedy transport of a sick relative to a hospital in a Jewish city,[17] to approve an application for entrance into Israel of relatives who had fled in 1948,[18] or to permit the marriage of an Israeli Arab man to a woman from the Jordanian-controlled West Bank.[19] Arab merchants who voiced open support for the Military Administration might be issued special permits exempting them from the necessity of regularly reapplying for licenses to keep their stores open.[20] In cooperation with the Histadrut Arab Department and the Arab Department of the Ministry of Labor the Military Administration might grant patriarchal leaders control over which villagers were to receive travel permits to work outside their localities.[21] In the 1950's the Military Administration, again in close cooperation with other government agencies, commonly allocated vouchers for relief work to hamula elders for distribution at their discretion.[22] Religious dignitaries might be accorded the right to grant or veto permission for the much-desired "Christmas visits" (between Israeli Arabs and their relatives) which took place annually at the Mandelbaum Gate in Jerusalem.[23]

With the formation of local councils in many Arab villages the Arab Department of the Ministry of the Interior, in cooperation with representatives of the Military Administration, decided how many representatives from which hamulas would be appointed to the first council, who they would be, and who the chairman of the council would be. In 1974 the policy of the ministry's Arab Department was to appoint council members only after consultation with the adviser's office, the Ministry of Police, and the Arab departments of the Ministries of Agriculture and Education.[24] With the passage of time the authorities have proved themselves to be extremely adept at influencing the course of intravillage politics. A common practice has been to provide cars and drivers to cooperative hamulas so that they may take their members to the polls "in style."[25] Cash payments for "campaign expenses" are also made available, along with promises of increased government aid.[26] Also, different organs of the government have established patron-client relations with different hamulas or hamula groups in the same village. Thus one clan may receive aid and promises from representatives of the Arab Department of the Labor Party while its arch rival receives similar support and corresponding promises from representatives of the Office of the Adviser to the Prime Minister on Arab Affairs, the Ministry of the Interior Arab Department, or the Arab Department of the Histadrut.[27]

For hamula leaders, participation in and control over the local council are matters of vital importance. A hamula left out of the governing coalition may well find itself paying a very high proportion of municipal taxes.[28] Participation in the ruling coalition and especially control over the chairmanship of the local council are likely to provide all sorts of benefits—including, with the approval of the Arab Department of the Ministry of Education, the right to hire and fire school administrators and teachers.[29] The ruling coalition may also choose subcontractors for public works sponsored by the council, decide near whose homes electrical transmission lines will be built, where roads in the village will be paved, and so on.[30] In villages without local councils, local headmen, or "trustees," as they are called by the Ministry of Interior, are assigned control over various registration procedures and over the distribution of various permits and licenses in return for their cooperation with the authorities.[31]

The departments of the Ministry of Religion in charge of Moslem, Christian, and Druse affairs also make full use of their powers to appoint imams, caretakers of religious facilities, *qadis*, marriage registrars, etc., to reward supporters of the government and to strengthen the position of traditionalist forces.[32] Most important in this connection is the government's control over the appointment of trustees for the Moslem Waqf. As a matter of practical policy it is the Adviser to the Prime Minister on Arab Affairs who has the major say in these appointments, and political considerations are crucial in the choices which he makes.[33] The appointment of ultra-orthodox feudalist figures as trustees of the Waqf in Acre, Jaffa, Haifa, Nazareth, Ramle, Lod, and Shfar-Am is an important aspect of the government's overall policy of cultivating and preserving traditionalist elements in the Arab sector.

Among the Druse this policy has found expression not only in the assignment of responsibility for the community's religious endowments to feudalist elements but also in the appointment of traditionalist elders to a committee empowered to grant religious exemptions from military service to Druse young men.[34] The government's decision to establish an independent judicial system for the Druse in 1962 also "helped to strengthen the traditional structure of the Druze sect, in spite of the dissensions surrounding competition for influential positions within the judiciary."[35]

On a formal basis local council chairmen, village trustees, and appointed clerical personnel receive stipends and a variety of other emoluments: paid vacations, junkets, conferences, expense accounts, etc.[36] But even more important than the formal prerogatives, stipends, and benefits granted to these individuals is the informal access which they can gain to important officials in the Jewish sector, such as regional representatives of the adviser's office, functionaries in the Arab departments of the large Jewish parties, the Jewish staff of the Histadrut's Arab Department, regional officers of the Ministry of the Interior, and so on. These are the officials who exercise direct control over the distribution of government funds in the Arab sector, the granting of various licenses and permits, and the hiring and firing of white-collar employees in those branches of the government that serve the Arab sector.[37] They also constitute the only sources for Israeli Arabs of *protectzia* or "pull," an all-important commodity in the context of Israel's big-city machine style bureaucracy. The personal ties which local notables can develop with these officials enhance their own status and their reputations as men who can "get things taken care of." For educated Arabs entertaining ambitions of working in government ministries or landing good jobs in the private sector, a close relative with such connections is practically a necessity. Such a reputation is also in and of itself likely to be of material importance, since it puts the individual in a position to charge substantial fees to villagers seeking intercession on their behalf in connection with some private petition or problem.

The range and importance of special favors and privileges granted to cooperative Bedouin chiefs by the government are especially striking. In the early years of Israel's existence Bedouin sheiks were permitted to charge fees to tribe members and fellahin in return for registering their names with the government. Since then, recognized Bedouin sheiks have also been given authority as "trustees" to register births and deaths, validate marriages, sign affidavits, etc. Typically, fees are charged for these services as well. In addition many heads of Bedouin tribes have been granted monopoly rights over the sale of food to members of their tribes. Bedouin sheiks have also been given control over the leasing of land to Bedouin, the distribution of relief work, and (during the tenure of the Military Administration) the issuance of travel permits. In the 1950's extra lands leased to Bedouin sheiks were often sublet to tribe members on a sharecropping basis. More recently the authorities have endeavored to reward cooperative Bedouin leaders by building schools near their encampments and by giving special preference to their sons in regard to university admission. All in all the prerogatives granted to Bedouin sheiks by the government have given these men enormous power over the lives of their tribes. A corollary of this point is that good relations with the authorities became absolutely necessary for a Bedouin chief to function effectively as "sheik."[38]

Most conspicuous among the traditional Arab elites coopted by the regime have been those notables chosen by the Labor Party's "Arabists"[39] to head the Knesset lists affiliated to the Labor Party.[40] Competition among prominent Israeli Arab personalities for "safe places" on these "minorities' lists" (as they are known) is intense, for membership in the Knesset has been, in terms of status and *protectzia*, the most an Arab can hope to achieve in Israeli society.[41]

The affiliated Arab lists, endowed by their Jewish creators in the Labor Party with such names as "Agriculture and Development," "Progress and Work," and "Cooperation and Brotherhood," are organized not as political parties but as "vote-catching tactics."[42] These lists are not and do not claim to be political parties. No membership exists; the names of the lists often change from election to election; their composition is determined immediately prior to Knesset elections.[43] Concerning the role of affiliated Arab lists in the Knesset election of 1965, Jacob Landau commented as follows:

> As formerly, the fact that the Alignment [i.e., the Labor Party] had formed slates of Arab candidates and was sponsoring their electioneering, both administratively and financially, conditioned the character of their propaganda. The candidates decided on a small number of local matters; otherwise the platform of both allied lists extolled the achievements of the Alignment and the advantages in supporting it and its Arab lists, as stabilizing factors. Such delicate subjects as the military administration and the Arab refugees were avoided. Other parties (chiefly RAQAH, MAPAM and RAFI) were attacked. However, these platforms were already well known, and greater importance attached to canvassing, personal visits, house meetings, and the like.[44]

The candidates chosen to run on safe places on these lists have been, uniformly, members of the upper stratum of Israeli Arab society: men who have commanded large religious, sectional, or kinship followings. For example, one Labor Party–affiliated Arab who has been elected to the Knesset, Seif a-din Zuabi, a Moslem landowner, is the leader of a large group of related hamulas in the Nazareth area. Other Moslems who have been elected to the Knesset on lists affiliated to the Labor Party are Salah Salim Suleiman, a prominent Galilean Arab; Faris Hamdan, a large landowner and former chairman of the Baka el-Gharbiyeh local council; Ahmed al-Daher, scion of an old and powerful landowning family in the Galilee; De'ib Obeid, a vegetable merchant and hamula leader from the Little Triangle; Mahmoud Nashef, a wealthy clothing merchant, also from the Little Triangle; and Hamad Abu Rabiah, a Bedouin sheik from the Negev. Of the Christian Arabs elected to the Knesset on lists affiliated to the Labor Party, Amin Jarjura was the head of a large and rich family in Nazareth, while Elias Nakhle, head of the powerful Nakhle clan in the Galilean village of Rama, and Masad Qasis, a large landowner from the western Galilee, were both chosen by the Labor Party primarily because of the strong support which they could garner among Greek Catholics. Of the Druse notables elected to the Knesset at various times on lists affiliated to the Labor Party, Jabber Muadi (deputy minister of agriculture, 1976) is a sheik from the Druse village of Yirka, Salah Khnefes was a Druse chieftain from the Arab town of Shfar-Am, and Labib Abu Rukun had been the chairman of the local council of Ussifiyah, a large Druse village atop Mt. Carmel.

Members of the Arab upper class exhibiting tendencies toward independence in their political stands have been excluded from the affiliated lists.[45] Moreover, failure on the part of these members of Knesset to support Labor Party policies with sufficient vigor, or the determination by Labor Party Arabists that a rotation of notables would yield a larger pro-Labor Arab vote, has been enough to result in their dismissal and the substitution of rival traditionalist candidates.[46]

THE GOVERNMENT AND THE DRUSE: CULTIVATING A SPECIAL RELATIONSHIP

The disproportionate number of Druse elected to the Knesset (as compared to the number of Moslem or Christian Arabs) is reflective of another aspect of the regime's cooptive policies. Government efforts to deepen the divisions between the Druse and other non-Jewish groups in Israel (see Chapter 4) have been accompanied by the extension of special benefits to the Druse community as a whole—part of an overall attempt to coopt the Druse on a communal basis—to convince them that by virtue of their "special relationship" with the regime life in Israel represents the best of all possible worlds.[47] As noted in Chapter 4 the government's policy in this regard has been implemented on the symbolic level by means of oft-repeated expressions of commendation for the Druse community's loyalty, bravery, and good citizenship. Official encouragement and widespread publicity have been provided for the annual pilgrimage of the Druse to their shrine at the Horns of Hittin in eastern Galilee. Traditionally, Israeli flags have abounded at the festival and high-ranking government officials have addressed the crowd concerning the unique role and honored status of the Druse community in the state of Israel. Another sign of the government's favor was the appointment (as of 1976) of five *qadis* for 40,000 Druse, as contrasted to six *qadis* for 420,000 Israeli Arab Moslems.

Equally if not more important has been the preference shown to Druse villages in regard to economic development. Statistics made available in 1960 show that between 1951 and 1959 the four Druse local councils in Israel received government contributions which exceeded, by an average of I£ 75,000, the revenues raised by the villagers themselves. The same statistics show that predominantly Moslem and Christian villages received an average of I£ 5,500 *less* in government contributions than the revenues raised by the villagers themselves.[48] According to the Ministry of the Interior district officer in charge of Arab affairs in western Galilee, Druse local councils received an average of I£ 30 per capita in government loans and grants in 1973/1974 compared to I£ 10 per capita for "cooperative" Moslem and Christian villages.[49] Of the five Arab villages in 1974 in which sizable light industries were located, three (Daliyaat al-Carmel, Ussifiyah, and Yirka) were Druse. Of the twenty-two factories operating in the Arab sector in 1976, eight—employing 38 percent of the total 1,405 workers—were located in Druse villages.[50]

The government has also shown a marked preference for Druse in hiring relatively high-level deputies, assistants, and advisers in the Arab departments of government ministries and Labor Party organs. The number of Druse in these positions far outweighs their proportion (8 percent) of the total non-Jewish population of Israel. In 1976 the highest-ranking non-Jew in the Arab Department of the Ministry of Education and Culture, Salman Falah, was a Druse. In 1974 two Druse served in the western Galilee, one as the assistant to the district officer for Arab affairs of the Ministry of the Interior, the other as the assistant to the director of the Labor Party's Arab branch. The first non-Jew to serve in any capacity in the Office of the Adviser to the Prime Minister on Arab Affairs, Mulla Ismaili, was a Druse. Zeidan Attassi, who became the first Arab to serve in the Israeli foreign service when he was attached to Israel's legation at the United Nations in 1976, was also a Druse.[51]

THE CAPTURE OF NONTRADITIONAL ELITES

The passage of time, the introduction of universal education in the Arab sector, and the exposure of the Arab population to all forms of mass media and to Israeli-Jewish lifestyles have resulted in the slow but steady erosion of traditional norms and patterns of behavior. Although parochial distinctions among the Moslem, Druse, and Christian communities are still meaningful, although patriarchal leadership remains dominant on the village and tribal level,[52] and although traditional customs and laws concerning inheritance, bride price, marriage, honor, and chastity continue to be enforced,[53] nevertheless, regular attendance at churches and mosques among young Arabs has become rare and various surveys have shown that personal commitment to traditional values among Israeli Arabs has been severely weakened.[54] Moreover, although the Arab rural lumpenproletariat remains dependent on the traditional village social structure (see Chapter 5), egalitarianism within kinship groups has increased with the contracting amount of agricultural land held by patriarchal types and with the substantial earnings of young Arab laborers in Jewish cities.[55]

Especially since the mid-1960's, the regime has shown itself to be sensitive to these processes.[56] While maintaining the support of members of the traditional elites, government and Histadrut officials responsible for the Arab sector have been careful as well to cultivate close ties with younger, more educated Arabs — grooming them to replace the older generation of notables as it gradually passes from the scene.[57] To these younger men the government and in particular the Histadrut have presented themselves as sympathetic to the frustrations of the new "modern" generation of Arabs as it confronts traditional social and political forces. To quote from a booklet published by the Histadrut's Arab Department:

... in 1959 the Arab and Druze workers became full members of the Histadrut. . . . They were afforded the feeling that within the Histadrut they were equals with all other working people. Here they know full well that the rights they enjoy do not come from the charity of the "effendi" . . . but derive from the strength of the big family of Arab and Jewish workers that is the Histadrut. Here . . . the Arab worker found not only a community of interest but obtained his first notion in equality, mutual aid, democracy, cooperation, and even a primary understanding of the complexities of socialism. All the forementioned phrases—so alien to the Arab way of life—are now being constantly integrated on an increasing scale into Arab society.[58]

Under the auspices of the Histadrut's Arab Department, an elaborate array of organizations and programs has been created in order to provide Arab Histadrut members with services, which for the most part are not available to Arabs, as a matter of standard procedure, from the general (Jewish) offices of the Histadrut. In the context of these activities the Histadrut, in cooperation with the Information Center—Arab Branch (attached to the Office of the Adviser to the Prime Minister on Arab Affairs), has been able to recruit hundreds of ambitious young Arabs willing to serve its interests in the Arab sector.[59] Such individuals are given positions, for example, as clerks and directors of branches of the Histadrut-owned Workers' Bank located in Arab towns; as officials in the Audit Union of Arab Cooperatives; as secretaries for Arab affairs attached to Histadrut labor councils in various municipalities; as scoutmasters for the Histadrut-sponsored Arab scout movement; as assistants and deputies in Histadrut Arab Department regional offices in Nazareth, Acre, Taiybe, and Beersheba; or as coordinators of Histadrut-sponsored sports activities (Hapoel) in Arab villages. Many Arab intellectuals have been given employment by the Histadrut as assistant editors and staff writers for *al-Anba*, Israel's Histadrut-sponsored Arabic daily newspaper, or as writers for Histadrut-sponsored Arabic periodicals. Educated Arabs also work for the Histadrut-owned Arabic Book Publishing House, which publishes Arabic journals and textbooks and the works of selected Israeli Arab authors and poets. A review of Histadrut activities in a sample year (1969) told of forty branches of the Hapoel Sports Organization in the Arab sector, one hundred Arab young men trained as youth leaders, 6,500 Arab boys and girls in the Histadrut's Arab scouts, seventeen Arab secretaries connected to Histadrut labor councils, 280 scholarships granted to Arab high school and university students, and fifty-two meetings, exchange visits, and excursions sponsored by the Arab Department's Society for Understanding and Friendship.

Among the most prominent of the Histadrut's Arab protégés, or "keymen," as they are called by Histadrut officials,[60] are Yusuf Khamis, a former member of Knesset on the Mapam list who now serves as deputy chairman of the Histadrut's Arab Department; Mahmoud Abassi, assistant editor of *al-Anba*, who was chosen to head an unsuccessful Labor Party affiliated list in 1977; Salim Joubran, a veteran official in charge of Arab affairs for the Histadrut's labor council in Haifa who has also served as chairman of the Histadrut-sponsored Arab-Jewish Association to Promote Fraternity and Peace; and George Saad, a Labor Party operative in Nazareth and chairman of the Nazareth Workers Council. The positions which men such as these hold, the numerous lectures and speeches which they are called upon to deliver, the informal associations with important Jewish figures which they develop, and their travels abroad, besides assuring them of a comfortable standard of living, also translate into prestige and influence in the Arab sector. Although these Arab officials seldom if ever exercise authority over matters pertaining to Jews or to the Jewish sector in general, nonetheless they represent the highest levels of achievement which so far have been open to the young generation of Israeli Arabs. Drawing upon the examples of men such as these the Histadrut stresses that for ambitious young Arabs roads to advancement, under its aegis, *are* open. The following quotes are taken from official descriptions of the careers of several Arab protégés of the Histadrut.

PROFILE OF AN ARAB COOPERATOR

The story of "Abu Kamal" (Zaki Abdullah Awisat), the cooperator from the prosperous village of Bak'a el-Gharbiyeh in the Central Region is indeed a tale of success. . . . On completing his schooling he joined his father in the fields of the family holdings. In the early 1950's he was appointed to the first Local Council set up to run the village affairs. Two years later elections were held and "Abu Kamal," as he came to be known among his friends, was returned to the Council, and subsequently elected as Vice-Chairman. A year later the Chairman of the local Council resigned and he succeeded him.

In 1958 Zaki Abdullah Awisat was chosen by the Arab local councils to represent them at the Union of Local Authorities in Israel. The body deputized him as part of its delegation to the Congress of the International Union of Local Authorities held in West Berlin in the latter half of 1958. On his return home Mr. Awisat entered the new phase of his activities, concerning the Cooperative Movement. . .

. . . later . . . Mr. Awisat was elected the first Chairman of the Arab Cooperative Audit Union . . . over the ensuing years, Mr. Awisat devoted himself to furthering the ideals of cooperation among the villagers in other areas. He became a sort of Father of Israeli Arab Cooperation. . . . By his personal example, the idea of cooperation has spread widely throughout Israeli Arab rural areas and has wrought many changes in that society.[61]

PROFILE OF ARAB TRADE UNION SECRETARY

Hanna Sussan is a typical Arab trade union keyman. . . . Until 1949 he struggled to make a living as an independent furniture maker and building worker. However, he enjoyed his first job security when obtaining employment with Solel Boneh, the large Histadrut contracting agency. The Building Workers Union provided a series of on-job vocational training courses and gradually he rose up the ladder of skills until he became a building foreman. In 1963 he was chosen by the Nahariya Labour Council to become Trade Union Secretary for all Arab workers in Western Galilee.[62]

PROFILE OF AN ARAB YOUTH LEADER

Zeidan Abu Attasheh, 29, is a typical youth leader drawn from the Druze village of Daliat-el-Carmel. . .

Young Ziedan completed his secondary education in Nazareth and on graduation proceeded to enlist alongside other young Druzes in the Israel Defence Forces. . . .

Upon his demobilization in 1963 he was chosen as secretary and instructor of the youths of the Druze community on the Carmel range for the Histadrut Noar-Haoved working youth organization.

. . . The Histadrut policy-makers had their eye on the young Druze and not much later on Zeidan was called to attend a special Histadrut training course for Arab and Druze youth leaders which lasted four months.

Then Zeidan . . . decided . . . to attend the Haifa University College. He chose as his subjects Arab language and literature, and political science. Zeidan managed to combine his youth work and his student life and in 1968 graduated with a B.A. degree. By then his talents had gained wider recognition, and he was asked to be in charge for Noar-Haoved of all its activities among Druze youth throughout Israel. It was his job to travel around the country, supervising the work of a number of local youth leaders.

    ... It may be safely said that Zeidan Abu Attasheh is looking far beyond his native village on the Carmel range, and indeed it is to be expected that ambitious, hard-working young men of his kind will surely lead their community in the future.[63]

In 1970 a five-year plan was adopted by the Arab Department of the Histadrut. One of its central aims was to make "a concentrated effort to form a large group of young active Arabs to serve as a fulcrum of the Histadrut in the Arab sector."[64] In response to unrest in the Arab sector generated by suppression of Land Day demonstrations in March 1976, the Histadrut Arab Department undertook a study of the Histadrut's policies toward Arabs. Among its primary recommendations were the hiring of one hundred Arab intellectuals by the Histadrut and its affiliated organizations, the development of a three- to four-month training program for "activists" to be chosen from various Arab villages, and substantial increases in scholarships and housing subsidies for Arab university students.[65]

Although the Histadrut is the primary vehicle for the cooptation of young potential Arab elites, the Arab Department of the Labor Party and the Office of the Adviser to the Prime Minister on Arab Affairs have also tried to adapt their techniques, contacts, and payoffs to the fact of the slow erosion of traditional authority structures in the Arab sector. The most common technique used by the adviser's office to coopt educated Arabs has been the recommendation of selected young, ambitious Arabs for employment as civil servants in the Arab departments of government ministries. In fact, since Shmuel Toledano assumed the adviser's post in 1966, the integration of university-educated Arabs into the ranks of the civil service has been characterized as the most important challenge facing the regime vis-à-vis the Arab minority: "Regarding the Arab sector, the serious problem facing us today is not the economic gap between Jews and Arabs. This gap *was* the problem, but the two five-year development plans which we implemented closed the gap and solved that problem. Today the main problem is the integration of educated Arabs into government offices."[66] In accordance with this aim the adviser's office has cultivated an image of itself as deeply concerned with the welfare of Arab intellectuals, and has coupled this image with a portrayal of most government ministries as distrustful of Arabs and willing to grant opportunities to non-Jews only as a result of pressure from the adviser's office. In a pamphlet written in early 1977 a spokesman for the adviser's office addressed this problem under the heading of the "Integration of Educated Arabs":

The number of high-school and university graduates in the Arab community is constantly increasing. For various social and occasionally even psychological reasons, many educated Arabs fail to get appropriate jobs, even though there is no unemployment in this sector of the population. Despite the economic difficulties facing the country at this time and the decision to freeze civil service employment, the government has decided to further integration of educated Arabs and expressed this purpose by creating 24 new civil service jobs of top and medium rank to be manned by educated Arabs. Naturally, a problem of this kind cannot be solved by integration in the Civil Service, which employs about 3 percent of Israel's work force. The solution must come through integration in appropriate jobs in the private sector, various institutions and organizations, and a positive attitude towards their social absorption among the general public.[67]

Thus recent advisers have adopted the posture of representing the interests of the Arab minority in the councils of government and toward the Jewish public. Arab intellectuals, uncomfortable with the thought of advancing their personal interests by drawing upon the influence of traditional Arab elites who stand in good stead with the Jewish authorities, have been encouraged to place their hopes and trust in the adviser, his deputies, and the *protectzia* which they command.

In Chapter 1, reference was made to a study commissioned by the Office of the Adviser to the Prime Minister on Arab Affairs, entitled *A Survey of Israeli-Arab Graduates from Institutions of Higher Learning in Israel (1961–1971)*. The study was based upon comprehensive interviews conducted with 78 percent of all Arabs who received university degrees in Israel between 1961 and 1971.[68] Published in 1973, it included data concerning fields of study, career records, work satisfaction, attitudes toward promotion, etc. The study, which stressed the growing social and political influence of young educated Arabs in the affairs of their community, was designed to provide the authorities with detailed information on which to base their policies toward the rapidly expanding number of Arab university graduates. The study was also intended to draw public attention to the problem of the integration of Arab intellectuals into the civil service and the private Jewish sector and to the special efforts of the adviser's office to solve the problem.

The extent to which the private Jewish sector is a "closed shop" in regard to the employment of Arabs is paralleled also in most of the government–public sector. Except for the Ministry of Education and Culture, which employs a considerable number of Arab and Druse teachers and inspectors, the higher administrative echelons of the Ministries integrate only a few of the Arab graduates. They are to be found scattered among various Ministries—Justice (mainly judges), Interior, Religion, Labour, Welfare, Health, Communications, and Finance, and the Central Office of Information—most of them in departments dealing with Arab affairs.

. . . Special note should be made of the repeated efforts of the Prime Minister's Office to change this atmosphere. . .[69]

The adaptation of the Labor Party's Arab Department to the growing importance of the Arab intelligentsia and to the sharpening generational struggle within the Arab sector was apparent in its decision to permit Arabs to become official members of the party: In 1970 Druse were admitted into the ranks of the party; in 1973 eligibility was extended to all Arabs in Israel.

Arabs accepted for party membership have tended to be between the ages of thirty and forty-five. These are men who have demonstrated a commitment to work for the Labor Party in local and in Knesset elections but who had resented their subordination to older (often illiterate) traditionalist figures. The symbolic value attached to party membership is substantial among this generation of Arabs. During conversations with such men in 1974, the fact that they were *chaverim* (members) of the Labor Party was usually the first bit of information offered. Such declarations were often followed by the dramatic display of party membership cards. For its part the Arab Department of the Labor Party, as well as certain officials of the Histadrut's Arab De-

partment who provide assistance in these matters, have endeavored to increase the symbolic value of Labor Party membership
by prolonging the application process and by strictly limiting
the number of applicants accepted.[70]

In general the government's policy, as implemented by all its
various branches in the Arab sector, has been to shift the locus
of its commitment and support from older to younger Arabs at a
tempo which corresponds to the rate at which actual authority
and influence within the Arab sector is being transferred. Thus
in small villages, where elderly hamula leaders are solidly entrenched, patriarchal types are given a monopoly on government
contracts and support. In large villages and in Arab towns,
where levels of education are higher, the regime has directed
substantial attention to the emergence of "reformist lists" in local elections. These groups, although usually basing their electoral support on particular hamulas, have typically attempted to
win additional votes by sponsoring young educated villagers as
candidates for the local council and by criticizing village hamula
leaders for their petty feuds and their inability or refusal to
modernize village services or sponsor economic development.

The regime's first reaction to such lists was one of hostility.
Soon, however, government Arabists learned that candidates on
such lists could be relatively easily coopted. For example, Labor
Party support on the level of local elections and personal favors
could be traded for the allegiance of these lists during Knesset
elections. Labor Party Arabists also decided to encourage older
hamula leaders to integrate younger members of their clans into
their lists for local council elections. Abraham Oved, director of
the Labor Party's Arab branch in the Nazareth area, explained
his department's policy in this way:

In Arab villages in the Nazareth area the power of the hamulas is di-
minishing, but [hamulas] are still the primary political factors. In any
given village, though, we modify our approach depending on the influence of traditionalist or more modernist elements. . . . We organize
and finance lists for *all* our supporters. We never throw out the old
hamula leaders. We encourage them to make combinations between
old notables and the young men of their hamulas.[71]

The gradual transfer of power from the older generation of
traditional leaders to younger men still loyal to their clans and

still committed to a traditionalist style of inter-hamula local politics is reflected in the fact that since 1969 the number of reformist lists winning representation on Arab local councils has fallen sharply. In 1973, although local council elections were held in thirty-four villages, such a list won representation on only one Arab local council.[72] Given this trend, and on the basis of surveys showing that the average age of Arab local council members has fallen steadily since the late 1960's, the Ministry of the Interior observed that "hamulas have succeeded in adapting to the spirit of the times by placing on their lists a considerable number of young men who still remain faithful to their clans."[73]

SERVICES PROVIDED BY COOPTED ARABS

Thus far the discussion of programmatic cooptation has concentrated on specifying the types of elites targeted by the regime and the various types of payoffs that have been employed. Although the side payments to traditional elites and to younger educated Arabs have been insubstantial in terms of the regime's political and economic resources, it is clear that limited funding has been available for these activities and that much of the time and energy of officials responsible for the Arab sector has been devoted to the identification of tractable Arab leadership figures and their cooptation. The question remains, then, as to precisely how coopted Arab elites have repaid the regime for the attention, favors, and personal privileges which they have been afforded.

One type of service performed by Arabs hopeful of obtaining the favor of the authorities has been to supply information concerning the sympathies and actions of other Arabs, especially members of rival hamulas. Thus, according to an article in *al-Fajer*, an Arabic monthly published by Mapam in the late 1950's, certain Arabs of one Galilean village came to be known as "Wednesday men." "Why? Because the military governor comes to the village every Wednesday, and is immediately surrounded by villagers anxious to get into his good books by supplying information and gossip against their neighbors."[74] Detailed knowledge and careful cataloging of private conversations among Arabs were revealed in a warning delivered by the adviser to the prime minister on Arab affairs to Israel's Arab population in August 1960. The government, said Uri Lubrani, was resolved to "take measures against Arabs who slander Israel." The adviser went on to quote "one Arab" as saying "that 'he who kills Jews will go to Heaven,' 'someone' as expressing his regret that 'Eichmann hadn't slaughtered all the Jews,' 'someone' else as saying in a bus that he 'would gladly drink the blood of the Jewish dogs,' etc., etc. Mr. Lubrani added that these were just a few remarks out of hundreds that had been overheard, and that those who had made them were mainly young people who could be described as intellectuals."[75]

In 1974 the official in charge of the Information Center—Arab Branch, which is located directly adjacent to the Office of the Adviser to the Prime Minister on Arab Affairs in Jerusalem, described the work of his office as follows:

At one time our office was officially located in the Ministry of Education. Subsequently we were transferred to the Office of the Adviser to the Prime Minister on Arab Affairs, though at present we are under the formal jurisdiction of the Ministry of Information. Despite these organizational changes our mission has remained the same.

It has been our job to provide Toledano with information on exactly what is going on in different villages. We sponsor many activities in the Arab sector—lectures, field trips, seminars, conferences, and social programs for which we provide funds and other assistance. As a result we have many friends in the Arab sector—Arabs who understand what goes on in their villages and who will tell us who is ours.

I personally brief Toledano once a week on current developments in the Arab sector. Our office also provides information to the Arab Department of the Histadrut and the Arab departments of various ministries.[76]

In addition to the use of informers, the authorities have found less surreptitious methods of using their allies in Arab villages to gather information. For example, during and immediately after the Yom Kippur War in 1973, the Ministry of the Interior's Arab Department sent out requests to all local council chairmen in Arab villages to raise money for the Voluntary War Loan. As reported by the local council treasurer in one large Galilean village, the committee designated by the local council to collect the funds was required to submit a list of the names of all contributors and the amounts donated to Yoram Katz, representative of the Office of the Adviser to the Prime Minister on Arab Affairs for the northern district.[77]

Besides supplying information, Arabs enjoying the favor of the authorities have also been expected to help the government legitimize its authority among the Arab population and to lend their assistance to the regime in its struggle against dissident political activity in the Arab sector. Accordingly, in speeches, in official messages sent to Jewish leaders, and in articles published in the government-sponsored Arabic press, notables and religious dignitaries have striven to portray Israel as a democratic state which, having done much to raise the material standards of the Arab minority, deserves the loyalty and vigorous support of its Arab citizens.[78] In reference to the stringent security problems which Israel has faced, these notables have counseled Arab citizens to be patient in their demands for full equality and tactful in the presentation of their grievances. Arab support given to communist or other "extremist elements" would, they have warned, only poison the minds of Jews toward Arabs and diminish the possibilities for progress toward complete equality.

Despise them [the communists], for they want to destroy the present brotherly coexistence between the Jewish and Arab communities in Israel. Struggle against them, for they want to rob the workers of power. Fight them, for they want to rob the people of cooperation between the two communities in Israel for fighting. Boycott them, for they want to prevent Arabs from working in Jewish institutions. Destroy them, for they want unemployment to prevail in the Arab sector. . . . Desert them, for they want disagreement to take the place of harmony between the two communities. Despise them, for they want to disrupt the life of Israeli Arabs.[79]

Nearly all Israeli Arab spokesmen, including coopted Arabs, have criticized the expropriation of Arab lands. Many of the latter, however, have also cooperated with the regime in its efforts to legitimize the land transfers by persuading Arab landowners to accept compensation and by persuading internal refugees to participate in resettlement schemes.[80]

Perhaps the most striking instance of the regime's manipulation of coopted Arab notables to support and legitimize government policy in the Arab sector occurred in connection with the Knesset vote in 1963 on whether or not to abolish the Military Administration. Deeply resented by Israeli Arabs for the restrictions which it placed on their daily lives and opposed by several Jewish parties because of its partisan political activity on behalf of the Labor Party, the Military Administration was a topic of heated parliamentary debate during the early 1960's. On November 20, 1963, a crucial vote was taken on a bill that would have abolished it. The bill was defeated by one vote, 57 to 56. Two of the votes against abolition came from Arab members of the Knesset elected on lists affiliated to the Labor Party.[81]

Since 1967 the regime has been particularly concerned about the possibility of widespread cooperation between Israeli Arabs and Palestinian guerrilla groups.[82] Responding to the upsurge in Palestinian-sponsored terrorism following the 1967 war, coopted Arab elites were quick to vilify Israeli Arabs discovered to have abetted the guerrillas. They called upon the authorities to show no mercy toward Arab citizens engaged in such activities. Following a series of bombings in 1969, for example, the ruling coalition of the Nazareth city council gathered in special session to pass the following resolution: ". . . We demand striking with an iron hand against every criminal who took part in these acts. The city council reaffirms its identification and solidarity with all other citizens of Israel against terrorism. If it is proved that a number of Arab citizens were indeed involved in these terrorist attacks, then they display sick minds and we dissociate ourselves from their criminal deeds."[83]

A week prior to the General Strike called by the Communist Party in March 1976 to protest expropriation of Arab lands, the Arab members of the Knesset affiliated to the Labor Party published a joint statement referring to the strike's organizers as "a minority which does not represent the bulk of the Arab community." They appealed to fellow Arabs "to refrain from helping 'negative elements' to wreck the framework of coexistence and understanding that had been set up at great pains over the years."[84] Late in March Shmuel Toledano paid a visit to a gathering of Arab mayors in Shfar-Am. Following his visit the mayors passed by an overwhelming margin a resolution protesting the expropriation of land but opposing the strike. Although the action of the mayors drew warm words of praise from government Arabists, Taufik Ziad—Communist mayor of Nazareth and one of the prime movers behind the strike—called the resolution "a stab in the back of the Arab masses."[85] One of the religious dignitaries who expressed his opposition to the scheduled strike was Ali Rashidi, chairman of the board of trust-ees of the Moslem Waqf in Jaffa. In a telegram to the prime min-ister he stated, on behalf of the board of trustees, his belief that "the Israeli Government will ensure that those whose lands are expropriated will be given fair compensation, whether these owners be Arabs or Jews. The committee regards the expropria-tions as a local matter and are against those groups who are at-tempting to turn it into a political issue . . ."[86]

In the aftermath of the strike and the violence accompany-ing it, Jabber Muadi, a Druse member of the Knesset affiliated to the Labor Party, called a news conference. As reported in *Maariv*:

Deputy Minister of Agriculture, Druse Sheik Jabber Muadi, de-manded yesterday that Rakah be declared an illegal organization "on account of its subversive activities and its agitation of the country's Arab population."

During a news conference with parliamentary correspondents Sheik Muadi gave the extremist group "el-Ard" as an example of an organization that had been banned. Once banned it ceased to exist and did not go underground, though while it existed el-Ard did great dam-age through its agitation in the Arab street.

Member of the Knesset Muadi accused Rakah of not in any way struggling against the expropriation of land, Rakah only wanted to sow confusion and disorder among the Arab community in Israel. . . . He warned that freedom and democracy in Israel were being exploited for evil by Rakah and other extremist elements who, in spite of every-thing, failed to gain the support of the majority in the Arab sector. "Even Sadat purged Egypt of Communist organizations," he said.[87]

On the local level the political assistance provided to the regime by traditional Arab elites has been more concrete than that afforded by Arab notables on the national level. For exam-ple, Ministry of Education regulations, which apply to Jewish as well as Arab localities, require the signature of the chairman of the local council for the hiring and firing of teachers and school administrators. Cooperative local council chairmen are therefore very important to the regime in its use of such positions to pun-ish political dissidence or reward good behavior. In general the heavy hand of patriarchal authority was seen, first by the Mili-tary Administration and later by civilian agencies in charge of Arab affairs, as an effective means of blocking unwanted political organization or activity. Thus hamula leaders, held responsible for the behavior of their sons, grandsons, and nephews, and fearful of jeopardizing their special ties to the government, have used their authority and their control over economic resources to threaten or punish clan members engaged in political activities not directly supportive of the government. "The structure of social control among the Arabs," as one military governor commented, "is closed and tight. . . . That is why in the 1950's, at least, Arab youth did not engage in extremist activities. Their hamulas simply wouldn't let them."[88] Regardless of the gradual weakening of the traditional social structure, its effectiveness as a mechanism of control is still apparent in the discipline which hamulas continue to exercise over their members in local council elections. In Arab local council elections held in 1969, 72.5 percent of the votes cast went to hamula-sponsored lists. In 1973 this figure was 77.2 percent, and for the localities which held elections in 1975 and 1976 (excluding the city of Nazareth) it was 73.4 percent.[89] The resistance of the traditional social structure to modern and potentially dissident forms of political organization is reflected in the relative failure of communist organizers to penetrate small Arab villages or Bedouin encampments, where traditional norms and patterns of authority remain essentially unchallenged. In the 1973 Histadrut elections, for example, although Rakah received 27.0 percent of the votes cast by Arabs, it received only 15.3 percent in Bedouin encampments and in Arab villages with fewer than five hundred eligible voters, and 11.1 percent in the thirty localities where fewer than one hundred votes were cast.[90]

Cooptation of selected educated Arabs, in addition to providing the Arab departments of the government, the Histadrut, and the Labor Party with administrative talent, also gives the regime access to the coteries of relatives, friends, and admirers surrounding well-spoken, dynamic young Arabs. More important, however, in the calculations of those responsible for the Arab sector, has been the effective removal of potential leaders from the public arena in the Arab sector. For having accepted a sinecure with a government or Histadrut agency, having appeared on speakers' platforms with prominent government Arabists, and/or having campaigned among Arabs on behalf of a

Zionist party, politically attractive young Arabs are permanently sullied from an Arab nationalist point of view. Subject to stinging condemnation by the Communist Party as traitors and opportunists, these individuals find that their credibility as trustworthy spokesmen for the Arab minority as a whole has been severely impaired.

Up until 1974, at least, government Arabists remained convinced that, for all the talk among young Arabs about the need for nonpartisan cooperation for the rapid economic development of Arab villages and about the need for sources of independent political expression for the Arab community as a whole, educated Arabs engaged in sustained criticism of regime policies could be dealt with in much the same manner as the regime had dealt with their fathers and grandfathers—by appealing to their *personal* economic and political ambitions.

When we notice young Arab extremists condemning the government and engaging in some kind of political organizing or agitation, we don't automatically put them on a blacklist. We always want to talk to them, to understand their problems, to understand what's really bothering them. Very often it's something very simple. Sometimes we have to pay them with a job of some kind, sometimes other sorts of favors are more appropriate.

There is a danger here, however, that by giving things to such "troublemakers" we will encourage other Arabs to engage in similar activities so that they too will receive favors. . . . A certain equilibrium is needed.[91]

The director of the Arab Branch of the Labor Party in the western Galilee agreed that cooptation was the best method for preventing educated Arabs from joining Rakah or forming independent political groups, but he complained that the resources provided by the regime for this purpose had not kept pace with the growing need for such "candies."

To block the trend to Rakah and the formation of other nationalist groups we must take care of young Arabs. We must give them party membership, and [what might be called] "directed democracy."

First of all we must identify those who criticize us and then join them to us. Then we must open more clubs in Arab villages and hire young Arabs to staff them. Through such clubs we can provide additional funds for musical performances, folklore groups, films, lectures, trips, and other activities which they want—make them feel a little

"Israeli." After they get these things, they'll forget about their nationalism . . . of course we have been doing these things but just look at how many of our clubs are closed down and dusty—we need more funds and workers to do what is necessary.[92]

A few specific examples should clarify the kinds of quid pro quos that have emerged in the context of regime attempts to coopt potential Arab leaders among the *doar hatzair* (young generation). In the mid-1960's Nawaf Masalha, a native of an Arab village in the eastern Galilee, was one of the Communist Party's most promising young leaders. Although he was of a poor Moslem family he had developed a considerable personal following among Christian as well as Moslem Arabs in the eastern Galilee. Then after being approached by representatives of the Histadrut's Arab Department, he accepted a Histadrut scholarship to study at Tel Aviv University. By 1974 he was working full time for the Histadrut's Arab Department as a coordinator of Histadrut programs among Arab youth. As a *chaver* (member) of the Labor Party, he has stressed that positive changes can only come about if Arabs work from within the ranks of the party. He opposes the formation of independent Arab political organizations and works to counter the influence of Rakah among young Arabs. He has been to the United States twice on Histadrut-sponsored tours of American college campuses as a representative of the "new generation of Israel's Arab citizens."

Although a Druse, Kemal Kassem was considered an "extremist" by the regime in the mid-1960's. Partly as a result of a song which he wrote—"a very anti-Israel song"[93]—he was, for a time, ordered confined to his village. As a university student he participated along with other young, educated Druse in an attempt to organize an independent list for the Knesset, an attempt which failed in the face of strong Labor Party opposition.[94] In 1972 he helped organize a group of Druse mayors critical of the Ministry of the Interior's discriminatory policies toward non-Jewish local councils.[95] In 1974 Kassem accepted a post as special adviser to the minister of commerce and industry concerning the development of industry in the Arab sector. Four months after his appointment, and after receiving his Labor Party membership card, Kassem expressed confidence that the government had, indeed, "made a basic policy decision to industrialize the Arab sector." He went on to voice his hope that the Labor Party would soon decide to open the ranks of its affiliated lists to younger educated Arabs such as himself.[96] Describing the cooptation of Kassem, one Labor Party Arabist commented, "It's always happened that way. As soon as troublemakers are given some kind of official position, they always settle down."[97]

The process according to which specific "troublemakers" with leadership capacity are selected by the authorities for cooptation was illustrated in microcosm during a two-day student conference sponsored jointly by the Histadrut Arab Department and the Information Center—Arab Branch, which was held in May 1974 in a facility complete with athletic field, television, hotel-type accommodations, and swimming pool. The official purpose of the meeting was to enable Jewish and Arab students to explore problems associated with "Coexistence on the Campus." Several guest lecturers, both Jews and Arabs, made presentations. In most cases the formal presentations were followed by long and heated debates on the major issues of concern among Arab students. All the while representatives of the Histadrut Arab Department hovered in the background.

During the discussions, both inside and outside the lecture hall, two Arab students in particular stood out for the harshness of the language which they "dared to use" in front of government and Histadrut officials. While most Arab students who spoke couched their critical remarks in a somewhat apologetic tone, these two students—one from Tel Aviv University and one from the Hebrew University in Jerusalem—spoke of the "crimes of Israeli fascism" and condemned "Zionism as the root of the problem." Their bearing was sullen, rebellious, and disdainful. Among the other Arab students I heard murmurs of admiration and amazement at the behavior of these two, both of whom were known as activists in Arab student groups on their campuses. I was told by a few Arab participants that although they shared such sentiments they would be willing to discuss them with me only at another time and place.

At the last session of the conference Yaacov Cohen, director of the Histadrut Arab Department, presented the Histadrut's view that separate Arab student organizations on Israeli campuses were detrimental to Jewish-Arab coexistence. But, said Cohen, the Histadrut would be willing to set up "coexistence committees" on each of Israel's campuses and to pay salaries to staff members on these committees, provided that they included both Jews and Arabs in their membership. Pandemonium ensued. The participants began talking and arguing about how much money the Histadrut would provide, that it wouldn't be enough, that there would be political strings attached, etc. The uproar was such that Cohen was forced, literally, to yell: "200,000 Lira with no strings attached!"

An hour later television cameras from Israel's national broadcasting authority recorded interviews with the two outspoken Arab students mentioned above. They had both accepted paid positions as coordinators of "coexistence committees" on their respective campuses.[98]

In the final analysis, regardless of whether coopted elites are traditionalist or modernist, they have been expected to deliver the political support of their constituencies. In its most salient form such support has been measured in terms of votes cast in Knesset and Histadrut elections for the ruling Jewish parties and for Arab lists affiliated to these parties. In the nine Knesset elections held between 1949 and 1977 the Labor Party, on average, drew approximately 36 percent of the total Jewish vote. Among Arabs it received an average of approximately 53 percent.[99] Approximately 11 percent of the Labor Party's electoral strength has, on average, been drawn from the Arab sector.[100]

The significance of the Arab vote and its importance to the Labor Party have been magnified by two factors: the highly fragmented character of the political party system in Israel and the relatively small "floating vote" in Knesset elections, of which the Arab vote has constituted a very sizable proportion.[101] Indeed, the maintenance of the Military Administration in Arab areas beyond the mid-1950's was due almost entirely to the importance which Labor Party leaders assigned to the Arab vote and to the ability of the Military Administration to establish and protect the Labor Party's supremacy in the Arab sector.[102] This was why repeated attempts by the communists and Mapam to abolish the Military Administration before 1966 received the strong support of right-wing parties, including Herut, the National Religious Party, and the General Zionists. These parties resented the Labor Party's electoral stranglehold in Arab areas under the Military Administration's jurisdiction.[103] In fact, the weakening of the Military Administration in the early 1960's and its abolition in 1966 largely explain the substantial increase in support for the National Religious Party among Arab voters, beginning with the election to the Sixth Knesset in 1965. No longer blocked by military governors vigorously supportive of the Labor Party, the National Religious Party—a participant in every Israeli government coalition since independence—was finally able to translate control over the Arab departments of the Ministries of Religion, the Interior, and Social Welfare into significant electoral support in the Arab sector.[104]

For Arab elites, Knesset elections have traditionally represented tests of their continued value to the various officials from whom favors and privileges have come in the past and from whom, it is hoped, such benefits will come in the future. During election campaigns these men receive visits from those government officials with whom they have had "special ties"—officers of the Military Administration (before 1966) and/or representatives of the sponsoring Jewish party, the adviser's office, the Histadrut Arab Department, and Arab department officials from assorted ministries. In the context of Israel's complicated proportional electoral system the Labor Party especially has been able to make efficient use of its diversified organizational presence in the Arab community. For example, in the 1973 Knesset election the adviser's office contacted "its hamulas" to mobilize their support for the Labor-affiliated "Bedouin and Villagers List" headed by Sheik Hamad Abu Rabiah. The Arab Department of the Labor Party did the same vis à vis "its hamulas" on behalf of the affiliated list headed by Seif a-din Zuabi and Jabber Muadi. Meanwhile the Histadrut Arab Department, using its protégés in the Arab sector, concentrated on encouraging less traditionally oriented Arabs to vote directly for the Labor Party list.[105]

In addition to instructing local notables as to exactly which list their constituents are expected to support, these officials may also distribute checks to heads of families for amounts calculated on a per-vote-promised basis—checks which can be cashed only *after* election day.[106] Typically, once assemblies of adult male members of hamulas are convened, the hamula leaders distribute ballots for the list they have endorsed and urge those present to strengthen their clan and maintain its honor by casting their votes faithfully. In isolated villages and especially among the Negev Bedouin, where the regime has been particularly anxious to receive a strong show of support, local Arabs appointed by the government to serve as election registrars have been encouraged to use their positions to see that an overwhelming vote for the government is indeed recorded.[107]

Besides the delivery of votes, another important type of political support provided to the regime by coopted Arabs has been the positive representation of the role and status of Arabs in Israeli society. For foreign dignitaries or reporters anxious to learn what *Arab* Israelis think of their country, the government can, depending on the visitor's particular interests and background, arrange interviews with noncommunist Arab members of Knesset, young protégés of the Histadrut Arab Department, Moslem religious dignitaries, government-hired Arab radio and television personalities, or prosperous and cooperative local council chairmen. Such figures can also be relied upon to issue statements of support for the government during times of crisis. During and after the 1973 war, for example, efforts by Arab notables to raise money for the Voluntary War Loan and to organize volunteer work details in Arab villages were given wide publicity.[108] No more fervent a supporter of Prime Minister Begin's hard-line stance toward the Arab world can be found than Amr Nasser E-din, a Druse member of Knesset elected in 1977 on the Likud list.[109] Indeed, the ability of the Israeli government to project an image of its Arab minority as marvelously contented with a standard of living far above that of their brethren in Arab lands and as fully equal citizens in a kindly and liberal democracy has been due, in no small measure, to the persuasiveness of these Arab elites and their desire not to appear disloyal by voicing strong criticism of the regime to foreigners.[110]

The Druse community has played an especially significant role in regard to Israel's image abroad. Daliyaat al-Carmel and Ussifiyah, for instance, two Druse villages atop Mount Carmel, have served as model examples of clean, prosperous, and well-serviced minority villages. They have been the only two Arab localities in Israel to which the Ministry of Tourism has scheduled visits for foreign tourists. There is little doubt, however, that the most important contribution which the Druse community has made to the Israeli regime has been the conscription of its men into the armed forces. In 1955 a group of Druse notables requested that Druse men be drafted into the army as a token of Druse loyalty and gratitude. Since 1956 Druse men have been drafted into the army and, serving primarily in the "minorities regiment" and in the border police, Druse soldiers have played a direct role in the control of Israel's Arab population. The minorities regiment, for a long time, was posted in the northern Negev, where it patrolled the Bedouin reservation and combatted smuggling. The border police have often been used to enforce curfews and put down disturbances in Arab localities.[111]

Cooptation as a Component of Control

The discussion of segmentation (Chapter 4) stressed the isolation of the Arab minority from the Jewish sector and its internal fragmentation. Regarding dependence (Chapter 5), the absence of autonomous centers of economic power in the Arab sector and the reliance of the overwhelming majority of Arabs on the Jewish economy for their livelihood were stressed. This chapter has shown how the cooptation of Arab elites has helped prevent the development of independent leaders in the Arab sector, has contributed to the conservation of traditional Arab social structures, and has helped the regime extract important resources from the Arab population. Thus, promise of personal gain has been used to persuade potential organizers and leaders of independent Arab political groups to work instead for the benefit of the regime in general and the Labor Party in particular. Government support for conveniently cooptable traditional elites has helped maintain the dominant position of hamula leaders in local Arab affairs. Coopted Arabs have aided the regime by supplying information, votes, and various other forms of political support. In short, "cooptation" has served as a noncoercive means of gaining access to members of the Arab minority and as a vehicle for their effective manipulation.

7.
Control as a System and the Future of Jewish-Arab Relations in Israel

In the course of this analysis the interaction of segmentation, dependence, and cooptation as components in a system of control has been noted. In general, however, analysis has focused on the relationships among factors operating on different levels of analysis "within" any one particular component. The following pages more explicitly identify and describe synergistic relationships *among* the three components. Such a "systemic" perspective enhances understanding of the reasons for the stability of control and its low cost to the regime and also permits discussion of system change. It makes it possible to link structural and institutional aberrations to the particular problems which the regime confronts in its effort to maintain effective, low-cost control over the Arab population. Comparison of the two most likely combinations of regime responses to current challenges is followed by consideration of the long-run prospects for a breakdown of Jewish control over the Arab population or the guided transformation of Jewish-Arab relations into patterns more consonant with models of pluralism or consociationalism.

A comprehensive description of how segmentation, dependence, and cooptation reinforce one another would be tedious as well as somewhat redundant. Nonetheless, that these components have not operated independently of one another and that the overall effectiveness of Israel's control of its Arab population has derived in large measure from mutually reinforcing relations among them warrant emphasis.

Financially, for example, the organizational fragmentation of the Arab population has contributed importantly to the economic dependence of the Arab sector. Since the Arab community possesses no country-wide financial institutions, the liquid capital which Arabs have accumulated is primarily deposited in Jewish-owned banks and used, ultimately, for investment projects in the Jewish sector. As suggested in Chapters 4 and 5, the Jewish-Arab segmentation of Israeli society, especially on the institutional level, has resulted in channeling national development funds into the economic development of the Jewish sector. This in turn has reinforced the structural underdevelopment of the Arab sector and increased Arab economic dependence on the Jewish community. In addition, the geographical and residential isolation of Arabs in Israel means that Arab workers are laid off first in a recession and rehired last after a business upturn, because Arabs in general commute to work in Jewish cities, while labor exchanges in those cities are required to give preference to local workers.[1]

The impact in Arab villages of a 1972 change in the property tax law illustrates how the institutional and ecological isolation of the Arab community from the Jewish population increases its economic insecurity independently of regime efforts to accomplish this end. Under the terms of the new law, property taxes were increased. "Rural" and/or "agricultural" land was still taxed at a lower rate than "urban," "nonagricultural" land, but the definitions used to categorize land were changed. By administrative fiat, localities of five thousand or more inhabitants were said to comprise urban areas, while the definition of an agriculturalist was changed from "the owner of an agricultural farm in a rural area" to "the owner of an agricultural farm, but where the farm is in an urban area . . . the owner thereof only if at least 50 percent of his income in one of the preceding two tax years . . . is from agriculture."[2]

The debate over the change in the law, though heated and prolonged, never touched on its possible implications for the Arab population. Nor does the language of the new law discriminate between Arab and Jew[3] (though special tax advantages are available for cooperative and collective agricultural settlements—*moshavim* and kibbutzim—all of which are Jewish). Yet the new law, while only marginally affecting private Jewish landowners, has had an enormous impact in the Arab sector and is forcing many Arab landowners to sell their land.

Almost all Jewish farm land qualifies for low tax rates, since no cooperative or collective farming settlement has more than two thousand inhabitants, and private Jewish plantation owners derive most if not all of their income from farming.[4] However, as the Arab population has soared, the number of Arab villages with populations of more than five thousand increased to fifteen in 1976. These villages are classified as "urban areas." Furthermore, due to expropriations, inheritance practices, and increased living costs, most Arab landowners use their small plots only to supplement the wages earned on Jewish farms and in Jewish factories. Thus the holdings of large numbers of Arab landowners, though located in thoroughly "rural" areas and used exclusively for agricultural purposes, are taxed at rates posted for urban nonagricultural land. Unable to afford these property taxes, Arab landowners have increasingly found themselves faced with a choice between bankruptcy and sale of their land to the state or the JNF.[5]

As noted in Chapter 6 the dependence of educated Israeli Arabs on Jewish-controlled white-collar jobs has made their cooptation relatively easy and inexpensive. If a substantial number of such positions were available in Arab-controlled institutions or companies, then at the very least the rewards offered to cooperative high school and university graduates would have to be greater, not only financially but socially and politically as well. The absence of autonomous centers of economic power in the Arab sector combined with the physical and linguistic segregation of Arabs and Jews provides the regime with thousands of teaching positions in Arab villages which are ideal for the cooptation of young educated Arabs. The teachers in Arab primary, intermediate, and secondary schools continue to reside in their villages and continue to live under the influence of hamulaism and inter- and intra-hamula politics. Extremely vulnerable to the retribution of politically victorious but hostile hamulas, they come to depend on the Ministry of Education and Culture as well as on their own hamulas to protect them and their salaries, promotions, and benefits. Kept under close surveillance by school administrators, they know that the exhibition of "extremist tendencies" will likely result in their dismissal. Furthermore, because they draw their salaries from the government and because they must teach from a strictly enforced government syllabus, their teaching roles sully them, from a political point of view, in the eyes of the children and other villagers.[6] Nor, in the course of their careers, do Arab school teachers gain any expertise or influence whatsoever concerning events in the Jewish sector.

But there are many ways, besides the concentration of educated Arabs in the teaching professions, by which "dependence" reinforces "cooptation." The economic dependence of Arabs on Jewish agriculture and industry, has, as indicated in Chapter 5 encouraged Arab workers to remain loyal to their traditional kinship groups and to those patriarchal leaders most conveniently coopted by the regime. At the same time the desire of all Arab villagers for the introduction of various municipal services and other amenities found in Jewish localities has encouraged local leaders to look to the government for assistance in achieving these goals. The dependence of local leaders on connections with the Jewish authorities has been reinforced by the loss of agricultural land—i.e., that which traditionally constituted the economic foundation of the power and prestige of local Arab elites. Bereft of private economic security and knowing that they are soon likely to be replaced by the representatives of rival hamulas, local council chairmen and deputy chairmen have typically exerted themselves while in office to establish connections in the Histadrut, the Arab departments of Zionist parties, the Office of the Adviser to the Prime Minister on Arab Affairs, and/or various ministries so that when they leave office sinecures of some kind will be available for themselves or their sons.

Segmentation has also reinforced cooptation. As suggested in Chapters 4 and 6, the fragmentation of Arab villages into fiercely competitive hamulas forces clan leaders to protect themselves from the ascendancy of their opponents by seeking support from the government. Furthermore, the relative isolation of Israeli Arabs from the Jewish-Zionist political arena and the predominance of the Labor Party in almost all spheres pertaining to the life of the Arab minority has meant that, in general, competition among Jewish parties for the loyalty of Arab elites has not been particularly intense. In this context the rewards offered to Arab notables to induce cooperation have remained minimal.

Finally, cooptation itself has contributed to the continued dependence of the Arab minority on the Jewish sector as well as to the internal fragmentation of the Arab population. Having sought out and supported traditionalist elements in Arab villages, the government has in effect helped give power to those in the Arab community who are often least desirous of rapid social and economic development (including the introduction of cooperatives, the establishment of local industries, the consolidation of scattered parcels of agricultural land, the abolition of the bride price, etc.). Furthermore, regardless of how desirous of socioeconomic change hamula leaders in particular villages may be, as a group they have been—in terms of their literacy rate, their understanding of the principles of modern management and accounting, and their command of other clerical and technical skills—particularly ill equipped to perform the required tasks. The incompetence of traditional elites is one important reason that some government monies officially budgeted for use by Arab villages have often been left untouched at the end of the fiscal year.[7] Many local Arab leaders have simply not mastered the techniques of applying for all the various loans available to them. Disputes among hamulas as to where roads are to be paved, to what homes the first electrical lines will be connected, and so on, have also interfered with the orderly economic development of Arab localities. Government officials are, indeed, quick to blame the incompetence of local Arab leaders, their traditionalist mores, and their petty family quarrels for the slow pace of economic development in the Arab sector. What bears emphasis here is that it is precisely the government's policy of coopting traditionalist elites which has been primarily responsible for the continued dominance of hamula leaders over local Arab politics.

The cooptation of rival local hamula leaders reinforces the fragmentation of the Arab population as well as its economic dependence. For their cooptation has given the regime valuable leverage in playing one clan off another and in creating, if and when it wishes, an atmosphere of intense suspicion and mistrust among rival kinship groups or local religious communities.

Multiple examples of how segmentation, dependence, and cooptation have reinforced one another on all three levels of analysis could be provided. The point, however, should now be clear. Deprived of facilities for united political action (segmentation), Israeli Arabs have found it difficult to protect their economic interests and to develop autonomous centers of economic power. Economically dependent, then, on the Jewish sector, Arab elites and potential elites have been relatively easy to co-opt. The access to the Arab population which cooptation has provided has, in turn, helped the regime maintain the fragmentation of the Arab sector and exploit its economic dependence. The stability of the system of control over Israeli Arabs, as reflected in the uniformity of government policy over time, the continued absence of mass-based Arab nationalist groups or political parties, and the insubstantial intrusion which the Arab-minority problem has made on the Israeli political scene, has been due, then, not only to multilevel patterns of segmentation, dependence, and cooptation but also to the synergistic relationships which have obtained among them.

Challenges to the System

Although the effectiveness of the system of control, as well as its stability and low cost has been accounted for, questions nevertheless remain regarding the possibility that control over Arabs is now weakening, that it will weaken substantially in the future, or that it may become substantially more costly to maintain. Indeed, there can be no doubt that the election of a communist mayor of Nazareth in December 1975, the general strike called by the Communist Party on March 30, 1976 and the local riots and killings that ensued, the growing Arab vote for Rakah in recent Knesset and Histadrut elections,[8] and the emergence of active Arab university student organizations and local radical groups known as Ibn el-Bilad (Sons of the Village) signal the need for the regime to adapt its techniques to new circumstances if it is to maintain that level of control over the Arab minority to which it has become accustomed.

The challenge to the system of control is basically three-pronged: (1) the slow but steady erosion of traditional beliefs and patterns of social interaction in the Arab sector; (2) the development among Israeli Arabs—Christians, Moslems, and Druse—of a strong sense of themselves as members of the Arab nation as a whole and the Palestinian nation in particular; and (3) the crystallization of frameworks for the expression of Arab discontent and opposition to Government policies—most importantly, the New Israel Communist Party (Rakah). Each of these trends undermines the three components of control. Their emergence can be traced to aberrations in otherwise "appropriate" structural and/or institutional conditions.

As previously suggested, the three components are mutually reinforcing. It is precisely because of this interdependence that aberrations in regard to the structural and/or institutional foundations of any one component have important ramifications for the integrity of all three. For example, the dominant pattern of the isolation of the Arab minority, detailed in Chapter 4 as one aspect of segmentation, is partially interrupted by the exposure which tens of thousands of commuting Arab workers have had to the opportunities, lifestyles, and attitudes prevailing in Jewish metropolitan areas. While relations between Jewish and Arab workers rarely extend beyond the contacts required in the workplace, this exposure has contributed to a breakdown in traditional mores and patterns of belief. In addition, as noted in Chapter 6, young Arab workingmen have derived a measure of autonomy from the fact that it is often their earnings which provide their families with whatever measure of economic security they enjoy.[9]

Along with universal suffrage, the extension of essentially modern educational norms into the Arab sector has been one of the most significant consequences of the existence of a "civic realm" where *Israelis*, Jews as well as Arabs, share certain rights and privileges qua Israeli citizens. The existence of such a civic realm, regardless of how attenuated and how lacking in symbolic accoutrements, stands in opposition to the dominant motif of Israel as a Jewish state and constitutes an important break in the institutional isolation of the Arab minority. In educational terms it has meant the introduction of near-universal primary schooling for Arab boys and girls and the graduation of thousands of Israeli Arabs from high schools and colleges. The presence of intellectually articulate young men in the villages, the limited introduction of coeducation in Arab school systems, and the generally high literacy rates in both Hebrew and Arabic among the Arabs of Israel have contributed to the gradual disintegration of the traditional social structure.

As power and influence in the Arab community continue to shift from patriarchal figures and sectarian leaders to larger numbers of younger educated men, cooptation as a strategy for gaining effective access to the Arab population becomes more expensive. For as power within the Arab community is diffused, the number of individuals whose cooperation the regime must induce in order to maintain the same level of control increases. Moreover, the types of rewards valued by educated elites— white-collar jobs, modern conveniences, and status and influence in Israeli society at large—are more difficult to provide than the types of favors with which traditional elites have typically been satisfied. In addition, these educated, nontraditional Arab elites are considerably more interested than their fathers and grandfathers in adopting a political stance that can be defended in terms of a coherent ideology. For this and other reasons Rakah attracts them more powerfully than it did the older generation of Arab notables.[10]

As has been previously argued, weakening the bonds of economic dependence tying sons to their fathers and grandfathers has been a major factor in weakening traditional Arab social structure and diffusing power within the Arab sector as a whole. This process has also had implications for the comparative ease with which the regime has been able to maintain the fragmentation of the Arab population. As detailed in Chapter 4 the regime's efforts to keep the Arab community divided have been based on attempts to maintain and encourage sectarian antagonisms, kinship-based rivalries, and sectional loyalties. With higher levels of education, a sharp decline in explicit religious commitment, and wider opportunities for Arabs to travel and associate freely (at work, at Israeli universities, and, for some, in the army), such parochial attachments and antipathies fade.

The pattern of fragmentation that has characterized the Arab minority since 1948 has also been weakened by the continuous development among Israeli Arabs of a strong positive identification, first with the pan-Arab movement, and subsequently with the struggle of the Palestinians. The pan-Arab identification of Israeli Arabs found its concrete expression in widespread adulation of Gamal Abdel Nasser. With the rise of the Palestinian guerrilla groups, the death of Nasser in 1970, and the Yom Kippur War of 1973, the focus of Arab political identity in Israel shifted from "Arab" to "Palestinian," especially among the younger generation.[11]

Although prior to 1967 Israeli Arabs had been physically isolated from political trends in the Arab world, including the nascent Palestinian movement, their isolation came to an abrupt end following the Israeli occupation of the West Bank and the Gaza Strip during the Six-Day War. The years of the occupation have provided ample opportunity for Israeli Arabs to develop sympathy for and identification with the Palestinian struggle. Many Israeli Arabs renewed ties with relatives and neighbors who had remained in camps on the West Bank and in Gaza after becoming refugees in 1948. Arabs in Israel witnessed the rise and fall of Palestinian guerrilla activity within the occupied territories (1968–1971) and the methods used to suppress it (deportations, mass arrests, housing demolitions). They also felt the effects of the struggle directly, in the form of condemnation by West Bank and Gaza Palestinians for "selling out" to the Israelis, requests from Palestinian underground groups for shelter and support, and greater Jewish suspicion of Arabs and frequent searches by the police. Most importantly, perhaps, they were exposed to a Palestinian Arab population, very similar in social structure and historical legacy to the Israeli Arab population, which possessed a full-blown nationalist ideology, thriving urban centers, a variety of political organizations, and a widely respected nationalist leadership. Moreover, especially following the Yom Kippur War and the shift in emphasis within the PLO toward achieving international legitimacy and establishing a separate Palestinian state, the struggle assumed a form that had direct bearing on the future of Israeli Arabs. For if the strategic goal of the PLO remains the creation of a separate Palestinian state alongside Israel rather than a single Arab state in all of Palestine, then the crucial question for the Palestinian movement becomes one of borders. Unavoidably this raises the issue of the political future of those sections of Israel, slated to become part of the Palestinian Arab state under the terms of the UN partition of 1947, which are still overwhelmingly Arab, viz., central and western Galilee and portions of the Little Triangle (see Maps 1 and 2). Meanwhile, on the tactical level, the demonstrations, strikes and tire-burnings which took place in West Bank cities during the winter and spring of 1976 and the repressive measures which they precipitated showed Israeli Arabs one way that the attention of the world could be effectively focused on the problems of Arabs living under Israeli jurisdiction.

The impact of the occupation of the West Bank and the Gaza Strip on the coalescence of a Palestinian identity among young Israeli Arabs would not have been as strong had it not been for the simultaneous growth of Rakah among the Arab population of Israel. Though active in the struggle against the Military Administration, the Communist Party did not achieve a solid position in the Arab sector until relatively recently. Its identification with an atheistic doctrine elicited the determined opposition of patriarchal village elites. Moreover, its close ties to the Soviet Union meant that when that country's relations with the Arab world cooled, as they did during the Khrushchev-Nasser feud of the late 1950's and early 1960's, the prestige and electoral performance of the party suffered. But as the restrictive ties of patriarchal supervision have weakened, young educated Arabs, more attuned to political appeals based on modern ideological and socioeconomic premises, have been attracted to vote for Rakah and to become active in its ranks. Moreover, since 1967 the Soviet Union has played a generally supportive role vis à vis the Arab cause as a whole and the Palestinian struggle in particular. It has consistently called for Israeli withdrawal from the West Bank and the Gaza Strip and for the establishment there of a Palestinian state.

In its widely read Arabic newspaper, *al-Ittihad*, Rakah has taken every opportunity to glorify the struggle of the inhabitants of the West Bank and the Gaza Strip against the occupation authorities. Firm in their support of Soviet policy toward the Arab-Israeli conflict as a whole and the Palestinian question in particular, Rakah's leaders have condemned the anomic terrorism of the Palestinian organizations but have been passionate in their attacks on the occupation itself. Among the issues

Rakah has raised most vigorously have been administrative detention, the demolition of houses, the deportation of Palestinian political figures, the erection of Jewish settlements in the occupied areas, and the failure of the Israeli regime to accept the principle of a separate Palestinian state. By organizing rallies and petitions and raising funds to aid the families of those imprisoned by the occupation authorities, Rakah has enlisted Israeli Arabs directly in its struggle against the occupation and for a Palestinian-state solution. Rakah's prestige was raised by the fact that, following the virtual elimination of underground guerrilla groups from the West Bank and the Gaza Strip in 1968–1971, the Communist Party in the West Bank and its front organization, the Palestinian National Front, came to serve as the primary framework for the expression of West Bank Palestinian opposition to the occupation. Rakah has also benefited from the informal participation of West Bank leaders in communist party election campaigns.[12]

Yet although Rakah's campaign on behalf of Palestinians in the occupied territories has served as a vehicle for the transmission of Palestinian identity to many Israeli Arabs, and although there is little doubt that many of Rakah's Arab leaders see themselves as Palestinian, the party has remained ambiguous as to whether the Arabs of Israel should be considered part of the "Israeli people" or the "Palestinian people," or both.[13] The basis of Rakah's activities among Arabs in Israel has been that both Arabs and Jews are citizens of the same state; that Arab and Jewish workers have identical interests; that they should unite to achieve their mutual goals; and that discrimination on the basis of nationality, whether practiced by the government, the Histadrut, or the national institutions, should be abolished.[14]

Reliable figures concerning Rakah membership are unavailable. Stendel estimated in 1973 that Rakah had only six hundred registered Arab members. On the other hand David Zechariah, director of the Labor Party's Arab Branch in 1972–1973, put Rakah's membership at two thousand Arabs and five hundred Jews.[15] Ever since Rakah's split from Maki in 1965 and its subsequent emergence as the official Communist Party of Israel (as defined by Moscow), Meir Vilner, a Jew active in the struggle for Israeli independence in 1948, has served as its general secretary. In recent years Jews have also served as secretary of Rakah's central committee, chairman of its central control commission, and general secretary of the Young Communist League. Participation in fraternal delegations sent to attend communist gatherings around the world and membership in the governing institutions of Rakah itself are apportioned on a fifty-fifty basis between Jewish and Arab activists. Thus the influence of Jewish communists in Rakah bears no relationship to the tiny proportion of the party's vote which comes from the Jewish sector.[16]

Unswerving in their support of the Soviet Union and in their use of the rhetoric of class struggle, Rakah's Jewish leaders, as well as certain of the party's veteran Arab leaders, are dedicated Marxist-Leninists.[17] The ethnic heterogeneity and the ideological orthodoxy of its leadership prevent Rakah from becoming a full-fledged Arab nationalist party, and its subservience to Moscow has hindered its ability to maneuver on issues of instrumental importance to Israeli Arabs. Nevertheless, because it is the only anti-Zionist political party (i.e., it opposes the "Jewish" character of the state, though it supports Israel's right to exist as a sovereign country), and because it has been the only party in more than a decade to devote substantial attention to the problems of the Arab minority, Rakah has become *the* electoral repository for Arab voters wishing to express their general dissatisfaction with government policy toward the minority population.[18]

If the 50 percent of its central committee, politburo, and Knesset delegation who are Jewish and the close ties between its leadership and the Soviet Communist Party ensure that Rakah will not become an independent Arab nationalist movement, nevertheless these are also the very factors which have made it so difficult for the regime to control the party's growth. Within the frame of reference of this study they represent aberrations in the structural and institutional isolation of the Arab minority. Communist party activities cannot be suppressed without harassing Jews as well as Arabs—Jews who in spite of their left-wing sentiments and their ostracism from the mainstream of Jewish society in Israel nevertheless *are* Jews, with Jewish friends, relatives, and acquaintances.[19] Moreover, the outright suppression of communists would open Israel to the same kind of criticism which its own propagandists direct toward Arab regimes which imprison communists and ban the party as an illegal organization.

In addition, since the Soviet Union's diplomatic break with Israel in 1967, the Israel Communist Party and its associated Israel–Soviet Union Friendship Movement have been among Israel's only regular links with Moscow. The constant exchange of fraternal delegations to and from the Soviet Union and the Eastern Bloc countries has served as a channel for information concerning Soviet views on Israeli policies and as a highly valued symbol of the Soviet Union's fundamental support of Israel's right to exist.[20] To ban the Communist Party or to harass it too severely would involve the risk of losing these contacts and the substantial contribution which they make to Israel's international legitimacy.[21]

For the Israeli Communist Party itself, its links with the Soviet Union have been absolutely crucial. By identifying itself with Soviet support for various Arab regimes Rakah raises its prestige among Israeli Arabs and counters the natural inclination of Moslem believers to dissociate themselves from "godless communism." That most of Rakah's veteran Arab leaders were born of Greek Orthodox parents reflects the assistance which the Eastern Church, based in Russia, provided to the Israel Communist Party (Maki) in the 1950's and early 1960's. It is generally accepted that Rakah received steady and substantial financial assistance from the Soviet Communist Party in order to fund its various newspapers and periodicals and its publishing house. Such monies are also available to pay scores of full-time party workers, to support a network of youth groups and front organizations, and to sponsor numerous lectures, field trips, and rallies. Thus, through its links with the Soviet Union, Rakah has become the only political force in the Arab sector with access to a center of economic power independent of the regime. This has proved to be of particular importance to young Arabs who wish to break out of their dependence on the regime. Rakah has been able to offer these individuals scholarships to study medicine, engineering, pharmacy, or journalism at universities in the Soviet Union and in Eastern Europe. Hundreds of Israeli Arabs, many of them the sons and daughters of the party faithful, have taken advantage of these opportunities.[22]

Besides university education and/or professional training in communist countries, Rakah can also offer young Arabs paid positions, on a part-time or full-time basis, as youth-group leaders, campaign workers, journalists, party organizers, etc. Indeed, the Communist Party is the only political organization in Israel within which ambitious, idealistic young Arabs can aspire to the highest positions of authority. Of course, by entering the communist "subculture" an Arab must give up nearly all hope of achieving economic security, social status, or political success outside of it. That is why Rakah's access to the economic and political resources which the Soviet Union can provide is so important: to the extent that such resources are available, they make full-time involvement in the Communist Party a viable choice for talented young Arabs.

Ever since the creation of the state of Israel, Maki and, after 1965, Rakah have striven to win the sympathy and electoral support of Israeli Arabs by publicizing and condemning all instances of discrimination, mistreatment, land expropriation, etc., in the Arab sector. Communist members of Knesset speak at length in parliamentary debates on any question touching upon the Arab minority. Although their efforts are inevitably tabled or rejected, communist members have offered hundreds of private bills of special interest to Israeli Arabs. Official question periods, during which government ministers are required to answer, however briefly, all questions put to them by Knesset members, give Rakah's members important opportunities to publicize specific grievances and to demonstrate their concern for the welfare of individual Arabs.

On a country-wide level the Communist Party's primary efforts in the 1950's and early 1960's were directed toward the abolition of the Military Administration and of the Defense Regulations upon which it was based—not least because so many communists were the target of travel restrictions and other types of harassment at the hands of military governors.[23] Since the early years of statehood, land expropriation, wage, price, and hiring discrimination against Arabs, unequal treatment of Arab and Jewish localities by government ministries, manipulation by national Jewish authorities of local Arab politics, and the corrupt practices of Arab notables who have cooperated with the regime have been constant themes in the campaign for Arab support. In recent years, in response to intensified regime efforts to "populate the Galilee"[24] and to "protect national land," Rakah and the Democratic Front for Peace and Equality which it formed in 1977 have concentrated special attention on the expropriation and threatened expropriation of Arab land.

As a result of government plans to expropriate tracts of Arab land in the Galilee, Rakah formed in late 1975 the National Committee for the Defense of Arab Lands, an organization similar to many others launched by the Communist Party in Israel in connection with a variety of specific issues. Its success, however, was far greater than that of any other Maki or Rakah attempt to mobilize Israeli Arabs on a mass basis. The committee declared March 30 Land Day and called upon Arabs to participate in a general strike on that day in protest against the slated expropriations. The Jewish and Arab members of the committee placed many paid advertisements in Hebrew newspapers explaining the reasons for the strike. In scores of Arab villages, "action committees" made up of Rakah supporters and members of the Young Communist League were organized to publicize the strike locally and to persuade Arab workers to participate. On the day of the strike curfews were placed on three villages in central Galilee, some of whose lands were to be expropriated. As a result of confrontation between villagers and army units sent in to enforce the curfews, several Arabs were killed, many wounded, and hundreds arrested.[25]

Although these events overshadowed the rather limited success of the strike itself, the obvious widespread sympathy for Rakah's efforts evinced by Arabs throughout Israel, the tremendous popular pressures to which notables who spoke out against the strike were subjected, and the international attention which the disturbances attracted reflected the unprecedented success Rakah had achieved vis à vis the political mobilization of the Arab population.[26] A month later, at Rakah's annual May Day rally in Nazareth, the speakers concentrated on the issue of the expropriation of Arab lands and the demand for a full investigation of the killings. Four thousand Arabs from Nazareth and villages throughout Galilee were in attendance.[27]

The featured speaker at the rally was Taufik Ziad, one of the prime movers behind the strike of March 30. Some months before, Ziad, a young communist elected to the Knesset in 1973, had been elected mayor of Nazareth. His election and the defeat of government-supported candidates stunned public opinion in Israel, though it came as no surprise to those familiar with the chaotic record of the Labor Party's machine in that city.[28] Containing the largest concentration of Arabs in Israel and the only city with an Arab majority, Nazareth has always been a center of communist strength. Rakah's successful campaign for control of the Nazareth municipality parallels other, less successful campaigns which the Communist Party has conducted in Arab local council elections throughout Israel in the last ten years. Nevertheless, although Rakah's record on the local level has been far less impressive than its performance in national elections, in recent years communist mayors have emerged in a number of Arab villages.

Rakah's standing among the Druse has also shown a marked increase. The Druse Initiative Committee, a communist-front organization active among the Druse since 1974, gained a good deal of attention by its disruption of the speeches of government spokesmen during Nebi Shueib celebrations in 1974 and 1975. The committee describes the Druse as "faithful sons of the Arab nation," condemns government attempts to distinguish between Druse and Arabs, and calls for an end to the conscription of Druse into the army.[29]

Rakah has also played an important role in the General Muslim Committee. The activities of this group, established in October 1977, have concentrated on the demand for control over Moslem Waqf funds, now supervised by trustees committees appointed by the government.[30]

Rakah and its front organizations are indisputably the most important framework for the expression of Arab grievances to have emerged in Israel, but since the Yom Kippur War three other significant forums have crystallized. In 1974 the Organization of Arab Local Council Chairmen was formed as an ad hoc group of Arab mayors concerned with raising the level of the

Ministry of the Interior's aid to Arab villages. Operating within the general framework of the ministry's Municipal Authorities Center, the group originally decided to exclude Arab mayors affiliated with Rakah and declared their opposition to the Land Day general strike. The Rabin government subsequently made some efforts to cultivate the mayors' committee as representative of "positive elements" in the Arab sector.[31] However, in the aftermath of the bloodshed on March 30, 1976, and the publication of the Koenig memorandum six months later, relations between the mayors and the government deteriorated. Taufik Ziad joined the group and, though ten mayors resigned in protest against the call for the removal of Koenig from his post, the mayors have continued to meet and pass resolutions on issues of concern to Israeli Arabs. Although the group declined to endorse the Democratic Front in the 1977 election, its chairman, Hanna Mois, joined the front and was elected to the Knesset.

Since 1975 the membership of Arab student committees on Israeli university campuses has expanded substantially and links have been established among them. Although these committees have not been accorded official recognition by the universities, some de facto contacts with administrative offices have developed. The activities of these student groups have primarily centered on coping with the housing, employment, and administrative problems faced by Arabs studying in overwhelmingly Jewish institutions. However, the national board (first elected by the individual campus committees in 1975), as well as the individual committees themselves, now regularly distributes leaflets of protest and sponsors demonstrations of solidarity in connection with issues such as land expropriation, occupation policies, and Palestinian national rights.

The student organizations have also become arenas for bitter competition between Rakah and young nationalist Arabs who reject Rakah's slogan of Jewish-Arab working-class solidarity, who wish to emphasize the possibility of national self-determination for Israeli Arabs in association with the PLO's struggle for a Palestinian state, and who support the use of "confrontationist" tactics such as general strikes, protest delegations to the United Nations, and demonstrations in front of the Knesset. Attacked by Rakah as effective allies of the regime in its effort to divide, weaken, and discredit the struggle for Arab rights in Israel, students holding these views nonetheless won a victory in the Jerusalem Arab-student-organization election in 1977 and increased their strength in the Haifa Arab student committee. At Bar Ilan, Tel Aviv, and Beersheva universities as well as at the Technion and in the national student committee, Rakah supporters maintained their dominant position.[32]

Rakah has also experienced challenges to its monopoly of organized dissent from Ibn el-Bilad, local associations of radical Israeli Arab intellectuals. These groups have sprung up in a number of large villages (the best known being located in Um el-Fahm, the largest Arab village in the Little Triangle), but there has not yet been an attempt to weld these local associations into a national movement. Initially concentrating their attention on reforming local politics, removing the blight of hamulaism, and striving for cooperative modernization of services and municipal facilities, these groups resembled the local reformist lists of young Arabs that emerged in the early 1970's only to be swallowed up by government-connected hamulas. However, Ibn el-Bilad groups have gone beyond local village politics to express the most radical position on national political issues since the dissolution of el-Ard in 1964. Along with some Arab students at the Hebrew University, Ibn el-Bilad has attacked Rakah for its refusal to embrace confrontationist tactics and its recent willingness to ally itself with politically powerful hamulas on the local level. Among the themes which Ibn el-Bilad groups stress and which have given them their radical reputation are self-determination for the Palestinians living in Israel (i.e., Israeli Arabs), rejection of political alliances with left-wing Jewish groups, explicit support for the PLO as the true representative of all Palestinians, and the eventual establishment of a single secular democratic state in all of Palestine.[33]

Before a discussion of the possible or likely response of the regime to the challenges it currently faces in controlling the Arab minority, one additional complicating factor must be noted. A sustained and spectacular rate of natural increase in the Arab sector (38.4 per thousand in 1976 as compared to 18.0 per thousand among Jews), falling levels of Jewish immigration, and increasing Jewish emigration (since the Yom Kippur War) have combined to raise the issue of the long-term stability of Israel's Jewish majority. For there is strong reason to believe that the growth of the Arab population relative to that of the Jewish population will accelerate in the future. In 1976, 49.4 percent of Arab Israelis were fourteen years of age or under. Among Jews the same figure was 30.1 percent.[34] Based on the assumption of a "migration balance" (emigration subtracted from immigration) of ten thousand Jews annually, Israel's Central Bureau of Statistics anticipates that Arabs will comprise 17.9 percent of Israeli citizens in 1985 and 20.6 percent in 1995 (as opposed to 13.5 percent at present).[35] In 1976 Arabs already constituted a solid majority in the western and central Galilee and were very close to a majority in the northern region as a whole[36] (see Map 4).

The components of control in Israel—segmentation, dependence, and cooptation—serve to fulfill what were referred to in Chapter 3 as the "functional requisites" of control. The challenges to the Israeli system of control described above can be seen as interfering with the fulfillment of these requisites. Most serious is the access which Israeli Arabs have gained to frameworks for united political action. Rakah and the Democratic Front provide organizational opportunities for Arabs to unite with sympathetic Jews (albeit with members of Jewish fringe groups only). Rakah, its front organizations, the Arab mayors group, and the national student committee also provide many Arabs with opportunities to establish personal relationships and political reputations on an "all-Israel" basis. The "Palestinianization" of Israeli Arabs contributes to the attractiveness and success of these organizations by providing a vocabulary of common struggle in the context of which kinship and sectarian jealousies can be more easily ignored. The gradual erosion of the traditional social structure frees young men (if not women) from close patriarchal supervision and makes them available for recruitment by these organizations. In addition, increased levels of education among young Arabs, combined with a stronger sense of themselves as Palestinians linked to an international struggle (however defined), interfere with the cooptation of attractive young leaders as a means of penetrating the Arab sector for purposes of surveillance and manipulation.

**Map 4. Arabs in Israel by
Natural Region, 1977.**

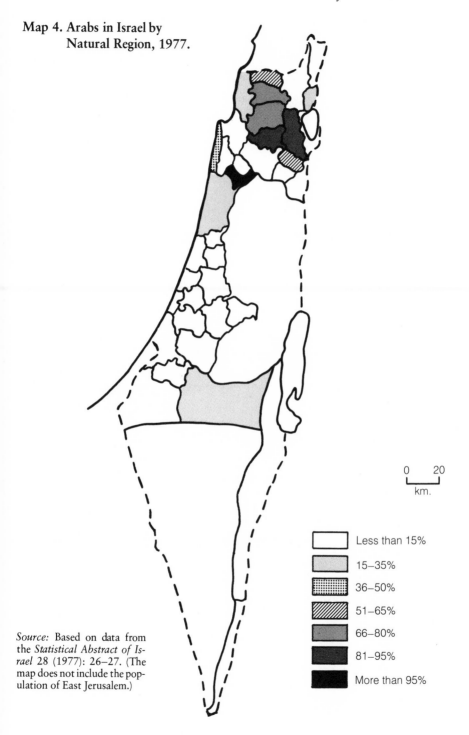

0   20
km.

Less than 15%

15–35%

36–50%

51–65%

66–80%

81–95%

More than 95%

Source: Based on data from
the *Statistical Abstract of Israel* 28 (1977): 26–27. (The
map does not include the population of East Jerusalem.)

Of the three requisites of control, perhaps the least affected by current trends is the absence of effective Arab access to independent sources of economic power. The Arab population as a whole has accumulated substantial liquid assets, but this capital is divided among thousands of small savers. The money, furthermore, is deposited in Jewish-owned banks.[37] While Rakah may provide opportunities to some highly motivated and skilled individuals to gain professional training, the mass of Arabs must continue to rely on the Jewish sector and the regime for jobs and for the provision of vital services.[38]

Regime Responses: System Adaptation, Breakdown, or Transformation

Within the conceptual framework employed in this study, calculated policies implemented by the Jewish regime have been seen as enforcing subordination or as reinforcing or exploiting convenient structural and institutional circumstances. Accordingly, as certain of the structural factors within the system of control weaken, more resources are required for the enforcement of control and more attention needs to be devoted to problems of policy design in the Arab sector. Following the disturbances of spring 1976 the regime did, in fact, devote more attention to the internal Arab problem than at any time since the early 1960's.

Before considering the development of policies since 1976, however, it must be stressed that although the triple challenge to the effective control of the Arab minority discussed above has turned the Arab minority into a problem of some consequence for the regime, it has not become and does not immediately threaten to become a critical issue for the Jewish state. The disturbances of spring 1976 did not signal the beginning of a sustained intrusion by Arab Israelis into the political arena. No independent Arab political party has formed; no independent Arab list was entered in the Knesset elections of 1977. Rakah has been careful since 1976 to refrain from the organization of general strikes and has put new emphasis on its Jewish-Arab-socialist character. Within the framework of the Democratic Front it has actively allied itself with fringes of the Zionist left and has responded harshly to attacks by nationalistic intellectuals who have condemned the party for its timidity in pressing Arab demands.[39] Although the proportion of Arab votes for the Labor Party decreased in 1977, this decrease was significantly lower than the decrease in the proportion of Jewish votes received by the Labor Party. Moreover, in spite of an extremely intense campaign effort by Rakah in the Arab sector and a semiofficial endorsement by the PLO, the Democratic Front received only five mandates in the Knesset election—only one more than Rakah itself won in 1974.[40] Also, from 1976 to 1977, security offenses by Arabs in the Galilee dropped by 35 percent, and in 1977 only five Israeli Arabs were charged with joining terrorist organizations.[41] Although mistreatment of Bedouin and Arab student protests received some attention in the Israeli press in 1978 and early 1979, news coverage of Arab affairs has remained sporadic, reflecting the continued success of the system of control in keeping the salience of the Arab minority problem low for Israeli society as a whole.

Thus it is not surprising that neither the Labor Party nor the right-wing Likud coalition which succeeded it in May 1977 has given any indication that a substantial change in the character of the regime's relationship with the Arab minority has been contemplated. For example, suggestions by a group of Arab mayors traditionally friendly toward the government that Israel develop an image of itself as a binational state, rather than as a Jewish state, were emphatically rejected by government spokesmen. "Israel," declared Prime Minister Yitzhak Rabin, "is a Jewish-Zionist state in which a minority of Arabs live with religious and cultural distinctions."[42] Editorials in leading Israeli newspapers echoed the government's position. The *Jerusalem Post*, Israel's semiofficial English language daily, found it "essential to reiterate to Israel's Arab citizens that while they have the inalienable right to fight for greater equality and more opportunities—a fight in which many Jews will enlist on their side—Israel is, and will remain, irrevocably Jewish."[43] *Haaretz*, Israel's most prestigious independent newspaper, was more specific in its distinction between rights accorded to Arab citizens as individuals and rights denied Arabs as a national or ethnic group.

The structure that Israel has adopted and will not part with has to allow the Arab citizens wide possibilities so that they can go on living as Arabs in the state of the Jews . . . But as a basis of representation we can not accept anything else but the Arab individual [in contrast to national or ethnic group representation].

We understand that this is not optimal from a national point of view. But the Arabs have to understand that this is the maximum they can expect as a minority . . . We do not ask from them more than Communist Rumania is asking from the Hungarian minority living there.[44]

Yet if the events of the spring of 1976 did not result in a fundamental reconsideration of the position of Arabs in Israeli society, they nonetheless did generate high-level Jewish criticism of the implementation of policy in the Arab sector. The overt use of coercion on a significant scale against Arab demonstrators, widespread and unfavorable international publicity, and the involvement of top decision-makers in the affairs of the Arab minority (if only for several weeks) represented costs which the regime has not been accustomed to pay in connection with the maintenance of a quiescent Arab minority. Thus, in spite of a declaration by the government in early April 1976 that its basic policies toward the Arab sector had been successful and continued to be appropriate, a number of ministers expressed their concern that the "implementation" of these policies had been "faulty or laggardly."[45] Other critics, such as Mattityahu Peled, a retired general and one of Israel's leading "doves," were harsher. "There is no need to evaluate the people who run the Arab departments; some of them are undoubtedly well meaning and conscientious workers. But the system as a whole is a disgrace. This is no way to handle the affairs of a whole segment of the population, it smacks of discriminatory tendencies and gives constant cause for discontent among the Arabs of Israel. But as was so well demonstrated . . . the system is above all inefficient from the point of view of those who deem it valuable."[46]

For the first time in more than ten years a review of government policy toward the Arab minority was undertaken by the cabinet in the late spring and summer of 1976. Indeed, government Arabists, intimately involved in the affairs of the Arab minority on a day-to-day basis, had long been aware of the difficulties which the three trends described earlier were creating for the maintenance of cheap, effective control in the Arab sector. They realized that the structural foundations of the Arab sector's fragmentation were eroding and that the cultural norms and social structures which contributed to the success of traditional cooptive techniques were disintegrating. They also appreciated that the routes of economic and social mobility available, on a limited basis, to Arabs within the communist structure loosened the dependence of educated young Arabs on the institutions of the regime. But only in the wake of the communist victory in Nazareth in December 1975 and of the disturbances of spring 1976 were the repeated requests by these officials for more staff, more money, and more attention by high level decision-makers given serious consideration.

In a very significant article written on the eve of Land Day, Ori Stendel, a former deputy to the adviser to the prime minister on Arab affairs who has maintained close ties with his office, warned of the need for certain adjustments to be made in government policy if the system of control over Arabs was to keep pace with the emergence of a nontraditional leadership, the growing "Palestinianization" of Israeli Arabs, and the growing power and prestige of the Communist Party. "The strong actions of the authoritative institutions help in blocking the efforts of extremist circles, but their effects will be shortlived, unless they are followed up within a short time, by a combined policy of encouraging, caring for, and integrating positive elements. Such a policy must be accompanied by the adoption of a strong, uncompromising stand against hostile elements and the creation of appropriate means to deal with the roots of the problem." Stendel left no doubt as to what he means by "hostile elements" and the "roots of the problem." "We must not shrink from taking practical measures against Rakah, which has proven its ability to change the balance of political forces and to use its success as a level for nationalist agitation. It is the primary factor behind the current unrest."[47] As outlined by Stendel and other Labor government spokesmen, future policy would emphasize two themes: (1) the identification and encouragement of "positive elements," and (2) the adoption of a harder line against Rakah and other "hostile elements."

In September 1976 the text of a confidential memorandum

written by two of the most prominent Arabists in Israel was published in the Hebrew press (see Chapter 3). Its main author, Israel Koenig, was (and is) district commissioner of the Ministry of the Interior for the Galilee, where most Israeli Arabs live.[48] The memorandum was an explicit attempt to analyze the impact of various trends which had weakened the government's ability to manipulate the Arab minority and to maintain political quiescence in the Arab sector. The specific measures suggested in the memorandum represented, in effect, a detailed extrapolation of Stendel's basic proposals: the intensification of Jewish settlement and land acquisition in order to break up the contiguity of Arab settlements in the Galilee; a more systematic "reward and punishment" of Arab villages and elites; the mobilization of all Jewish parties to refrain from competing with one another for support in the Arab sector; the coordination of a smear campaign against Rakah activists; and the harassment of "all negative personalities at all levels and at all institutions."[49] Various specific techniques were also proposed for reducing the level of liquid savings (available for contribution to political causes) in the Arab sector, for encouraging the emigration of Arab intellectuals, and for degrading the effectiveness of Arab university student organizations.

There has been evidence, though, of substantive disagreements within official circles with respect to exactly how government policy might best be adapted to the basic changes that have taken place in the Arab sector. In February 1977 Shmuel Toledano resigned from the Labor Party and from his post as adviser to the prime minister on Arab affairs (an office he had held since 1966) in order to run for the Knesset as part of Yigal Yadin's new Democratic Movement for Change. Though uncompromising in his opposition to "extremist" or "nationalist" political activity by Arabs, Toledano was generally known for his "liberalism," which in the context of Jewish-Arab relations in Israel refers to his support for increased welfare and development expenditures for Arabs and his vision of Israeli Arabs as a community with conflicting loyalties which should not be obliged to express its full support for Zionism or the Jewish state. In the last years of his tenure as adviser, Toledano drew criticism for his attempts to block new large-scale land expropriations from

Arabs in the Galilee, for his support of the efforts of Arabs from Ikrit and Biram, two villages evacuated in 1948, to return to their homes, and for his efforts to convince Jewish businesses and government agencies to hire more Arab university graduates.

The specific recommendations approved by the Labor government were discarded by the Likud when it came to power. Preoccupied with the fighting in Lebanon and peace negotiations with Egypt, the Begin cabinet has not, in the first two and a half years of its tenure, directed serious attention to the Arab minority problem. In October 1977, Moshe Sharon, a lecturer in Islamic studies at Bar Ilan University and a former military governor of the West Bank, was appointed adviser to the prime minister on Arab affairs. He had no previous experience in the Arab sector of Israel, and following his appointment he concerned himself primarily with administrative reforms. In public statements he stressed the nonpartisan character of his office, the necessity to treat Arabs and Jews alike, and his desire to minimize the significance of nationalist sloganeering in the Arab sector. After failing to interest Prime Minister Begin in the problems of his office, he resigned in February 1979. His immediate predecessor, Benyamin Gur-Aryeh, was again named acting adviser to the prime minister on Arab affairs.[50]

The adviser's office under the Likud government has not, to date, developed and applied vigorous new policies toward the Arab minority, but Jewish officials with responsibilities for or interest in Arab affairs—in government ministries, in the security services, in the Histadrut, and in the Knesset—have continued the search for innovations in policy which could increase the efficiency of control over the Arab population. Of these officials associated with Likud, Arik Sharon, minister of agriculture and chairman of the Interministerial Committee on Land Settlement, and Member of Knesset Amnon Linn, formerly head of the Arab Department of the Labor Party, have had the greatest influence. Both are known for their "toughness" in dealing with Arabs.

In the 1950's and 1960's Arik Sharon was the commander of "Unit 101," a special regiment with a reputation for devastating retaliation raids against Arab villages in the West Bank.

Sharon was also the commander called upon to subdue the population of the Gaza Strip when armed resistance to the occupation was at its peak. Sharon's interest in the Arab minority problem has expressed itself mainly in connection with the land issue. All Arab villages have experienced a population explosion over the last twenty years. Yet, because of land expropriations, these villages do not have room to expand. As a consequence homes are built adjacent to Arab villages, on land which the Arab inhabitants claim as their own but which the government considers "state" or "national" land. As discussed in Chapter 5, houses built on such land are liable to be demolished by order of the Ministry of the Interior (in consultation with the Israel Land Authority, over which Arik Sharon, as minister of agriculture, exercises considerable influence). In November 1977, one Arab was killed by security forces, twelve injured, and thirty arrested following the demolition of an illegal house in the Arab village of Majd el-Krum.[51] Similar measures, including the use of roving Green Patrols to destroy Bedouin encampments and confiscate livestock grazing on state lands, have been part of an "energetic offensive" which, in Sharon's words, "I have launched to stem the hold of foreigners on state lands . . ."[52] The use of the word "foreigners" to describe Arab citizens of Israel and Sharon's use of the phrase "Yehud ha·Galil" (Judaization of the Galilee) in place of the euphemisms used by the previous Labor government are reflections of an approach which is much more explicit, in its characterization of the Arab minority as a threat to the Jewish state and in its commitment to effectively control the Arab population, than any Labor government had been since the abolition of the Military Administration in 1966.

Member of Knesset Amnon Linn (Likud) is known for his long-time opposition to Toledano's policy of encouraging Arabs to maintain a low political profile while minimizing the use of strong-arm methods. Linn's position has been that Israeli Arabs should be called upon to demonstrate their loyalty to the state by adopting an "Israeli-Arab ideology" and by offering positive, active proof of their commitment to Israel and its Jewish-Zionist mission.[53] Accordingly, he once proposed the establishment of a school in the Galilee which would instill "Israeli-Arab consciousness" among the non-Jewish inhabitants of the area and has also argued for the acceptance of Arab army veterans for genuine participation in the ranks of Zionist political parties. With encouragement from Linn a group of Druse veterans formed a Druse-Zionist Committee in 1975. The head of that committee, Amr Nasser E-din, was subsequently elected to the Knesset in May 1977 on the Likud ticket.[54]

For those Arabs unwilling to voice their positive support of the government and its policies, Linn has consistently favored the use of the "strong hand," e.g., the expulsion of Arabs suspected of involvement in guerrilla organizations, the banning of radical Arabs from Israeli universities, an increase in the use of administrative detention, the firing of Arab teachers and other government employees who support the Communist Party, and the use of tough police and border patrol units to quell demonstrations in Arab villages. Commenting on the strong-hand aspects of his proposals Linn explained that "though my policy is a little brutal, the future of Israeli Arabs is very complicated and that is the only way."[55]

The influence of Linn's ideas is evident in the government's categorical refusal to allow the Arabs of Biram and Ikrit to return to their villages (a reversal of the position on this issue adopted by the Likud before the 1977 elections) and in the multiplication of incidents of police brutality and political harassment.[56] But Linn has made known his deep dissatisfaction with what he sees as the lackadaisical response of the Begin cabinet and its Arab affairs adviser to the erosion of effective control in the Arab sector. On March 5, 1978, Linn announced plans to convene a closed meeting of one hundred officials who work or have worked in the Arab sector. The purpose of this conference would be to discuss "the dangerous deterioration in the Arab sector caused by extremist nationalists who identify with the PLO and whose [activities] are creating a very serious crisis between Jews and Arabs. The seriousness of the consequences of this crisis cannot be overestimated."[57] Linn clearly hoped the conference would aid his efforts to move the government toward a more systematic response to the loosening of control. He described the goal of the meeting as the formulation of "recommendations to the government of ways to put a stop to elements that endanger the existence of the state of Israel."[58]

What may be termed the Toledano-Histadrut approach and the Linn-Sharon (Arik) approach are fundamentally similar in their conception of the Arab minority problem as one of "control," in their determination to devote more regime resources to the control of the Arab minority, and in their commitment to sharpen policies of reward and punishment toward elements in the Arab sector deemed "positive" or "negative." But the adoption of one or the other approach will have very different implications for the future shape of Arab-Jewish relations in Israel. For the regime each approach has advantages and disadvantages.

The Toledano-Histadrut approach is based on an attempt to maintain the organizational fragmentation of the Arab sector by expanding the scope and increasing the rewards of cooptation. If distribution of development aid, white-collar jobs, and political support were diversified through a variety of agencies administered by rival Jewish political factions or personalities, young Arab elites would be encouraged to trade loyalty to factions or individuals within the Jewish sector for assured economic and political assistance. Although the rivalries between politically ambitious Jews in the agencies responsible for Arab affairs are of little consequence in the overall context of Israeli politics, the recruitment of coteries of Arab supporters by these personalities and factions as a means of advancing their own political fortunes would help to divide the "young generation" of Arab leaders into rival cliques. Each clique would argue, essentially, that its particular set of attachments and contacts and the particular approach of the officials or department with which it associates hold the only true promise of future equality for Arabs and Jews.[59]

As discussed in Chapter 6, the Arab Department of the Histadrut, more than any other single agency, has cultivated support among young educated Arabs. A study of policy in the Arab sector undertaken by the department in response to the events of Land Day was published in October 1976. Its recommendations were very much in line with the Histadrut's traditional emphasis in the Arab sector. The authors of the report suggested that:

(1) greater publicity be given to the Arab Department's contribution to the social and economic progress that has been made by the Arab population;

(2) the activities of the Histadrut be publicly differentiated as

clearly as possible from official government programs in order to facilitate recruitment of potential dissidents;

(3) the number of Arabs appointed to committees and secretariats which administer the multitude of internal and affiliated Histadrut organs (sports leagues, health-care facilities, occupational associations, etc.) be increased and one Arab representative be placed on the twenty-one–member Executive Bureau;

(4) Histadrut clubhouses in Arab villages be revitalized and the budgets allocated for locally hired directors be increased;

(5) special three- to four-month Histadrut seminars be established to recruit and train young Arab activists;

(6) the number of high school and college scholarships awarded by the Histadrut to Arab students be increased;

(7) the activities of the Arab arm of the Histadrut's youth organization be expanded;

(8) the Histadrut create one hundred white-collar jobs for Arab high school and university graduates;

(9) the Histadrut, in cooperation with the government, extend small investment loans to Arab members of the Histadrut for the construction of workshops in their villages; and

(10) Hevrat Ovdim (the corporate arm of the Histadrut) build specially designed industrial projects in selected Arab localities.[60]

In general the report stressed the need for the leadership of the Histadrut to take a more direct and sustained interest in the Arab minority problem than it had in the past. The authors criticized the attitude of Jewish Histadrut officials who "refuse to 'go in to the field' to meet with the Arab population."[61] In response to the report, Labor Party leader Yigal Allon announced his intention, in June 1977, of engaging in intensive activity in the Arab sector. At the same time it was revealed that George Saad, a long-time Labor Party and Histadrut politician from Nazareth, would be appointed by the Labor Party to one of its places on the Executive Bureau.[62] In 1978 Mapam, part of the Labor Alignment, made known its intention to appoint two of its Arab members to the management of Hevrat Ovdim. The Histadrut Arab Department also indicated that new efforts were underway to sponsor joint Jewish-Arab investments in Arab communities.[63]

For the regime the benefits of the Toledano-Histadrut approach are fairly clear. It provides an opportunity to compete credibly, though not necessarily successfully, with Rakah for the support of young Israeli Arabs without giving up the capacity to take stronger measures against the communists or other Arab political groups if necessary. This means votes for the Zionist parties involved in the Arab sector, the siphoning of attractive potential elites from dissident activity, positive international publicity concerning increasing numbers of Arabs in the civil service and increased funding of Arab development projects, and the continued availability of accurate information regarding trends, personalities, and threats in the Arab community.

One obvious disadvantage of this approach is the necessity to commit substantial economic resources to the cooptation of larger and larger numbers of Arabs. Since these younger edu-cated Arabs have narrower constituencies than the old Arab elites, more need to be coopted to achieve the same degree of access to Arabs than when the patriarchal chiefs of large clans were the primary targets of cooptation. Moreover, as indicated earlier, white-collar jobs, respectable salaries, and meaningful development projects (sewer systems, high-tension power lines, water works, etc.) are considerably more expensive than the kind of personal favors that satisfied the ambitions of tradi-tionalist elites. Furthermore, given the rising expectations of these younger Arabs, the discontent engendered by not satisfy-ing their desires would likely be more intense than that triggered by the disappointment of patriarchal types.

Indeed, the most fundamental problem with this approach involves the possibility that the new generation of young Arab elites will not be "cooptable," i.e., that they will ultimately ob-ject to the "Zionist" character of the organizations and institu-tions into which they are introduced. Mapam and, more re-cently, Moked (Shelli), two leftist-Zionist parties with strong sympathies for Israeli Arabs, have had enormous difficulties at-tracting members and finding ideological formulas with which they can feel comfortable. It may be expected that with some traditionalist support these new Arab elites, unable to derive emotional or ideological satisfaction from their new positions, will use their new status, their education, and their social con-nections in the Jewish sector to organize some sort of sustained civil rights movement for Israeli Arabs. Though Toledano has suggested that banning the Communist Party would be an effective, enforceable, and possibly necessary part of any effort to maintain the organizational fragmentation of the Arab sector,[64] it would be extremely difficult for the government to use a strong hand against an Arab civil rights movement, the loyalty of whose leadership had been established by the Zionist parties themselves and by ongoing links with sympathetic Jewish circles. With resources at their command, with organizational frameworks available for united political action, and having been ascribed public legitimacy, Arab elites would be in a position to aggregate and represent Arab interests. Individual leaders might then come to decide that political action, and not only collaboration, can satisfy personal ambition. Such elites are likely to begin bargaining on behalf of the Arab minority for political and economic goods rather than to satisfy parochial interests through personal arrangements. Moreover, an Arab civil rights movement would raise extremely uncomfortable demands for cultural autonomy, for the appointment of Arabs to key decision-making positions, and for recognition of Israel as a binational Jewish-Arab country rather than as a Jewish-Zionist state.

In this connection Toledano has argued that "integration" of Arabs into Jewish political parties and other decision-making bodies—i.e., the loosening of the Arab minority's isolation from centers of Jewish power and status—need not be viewed with alarm as long as the economic dependence of the Arab population on the Jewish sector continues to be overwhelming. "All the economic positions in the country are filled by Jews, the Jews control all the banks, all the corporations. In politics and in the Histadrut, they have all the power. There is nothing to fear from the integration of Arabs in our democratic life to the greatest extent possible . . . I am not speaking about integration into key positions. I am talking only about the appointment of Arabs to head branch offices, to direct departments. What is bad about that? What is there to fear?"[65]

The Linn-Sharon approach to the Arab problem contrasts most strongly with the Toledano approach in its abandonment of cooptation as the primary mechanism for penetrating the Arab sector. Although traditional elites, especially in small villages and among the Bedouin, would still be supported in return for the access which they could provide to their constituencies, no sustained effort would be made to induce large numbers of young educated Arabs to trade political docility or collaboration for white-collar jobs, civil service positions, the status of association with prominent Jewish politicians, or local development projects. A sharp distinction, in the context of this approach, is made between army veterans (Druse, Circassians, some Bedouin, and a few Christians) and Arabs who do not serve in the armed forces. Army veterans would be encouraged to participate actively, either in Zionist political parties or in Arab groups explicitly committed to Israel's Jewish-Zionist destiny. From their ranks would likely be drawn most if not all of the non-Jewish staff of agencies responsible for Arab affairs as well as a large proportion of the security personnel used to police Arab areas. They would also provide what propaganda and political support the regime would extract from the Arab sector. While in return these Arabs would be granted wide access to the economic and educational resources of the Jewish sector, this would not be intended as an effort to mobilize the bulk of the Arab population to support the government.

If this approach were implemented, the organizational fragmentation of the Arab sector would almost certainly yield to the near total dominance of Rakah in Arab towns and large villages—assuming, of course, that it is not suppressed (the likely fate of explicitly Arab nationalist organizations). On the other hand, in the context of a long overdue and generally favored reform of Israel's proportional electoral system, gerrymandering in the Galilee and the central district could sharply reduce, if not eliminate, Rakah representation in the Knesset.[66] As suggested in the Koenig memorandum, more rigorous tax collection in Arab villages, additional land expropriations, cuts in government development aid to the Arab sector, and the blacklisting of Arabs suspected of communist or nationalist activities would help to deepen the economic dependence of the Arab minority and make it exceedingly difficult for the Arab population to sustain general strikes or other mass political actions. Some Likud spokesmen have also suggested conscription of Arabs for two or three years of noncombat "alternative service" as a means of re-

ducing the capital available to the Arab population (by removing a substantial percentage of its active labor force) and as a
means of encouraging emigration.[67]

To compensate for the loss of cooptation as the primary
means of penetrating the Arab sector and for the anticipated increase in the political solidarity of the Arab community, the regime would seek to intensify the ideological, psychological, and
social isolation of the bulk of the Arab population from the Jewish sector. Explicit characterization of the majority of Arabs as
communist extremists and nationalist fanatics who ultimately
threaten the territorial integrity and security of the state not
only would reduce the international impact of Arab dissent, but
also would permit the freer use of coercion and administrative
harassment as means of eliciting cooperation when needed. An
adequate flow of information could be ensured by means of frequent arrests, formal interrogations, and a system of dedicated
informants. Linn himself believes that "less than a score of anti-
subversive activists in every village, to be mobilized from among
the new generation of intellectuals in every *hamula*, could do the
job."[68]

The costs of this kind of response to the internal Arab problem would be high, particularly in regards unfavorable publicity
in the international arena. The dispersal of demonstrations in
Arab areas often results in scores of injuries and even more arrests. Occasional fatalities spark further demonstrations during
funerals and commemorative services. Though neither Israeli
nor Western television news teams have penetrated the Arab sector in Israel, these clashes are reported in leading newspapers
throughout the world, and charges of anti-Arab racism made in
the United Nations and other international forums are seen to
find support. In light of the current American emphasis on hu-
man-rights violations in countries linked to the United States,
the consistent use of strong-arm measures against Arab citizens
might have much more serious international repercussions than
in the past. The Linn-Sharon approach would also almost certainly result in a higher level of social tension between Jews and
Arabs in Israel. At times of such tension in the past it has not
always been possible to prevent attacks by bands of Jewish "hot-
heads" on the Arab quarters of the mixed cities.

The West Bank, The Gaza Strip, and the Future of the Arab Minority in Israel

The shape of an eventual settlement of the Arab-Israeli conflict, especially as it pertains to the disposition of the West Bank and the Gaza Strip, will have enormous consequences for the future of the Arab minority in Israel. Indeed, the attractive features of the Linn-Sharon approach for maintaining Jewish control over the Arab minority can be appreciated only in the context of a discussion of this problem. Notwithstanding return of the Sinai peninsula to Egyptian sovereignty, present indications are that if formal annexation of the West Bank and Gaza is not being pursued by the Likud government, some relationship with these territories is being sought which will permanently tie them to the state of Israel. But, as Israeli doves have always stressed, annexation or the permanent de facto incorporation of these areas would result in an Arab minority of 40–45 percent. Given the political sophistication of Palestinian elites in these areas, their cohesion, their economic resources, and their loyalty to the PLO's ideology, leadership, and organizational framework, the task of preventing mass Arab nationalist activity would prove next to impossible without employment of techniques of control much more similar to those used by Israeli military forces in the occupied territories since 1967 than those used by the regime within Israel for the past thirty years.[69] Thus the incorporation of these areas into Israel, under one juridical formula or another, would tend to push the regime toward the Linn-Likud combination of policies. *Ironically, the implications for Israeli Arabs of the opposite scenario, the crystallization of a comprehensive peace settlement including the emergence of some sort of Palestinian entity in the West Bank and the Gaza Strip, are much the same.*

Since 1967 many Israelis, and in particular leftist Zionists who have taken a strong interest in the Palestinian question, have argued that the creation of an independent, nonbelligerent Palestinian state on the West Bank and the Gaza Strip, besides fulfilling the "legitimate national rights of the Palestinian people," would also go far toward eliminating the psychological and political disabilities of Israeli Arabs. Such a Palestinian state, it is argued, would do for Israel Arabs what the creation of Israel has done for the standing of Jewish minorities in the diaspora.[70]

There can indeed be no question that a reduction in tension between Israel and the Arab world, on whatever scale, would tend to make the day-to-day relations between Jews and Arabs in Israel less fraught with fear and suspicion. Peace agreements would help defuse the security issue, and the emergence of a Palestinian political entity would no doubt ease the psychological identity problem of Israeli Arabs.

However, there are strong reasons to believe that, vis à vis the Arab minority, the most significant effects of a peace settlement and/or the establishment of a Palestinian state would be to intensify the efforts of Israeli Arabs to gain power, status, and autonomy; to increase substantially the costs of regime attempts to maintain control over the minority population by coopting Arab elites; and to strengthen the position of those who argue for the need to make the conflictual character of the regime's relationship with the minority explicit. It can be imagined, for example, that in five to ten years, hundreds and thousands of middle-aged Arab school teachers in Israel would be considerably more discontented with their lot if across the fields from their villages were a state where friends and relatives could aspire to and hold not only skilled technical positions, directorships in banks, factories, and commercial institutions, editorial positions with prominent newspapers, senior civil service posts, etc., but also the highest military and political offices in the land. Under such circumstances it is quite likely that, in their struggle for greater equality as Israeli citizens and for recognition of Arab prerogatives to cultural and regional autonomy, these individuals would come to make secessionist demands. Demands in heavily Arab areas for plebiscites on whether or not to join the Palestinian entity would most probably elicit strong political and material support from Palestinians across the border.[71]

Finally, one must remember that Israeli withdrawal from the West Bank and the Gaza Strip and the emergence of some sort of Palestinian homeland there would represent an enormous concession, in Israeli eyes, to Arab demands and to the rights of the Palestinians. It is very likely that following such a sacrifice the regime would redouble its efforts to develop Israel proper as a Zionist state and to create within it as much room as possible for future Jewish immigrants. Under such circumstances the Arab minority's demands for a more active role in Israeli politics and for the commitment of a larger share of the country's resources to the development of the Arab sector would be likely to be firmly dismissed. The capacity of the regime to suppress Arab dissent and to implement the policies suggested in the Linn-Sharon approach would also be greatly increased by withdrawal from the occupied territories. For, as a result, the entire apparatus of the military government in those areas, including hundreds of officers and political operatives trained in the control of Arab political activity, would be available for use inside Israel.

Conclusion

The most common observation made by sympathetic Israeli critics of the government's internal Arab policy, from 1948 to the present, has been that it has not had one; that it has failed to enunciate or guide the implementation of a clear over-arching policy toward the Arab minority. The most common warning issued by these critics has been the need to develop a coherent, explicit, and comprehensive approach to this sector.[72] With regard to the programs decided on and implemented by the Israeli cabinet, these observers have been correct. Indeed, a purpose of my analysis has been to explain the capacity of relatively low-echelon officials to enforce the subordination of the Arab population without relying on the resources commanded by their superiors and without having to make the purposes of their activities explicit. As I have argued, the ambiguity of official policy in the Arab sector (Arabs are to be treated as equal Israeli citizens; yet, since they are neither obliged to identify with the state's Jewish-national goals nor conscripted into the army, they are not to expect full privileges) has helped the system of control serve the ideological ends of Zionism while reaping propaganda benefits for Israel among liberal circles abroad.

However, the single clearest conclusion that can be drawn from consideration of the eroding structural foundations of effective control is that the regime can much less afford to ignore the advice of these critics now than it has in the past. For, as the trends analyzed in this chapter gain strength, more attention by high-level decision-makers, the commitment of a greater proportion of the resources they command, and more explicit formulas to facilitate systematic and comprehensive policy adjustments will be increasingly required. In recent years, although there is evidence that a somewhat higher level of resources has been devoted to the problem than in the past, the increase has not matched the need. Accordingly, the regime has experienced a real decrease in its ability to manipulate the Arab population.

At some point the consequences of this deterioration will force the highest echelons to make a decision between accepting a lower level of control over the Arab minority than that to which they have been accustomed or paying the costs (in time, energy, money, and, possibly, unfavorable international publicity) of reversing the trend. Until that point comes it is unlikely that policy toward Israeli Arabs will diverge more than incrementally from the patterns described on the programmatic level of analysis in Chapters 4–6. While Arabists who favor the Toledano-Histadrut approach will push for successive increases in funds and staff devoted to cooptation of young Arabs, Arabists who support the ideas of Amnon Linn and Arik Sharon will encourage a confrontationist attitude in the Jewish sector and the intermittent use of strong-arm methods.

Though it has been possible to trace the logic inherent in the options open to the regime for adapting the system of control and to compare the advantages and disadvantages of each, it is not possible to predict which approach, if either, will ultimately be followed. The answer depends partly on how long Israel continues to experience political, economic, and security crises that overshadow the internal Arab problem. It depends, as I have indicated, on how long the occupation of the West Bank and Gaza continues and on the eventual juridical disposition of those areas. It also depends on the perspicacity of the Israeli leadership and on the balance between its liberal and Zionist ideological commitments.

Concentration on how and when the system of control might be adapted to changing circumstances seems justifiable only if its breakdown or the guided transformation of Jewish-Arab relations from "control" to more consociational or pluralist arrangements is deemed unlikely. To be sure, there are some Jewish groups, such as Shulamit Aloni's Civil Rights Movement, Mapam, and "Shelli," on the left wing of the Labor-Zionist Movement, which emphasize the importance of the legal status of Arab Israelis as citizens of the state who deserve equal treatment and a proportionate share of the country's wealth. Implicit in their call for equal economic development in the Arab sector, nondiscrimination, and complete political freedom for Arabs has been a pluralist vision of a multiethnic Israeli state and society. It is the belief, among Arabs, in the fundamental contradiction between the reforms these groups advocate and their firmly held Zionist commitments which has hampered the efforts of Mapam, Shelli, and the Civil Rights Movement to woo Arab voters from Rakah.[73] Though they have expressed their opposition to the treatment of Arabs as "second-class citizens," these groups have continued to support the idea of Israel as a Jewish and Zionist state and explicitly reject binationalist formulas. Thus these groups have not faced the basic problem: whether their support for the symbolic and institutional expressions of Zionism in Israel—e.g., "Hatikvah" as the national anthem, the Star of David on the national flag, the Law of Return, the continued operation of the JNF and the Jewish Agency, the massive involvement of the government in immigrant absorption and other Zionist tasks—is compatible with the reforms which they advocate (including Arab participation in the governance of Israel's major institutions).[74]

At any rate, Israeli Jews who hold such opinions comprise not more than 5 percent of the Jewish population (as measured by Knesset representation). Therefore, since the political program they espouse is not likely to be implemented, the contradiction within it is not likely to be experienced. For the overwhelming majority of Israeli Jews, as well as for the political, social, and economic elites, the permanent character of the state as an expression of the political will of Jews is not a matter for debate or even speculation. Their vision of Israel is not of a state that is to serve, ultimately, as a neutral umpire between Jewish and Arab ethno-national groups apportioning or competing for its resources, but of an organizational tool in the continuing struggle of the Zionist movement to solve what is seen, more or less vividly, as the international Jewish problem.

In the absence of a political base for a Jewish leadership committed to changing the fundamental terms of the relationship between Jews and Arabs in Israel, the guided transformation of Israel toward a consociational or pluralist society will not take place. However, if control over the minority breaks down, accompanied either by the crystallization of a mass-based Arab political organization with electoral and economic bargaining power or by widespread violent protest, a radical reassessment of the position of Arabs in Israel will be required. Under such circumstances pluralist or consociational futures could become relevant; on the other hand, so might the possibility, now discussed publicly only in ultranationalist circles, of eliminating the problem through mass expulsions. But for the next ten to fifteen years, unless the masses of Palestinian Arabs in the West Bank and the Gaza Strip are incorporated into the state, it is unlikely that either the resources or the political ingenuity of the regime will be seriously strained by the task of controlling the Arab population.

Notes

1. The Quiescence of Israeli Arabs: Explaining Stability in a Deeply Divided Society

1. I find Milton Esman's definition of "communalism" as "competitive group solidarities within the same political system based on ethnic, linguistic, racial, or religious identities," to be perfectly satisfactory for my purposes (Milton J. Esman, "The Management of Communal Conflict," *Public Policy* 21, no. 1 [Winter 1973]: 49). Because I shall make no assertions concerning the possible political implications of various modes of group identification, I shall use such terms as "ethnic" and "communal" interchangeably.

2. For a survey and discussion of this literature, see Arend Lijphart, *The Politics of Accommodation*, pp. 1–15.

3. For a survey of over fifty contemporary cases of ethnic discord, see Cynthia Enloe, *Ethnic Conflict and Political Development*.

4. For discussion of the need for this suppositional switch, see Clifford Geertz, "The Integrative Revolution: Primordial Sentiments and Civil Politics in the New States," in Jason L. Finkle and Richard W. Gable, eds., *Political Development and Social Change*; and Walker Connor, "Nation-Building or Nation-Destroying," *World Politics* 24, no. 3 (April 1972): 319–355.

5. Samuel P. Huntington, *Political Order in Changing Societies*, p. 39.

6. Robert Melson and Howard Wolpe, "Modernization and the Politics of Communalism: A Theoretical Perspective," *American Political Science Review* 64 (December 1970): 1112–1130.

7. Enloe, *Ethnic Conflict and Political Development*, pp. 261–274.

8. Alvin Rabushka and Kenneth A. Shepsle, *Politics in Plural Societies: A Theory of Democratic Instability*, pp. 20–21, 213, 217.

9. Arend Lijphart, "Consociational Democracy," *World Politics* 21, no. 2 (January 1969): 207–225.

10. Donald Rothchild, "Ethnicity and Conflict Resolution," *World Politics* 22, no. 4 (July 1970): 597–616.

11. Eric A. Nordlinger, *Conflict Regulation in Divided Societies*, p. 117.

12. Nordlinger's definition of "open" is somewhat vague: "Democratic regimes, featuring universal suffrage, free elections, and genuine competition between two or more parties clearly qualify as open regimes. . . . In contemporary terms practically all western regimes, as well as some non-western ones, such as Malaysia, Lebanon, and India qualify as open" (ibid., pp. 10–11). For my purposes it is significant only to note that Israel would most certainly be classified as an "open regime" according to Nordlinger's usage.

13. Sidney Verba, "Some Dilemmas in Comparative Research," *World Politics* 20, no. 1 (October 1967): 127. For an analysis of the assumptions upon which consociational approaches to an explanation of stability in deeply divided societies rest, and for a comparison of these assumptions and those which underlie the "control" approach used in this study, see Ian Lustick, "Stability in Deeply Divided Societies: Consociationalism vs. Control," *World Politics* 31, no. 3 (April 1979): 325–344.

14. This figure is more than 2 percent lower than official estimates of the non-Jewish population of Israel. This is because since 1967 the government's Central Bureau of Statistics has included in this category the inhabitants of the Arab or Eastern sector of Jerusalem, occupied by Israeli forces in June 1967. Although "Arab Jerusalem" has been incorporated into the municipality of West or "Jewish Jerusalem," it has not been annexed by Israel, and Israeli citizenship has not been extended to its inhabitants. Socially and politically it is the center of the West Bank. Nor do the Arab residents of East Jerusalem vote in Israeli parliamentary elections.

    This study concerns *only* those Arabs (approximately 503,000 in Fall 1979) living inside the "Green Line," i.e., within the 1949–1950 armistice lines. However, when post-1967 official statistics are quoted, the reader should be aware that they include (unless otherwise specified) the Arab population of East Jerusalem (estimated at 110,000 in 1979).

15. There are two important exceptions: (1) The Law of Return makes it possible for any Jew, from anywhere in the world and solely by virtue of Jewishness, to acquire Israeli citizenship automatically upon entrance into the country. (2) A separate though related measure known as the Nationality Law, passed in 1952,

places special conditions on the naturalization of non-Jewish residents of Israel who had not acquired Israeli citizenship by that date. For a discussion of the provisions of the Nationality Law, see Don Peretz, *Israel and the Palestine Arabs*, pp. 121–126.

16. The Israeli Communist Party, both before and after its split in 1965, has played an important role in the articulation of Arab grievances. However, it is neither independent in its policy line nor communal in its orientation. It is and always has been, except for the now essentially defunct "Maki" branch, closely aligned with and supported by the Soviet Union. Its present leadership was active in the Palestinian Communist Party before the creation of the state, and, although many of its top-echelon cadre and most of its votes are Arab, its leader, Meir Vilner, and half of its administrative hierarchy are Jewish.

The role of the Communist Party vis-à-vis the Arab minority in Israel is discussed at some length in Chapters 4 and 7.

17. The furor among Jewish political parties in the early 1960's over abolition of the Military Administration was perhaps the most significant intrusion into Israeli politics of an issue directly relating to the Arab minority.

Most studies of the politics of communalism do not draw upon the Israeli case for exemplification or comparison. When Israel is included in such studies, attention is almost always directed to the division between Ashkenazic Jews (European and American) and Oriental Jews (those from African and Asian countries). In those few cases where the Jewish-Arab segmentation of Israeli society is considered, the lack of hard information is manifest in the naïveté of the analysis. Thus one purpose of this study is to add information about Israel to the data base of scholars undertaking the study of deeply divided or multi-ethnic societies.

See for example Enloe's discussion of Arab-Jewish relations in Israel, *Ethnic Conflict and Political Development*, pp. 21–22. *Israel: Pluralism and Conflict* by Sammy Smooha is valuable for an accurate assessment of the basic character of the Arab-Jewish relationship in Israel, though the author's attention is directed almost exclusively to the Ashkenazic-Oriental segmentation of the Jewish sector.

18. Dan Bavli, in *Davar*, June 29, 1975, p. 7. On the political quiescence of the Arab sector see Moshe Keren, "Have We an Arab Policy?" *Haaretz*, January 14, 1955; Eli Elad, "The Tired Arabists," *Haaretz*, January 30, 1970; Mattityahu Peled, "The Arab Minority in Israel," *Maariv*, August 1, 1975, reprinted in *SWASIA*, September 19, 1975.

19. Nadav Safran, "Israel's Internal Politics and Foreign Policy," in Paul Y. Hammond and Sidney S. Alexander, eds., *Political Dynamics in the Middle East*, pp. 155–185.

20. Nordlinger, *Conflict Regulation in Divided Societies*, pp. 21–29. The fundamental reason for the inapplicability of the conflict-regulating or consociational approach in the Israeli context is the assumption made by these analysts that in a democratic or open society communal identities will, almost automatically, be politically mobilized. In Israel it is precisely the absence of "Arab" political mobilization that I wish to explore. See in this regard Hans Daalder, "The Consociational Democracy Theme," *World Politics* 26, no. 4 (July 1974): 604–621.

21. For a discussion of the influence of these factors on the intensification of interethnic conflict see Myron Weiner, "The Macedonian Syndrome: An Historical Model of International Relations and Political Development," *World Politics* 23, no. 4 (July 1971): 665–683. See also Rupert Emerson, *From Empire to Nation*, p. 331.

22. Verba, "Some Dilemmas in Comparative Research," p. 127.

23. David Ben-Gurion, *Israel: A Personal History*, p. 348.

24. Ibid., p. 349.

25. Verba, "Some Dilemmas in Comparative Research," p. 217.

26. Yitzhak Oded, who has studied the question of the expropriation of Arab land more closely than anyone else, wrote in 1964 that "almost all Arab land in the valleys and the coastal plain . . . was taken over" ("Land Losses among Israel's Arab Villagers," *New Outlook* 7, no. 7 [September 1964]: 11). Although estimates of the precise amount of land confiscated in one way or another from Arab residents of Israel vary widely (there are no official figures), it would seem that between 65 and 75 percent of the lands owned by Israeli Arabs in 1948 have been expropriated. A more detailed examination of the issue is presented in Chapter 5.

27. According to the *Statistical Abstract of Israel* 24 (1973): 79, 119; 29 (1978): 271. The data in the figure refer to all Jewish families who live in localities with a population of 2,000 or more. However, the non-Jewish figures refer only to those non-Jews who live in "towns" (population 10,000 or more). This has the effect of excluding many large Arab villages (population 4,000–10,000). Judging from a comparison of living conditions in these villages with those prevailing in the towns, there is every reason to think that had the large villages been included in the survey, the gap between Jewish and Arab incomes would be shown to be considerably wider.

Prior to the Yom Kippur War of 1973 the value of the Israeli lira was officially pegged at I£ 4.20 = $1.00. Inflationary pressures have forced the government into a series of devaluations. The rate of exchange in the summer of 1976 was more than 7 lira to the dollar. The large absolute increase in Jewish and Arab incomes from 1967 to 1976 was due, primarily, to inflation.

28. Computed from statistics provided in the *Statistical Abstract of Israel* 28 (1977): 263.

29. Eliahu Gutman, Haim Klaf, and Shulamith Levi, *The Histadrut and Its Activities in the Arab Sector: Research on the Status, Opinions and Behavior of Arab Villagers in Israel*, p. 20 (Hebrew).

30. Oded Remba, "Income Inequality in Israel: Ethnic Aspects," in Michael Curtis and Mordechai Chertoff, eds., *Israel: Social Structure and Change*, p. 207.

31. On the absence of a national leadership of Israeli Arabs, see Jacob M. Landau, "A Note on the Leadership of Israeli Arabs" (reprint from *Il Politico* [University of Pavia, Milan] 27, no. 3 [1962]).

32. Yochanan Peres and Nira Yuval-Davis, "Some Observations on the National Identity of the Israeli Arabs," *Human Relations* 22, no. 3 (June 1969): 230.

33. Yochanan Peres, "Modernization and Nationalism in the Identity of the Israeli Arab," *Middle East Journal* 24, no. 4 (Autumn 1970): 491.

34. Yochanan Peres, "Ethnic Relations in Israel," *American Journal of Sociology* 76, no. 6 (May 1971): 1039. Regarding the attitudes of Jewish Israelis toward the Arab minority, see Chapter 4.

35. Sammy Smooha, "Control of Minorities in Israel and Northern Ireland," paper presented at the Ninth World Congress of Sociology in Uppsala, August 1978, pp. 18–19.

36. Ellen Joyce Kubersky Geffner, "Attitudes of Arab Editorialists in Israel, 1948–67: An Analysis of AL-ITTIHAD, AL-MIRSAD, and AL-YAWM" (Ph.D. dissertation, University of Michigan, 1973), pp. 11–12. These circulation figures are for 1966.

37. Ibid., p. 148.

38. Ibid., p. 139.

39. Ibid., p. 143.

40. Avraham Yinnon, "Some Central Themes of the Literature of Israeli Arabs," *Hamizrah Hechadash* 15, no. 1 (1965): 57 (Hebrew). See also Ori Stendel, *The Minorities in Israel*, pp. 170–174; and Jacob M. Landau, *The Arabs in Israel*, pp. 64–68.

41. Yinnon, "Some Central Themes of the Literature of Israeli Arabs," p. 57.

42. Emile A. Nakhleh, "Wells of Bitterness: A Survey of Israeli-Arab Political Poetry," *The Arab World* 16, no. 2 (February 1970): 34.

43. Yinnon, "Some Central Themes of the Literature of Israeli Arabs," pp. 60–61.

44. Shmuel Moreh, "Arabic Literature in Israel," *Middle Eastern Studies* 3, no. 3 (April 1967): 290.

45. Nakhleh, "Wells of Bitterness," p. 33.

46. Jacob M. Landau, in *Encyclopaedia Judaica* 9 (1974): 1042.

47. Nakhleh, "Wells of Bitterness," p. 33. For more information concerning the political thrust of Arab literature in Israel, see Emile Marmorstein, "Rashid Hussein: Portrait of an Angry Young Arab," *Middle Eastern Studies* 1, no. 1 (January 1964): 3–20; Landau, *The Arabs in Israel*, pp. 57–68.

48. *Al-Yaum*, December 24, 1950; reprinted in *Ner* 2, nos. 9–12 (March 1951): 19 (Hebrew).

49. Naim Makhoul, "The Arab Village in Israel," *Ner* 9, nos. 8–9 (May–June, 1958): 48.

50. Sheik Musa al-Atawna, "What the Bedouin Want," *New Outlook* 3, no. 9 (September 1960): 16.

51. "An Appeal from Galilee," reprinted from *al-Hamishmar* in *Ner* 14, nos. 7–9 (March–May, 1963): xlvii.

52. Massad Kassis, "Outcry in the Knesset," *Ner* 4, no. 11 (July 1953): 47.

53. Walid Fahoum, "A Socialist Perspective on the Arab-Israeli Conflict," *Student World* 62, no. 1 (First Quarter 1969): 95.

54. *Haaretz*, February 26, 1976, reprinted in *Israleft*, no. 79 (March 1, 1976). For details concerning Arab protests against land expropriations in the Galilee in 1976, see Chapter 7.

55. Interview with Suleiman Hasan, Abu-Krinat tribe, *Zoo Haderech*, May 31, 1978. Regarding the activities of the "Green Patrol," established in 1977 to enforce Jewish claims to Negev lands, see Chapter 7.

56. Yitzhak Oded, "Israel's Arab Villagers Are Being Driven from Their Land," *Ner* 13, nos. 11–12 (July–August 1963): iii. See Chapter 5 of this book for a detailed discussion of compensation for expropriated land.

57. Elias N. Koussa, "Israel and the Arab People," *Ner* 4, no. 1 (October 1952): 23–24.

58. Ibid., p. 22.

59. Elias N. Koussa, letter dated March 12, 1952 in *Ner* 3, nos. 13–14 (June 1952): 20.

60. Ibid., p. 19.

61. Yaacov Friedler, "Arab Villagers and Minister on Give-and-Take Projects," reprinted from the *Jerusalem Post* in *Ner* 8, nos. 10–12 (July–September 1957): 46.

62. *Ner* 13, nos. 3–4 (November–December 1961): xxv.

63. Yehoshua Guilboa, "Envious Arab Boys," *Ner* 9, nos. 1–2 (October–November 1957): 40–41.

64. Ibid.

65. Ibid., p. 40.

66. Eliezer Ben Moshe, "Does Arab Youth Have a Future in Israel?" *Ner* 15, nos. 4–5 (December 1964–January 1965): xxiv.

67. *Statistical Abstract of Israel* 24 (1973): 378.

68. Mohammed Sirhan, "Is There a Solution to the Problem of the Israeli Arabs?" *Student World* 62, no. 1 (First Quarter 1969): 81. Concerning Jewish Agency subsidies for Jewish agriculture, see Chapter 5.

69. Khalil Aboud, Letter to the *Jerusalem Post*, reprinted in *Ner* 9, nos. 1–2 (October–November 1957): 38.

70. "The rapid growth of the Israeli economy since the establishment of the state is one of the most outstanding phenomena on the world economic scene since World War II. From a relatively backward, underdeveloped economy, with a per capita income of $580 in 1950, by 1972 she had reached a per capita income of $1,330 (both measured in 1955 dollars). During this same period the population increased more than three and one-half times, from 900,000 to 3.2 million, while the real gross national product increased eight times. In the course of this rapid economic development, houses were constructed to meet the needs of a massive immigration, new towns were built, new agricultural settlements were established, a modern agricultural system was developed, industry was modernized and a whole new infrastructure for the economy and society was built" (Abba Lerner and Haim Ben-Shahar, *The Economics of Efficiency and Growth: Lessons from Israel and the West Bank*, p. 67).

71. Personal interview with a resident of the Arab village of Eilabun in the central Galilee, March 30, 1974.

72. Sirhan, "Is There a Solution to the Problem of the Israeli Arabs?" p. 81.

73. Rustum Bastuni, "Whither the Arab Minority?" *Ner* 7, nos. 10–11 (June–July 1956): 16 (Hebrew) (emphasis in original).

74. Personal interview with Nawaf Masalha, Tel Aviv, April 24, 1974. Concerning the slow rate of economic development in the Arab sector, see Chapter 5.

75. Personal interview with Mahmoud Bayadsi, Baka el-Gharbiyeh, April 20, 1974.
76. Personal interview with Yusuf Khamis, Tel Aviv, April 18, 1974.
77. Attalah Mansour, "Arab Intellectuals Not Integrated," *New Outlook* 7, no. 3 (June 1964): 28.
78. Eli Rekhess, *A Survey of Israeli-Arab Graduates from Institutions of Higher Learning in Israel (1961–1971)*, p. 9.
79. Mustafa Yahia, "Reflections on the National Identity of the Arabs in Israel," *Student World* 62, no. 1 (First Quarter 1969):73.
80. *Ner* 13, nos. 9–10 (May–June 1963): xi–xii.
81. Eli Rekhess, *Arabs in Israel and the Land Expropriations in the Galilee: Background, Events, and Implications* (Hebrew). See as well Jalal Abu-Tama, "Viewpoints of Israeli Arabs," *Maariv*, December 8, 1974.
82. Yahia, "Reflections on the National Identity of the Arabs in Israel," p. 75.
83. Quoted from an interview with an Arab writer and journalist in Rekhess, *A Survey of Israeli-Arab Graduates from Institutions of Higher Learning in Israel (1961–1971)*, p. 29. His findings "confirm the assumption that the younger generation of Israeli Arabs measure their own position by comparison with Jewish society . . ."
84. "Arab Youth in Israel," *Ner* 13, nos. 1–2 (September–October 1961): viii.
85. According to official government sources "there has been hardly any Arab emigration from Israel since the establishment of the State" ("Minority Groups in Israel," Prime Minister's Office, Bureau of the Adviser on Arab Affairs [Jerusalem, 1970], p. 2). This is because an Arab who chooses, formally, to emigrate must renounce the right ever to return, even for a visit. Extremely close family ties among Arabs in Israel make such a decision almost impossible. More meaningful data can be gleaned from Table IV/I of the *Statistical Abstract of Israel* 28 (1977): 110, entitled "Arrivals and departures, by category of visa." According to this table, 18,497 Arabs who departed from Israel between 1948 and 1976 had not returned by the end of 1976.
86. Personal interview with participants in a "Seminar on Coexistence on the Campus," sponsored by the Histadrut, Ramat Gan, May 3, 1974. For a discussion of the particularly acute employment problems facing Arab engineers in Israel see Rekhess, *A Survey of Israeli-Arab Graduates of Institutions of Higher Learning (1961–1971)*, pp. 18–19.

87. Personal interview, Sakhnin village, March 2, 1974.

88. Ben Moshe, "Does Arab Youth Have a Future in Israel?" pp. xxiv–xxv.

89. In the 1976 survey of Israeli Arab opinion referred to above, two-thirds of those questioned favored the formation of independent Arab organizations as a means of political struggle (Smooha, "Control of Minorities in Israel and Northern Ireland," p. 19).

90. Bishop James A. Pike, "A Good Word for Israel," *New Outlook* 6, no. 3 (March–April 1963): 25.

91. Quoted from a court decision written by Justice Moshe Landau of the Israeli Supreme Court by Ori Stendel, *The Arab Minority in Israel* (reprinted from *Israel Yearbook on Human Rights*, vol. 1 [Tel Aviv University, Faculty of Law, 1971]), p. 145. Several authors have remarked on the lack of independent political activity on the part of Israeli Arabs as well as on the absence of an accepted leadership for the Arab minority. For example, see Landau, *The Arabs in Israel*, p. 71; and, by the same author, "A Note on the Leadership of Israeli Arabs." See also Stendel, *The Minorities in Israel*, p. 107; Peled, "The Arab Minority in Israel"; Peres and Yuval-Davis, "Some Observations on the National Identity of the Israeli Arabs," p. 225.

92. Israel Information Center, "Minorities in Israel," Information Briefing 9, October, 1973.

93. Stendel, *The Minorities in Israel*, pp. 107–111.

94. Micah Nino, "The Situation of Minorities and of Christian Communities under Israeli Jurisdiction," *International Problems* 11, nos. 3–4 (December 1972): 12.

95. Landau, *The Arabs in Israel*, pp. 71, 74.

96. Sami Hadawi, *Israel and the Arab Minority*, Information Paper No. 7 (New York: Arab Information Center, July 1959); Sabri Jiryis, *The Arabs of Israel*; Fouzi el-Asmar, *To Be an Arab in Israel*. An expanded and updated version of Sabri Jiryis' book was published in 1976 by Monthly Review Press, New York.

97. Maxim Ghilan, *How Israel Lost Its Soul*, pp. 201–204.

98. Elia T. Zureik, "Transformation of Class Structures among the Arabs in Israel: From Peasantry to Proletariat," *Journal of Palestine Studies* 6, no. 1 (1976): 39–66. See also, by the same author, *Palestinians in Israel: A Study in Internal Colonialism*.

99. Smooha, "Control of Minorities in Israel and Northern Ireland." See also, by the same author, *Israel: Pluralism and Conflict*.

2. Zionism and the Idea of an Arab Minority: Regime Objectives and Israeli Arabs in the First Years of Statehood

1. James G. MacDonald, *My Mission in Israel, 1948–1951*, p. 176.
2. Theodor Herzl, *The Complete Diaries of Theodor Herzl*, ed. Raphael Patai, 2:581.
3. Leonard Stein, *The Balfour Declaration*, pp. 464–470.
4. Enzo Sereni, "Historical Survey," in Enzo Sereni and R. E. Ashery, eds., *Jews and Arabs in Palestine*, p. 42a. Weizmann made the statement in 1919.
5. For an extended discussion of how pronouncements of the Zionist leadership concerning the official objectives of the movement were adjusted and readjusted after 1897 and 1948 as a result of a combination of changing circumstances and an unwavering commitment to an ultimate goal—Jewish statehood—see Ben Halpern, *The Idea of the Jewish State*, esp. pp. 281–343.
6. David Ben-Gurion, "Planning Zionist Policy," in Sereni and Ashery, eds., *Jews and Arabs in Palestine*, pp. 143–144.
7. Halpern, *The Idea of the Jewish State*, p. 340.
8. Eliezer Liebenstein (Livne), "A New Zionist Foreign Policy," in Sereni and Ashery, eds., *Jews and Arabs in Palestine*, pp. 231–233.
9. In contrast to the exhaustive treatment accorded to various minute points of ideology and political tactics during the twenty-two Zionist congresses which preceded the establishment of the state, the record of these meetings shows almost no serious public consideration of the question of the actual role and the status of an Arab minority in the future Zionist entity. For a whimsical but seriously intended treatment of the problem, see Theodor Herzl's novel *Alteneuland*, pp. 121–124.
10. Susan Lee Hattis, *The Bi-National Idea in Palestine during Mandatory Times*, p. 91.
11. Ibid., p. 98.
12. Ibid., p. 167.
13. *Palestine Royal Commission Report*, Cmd. Paper 5479, p. 289.
14. Hattis, *The Bi-National Idea in Palestine*, p. 254.
15. On the efforts and eventual failure of binationalist Zionists, see Hattis, *The Bi-National Idea in Palestine*. The various usages of the term "parity" discussed in this section refer to formulas put forward by mainstream Labor Zionist spokesmen. On the fringes of the Zionist movement, among those associated with Ihud, "parity" was used to mean quite a different thing, viz., fixed ratios of Jewish and Arab populations in Palestine.

16. *The Jewish Case: Before the Anglo-American Committee of Inquiry on Palestine as Presented by the Jewish Agency for Palestine*, p. 69.
17. See David Ben-Gurion's testimony in *Palestine Royal Commission Report*, pp. 289–290.
18. Testimony of Moshe Sharett (Shertok), in *The Jewish Case*, p. 37.
19. Ibid., p. 71.
20. United Nations Special Committee on Palestine (UNSCOP), *Report to the General Assembly* (1947), p. 64.
21. Testimony of David Ben-Gurion, in ibid., p. 40.
22. *The Jewish Case*, pp. 77–78. For a similar analysis of the future role of the Arab states see the testimony of Chaim Weizmann in *The Jewish Case*, pp. 23–24.
23. UNSCOP, *Report to the General Assembly*, pp. 65–66.
24. Moshe Dayan, "Israel's Border Problems," *Foreign Affairs* 23, no. 2 (January 1955): 261.
25. Quoted by Natan Hofshi in *Ner* 1, no. 1 (February 1950): 5.
26. Under the terms of the United Nations partition resolution, Israel's area was to have been 14,400 square kilometers. After the fighting and the signing of the armistice agreements, Israel encompassed an area of 20,662 square kilometers. See Maps 1 and 2.
27. Don Peretz, *Israel and the Palestine Arabs*, p. 156.
28. David Ben-Gurion, *Israel: A Personal History*, p. 318.
29. Granott, *Agrarian Reform and the Record of Israel*, p. 104. Granott was chairman of the board of directors of the JNF, 1945–1960. Land purchased by the JNF was considered to have become an unalienable part of the "national patrimony." As such it could not be sold and was under various restrictions regarding its use by non-Jews.
30. Zvi Zinger, "State of Israel (1948–1972)," in *Immigration and Settlement*, pp. 54–55.
31. United Nations, *Progress Report of the United Nations Mediator on Palestine* (1948), p. 5.
32. Rony E. Gabbay, *A Political Study of the Arab-Jewish Conflict*, p. 224. Indeed, in 1948 and early 1949 overt British military intervention against the new state was one of the primary concerns of Israel's leaders. See Ministry of Foreign Affairs, Press and Information Division, *Review of the Hebrew Press*, November 1948–March 1949.
33. *Haaretz*, June 10, 1949; August 14, 1949. See also James G. Macdonald, *My Mission in Israel, 1948–1951*, p. 181.
34. Granott, *Agrarian Reform and the Record of Israel*, pp. 99–100, 102.

35. On the development and structure of the Palestinian national movement, see Jacob Shimoni, *Arabs of the Land of Israel;* Ann Mosely Lesch, "The Palestine Arab Nationalist Movement under the Mandate," in William Quandt, Fuad Jabber, and Ann Mosely Lesch, *The Politics of Palestinian Nationalism;* Aharon Cohen, *Israel and the Arab World,* Chapters 5–8.

36. Personal interview with Yehoshua Palmon, Jerusalem, December 10, 1973. See also Yosef Waschitz, "Changes in the life of Israel's Arabs," *Hamizrah Hechadash* 1, no. 4 (August 1950).

37. See Yaacov Shimoni, "The Arabs of the Land of Israel: Pride and Catastrophe," *Molad* 3, no. 15 (June 1949): 152 (Hebrew). There was, however, a Communist Party–sponsored labor organization—the Arab Workers Congress—which was active in 1948 and 1949, but its membership was quite small and it soon disappeared.

38. Granott, *Agrarian Reform and the Record of Israel,* p. 114.

39. For details concerning the question of the "internal refugees," see Chapter 5.

40. Prior to his command of the Military Administration, Elimelech Avner (Zelikowitz) had served as director of the Tel Aviv municipality's Department of Housing. In 1949 he was appointed director-general of the national Ministry of Housing.

41. G. Shamir, "The Establishment of the 'Military Administration' over the Arab Population in Israel during the War of Independence" (seminar paper for Professor Meir Pa'il, Tel Aviv University, 1973), pp. 12–13 (Hebrew).

42. Foreign Minister Moshe Sharett was the only Israeli leader to take an interest in the internal Arab problem, but there is no evidence that he affected internal Arab policy in any substantial respect.

43. Shamir interviewed Mor and a number of the early military governors; these quotations are taken from Shamir's record of his interviews with them ("The Establishment of the 'Military Administration,'" pp. 13–14).

44. Michael Assaf, "The Arab Refugees and the State of Israel," in *Palestine Yearbook and Israel Annual, 1948–1949* 4 (August–September 1948): 234. Consider, for example, the reaction of Moshe Sharett, long-time head of the political department of the Jewish Agency and Israel's first foreign minister: "I am particularly amazed by the flight of the Arabs. This is a more extraordinary episode in the annals of this country than the establishment of a Jewish State. . . . Truly astonishing is that the Arabs have dis-

appeared from a whole section of the country. . . . We must explore the enormous impact of this change on settlement and security. . . . This is one of those revolutionary events that alter the course of history. There can be no return to the status quo ante . . ." (quoted by Ben-Gurion, *Israel: A Personal History*, p. 149).

45. *Israel and the Arab Refugees* (1950), pp. 12–13; quoted by Gabbay, *A Political Study of the Arab-Jewish Conflict*, p. 292.

46. UNSCOP, *Report to the General Assembly*, p. 54. This percentage is based on the projected establishment of Jerusalem as a *corpus separatum*, and does not include an estimate of anticipated Jewish immigration.

47. Yigal Allon, *A Curtain of Sand*, p. 322. See also Peretz, *Israel and the Palestine Arabs*, p. 94.

48. Moshe Keren, "In a Vicious Circle," *Haaretz*, December 29, 1954 (Hebrew).

49. Israel Office of Information, *The Arabs in Israel* (1952), p. 15.

50. Personal interview with Yoshua Verben, Rehovot, December 14, 1973.

51. Israel Office of Information, *The Arabs in Israel* (1952), p. 16.

52. See Hal Lehrman, "Arabs in Israel," *Commentary* 8, no. 12 (December 1949): 524.

53. Judd L. Teller, "Israel Faces Its Arab Minority," *Commentary* 10, no. 12 (December 1951): 553.

54. Israeli Ministry of Foreign Affairs, *The Arabs in Israel* (1961), p. 27.

55. Yaacov Aviel, "The Military Government," *Haaretz*, December 31, 1954.

56. Teller, "Israel Faces Its Arab Minority," p. 553.

57. Ben-Gurion, *Israel: A Personal History*, p. 304.

58. Granott, *Agrarian Reform and the Record of Israel*, pp. 95, 115.

59. Efraim Orni, *Agrarian Reform and Social Progress in Israel*, p. 33.

60. Granott, *Agrarian Reform and the Record of Israel*, p. 99.

61. See Peretz, *Israel and the Palestine Arabs*, pp. 141–142, 149, 155, 159, 162, 163; Shamir, "The Establishment of the 'Military Administration' over the Arab Population in Israel during the War of Independence," p. 14; Yaacov Aviel, "The Uprooted and the Abandoned," *Haaretz*, January 7, 1955; Aharon Liskovsky, "The Present Absentees, in Israel," *Hamizrah Hechadash* 10, no. 3 (1960): 187 (Hebrew).

62. Don Peretz, "Problems of Arab Refugee Compensation," *Middle East Journal* 8, no. 4 (Autumn 1954): 403.

63. Israel Office of Information, *The Arabs in Israel* (1955), p. 27. For a close examination of the issue of the expropriation of absentee lands, see Chapter 5.

64. Shimoni, *Arabs of the Land of Israel*, p. 213.

65. *Yearbook of the United Nations*, 1950, p. 314.

66. Hal Lehrman, *Israel: The Beginning and Tomorrow*, p. 60.

67. Peretz, *Israel and the Palestine Arabs*, p. 143.

68. K. Menachem, "The Affair of Abasiye [Ghabasiyeh] Village," reprinted from *Davar* in *Ner* 1, no. 3 (March 1950): 5. For information on other Arab villages whose inhabitants were expelled after the end of hostilities, see Peretz, *Israel and the Palestine Arabs*, p. 153; Sabri Jiryis, *The Arabs in Israel*, pp. 56–67.

69. For an explanation of the various categories of the Waqf in Israel, see Aharon Layish, "The Muslim Waqf in Israel," *Hamizrah Hechadash* 15, nos. 1–2 (1965).

70. The Palestinian pound was equal, at the time, to the British pound sterling.

71. Peretz, "Problems of Arab Refugee Compensation," pp. 404–408.

72. Peretz, *Israel and the Palestine Arabs*, p. 142. For a detailed discussion of the Absentee Property Law and the problem of the "present absentees" see Chapter 5.

73. Editorial, *Palestine Post*, March 30, 1949.

74. Yoram Ben-Porath, *The Arab Labor Force in Israel*, p. 51.

75. Israel Office of Information, *The Arabs of Israel* (1955), p. 32.

76. Amin Jarjura, address reprinted from *Divrei Haknesset* in *Ner* 1, no. 12 (July 28, 1950): 8–10. See also Moshe Aram, *Divrei Haknesset* 4 (February 7, 1950): 947–948; Jiryis, *The Arabs in Israel*, pp. 156–163.

77. E. N. Koussa, "Memorandum on Properties Belonging to Arabs Living in Israel," *Ner* 2, no. 18 (July 13, 1951): 27.

78. Michael Assaf, "The Process of Integration of Arabs in the State of Israel," *Hamizrah Hechadash* 1, no. 1 (October 1949): 2–7 (Hebrew).

79. United Nations Conciliation Commission for Palestine, *General Progress Report and Supplementary Report, December 11, 1949–October 23, 1950*, p. 12.

80. Ibid., p. 16.

81. Aubrey S. Eban, *Israel: The Case for Admission to the United Nations* (address delivered before the Ad Hoc Political Committee of the United Nations, May 5, 1949, published by Israel Office of Information), p. 41.

82. Allon, *A Curtain of Sand*, pp. 322–337. There were, of course, differences among Israeli leaders. Generally speaking, those who

tended to be more respectful of international opinion and the United Nations as factors of importance on the international political scene, such as Moshe Sharett, were more concerned with the problem of the Arab minority, while those, such as Ben-Gurion, whose attitude toward the United Nations verged on contempt, showed less concern for the issue.

83. UNRWA, *Assistance to Palestine Refugees*, Interim Report of the Director of the UNRWA for Palestine Refugees, p. 5.
84. *Divrei Haknesset* 4 (1950): 1949–1950.
85. Editorial, *Palestine Post*, November 12, 1948.
86. Jon Kimche, "Nazareth—Political Cameo of Jewish-Arab Relations," *Palestine Post*, August 3, 1948.
87. See, for example, Eban, *Israel: The Case for Admission to the United Nations*, p. 41; and Editorial, *Palestine Post*, August 3, 1948.
88. Koussa, "Memorandum on Properties Belonging to Arabs Living in Israel," p. 26.

3. Control of Arabs in Israel: An Analytic Framework

1. *Jerusalem Post*, June 9, 1976.
2. Yigal Allon, *A Curtain of Sand*, pp. 322, 337.
3. Gideon Spiegel, "We Did Not Come in Order to Be Absorbed by the Inhabitants of This Area," *Ramzor* (a publication of the Central Committee of Mapai), March 1967 (Hebrew).
4. As one Israeli specialist on the Arab minority has put it, the adviser to the prime minister on Arab affairs "is in effect the coordinator of all official, as well as non-governmental institutional policy towards the Arabs who live in Israel" (Yosef Goell, *Jerusalem Post*, April 4, 1976). Since 1976 the authority of the adviser's office has continued to be limited to those Arabs under Israeli jurisdiction who are citizens of the state, i.e., the adviser does not have responsibility for Arabs in the West Bank, the Gaza Strip, or East Jerusalem.
5. Shmuel Toledano, *The Israeli Arabs—Achievements and Perplexities* (Labor Zionist Movement, Tel Aviv, 1974), p. 1.
6. Walter Schwarz, *The Arabs in Israel*, p. 119 (emphasis in original).
7. Ruth Gruber, *Israel Today: Land of Many Nations*, p. 176.
8. Allon, *A Curtain of Sand*, p. 327.
9. Ibid., pp. 328, 331.
10. *Jerusalem Post*, January 21, 1962.
11. Zeev Schiff, "If I Were an Arab," *Haaretz*, April 4, 1961.

12. Ibid.
13. *Davar,* February 25, 1975, quoted in *Middle East International,* no. 47 (May 1975): 21.
14. *Yediot Acharonot,* September 9, 1976.
15. *Israleft,* no. 90 (September 15, 1976): 5.
16. The "Koenig Memorandum," translated from *al-Hamishmar* in *SWASIA* 3, no. 41 (October 15 1976): 1–8. Concerning the Koenig memorandum, see below, Chapters 4–7 passim.
17. Quoted by M. G. Smith, "Some Developments in the Analytic Framework of Pluralism," in Leo Kuper and M. G. Smith, eds., *Pluralism in Africa,* p. 418.
18. Leo Kuper, "Plural Societies: Perspectives and Problems," in Kuper and Smith, eds., *Pluralism in Africa,* p. 21.
19. M. G. Smith, "Pluralism in Precolonial African Societies," in Kuper and Smith, eds., *Pluralism in Africa,* p. 96; Smith, "Some Developments in the Analytic Framework of Pluralism," in ibid., p. 445.
20. See Ira Katznelson, "Comparative Studies of Race and Ethnicity," *Comparative Politics* 5, no. 1 (October 1972): 143.
21. Smith, "Developments in the Analytic Framework," p. 430. See also Leo Kuper, "Ethnic and Racial Pluralism: Some Aspects of Polarization and Depluralization," in Kuper and Smith, eds., *Pluralism in Africa,* p. 473.
22. Pierre Van den Berghe, "Pluralism and the Polity: A Theoretical Exploration," in Kuper and Smith, eds., *Pluralism in Africa,* p. 81n.
23. Alvin Rabushka and Kenneth A. Shepsle, *Plural Societies: A Theory of Democratic Instability,* p. 90.
24. Milton J. Esman, "The Management of Communal Conflict," *Public Policy* 21, no. 1 (Winter 1973): 56.
25. Ibid., p. 57.
26. Leo Kuper, "Political Change in White Settler Societies: The Possibility of Peaceful Democratization," in Kuper and Smith, eds., *Pluralism in Africa,* pp. 177–182.
27. Kuper, "Ethnic and Racial Pluralism," p. 475.
28. Kuper, "Political Change in White Settler Societies," p. 182.
29. Heribert Adam, *Modernizing Racial Domination,* p. 15.
30. See James D. Cockcroft, et al., eds., *Dependence and Underdevelopment,* esp. Chapters 1 and 10. For an interesting critique of this material see Harold Wolpe, "The Theory of Internal Colonialism: The South African Case," in Ivar Oxaal, et al., eds., *Beyond the Sociology of Development,* pp. 229–250.
31. Several proponents of the "internal colonialism" approach have

indicated their awareness of this difficulty. See Michael Hechter, *Internal Colonialism: The Celtic Fringe in British National Development, 1536–1966*, pp. 33n, 349–350; Dale Johnson, "On Oppressed Classes," in Cockcroft, et al., eds., *Dependence and Underdevelopment*, p. 279n.

32. Wolpe, "The Theory of Internal Colonialism," pp. 244–250. For an attempt to apply Marxist theories of internal colonialism to Arab-Jewish relations in Israel, see Elia Zureik, *Palestinians in Israel: A Study in Internal Colonialism.*

33. This use of the concept of "cooptation" is very different from that made popular by Philip Selznick in *TVA and the Grass Roots.* For Selznick, "cooptation" involves the absorption of new elements into decision-making processes as a method of stabilizing an organization. My notion of "cooptation" as a technique of manipulation based on "side payments" or "bribes" is closer to what Selznick refers to as "formal cooptation" (p. 261).

4. Segmentation as a Component of Control: The Isolation and Fragmentation of the Arab Minority

1. Abner Cohen, *Arab Border Villages in Israel: A Study of Continuity and Change in Social Organization*, p. 149.

2. *Statistical Abstract of Israel* 28 (1977): 51.

3. Concerning hamula-inspired attacks on Arab communists in Nazareth, see *Zoo Haderech*, May 17, 1978.

4. Yechiel Harari, ed., *The Arabs in Israel: Facts and Figures*, pp. 2, 10; *Statistical Abstract of Israel* 28 (1977): 36–37. Statistics exclude Arabs living in Jerusalem.

5. In a 1973 study of Arab-Jewish community relations in Acre, Erik Cohen, an urban sociologist, wrote that there is "separation and little social contact between the two groups. . . . Though Acre is a mixed city, Jews and Arabs are still much segregated, reflecting the pervasive segregation of the two communities in the country" (*Integration vs. Separation in the Planning of a Mixed Jewish-Arab City in Israel*, pp. 5–7).

6. Sammy Smooha and John Hofman, "Some Problems of Arab-Jewish Coexistence," *Middle East Review* 9, no. 2 (Winter 1976/1977): 12.

7. Yochanan Peres, "Ethnic Relations in Israel," *American Journal of Sociology* 76, no. 6 (May 1971): 1039.

8. Sammy Smooha, "Control of Minorities in Israel and Northern Ireland" (paper presented at the Ninth World Congress of Sociology in Uppsala), pp. 16–17.

9.   *Haaretz*, September 20, 1974, reprinted in *Israleft*, no. 48 (October 15, 1974).

10.   Ibid. For an extended though quite impressionistic discussion of Jewish-Israeli attitudes toward Arabs and Arab attitudes toward Jews, see Edward Alan Robins, "Pluralism in Israel: Relations between Arabs and Jews" (Ph.D. dissertation, Tulane University, 1972). See also in this regard Amos Elon's discussion of Meir Har Zion as an Israeli culture hero (*Israelis: Founders and Sons*, pp. 302–307).

11.   For example, on September 4, 1968, three explosions in the central bus station of Tel Aviv killed one man and left many persons wounded. A majority of the fifty-nine persons hurt that day received their injuries in the rioting that followed the explosion, as groups of Jewish "hot-heads" roamed the streets with steel bars and wooden clubs "hunting Arabs" (*Davar*, September 15, 1968). On February 25, 1969, two thousand angry Jewish residents of Lod surged toward the Arab quarter of that town after a bomb exploded in the marketplace. Only the presence of reinforced police units prevented widespread violence (*Haaretz*, February 26, 1969; *Jerusalem Post*, February 26, 1969). On April 11, 1974, eighteen Jews, mainly women and children, were killed in Kiryat Shmona by Arab infiltrators. After several Druse passers-by were assaulted by furious Jewish residents, the town had to be closed to Arabs for almost two weeks. Meanwhile incidents of Arabs being attacked or prevented from entering their places of work spread to other cities throughout the country (*Jerusalem Post*, April 12, 19, and 21, 1974; *Israleft*, no. 39). For a description of serious anti-Arab riots in Ramle in 1965, see Terence Prittie, *Israel's Miracle in the Desert*, pp. 131–132. For a more recent example of an attempted lynching following a terrorist bombing in Tel Aviv, see the *New York Times*, August 4, 1978.

12.   For details of the Kfar Kassem massacre, see the translation of court proceedings from the court martial of the soldiers involved provided by Sabri Jiryis in *The Arabs in Israel*, pp. 96–115. See also the *Jerusalem Post*, March 26 and 27, 1957.

13.   Mohammed Watad, Co-existence (*Du-Kiyum*), in *New Outlook* 13, no. 7 (September–October 1970): 72. For comment on the meaning of Kfar Kassem to Israeli Arabs, see also Abdul Karim, in *Ner* 13, nos. 5–7 (February–April 1958): 26.

14.   Fouzi el-Asmar, *To Be an Arab in Israel*, p. 58.

15.   Eliezer Schweid, "Israel as a Zionist State," in American Zionist Youth Foundation, *Zionism: Israel—Vision and Realization*, p. 5.

16. Quoted from the statement of David Ben-Gurion before the Anglo-American Committee of Inquiry on Palestine, as reprinted in *The Jewish Case: Before the Anglo-American Committee of Inquiry on Palestine as Presented by the Jewish Agency for Palestine*, p. 66. For a recent discussion of how the concept of a "Jewish state" should be operationalized, see an interview with Zevulun Hammer conducted soon after his appointment as minister of education and culture (reprinted from *Haaretz*, June 10, 1977, in *Israleft*, no. 109).

17. Schweid, "Israel as a Zionist State," pp. 4–6.

18. These figures are based on the personnel listings provided by Israeli ministries and agencies in the *Israel Government Yearbook, 1976.*

19. In an interview with the official spokesman for the Ministry of Housing, for example, I asked about housing projects for Arabs. "We build Jewish housing here," the spokesman answered. "I don't know what we do for the Arab nation." Eventually I was directed to the Arab Department of the ministry—a small, one-man office in a separate building. The conception which the Ministry of Housing has of itself as an agent of the Jewish people is reflected in the fact that of the 19,100 apartments which the ministry planned to complete in 1971–1972, only 250 were to be made available to non-Jewish Israelis (Zeev Sharef, *On the Activities of the Ministry of Housing: Report to the Knesset by the Minister of Housing*, June 28, 1971 [Hebrew]). For an explicit statement of the priority accorded to the Jewish sector by the ministry, see excerpts of "The Kubersky Committee Report on Illegal Construction and Takeover of Land in the Minorities Sector," *Middle East Review* 9, no. 2 (Winter 1976/1977): 30. For an argument by a high-ranking civil servant justifying the dedication of government ministries to the pursuit of Jewish national goals, see an interview with Chaim Kubersky, director-general of the Ministry of the Interior, in *Maariv*, September 10, 1976.

20. The Labor Party was in control of the governing coalition without interruption from 1948 to 1977. Therefore, although this particular statement of the government's program was submitted to the Knesset by the cabinet of Yitzhak Rabin when he assumed the premiership, it is fair to say that this document expressed the outlook of all preceding governments as well.

21. Israel Information Center, "Basic Principles of the Government's Programme," Information Briefing 24, p. 16. Significantly, nowhere in this list of eleven central domestic objectives were issues relating to Israel's Arab population mentioned.

22. Ibid., p. 5.

23. *Israleft*, no. 109 (July 1, 1977): 10. As was the case in similar documents issued by previous Labor governments, no explicit mention was made of issues relating to the Arab minority.

24. Israel Information Center, "Basic Principles of the Government's Programme," p. 14. Similar language has been used by the Likud government to characterize its official policy toward Arabs in Israel, though spokesmen have been more apt to note the difficulties associated with "extensive integration." See an interview with Defense Minister Ezer Weizmann reprinted from *Haaretz*, May 27, 1977, in *SWASIA* 4, no. 17, and an interview with the Adviser to the Prime Minister on Arab Affairs, Moshe Sharon, in the *Jerusalem Post Weekly*, April 4, 1978.

25. Moshe Keren, "In a Vicious Circle," *Haaretz*, December 24, 1954. For another such contrast, see Amos Elon, "The Tragedy of Ghabisiye and Israeli Justice," *Haaretz*, October 19, 1951.

26. Concerning the bureaucratic segregation of Jews and Arabs in the Ministry of Health in 1975, see Shulamit Aloni, "Discrimination against Arab Settlements," *Yediot Acharonot*, October 10, 1975, reprinted in *SWASIA* 2, no. 45 (November 14, 1975).

27. Excluding, that is, many ultra-orthodox Yeshiva students, those exempted for medical reasons, married women, and women who have been exempted on religious grounds.

28. For a characterization of the Israeli armed forces as "a Zionist army," see the text of an interview with the chief education officer of the Israel Defense Forces, Avner Shilo (translated from *Haaretz*, July 14, 1978, in *Israleft*, no. 131 [August 1, 1978]).

29. For example, although all children in large families are eligible for allowances from the National Insurance Institute, those whose parents, grandparents, or brothers served in the Israel Defense Forces receive 40 percent more. Thus most Arab children as well as the children of orthodox Jewish students in religious seminaries (who are exempted from army service) are ineligible for the higher payments. The latter, however, receive compensatory payments from a special fund under the control of the Ministry of Religion. See *Davar*, March 14, 1978.

30. Dan Horowitz and Baruch Kimmerling, "Some Social Implications of Military Service and the Reserves System in Israel," in Reuven Kahane and Simcha Kopstein, eds., *Israeli Society, 1967–1973*, p. 121.

31. Zvi Sussman, "The Policy of the Histadrut with Regard to Wage Differentials: A Study of the Impact of Egalitarian Ideology and

Arab Labour on Jewish Wages in Palestine" (Ph.D. dissertation, Hebrew University, 1969), p. 162.

32. Yoram Ben-Porath, *The Arab Labor Force in Israel*, pp. 52–55. See also Michael Assaf, "The Evil Story of the Military Administration," *Beterem* (May 1953): 8–9 (Hebrew).

33. For a description of this organization and other small groups which work on an interpersonal level to establish links between Jews and Arabs, see Harry M. Rosen, *The Arabs and Jews In Israel: The Reality, the Dilemma, the Promise*.

34. For a discussion of continuity and change in the organizational purposes of the Histadrut since 1948, see Edwin M. Epstein, "The Social and Economic Role of Hevrat Ovdim in Israel, 1923–1973: An American Perspective," *Annals of Public and Cooperative Economy* 45, no. 2. Epstein observes that, "Notwithstanding the strains resulting from the necessity for the Histadrut to accommodate itself since 1948 to governmental leadership rather than operating as a largely autonomous entity in the Yishuv, Hevrat Ovdim has maintained as its basic social and economic rationale a task which dates from its founding: *facilitating the growth, development and economic self-sufficiency of a Jewish State*" (p. 135, emphasis in original). Concerning the Zionist character of the Histadrut in the poststate era, see also Maurice Hindus, *In Search of a Future: Persia, Egypt, Iraq, and Palestine*, pp. 237–251.

35. When the state of Israel was established, the World Zionist Organization and the Jewish Agency were, essentially, two names for the same institution. In 1971 an important reorganization took place. As a result of what was called the "reconstitution" of the Jewish Agency, the World Zionist Organization maintains a separate organizational existence from the Jewish Agency, though it continues to participate in Jewish Agency activities and decisions as a kind of senior partner. The activities undertaken solely by the World Zionist Organization include propaganda, Zionist education, leadership training, and other political operations which would endanger the Jewish Agency's tax-exempt status (as far as American contributions are concerned) if undertaken by that organization. The World Zionist Organization is financed by the Basic Fund (Keren Hayesod), which receives contributions from Jewish communities outside the United States. The World Zionist Organization will not be examined in detail; its activities are primarily directed toward the Jewish diaspora. For an excellent discussion of the background to the Jewish Agency reorganization,

see Ernest Stock, "The Reconstitution of the Jewish Agency: A Political Analysis," *American Jewish Yearbook* 73 (1972): 178–193. Also, see Zelig S. Chinitz, "The Meaning of the Reconstitution of the Jewish Agency," *Dispersion and Unity* 10 (Winter 1970): 97–103.

36. "Keren Kayemeth Le'Israel—The Jewish National Fund," *Who's Who in Israel*, p. 416.

37. See Map 4 for an indication of Jewish and Arab population densities.

38. "The JNF is headed by a board of directors consisting of 26 members elected by the Zionist General Council and up to three governors nominated by the Zionist Executive" (Jacob Tsur [former chairman of the board of directors of the JNF], "The Jewish National Fund," in *Immigration and Settlement*, p. 116).

39. Abraham Granott, *Agrarian Reform and the Record of Israel*, pp. 103–104.

40. Ibid., p. 106.

41. *Who's Who in Israel*, p. 416.

42. Joseph Weitz (former director of the Development Authority of the JNF), "Land Ownership," in *Immigration and Settlement*, p. 108.

43. The budget of the JNF averaged about I£80 million annually in the 1960's (Tsur, "The Jewish National Fund," p. 115). Its official budget for 1977/1978 was I£ 374.5 million. JNF plans for the future include investment of I£ 2.5 billion in eighty new Jewish settlements (*Maariv*, March 30, 1978).

44. Orni, *Agrarian Reform and Social Progress in Israel*, pp. 32–33.

45. These tasks include land purchases, road construction, and other development projects in the territories occupied by Israel in 1967. According to Moshe Rivlin, chairman of the board of directors of the JNF, 69 of 102 Jewish settlement sites prepared by the JNF in 1967–1977 were in these areas (*Maariv*, March 30, 1977).

46. One finds almost no consideration of the impact of land development programs on the Arab community by those in the government and in the JNF responsible for analysis and consultation regarding land policy. See for example Simon Ben Shemesh, "Toward a Second Land Reform," *Karka* (Autumn–Winter 1973/1974): 73–79 (Hebrew), as well as various articles dealing with long-range land policy that have appeared in subsequent issues of this journal.

47. Zvi Zinger, "State of Israel (1948–1972)," in *Immigration and Settlement*, pp. 50–51.

48. Raanan Weitz (member of the World Zionist Executive and formerly director of the Jewish Agency Land Settlement Department), "Settlement," in *Immigration and Settlement*, pp. 95–97.
49. *Settlement of the Land* (pamphlet) (Hebrew). These figures include forty-four settlements established in the occupied territories between June 1967 and September 1973.
50. "The Jewish Agency: Land Settlement Department," in *Who's Who in Israel*, p. 407.
51. Personal interview with Adam Kahan, official spokesman, Jewish Agency Finance Department, April 10, 1974, Jerusalem. These figures do not include expenditures in the occupied territories. Kahan indicated that expenditures on these and other items were rising annually. By April 1974, for example, according to Kahan, the total Jewish Agency expenditure on agricultural settlements alone equaled $1.2 billion. For more information concerning the institutionalized transfer of funds from abroad to the Jewish sector, see Chapter 5.
52. Jewish Agency for Israel, Finance Department, *Proposed Budget for the Year 1973–1974*, p. 3; *Statistical Abstract of Israel 75* (1974): 574. The figure given here for the 1972–1973 Israeli government development budget (i.e., that part of the budget representing projects undertaken by the government that are not included in the ministries' "ordinary" budgets) excludes debt repayment. Jewish agency figures were provided in the original source in dollars. Israel government figures for 1972–1973 were converted from Israeli lira to dollars on the basis of an estimated average free market exchange rate during that period of $1 = I£ 4.80.
53. Personal interview with Yosef Lichtman, coordinator of the board of directors of the Land Settlement Department of the Jewish Agency, April 10, 1974, Jerusalem.
54. "The Jewish Agency: Land Settlement Department," in *Who's Who in Israel*, p. 407.
55. Personal interview, Jerusalem, April 10, 1974. This plan has since been approved and published. See Israel Information Center, "The New Plan for the Development of the Galilee," no. 51 (January 1976) (Hebrew).
56. Zinger, "State of Israel (1968–1972)," in *Immigration and Settlement*, p. 70.
57. "Rassco: Rural and Suburban Settlement Co., Ltd," in *Who's Who in Israel*, (1972), p. 585.
58. "Jewish Agency Companies Bureau," in *Who's Who in Israel*, (1972), p. 409. (Figures in this paragraph are for 1972. Note that

I£ 100 million in 1972 is equivalent to I£ 640 million in 1979 values.)

59. *Middle East International*, no. 75 (September 1977): 26. Concerning American Jewish contributions to Israel, see the American Jewish Committee's *American Jewish Year Book, 1978*, pp. 179–191.

60. Ministry of Information, *Facts about Israel* (1975) p. 124; The Jewish Agency for Israel, *25 Years of Partnership 1948–1973*; *Maariv*, July 1, 1977.

61. Ernest Stock, "The Reconstitution of the Jewish Agency: A Political Analysis," *American Jewish Yearbook* (1972): 187–188.

62. Interview with Yitzhak Efron, Jerusalem, April 10, 1976.

63. Interview with Yosef Lichtman, Jerusalem, April 10, 1974.

64. Personal interview with Adam Kahan, Jerusalem, April 10, 1974.

65. Orni, *Agrarian Reform and Social Progress in Israel*, p. 32.

66. The total area of lands belonging to Arab refugees who left the country in 1948 (excluding the Negev) has been estimated at approximately 3,196,000 dunams. More than a million dunams of land have been expropriated from Israeli Arabs since 1948, including the lands of "internal refugees" or "technical absentees." For statistics on the question of the extent of land expropriations, see especially Don Peretz, "Problems of Arab Refugee Compensation," *Middle East Journal* 8, no. 4 (Autumn 1954): 405; Yaacov Aviel, "The Uprooted and the Abandoned," *Haaretz*, January 7, 1955; Yitzhak Oded, "Land Losses among Israel's Arab Villagers," *New Outlook* 7, no. 7 (September 1964): 10–24; Ran Kislev, "Land Expropriations: History of Oppression," *New Outlook* 19, no. 6 (September–October 1976): 23–32. See also Chapter 5.

67. Joshua Weisman, "The Land Law, 1969: A Critical Analysis," *Israel Law Review* 5, no. 3 (1970): 399n.

68. See for example the comments of Member of Knesset Shmuel Shoresh, *Divrei Haknesset* 47 (October 31, 1966): 166, and Agriculture Minister Haim Givati, ibid., p. 155.

69. In many cases individual Arabs have been sublet, or have been hired to work, the very same lands which were expropriated from them. See, for instance, *Haaretz*, October 14, 1966, in connection with lands formerly belonging to inhabitants of the Arab village of Fassuta; and *Divrei Haknesset* 47 (October 31, 1966): 1965, regarding lands formerly belonging to inhabitants of the Arab village of Baram.

70. "Ishmael's National Fund," *Haaretz*, October 14, 1966 (supplement).

71. This law by no means solved the problem, especially in light of an intensified labor shortage following the 1967 war. In September 1975 it was reported that a special committee, headed by the minister of agriculture, had been established to deal with the problem of the widespread employment of non-Jews by Jewish agricultural settlements—something which the director general of the Ministry of Agriculture termed a "national problem of first priority." The committee was charged to "take vigorous action against the irregular use of national land . . . the committee has thus far dealt with scores of such irregularities by kibbutzim, moshavim, and individual farmers . . ." (*Maariv*, September 18, 1975). See also *Haaretz*, July 21, 1975, for more information on the activities of this committee, and Sabri Jiryis, "Recent Knesset Legislation and the Arabs in Israel," *Journal of Palestine Studies* 1, no. 1 (Autumn 1971) for an analysis of the 1967 Agricultural Settlement Law. In 1976 several hundred thousand pounds in fines were levied against seven Jewish settlements engaged in the lease of agricultural land to Arabs (*Middle East International* 63 [September 1976]: 20).

72. David Ben-Gurion, *Israel: A Personal History*, pp. 838–839. Since 1970, former Jewish residents returning to live in Israel have been required to apply to the World Zionist Organization for the benefits (loans, permits to buy duty-free goods, etc.) which had previously been administered by government offices. This change was triggered by claims for such benefits by an Arab from the village of Arara who had left Israel after 1948 but had been permitted to return (see *Yediot Acharonot*, August 30, 1970).

73. These include the Broadcasting Authority, the Vegetable Production and Marketing Board, the National Water Authority, the Water Board, the Interministerial Committee on Settlement, etc.

74. The Jewish Agency for Israel, *25 Years of Partnership, 1948–1973*.

75. The careers sketched here are of persons working at the highest levels of authority, but parallel patterns can easily be traced at lower levels as well. The ascendance of Yitzhak Rabin, a former army chief of staff, to the premiership in 1974 has significance in that it reflects the growing importance of the military as somewhat of an alternative route to power. Nevertheless Rabin, a Labor Party member of Knesset and a long-time party member, became prime minister only as a result of being chosen by the Labor Party Central Committee—a choice heavily determined by such Mapai stalwarts as Pinchas Sapir and Yehoshua Rabinowitz.

76. For an analysis of Israel as a "Partienstaat," see Leonard Fein, *Politics in Israel*, Chapter 3. For a more recent treatment see Efraim Torgovnik, "Israel: The Persistent Elite," in Frank Tachau, ed., *Political Elites and Political Development in the Middle East*, pp. 219–254.

77. Personal interview with David Zechariah, chief of the Labor Party Arab Division, Tel Aviv, January 29, 1974. At the end of 1976 it was reported that the Labor Party had fewer than five thousand Arab members (*Haaretz*, November 21, 1976).

78. For a detailed discussion of the role of Rakah in the Arab sector, see Ch. 7. Concerning Rakah's electoral strength in the Arab sector, see Table 9.

79. "Knesset Election Results 1949–1973," *Facts About Israel* (1975), pp. 96–97.

80. See, for example, David Ben-Gurion's outburst in the Knesset as reported by the *Jerusalem Post*, July 3, 1959.

81. In the 1977 Knesset elections Rakah sponsored a "front" list, the Democratic Front for Peace and Equality. In a serious attempt to mobilize support among poor Sephardic Jews it awarded one of its "safe" seats to a noncommunist leader of the "Black Panthers," a radical Sephardic group. In spite of such efforts, support for Rakah in Sephardic neighborhoods remained negligible.

82. Personal interview with Jalal Abu Tama, Arab youth leader and, in 1976, chairman of the local council of Baka el-Gharbiyeh, April 19, 1974, Baka el-Gharbiyeh. See the remarks of Simcha Flapan, former director of the Arab Department of Mapam, in a symposium on "Israel's Arabs after October 1973," *New Outlook* 18, no. 7 (October–November 1975): 76.

83. Keren, "In a Vicious Circle."

84. For information on the Arab-Jewish Committee and government reaction to it, see "Israeli Arabs Call for Action," *Jewish Observer and Middle East Review*, August 5, 1966, p. 16, and A. Ben-Ami, "Israeli Jews and Israeli Arabs: A Symposium," *Jewish Frontier* 33, no. 9 (November 1966): 15–24. See Uri Avnery, *Israel without Zionists*, and an interview with the "Canaanite" poet Yohonatan Ratosh, in *Maariv*, August 13, 1976.

85. Cohen, *Arab Border Villages in Israel*, p. 118.

86. Similar patterns in the villages of Rama and Baka el-Gharbiyeh are discussed by Shimon Shamir, "Changes in Village Leadership," *New Outlook* 5, no. 3 (March–April 1962): 64–71, and by Jalal Abu Tama, "The Arabs in Israel and the Elections to Local Authorities" (seminar paper, Bar-Ilan University, 1972).

87. Cohen, *Arab Border Villages in Israel,* p. 104n. See pp. 94–104 for Cohen's explicit treatment of the role of the local council system in reviving the political significance of hamula cleavages, a "pattern of change" which he says "occurred in almost all the Triangle villages."

88. Subhi Abu-Ghosh, "The Politics of an Arab Village in Israel," (Ph.D. dissertation, Princeton University, 1965), p. 33.

89. Ibid., p. 3.

90. Ibid., p. 25.

91. See Shlomo A. Deshen, *Immigrant Voters in Israel.*

92. In a Galilean Arab village studied by social-anthropologist Henry Rosenfeld, the number of intra-hamula marriages nearly doubled from 1954 to 1969 (Professor Henry Rosenfeld, lecture, Hebrew University, February 1974). For more information concerning marriage patterns in Arab villages in Israel, see Henry Rosenfeld, "Processes of Change and Factors of Conservation in the Rural Arab Family in Israel," *Hamizrah Hechadash* 19, no. 3 (1969) (Hebrew), and, by the same author, "The Contradictions between Property, Kinship and Power as Reflected in the Marriage System of an Arab Village," in J. G. Peristiany, ed., *Contributions to Mediterranean Sociology: Acts of the Mediterranean Sociological Conference,* pp. 247–260.

93. Yechiel Harari, *The Arabs in Israel—1976,* p. 28 (Hebrew). Figures are not available on the number of lists that competed for seats but failed to win representation.

94. See Yechiel Harari, *The Arabs in Israel—1974,* pp. 39–40; Ministry of the Interior, "Elections for Eight Local Councils in the Arab Sector in the Years 1971 and 1972," (Jerusalem, June 1972) (Hebrew), and Jacob M. Landau, *The Arabs in Israel,* Chapter 6.

95. *Israel Government Yearbook,* 1953/1954, p. 111.

96. H. Baruch, "Facing the 180,000: How the Military Government Rules," reprinted from *Davar* in *Ner* 10, nos. 3–4 (December 1958–January 1959): 40. According to the *Jerusalem Post,* April 4, 1956, eight hundred of Um el Fahm's six thousand inhabitants had travel permits. The village is the largest in the Little Triangle.

97. Although the Military Administration was officially assigned to designated geographical areas, which contained Jews as well as Arabs, military governors were allowed under the law to exercise discretion in the enforcement of travel restrictions. Thus Jews, with some significant exceptions, were allowed to travel freely in and out of these areas.

98. See for example the observations of Allon in *A Curtain of Sand*, pp. 328–329. Pinchas Rosen, a former minister of justice and chairman of a ministerial committee that in 1962 was charged with evaluating the performance of the Military Administration, declared during a Knesset debate "that on the basis of what he had learned as Chairman of the Ministerial Committee ... the Military Government was not necessary for security purposes" (*Jerusalem Post*, November 15, 1962).

99. Samuel Divon, former Adviser to the Prime Minister on Arab Affairs, as quoted by Walter Schwarz, *The Arabs in Israel*, p. 141.

100. Gideon Weigert, *The Arabs in Israel* (mimeo published by the Information Department of the Ministry of Foreign Affairs, undated, but by its contents written in 1967 or 1968).

101. Baruch, "Facing the 180,000," pp. 42–43.

102. Ibid., p. 38.

103. *Jerusalem Post*, June 28, 1959.

104. *Jerusalem Post*, October 8, 1959.

105. *Haaretz*, April 1, 1962.

106. *Haaretz*, September 14, 1962.

107. *Jerusalem Post*, December 6, 1962; *Haaretz*, December 6, 1962.

108. *Jerusalem Post*, August 25, 1963.

109. *Haaretz*, April 27, 1964; *Jerusalem Post*, April 27, 1964. For a description of the overall limitations on Arab sports activities by the government, see an article by Zvi Kaufman in *Maariv*, August 21, 1973.

110. For more detailed accounts of el-Ard and its fate by members of the organization, see Jiryis, *The Arabs in Israel*, pp. 130–140; el-Asmar, *To Be an Arab in Israel*, pp. 65–75. For the government's view, see Ori Stendel, *The Minorities in Israel*, pp. 138–146.

111. Abu N., "The Arabs and the Knesset Elections," *Ner* 10, nos. 5–7 (February–April 1959): 51.

112. *Jerusalem Post*, January 28, 1962.

113. Personal interview with Uri Thon, Jerusalem, April 16, 1974. See Map 4.

114. For a detailed map depicting plans for the establishment of twelve Jewish villages and the expansion of thirty-seven more in the heavily Arab central and upper Galilee, see Israel Information Center, *The New Plan for the Development of the Galilee*, no. 51 (January 1976), p. 4 (Hebrew).

115. The deportation of whole Arab villages, described by Toufik Toubi, a communist member of Knesset, during Knesset debate in 1949 (*Jerusalem Post*, November 14, 1949), and by Jiryis in *The*

Arabs in Israel, p. 57, was confirmed in a personal interview conducted with Zvi Alpeleg (Tel Aviv, April 24, 1974).

116. Personal interview with Zvi Alpeleg, Tel Aviv, April 24, 1974.

117. *Encyclopaedia Judaica*, 9: 374, map of the Little Triangle, and *Atlas of Israel*, XI/I Survey of Israel, Ministry of Labour.

118. *Zoo Haderech*, November 19, 1975. For more recent statistics regarding the population-to-land ratio in upper and lower Nazareth, see *Zoo Haderech*, July 26, 1978.

119. M. Rahat, *Maariv*, March 19, 1971, quoted in Erik Cohen, *Integration vs. Separation in the Planning of a Mixed Jewish-Arab City in Israel*, pp. 9–10.

120. Cohen, "*Integration vs. Separation*," p. 14 (emphasis in original).

121. Ibid., p. 9.

122. Ibid., p. 15.

123. *Statistical Abstract of Israel* 28 (1977): 37.

124. *Jerusalem Post*, November 21, 1962.

125. See, for example, the statistics provided by the Ministry of the Interior in a publication entitled *Arab Local Councils in Israel*, no. 3, p. 20. Concerning the government's policy of favoritism toward the Druse, see Chapter 6.

126. Emanuel Marx, *Bedouin of the Negev*, p. 50.

127. Sheik Mussa al-Atawna, "What the Bedouin Want," *New Outlook* 3, no. 9 (September 1960): 16.

128. Marx, *Bedouin of the Negev*, p. 62.

129. Yochanan Peres, Avishai Erlich, and Nira Yuval-Davis, "The National Education of Arab Youth in Israel: A Comparison of Courses of Studies," *Megamot* 16, no. 1 (October 1968): 28 (Hebrew).

130. Elias Dalal, "Arab Education in Israel," reprinted and translated in *Ner* 9, nos. 1–2 (October–November 1957): 42.

131. Peres, Erlich, and Yuval-Davis, "National Education of Arab Youth in Israel," p. 30.

132. Fouzi el-Asmar, *To Be an Arab in Israel*, pp. 48–50.

133. Landau, *The Arabs in Israel*, p. 186.

134. Concerning the parochial considerations on the basis of which the Labor Party sponsored three separate affiliated lists in 1977, see *Maariv*, January 30, 1977; March 27, 1977; and April 13, 1977.

135. Cohen, *Arab Border Villages in Israel*, pp. 154–155.

136. Quoted from a lecture given by Yehoshua Palmon in Baka el-Gharbiyeh, April 1972. Abu Tama, "The Arabs in Israel and the Elections to Local Authorities," p. 2.

137. Such a sequence of events occurred in the village of Baka el-Gharbiyeh in the spring of 1974.
138. Interview with Shmuel Toledano, in *Maariv* supplement *Yamim ve'Lylot*, November 26, 1969.
139. In November 1975, new elections were held in Arrabe and again, despite government efforts to the contrary, a communist-controlled coalition emerged (*Zoo Haderech*, November 19, 1975). It should also be noted that in the 1973 Knesset elections the communists received a higher percentage of the votes in Arrabe than in any other Arab village. The information presented here concerning the disbanding of the Arrabe local council is based on personal interviews conducted in Arrabe and surrounding villages in late March 1974 as well as interviews with Yoram Katz, Galilee representative of the Office of the Adviser to the Prime Minister on Arab Affairs, and Sasoon Rashdi, representative of the Arab Department of the Ministry of the Interior in Acre.
140. Abu-Ghosh, "The Politics of an Arab Village in Israel," p. 104.
141. Kassem Zayad, "Am I a 'Positive' or a 'Negative' Arab?" translated from *al-Hamishmar* in *Israel Horizons* 24, no. 6 (June–July 1976): 11; *Zoo Haderech*, August 31, 1977.
142. Both Tuma and Fahoum were arrested on suspicion of contacts with terrorist organizations. Tuma's conviction was based on the fact that a friend of his, Ahmed Khalifa, an East Jerusalem Arab who had stayed in Tuma's house for ten days, was a member of the Arab Nationalist Movement (later known as the Popular Front for the Liberation of Palestine), an organization banned by the occupation authorities in the West Bank. The court determined that in fact Tuma did not know of Khalifa's involvement with the ANM, but under Israeli law such knowledge is not necessary for conviction.
143. The two students were arrested when they arrived at a news conference which they called to discuss cooperation between police and the administration of Haifa University (*Zoo Haderech*, June 8, 1977).
144. For examples of the harassment of Arab student activists, see *Zoo Haderech*, May 22, 1975; December 25, 1974; January 15, 1975; February 5, 1975; January 8, 1975; March 16, 1975. See also Shmuel Toledano's public condemnation of Arab student committees: *Yediot Acharonot*, January 27, 1975; January 26, 1979; *Haaretz*, June 7, 1977; June 8, 1977.
145. For information concerning "consultation" between university administrators and the Shin Bet regarding Arab students, see ac-

counts of the case of Mahmoud Meari, an Arab sociologist and graduate of the Hebrew University who was denied employment at the University of Haifa in 1971 (*New Outlook* 14, no. 2 [March 1971]: 121).

146. Eli Rekhess, *A Survey of Israeli-Arab Graduates from Institutions of Higher Learning in Israel (1961–1971)*, p. 31.

147. This is how official government policy is usually stated (see, for example, Israel Information Center, "Basic Principles of the Government's Programme," Information Briefing 24, Jerusalem, March 1974, p. 14).

148. Yaacov Aviel, "The Military Government," *Haaretz*, December 31, 1954 (Hebrew).

149. Baruch, "Facing the 180,000," p. 39.

150. Personal interview with Zvi Alpeleg, April 24, 1974.

151. See, for example, the *Jerusalem Post*, February 13, 1966, for an account of one attempt by Uri Avnery (a former member of Knesset) to lead a "fraternal convoy" of Jewish well-wishers into the Little Triangle.

152. Personal interview with Simcha Flapan, Tel Aviv, December 19, 1973.

153. For an example of such a complaint, see the letters-to-the-editor section of *Maariv*, March 27, 1977. Although the major Hebrew newspapers regularly carry feature articles on events or problems in the Arab sector, the only Hebrew newspaper which reports news in the Arab sector as comprehensively as the general Israeli press reports news in the Jewish sector is the Hebrew organ of Rakah, *Zoo Haderech*. Its circulation, however, is extremely small.

154. This is a constant refrain. See, for example, Ezekiel Shemesh, "Israel's Arabs—1975," *New Outlook* 18, no. 7 (October–November, 1975): 24.

155. This, for example, is the opinion of Simcha Flapan, director of the Arab Department of Mapam, 1954–1965. According to Mr. Flapan, during the late 1950's and early 1960's, when Mapam was quite active in the Arab sector, "Mapai regarded the Mapam cadres as more dangerous than the communists . . . Mapai could easily use the growth of Rakah influence to frighten the Arab community because Rakah presented the potential danger of loyalty to the state of Israel. So, too, could the government use the influence of Rakah to justify, in the eyes of the Jewish population, the maintenance of the Military Administration, stressing how communist agents of a foreign power were building up their

strength and had to be kept under control. On the other hand Arabs associated with Mapam could not be automatically impugned with regard to their loyalty" (personal interview, Tel Aviv, December 19, 1973). For official fears that the wall of ostracism around Rakah was breaking down somewhat, see *Israleft*, no. 59 (April 6, 1975); no. 66 (August 15, 1975).

156. Daniel Bloch, "Expected Adjustments in the Partisan Map," *Davar*, March 10, 1975.

157. Lecture delivered by Shmuel Toledano at the Center for Arab and Afro-Asian Studies, Givat Haviva, Israel, February 21, 1974.

158. In Chapter 7 these and other current developments in Israel are discussed in terms of their implications for the present and future operation of the system of control.

5. Dependence as a Component of Control: The Economics of Arab Subordination

1. Henry Rosenfeld, "From Peasantry to Wage Labor and Residual Peasantry: The Transformation of an Arab Village," in Robert A. Manners, ed., *Process and Pattern in Culture*, p. 229.

2. Yosef Waschitz, *The Arabs of the Land of Israel*, pp. 383–384 (Hebrew).

3. Ibid., p. 38.

4. I would like to thank Rachel Tachau for information concerning the Palestinian Arab labor movement in the 1940's.

5. For additional information concerning the structure of Arab society in Palestine before the creation of the state of Israel, see Henry Rosenfeld, *They Were Peasants* (Hebrew); Yaacov Shimoni, "The Arabs of the Land of Israel: Pride and Catastrophe" *Molad* 3, no. 15 (June 1949): 150–156 (Hebrew); Jacob Shimoni, *Arabs of the Land of Israel*. See also Chaim Arlosoroff, "Economic Background of the Arab Question"; Zev Abromovitz, "Social-Economic Structure of Arab Palestine"; and David Hurwitz, "Agrarian Problem of the Fellahein"; all in Enzo Sereni and R. E. Ashery, eds., *Jews and Arabs in Palestine*, pp. 3–74.

6. P. J. Loftus, *National Income of Palestine, 1944*, p. 24.

7. Robert Szerszewski, *Essays on the Structure of the Jewish Economy in Palestine and Israel*, pp. 81–82.

8. Loftus, *National Income of Palestine, 1944*, p. 27.

9. Ibid., p. 6. For Jews in 1944 income from nonagricultural sources represented 88 percent of total income while the comparable fig-

ure for the Arab population was 59 percent (calculated from figures provided by Loftus, *National Income of Palestine, 1944,* p. 27).

10. *The Jewish Case: Before the Anglo-American Committee of Inquiry on Palestine as Presented by the Jewish Agency for Palestine,* p. 441.

11. The total amount spent by the national institutions of the Zionist movement in Palestine between 1917 and 1946 has been estimated at more than £P 52,675,000 (A. Ulitzur, "Jewish National Finances 1881–1946," *Palestine Yearbook* 3:379). This may be compared to the amount spent by the British mandatory administration in Palestine from 1920 to 1944, £P 104,039,000 (R. Nathan, O. Gass, and D. Creamer, eds., *Palestine: Problem and Promise,* p. 357).

12. See "Activities of the Labor Movement in Palestine during and after the War," *Palestine Yearbook* 2: 154–168.

13. *The Jewish Case,* p. 213.

14. Ibid., p. 278.

15. In 1948 Nazareth was the only Arab locality in Israel that had electricity. Not one Arab village had piped water. The "backwash effect," as Gunnar Myrdal has referred to it (*Economic Theory and Under-Developed Regions,* Chapter 3), is discussed in a comparative context by J. G. Williamson in "Regional Inequality and the Process of National Development: A Description of the Patterns," *Economic Development and Cultural Change* 13 (1965): 3–45. For a specific discussion of this problem with reference to the Arab minority in Israel, see Fred M. Gottheil, "On the Economic Development of the Arab Region in Israel," in Michael Curtis and Mordechai Chertoff, eds., *Israel: Social Structure and Change,* pp. 237–248.

16. For details of these contradictions and the tensions and stresses which they produce, see Henry Rosenfeld, "Change, Barriers to Change, and Contradictions in the Arab Village Family," *American Anthropologist* 70, no. 4 (August 1968): 732–752.

17. Ibid., p. 733. It is instructive to note that in neighboring Arab countries such as Syria and Egypt, not usually thought of as more modern in social fabric than Israel, the *mohar,* or bride price, has become little more than a formality. In contrast, among Israeli Arabs a typical bride price may range from I£ 10,000 to I£ 15,000 (1974 values). The groom and/or his family may even be required to provide a newly constructed house.

18. Ibid., p. 739 (emphasis in original).

19. Rosenfeld, "From Peasantry to Wage Labor and Residual Peasantry."

20. Shaul Zarhi and A. Achiezra, *The Economic Conditions of the Arab Minority in Israel*, p. 16.

21. Oded Remba, "Income Inequality in Israel: Ethnic Aspects," in Curtis and Chertoff, *Israel: Social Structure and Change*, p. 207.

22. *Statistical Abstract of Israel* 28 (1977): 291–292.

23. Personal interview with Aga Schwartz, Jerusalem, March 11, 1974. The percentage would be higher except for the fact that it excludes Bedouin encampments, both in the north and in the south. Although the minister of commerce and industry announced in 1977 that electricity would not be provided to all Arab villages until 1980 or 1981, the connection of Arab villages to the national power grid was accelerated significantly in 1975 and 1976. In 1976, 62 of 160 Arab localities, including approximately 78 percent of Israeli Arabs, were serviced by the Israel Electric Corporation. Recent statistics concerning the percentage of Arab households linked to the grid, however, are unavailable. See *Israleft*, no. 98 (January 15, 1977): 6, and Yechiel Harari, *The Arabs in Israel—1976*, pp. 44–45 (Hebrew).

24. *Statistical Abstract of Israel* 28 (1977): 93.

25. Yechiel Harari, *Arabs in Israel in Numbers, 1971*, p. 47 (Hebrew); *Statistical Abstract of Israel*, 24 (1973): 320.

26. Yechiel Harari, *The Arabs in Israel: Facts and Figures*, p. 50. A study conducted in 1976 counted only 1,405 Arabs as employed in industrial enterprises located in the Arab sector, most of these branches of Jewish-owned firms (A. Harel, et al., *The Conclusions of the Committee Concerning the Activities of the Histadrut in the Arab Sector*, pp. 35–37 [Hebrew]). For an overall assessment of the slow rate of industrialization in Arab villages, see Yosef Waschitz, "Commuters and Entrepreneurs," *New Outlook* 18, no. 7 (October–November 1975): 45–53. Regarding the proliferation of small workshops in Arab villages (mostly to employ unskilled women), see Yechiel Harari, *The Arabs in Israel—1976*, pp. 40–41 (Hebrew).

27. Simcha Flapan, "Planning for the Arab Village," *New Outlook* 6, no. 8 (October 1963): 28; Waschitz, "Commuters and Entrepreneurs," p. 49; Khalil Nakhleh, "Shifting Patterns of Conflict in Selected Arab Villages in Israel" (Ph.D. dissertation, University of Indiana, 1973), pp. 34–37, 44–46.

28. The Jewish Agency for Israel, *25 Years of Partnership, 1948–1973*; The Jewish Agency for Israel, Finance Department, *Pro-*

posed Budget for the Year 1973/1974, p. 2; David Lazar, "Not Almogi, not Dulzin," in *Maariv*, November 21, 1975; April 1, 1976; July 1, 1977; the $5 billion figure does not include funds donated to and distributed by the JNF, the American Jewish Joint Distribution Committee, the Histadrut, and other Jewish-Zionist fund-raising organizations (see the *American Jewish Yearbook, 1978,* pp. 177–191). From 1974 to 1976, the government transferred more than $34 million of Israel Land Administration funds to the JNF. See *Israel Government Yearbook,* 1978, p. 204 (Hebrew).

29. For an illustrative study of the impact of the Jewish Agency's industrialization program on one kibbutz, see Robert Nobel, "Industry's Impact on the Kibbutz," *Israel Yearbook, 1978,* pp. 251–253.

30. Simcha Flapan, "Planning for Arab Agriculture," *New Outlook* 6, no. 9 (November–December 1963): 72; The Executive of the Jewish Agency, "Re: Jewish Agency Investments in Companies" (memo), description of Idud (loan company); Raanan Weitz and Avshalom Rokah, *Agricultural Development: Planning and Implementation,* pp. 318–319.

31. Personal interview with Mr. Abu-Nasr, Nazareth, March 29, 1974.

32. Yoram Ben-Porath, *The Arab Labor Force in Israel,* p. 53.

33. Ibid., p. 55.

34. Sabri Jiryis, *The Arabs in Israel,* pp. 164–165. See also E. N. Koussa, "Israel and the Arab People," *Ner* 4, no. 1 (October 1952): 23–24.

35. Ben-Porath, *The Arab Labor Force in Israel,* pp. 53–55.

36. For an in-depth analysis of the stagnation of Arab agriculture in Israel, see Flapan, "Planning for the Arab Village," pp. 23–31; and, by the same author, "Planning Arab Agriculture," pp. 64–73. See also S. Zarhi and A. Achiezra, *The Economic Conditions of the Arab Minority in Israel,* pp. 20–22; and Emmanuel Yalan, et al., *The Modernization of Traditional Agricultural Villages: Minority Villages in Israel.*

37. *Statistical Abstract of Israel* 28 (1977): 360.

38. Zarhi and Achiezra, *The Economic Conditions of the Arab Minority,* p. 21.

39. This approximation was calculated from statistics provided in the *Statistical Abstract of Israel* 28 (1977): 366–367.

40. The failure of the cooperative movement in the Arab sector has been due, in large measure, to the continuing vitality of the tradi-

tional social structure. See Gad Ben-Meir, "The Development of Arab Cooperation in Israel," *New Outlook* 5, no. 7 (July 1961): 31–36; and, by the same author, "Arab Water Supply Cooperatives," *Ner* 13, nos. 1–2 (September–October 1961): xii; Abdul Magid Zubi, "A Plan for Arab Agriculture," *New Outlook* 1, no. 3 (September 1957): 16; Y. Arnon and S. Molcho, *Trends in Agriculture in Two Arab Villages (1948–1970)* (Ministry of Agriculture) (Hebrew); Histadrut Agricultural Center, *The Agricultural Histadrut and Its Activities*, p. 33.

41. Personal interview with Yusuf Khamis, April 18, 1974; personal interview with Yaacov Cohen, Tel Aviv, April 30, 1974. For a description of the reorganization of these agencies and their various spheres of activity, see Histadrut Agricultural Center, *The Agricultural Histadrut and Its Activities*, pp. 157–165.

42. *Statistical Abstract of Israel* 27 (1976): 360; 28 (1977): 421. For a discussion of the significance of the absence of cooperatization in the Arab sector, see Flapan, "Planning Arab Agriculture," pp. 71–72.

43. Attalah Mansour, "Arab Land: Sale or Requisition?" *New Outlook* 7, no. 3 (March–April 1964): 82–84.

44. For specific discussion of how the confiscation of land and the inability of Arabs to acquire additional arable land stunted the development of Arab agriculture in particular villages, see Arnon and Molcho, *Trends in Agriculture in Two Arab Villages*, and Arie Bitan-Buttenwieser, "Changes in Settlement and Land Use in Eastern Lower Galilee from the Beginning of the 19th Century until the Present Day" (Ph.D. dissertation, Hebrew University, 1969), esp. pp. 246–247 (Hebrew).

45. Yitzhak Oded, "Israel's Arab Villagers Are Being Driven from Their Land," *Ner* 13, nos. 11–12 (July–August 1962): vi. In 1975 Jacob Tsur, former chairman of the board of the JNF, characterized the acquisition of land in Eretz Israel as "the Fund's primary obligation towards the Jewish people" ("The Work of the JNF: Planning for the Future," in L. Berger, ed., *Immigration and Israel's Survival*, p. 17).

46. JNF, *The Blue Box That Keeps Israel Green*. JNF land holdings amount to nearly 4.5 million dunams, but this includes state land for which the JNF has been given exclusive administrative control without official ownership.

47. Calculated on the basis of statistics and information provided by Joseph Lador-Lederer, "In the State of Israel," in *Society*, p. 187; Abraham Grannot, *Agrarian Reform and the Record of Israel*, p.

94; Ran Kislev, "Land Expropriation: History of Oppression," *New Outlook* 19, no. 6 (September–October 1976): 28. Kislev reports that official Israel Land Authority figures show that in 1973 Arab villagers owned and cultivated a total of 391,435 dunams outside of the Negev.

48. Yitzhak Oded, "Land Losses among Israel's Arab Villagers," *New Outlook* 7, no. 7 (September 1964): 11.

49. Concerning the proletarianization of Arab villagers as that process relates to the loss of land in the Arab sector, see Sami Farah Geraisy, "Arab Village Youth in Jewish Urban Centers: A Study of Youth from Um el Fahm Working in the Tel Aviv Metropolitan Area," (Ph.D. dissertation, Brandeis University, 1971), pp. 62–89; and Henry Rosenfeld, "Wage Labor and Status in an Arab Village," *New Outlook* 6, no. 1 (January 1963): 5–9.

50. In 1974 the connection of electricity to an Arab village, depending on its distance from the nearest existing transmission line, cost anywhere from I£ 400,000 to I£ 3,000,000 (personal interview, Public Relations Officer, Israel Electric Company, Haifa, April 5, 1974). This would not include the connection of individual households within the village. The financial burden which electricity constitutes for an Arab village can be better appreciated if one considers that the average *total* budget for an Arab local council in 1972 was approximately I£ 660,000. For more recent statistics in the context of the specific case of the village of Musmus, see *Zoo Haderech*, August 18, 1976.

51. *Statistical Abstract of Israel* 28 (1977): 610.

52. Government of Israel, *Comptroller's Report*, no. 22 (1972): 22–23, 319, 328 (Hebrew). In 1974/1975 a majority of Arab teachers still lacked appropriate training (*Statistical Abstract of Israel* 28 [1977]: 606).

53. *Statistical Abstract of Israel* 28 (1977): 602, 619.

54. *Divrei Haknesset*, July 23, 1975, p. 3872. Estimates of the shortage of classrooms in Arab villages in 1977 ranged from 4,500 to 6,000 (see *Zoo Haderech*, July 6, 1977; November 23, 1977). The increasingly severe shortage of classrooms has forced most Arab schools to rent rooms in private homes scattered throughout their villages. For a graphic description of this problem in the village of Um el-Fahm, see *New York Times*, January 31, 1979.

55. Concerning the government's efforts to solve the problem of "closing the gap between 'the first Israel' and 'the second Israel,'" see Ahron Amir, "Intercommunal Problems," in *Society*, pp. 58–

61. For a variety of articles on the subject, see Curtis and Chertoff, eds., *Israel: Social Structure and Change*, pp. 281–360.
56. Oded, "Land Losses among Israel's Arab Villagers," p. 14.
57. Ibid., p. 14.
58. Ibid., p. 11.
59. *Israel Government Year Book*, 1950, pp. 73–74.
60. *Laws of the State of Israel* 2 (1948/1949): 72.
61. Ibid. 4: 3.
62. Amos Elon, "Land-Acquisition: The Tragedy of Ghabasiyeh and Israeli Justice," *Haaretz*, October 18, 1951, translated and reprinted in *Ner* 4, no. 11 (July 1953): 40–42; no. 12 (August 1953): 25–26; Elieser Ben Moshe, "The Tragedy of Kfar Bir'am," *Ner* 12, nos. 1–2 (November–December 1960): xviii–xxi; *Israleft*, no. 66 (August 15, 1975): 9–10; no. 69 (October 1, 1975): 4–5; Yaacov Aviel, "The Uprooted and the Abandoned," *Haaretz*, January 7, 1955.
63. "'Absentee' means—

"(1) a person who, at any time during the period between the 16th of Kislev, 5708 (November 29, 1947) and the day on which a declaration is published, under section 9 (d) of the Law and Administration Ordinance (5708-1948) that the state of emergency declared by the Provisional Council of State on the 10th Iyar, 5708 (19th May, 1948) has ceased to exist, was a legal owner of any property situated in the area of Israel or enjoyed or held it, whether by himself or through another, and who, at any time during the said period—

"(i) was a national or citizen of Lebanon, Egypt, Syria, Saudi Arabia, Trans-Jordan, Iraq, or the Yemen, or

"(ii) was in one of these countries or in any part of Palestine outside the area of Israel, or

"(iii) was a Palestinian citizen and left his ordinary place of residence in Palestine

"(a) for a place outside of Palestine before the 27th Av, 5708 (September 1, 1948); or

"(b) for a place in Palestine held at the time by forces which sought to prevent the establishment of the State of Israel or which fought against its establishment . . ." *Laws of the State of Israel* 4 (1949/1950): 68.
64. *Laws of the State of Israel* 4: 74–75, 152.
65. Concerning those "present absentees" actually displaced from their villages, see "The Precedent of the Displaced Persons: Inhabitants of Twenty-one More Villages Demand to Return to

Their Villages," translated from *Haaretz*, July 28, 1972, and reprinted in Uri Davis and Norton Mezvinsky, eds., *Documents from Israel, 1967–1973*, pp. 34–38.

66. *Laws of the State of Israel* 2:72, Emergency Regulations (Cultivation of Waste Lands) Ordinance, Section 5, article (a).

67. *Laws of the State of Israel* 4:3, Emergency Land Requisition (Regulation) Law, Section 4, article (b).

68. *Laws of the State of Israel* 4:69, Absentees' Property Law, Section 4, article (a), part (1).

69. *Laws of the State of Israel* 7:43, Land Acquisition (Validation of Acts and Compensation), Law, Section 2, article (a).

70. Ibid., Section 2, articles (a), (b), and (c); 4:68, Absentees' Property Law, Section 4, articles (a) and (b).

71. Aharon Liskovsky, "The Present Absentees in Israel," *Hamizrah Hechadash* 10, no. 3 (1960):189–190 (Hebrew).

72. Oded, "Land Losses among Israel's Arab Villagers," p. 21.

73. Moshe Keren, "Have We an Arab Policy?" *Haaretz*, January 1, 1955.

74. *Laws of the State of Israel* 12:129, Law of Prescription.

75. Oded, "Land Losses among Israel's Arab Villagers," p. 13 (emphasis added).

76. Ibid., p. 15. For additional details concerning the battle over the registration of Arab village lands, see Ran Kislev, "Land Expropriations: History of Oppression," pp. 27–28.

77. One Arab who had owned a pottery workshop on this land took legal action. Fearing an adverse judgment, the government chose to settle with him out of court. Other Arab landowners who filed similar charges were told they had waited too long to make their complaints (Oded, "Israel's Arab Villagers Are Being Driven from Their Land," p. ii; Yosef Alghazi, in *Zoo Haderech*, July 30, 1975).

78. Jiryis, *The Arabs in Israel*, p. 84. See also Attalah Mansour, in *Haaretz*, March 26, 1976.

79. Officially the "public purpose" for which the expropriations were carried out was "security," but in defense of its action the government has always emphasized the political importance of increasing the Jewish population of the Galilee. Carmiel, Upper Nazareth, Ma'alot, and Shelomi are development towns regularly cited by the government as evidence of its vigorous efforts to Judaize the Galilee (Oded, "Land Losses among Israel's Arab Villagers," p. 23; *Ner* 13, nos. 7–9 [March–May 1963]: xlvii; Fouzi el-Asmar, *To Be an Arab in Israel*, pp. 107–109).

80. Shimon Peres, "The Military Government Is the Product of the 'War Regime,'" *Davar*, January 26, 1962. For an example of how this technique has been employed, see the description of the case of *Mahmoud Yunis* v. *Ministry of Finance*, as set forth in the *Jerusalem Post*, March 16, 1954. Also see Yaacov Aviel, "The Uprooted and the Abandoned," *Haaretz*, January 7, 1955; Yosef Alghazi, in *Zoo Haderech*, September 3, 1975; and *Ner* 13, nos. 11–12 (July–August 1962): xxvi.

81. The figures for nos. 3, 5–8 are from Aharon Cohen, *Israel and the Arab World*, p. 529 (Hebrew); for no. 2, from Elias Koussa, "Memorandum on the Proposed Expropriation of Arab Agricultural Lands," *Ner* 4, nos. 7–8 (April 1953): 46; for no. 1, from S. Shereshevsky, "Against the Agricultural Lands Consolidation Law," *Ner* 12, nos. 5–6 (March–April 1961): ii, and Koussa, "Memorandum on the Proposed Expropriation of Arab Agricultural Lands," p. 46; for no. 9, from *Haaretz*, January 18, 1976; for no. 10, from Geraisy, "Arab Village Youth," p. 64; for no. 11, from Yosef Alghazi, in *Zoo Haderech*, September 3, 1975; for no. 12, from Oded, "Israel's Arab Villagers Are Being Driven from Their Land," p. 5 (the statistics for no. 12 refer to cultivated land and quarries only); for no. 4, from Zeev Schiff, in *Haaretz*, April 4, 1961; for no. 13, from Nakhleh, "Shifting Patterns of Conflict," pp. 42–43; for no. 14, from Jamal Kanann, "Symposium: Israel's Arabs after October 1973," *New Outlook* 18, no. 7 (October–November 1975): 79; for nos. 15–17, from Ran Kislev, in *Israleft*, no. 89 (September 1, 1976): 11; for no. 18, from *Zoo Haderech*, November 16, 1977. The proportion of Negev Bedouin lands expropriated by the authorities has been considerably higher than that expropriated from Arab villagers (see Yitzhak Oded, "Bedouin Lands Threatened by Takeover," *New Outlook* 7, no. 9 [November–December 1964]: 45–52; Emanuel Marx, *Bedouin of the Negev*, p. 52). Since 1974 the government has advanced claims to 1.5 million dunams of Bedouin land in the Negev.

82. *Israel Government Year Book*, 1971/1972; 1975/1976; Oded, "Land Losses among Israel's Arab Villagers," pp. 20–21. Figures for land acquired and compensation provided from 1964 to 1966 were unavailable. Averages of statistics available for other years were used for this period in the computation of these estimates.

The significance of the practice of basing compensation on land values that prevailed in 1950 is related, in the observation of the *Israel Economist* (May 1951), to the fact that "the property of the [JNF] has lately grown considerably through the acquisition of large tracts of state land. Its holdings at the end of the last fiscal year (September 30, 1950) totalled 2,085,000 dunams at a cost price (including outlay for development work) of I£ 40.5 million; and their present value, at a conservative estimate is at least five times as high" (p. 109). For information concerning compensation rates offered to Negev Bedouin for expropriated land in 1976, see *Zoo Haderech*, August 11, 1976.

83. *Laws of the State of Israel* 7:43.
84. Oded, "Land Losses among Israel's Arab Villagers," p. 18.
85. Ibid., pp. 18–19. An extra half-unit is sometimes provided for the first married son of an Arab landowner. In 1951 more than 40 percent of Arab farms were larger than thirty dunams. These farms included more than 80 percent of the land cultivated by Arabs (*Israel Economist*, July 1951, p. 171).
86. In 1963 standard farming units allotted to Jewish settlers with small nuclear families were forty-five dunams, complete with irrigation facilities (Oded, "Land Losses among Israel's Arab Villagers," p. 19. For statistics on discrimination against Arab farmers in regard to water allotments, see Bitan-Buttenwieser, "Changes in the Settlement and Land Use in Eastern Lower Galilee," p. 247).
87. Personal interview with Mr. Dror, Jerusalem, April 23, 1974; personal interview with Yitzhak Efron, Jerusalem, April 10, 1974. See also "Arab Farmers," *Ner* 13, nos. 11–12 (July–August 1962): xxvii.
88. On average just under half the crop area cultivated by Arabs in any given year is land leased in this manner, the great bulk of it by Negev Bedouin. For additional information regarding discrimination against Arab farmers concerning the lease of agricultural land, see "The Position of the Arabs in the State of Israel," *Ner* 4, (February 1953): 22; *Haaretz*, April 17, 1956; *Ner* 13, nos. 11–12 (July–August 1962): xxvii; *Zoo Haderech*, July 26, 1978.
89. Israel Information Center, "Minorities in Israel," Information Briefing 9 (October 1973): 15.
90. Ibid., p. 17.
91. For example, a tour of Arab villages will quickly reveal that where "cultural clubs" do exist they have usually long since been closed for lack of funds, that most electric lighting in Arab villages (in 1974) came from small, privately owned generators operating for a few hours in the evening, and that refrigerators are

often owned but not used, because where electricity is available it is not dependable enough to ensure against food spoilage.

92. *Maariv*, October 3, 1972.

93. Personal interview with Aga Schwartz, Jerusalem, March 11, 1974.

94. Personal interview with Kemal Kassem, Haifa, April 3, 1974.

95. Personal interview with Yaacov Cohen, Tel Aviv, April 30, 1974.

96. Personal interview with Yusuf Khamis, Tel Aviv, April 18, 1974.

97. H. Baruch, "Facing the 180,000: How the Military Government Rules," *Ner* 10, nos. 3–4 (December–January 1958/1959): 39.

98. Personal interview with Dan Tichon, Jerusalem, March 18, 1974.

99. *Divrei Haknesset* 4 (1950): 947–948; Jiryis, *The Arabs of Israel*, p. 156; personal interview with Yehoshua Palmon, Jerusalem, December 10, 1973.

100. *Divrei Haknesset* 4 (1950): 947–948, 977; Ben-Porath, *The Arab Labor Force in Israel*, p. 62. Ben-Porath has estimated that between 1949 and 1952, "Arab wages were roughly 35% to 70% of Jewish wages for similar work" (p. 55).

101. Ben-Porath, *The Arab Labor Force in Israel*, p. 62.

102. Ibid., p. 53.

103. Ernest Stock, *From Conflict to Understanding*, p. 66.

104. *Israel Government Year Book*, 1962/1963, p. 256.

105. Zeev Sharef, *On the Activities of the Ministry of Housing: Report to the Knesset by the Minister of Housing*, June 28, 1971, p. 8 (Hebrew).

106. Personal interview with Akiva Feinstein, Jerusalem, April 9, 1974.

107. Personal interview with the official spokesman of the Ministry of Housing, Jerusalem, April 9, 1974. In 1975 the government announced plans for the construction of eight hundred housing units a year in the Arab sector from 1975/1976 to 1980/1981 (Ezekiel Shemesh, "Israel's Arabs—1975," *New Outlook* 18, no. 7 [October–November 1975]: 29). Concerning the slow progress made by the government in meeting the severe housing shortage in the Arab sector, see Harel et al., *The Conclusions of the Committee Concerning the Activities of the Histadrut in the Arab Sector*, p. 39.

108. Ministry of Finance, Investment Authority, *Israel: Investor's Manual*, p. 44.

109. Ibid., p. 44–45.

110. According to the Office of the Adviser to the Prime Minister on Arab Affairs, three "approved industries" were established in the Arab sector under the terms of the capital investment incentive law (Shemesh, "Israel's Arabs—1975," p. 29).

111. *Zoo Haderech*, January 16, 1974. For a more recent comparison of the budgets of comparable Arab and Jewish localities, see *Zoo Haderech*, November 23, 1977.

112. Lecture delivered by Kamal Tibi, Conference of Local Authorities, May 8, 1974, Jerusalem. For details of the findings of the Jerisi Committee, see *Divrei Haknesset*, July 23, 1975, p. 3872.

113. Yosef Burg, *The Activities of the Ministry of the Interior: Report by the Minister of the Interior for the Fiscal Year 1973/1974*, p. 143 (Hebrew).

114. *Statistical Abstract of Israel* 24 (1973): 602.

115. Mahmud Bayadsi, "The Arab Local Authorities: Achievements and Problems," *New Outlook* 18, no. 7 (October–November 1975): 59.

116. This estimate of the extent of Waqf lands is exclusive of lands in the Negev (from Shimoni, *The Arabs of the Land of Israel*, pp. 86–88).

117. Shimoni, *The Arabs of the Land of Israel*, pp. 63–64; Jacob Yehoshua, "Muslims," in *Religious Life and Communities*, pp. 41–42.

118. Text of speech delivered on the floor of the Knesset by Member of Knesset Taufik Ziad, reprinted in *Zoo Haderech*, August 6, 1975.

119. Avraham Rotem, "The Leasing of Cemeteries, the Throwing of Grenades," *Maariv*, November 21, 1975.

120. For a very instructive description of the relationship between the government and the board of trustees of the Muslim Waqf in Jaffa, see Moshe Shokeid, "Strategy and Change in the Arab Vote: Observations in a Mixed Town," in Asher Arian, ed., *Elections in Israel–1973*, pp. 145–166.

121. Interview with Shmuel Toledano, in *Davar*, December 26, 1969.

122. Israel Information Center, "Minorities in Israel," Information Briefing 9, p. 16.

123. For additional information concerning the implementation of the five-year plans and their impact on the development of the Arab sector, see Waschitz, "Commuters and Entrepreneurs," pp. 52–53; Moshe Dayan, "Minister Dayan Answers *New Outlook*," and Simcha Flapan, "The Minister Admits He Has No Plan," in *New Outlook* 7, no. 3 (March–April 1964): 85–90; Aharon Cohen, *Israel and the Arab World*, p. 499; Harari, *The Arabs in Israel–1976*. Concerning the water and sewage crises that have plagued Arab villages in recent years and the financial impossibility for Arab localities to provide these basic services for

themselves, see Harari, *The Arabs in Israel—1976*, p. 40. For graphic descriptions of drinking water and sewage problems in various Arab towns and villages, see *Zoo Haderech*, August 10, 1977; October 12, 1977; November 9, 1977; July 26, 1978.

124. Stendel, *The Minorities in Israel*, pp. 65–67; "The Development Plans for the Israel Minorities" (mimeo in the files of the American Jewish Committee, Jerusalem); Gideon Weigert, *The Arabs of Israel* (mimeo distributed by Israeli Ministry of Foreign Affairs), p. 7.

125. Binyamin Shidlovsky, "Changes in the Development of the Arab Village in Israel," *Hamizrah Hechadash* 15 (1965): 27 (Hebrew).

126. S. Zarhi and A. Achiezra, *The Economic Development of the Arab Region in Israel*, pp. 23–24.

127. Fred M. Gottheil, "On the Economic Development of the Arab Region in Israel," in Curtis and Chertoff, eds., *Israel: Social Structure and Change*, p. 246. Estimates quoted here and above, it should be noted, are based on prices and the value of the Israeli lira current at the time the analysis was undertaken.

128. *Statistical Abstract of Israel* 13 (1962): 442; 14 (1963): 576; 17 (1966): 552–553; 18 (1967): 492–493; 20 (1969): 510–511; 24 (1973): 592–593; Flapan, "Planning for the Arab Village," p. 29; Shidlovsky, "Changes in the Development of the Arab Village in Israel," p. 27; Stendel, *The Minorities in Israel*, p. 66. The categories used to compute overall development budget expenditures were Agriculture, Industry and Crafts, Mines and Quarries, Electricity, Transport, Housing, and Loans to Local Councils. Comprehensive statistics regarding annual government expenditures in the Arab sector are not available for years after 1972.

129. In the words of a prominent Labor Party ideologue, "The Military Government's main task is to keep as many Arabs as possible dependent upon the dominant party's institutions, enterprises, and protection" (Eliezer Livne, "Israeli Democracy and the Arabs," *New Outlook* 3, no. 7 [June, 1960]: 48).

130. Personal interview with Yoshua Verben, Rehovot, December 14, 1973.

131. See, for example, the editorial of the *Jerusalem Post*, November 24, 1969.

132. See interview with Benjamin Azkin and articles by Henry Rosenfeld and Zeev Schiff concerning the role of the Shin Bet in connection with the hiring and firing of Israeli Arab intellectuals (*New Outlook*, 14, no. 2 [March 1971]: 10–24). See also in this regard Eli Rekhess, *A Survey of Israeli-Arab Graduates from Institu-*

tions of Higher Learning in Israel (1961–1971), pp. 30–31; interview with Uri Lubrani, adviser to the prime minister on Arab affairs, *Ner* 13, nos. 9–10 (May–June 1962): x–xii; Zeev Schiff, "The Problem of the Arab Minority and Its Relationship to the State," *Temurot*, nos. a–b (November 1960): 10 (Hebrew).

133. A description of feelings of dependence and fear among Arab school teachers can be found in a lecture delivered by Elias Dalal, principal of the Orthodox Community Secondary School in Haifa, reprinted in *Ner* 9, nos. 1–2 (October–November 1957): 41–44.

134. See, for example, Subhi Abu-Ghosh, "The Politics of an Arab Village in Israel" (Ph.D. dissertation, Princeton University, 1965), pp. 113–115, for a description of the dependence of teachers and other white-collar workers and its political implications. Arab laborers are relatively immune from the threat of blacklisting as long as there are serious labor shortages in the Israeli economy as a whole. As one official in the Labor Party responsible for Arab affairs told me in 1974, "The economic situation in this country is now a little too good. With full employment an Arab worker knows that if I recommend to his employer that he be fired another job will become available immediately" (personal interview with Eliyahu Ronen, Acre, April 1, 1974).

135. These examples are based on information supplied by villagers in Deir Hana, Kfar Yasif, and Arrabe and by officials of the Israel Electric Corporation, the Ministry of Development, and the Haifa Branch of the Office of the Adviser to the Prime Minister on Arab Affairs.

136. Open letter, mimeographed, distributed by Arab local council chairmen at the Conference of Local Authorities, Jerusalem, May 7–8, 1974; *Divrei Haknesset*, July 23, 1975, p. 3872. Concerning official inaction in the approval of master plans, see Ariel Weinstein, in *Maariv*, July 2, 1976; *Zoo Haderech*, November 23, 1977, and November 7, 1979.

137. *Maariv*, September 23, 1976; September 10, 1976.

138. *Zoo Haderech*, July 6, 1977. In an interview on September 9, 1977, Agriculture Minister Arik Sharon accused the previous Labor government of "laxity" in the defense of national lands from intrusions by Israeli Arabs. In the coastal strip alone, he declared, "some tens of thousands of Arabs settled, building about 800 dwellings on national land. In the Galilee, state lands are a real no-man's land; we talk of Judaizing the Galilee while the region is again the Galilee of the gentiles. I've begun intensive activity, as

the one responsible for the Lands Authority, along with other elements, to prevent control of state lands by strangers [or 'foreigners,' i.e., Israeli Arabs]" (*Maariv*, September 9, 1977).

139. *Zoo Haderech*, July 6, 1977.

140. For information concerning the problem of obtaining building permits and regarding the destruction or threatened destruction of unlicensed buildings in the villages of al-Suad, Iksal, Shaab, Ein Mah'l, Um el-Fahm, and Pekien, see *Haaretz*, February 14, 1976; February 26, 1976; *Zoo Haderech*, April 3, 1974; September 19, 1974; April 9, 1975; April 14, 1975; August 27, 1975; and esp. September 13, 1975. See also Kassem Zayad, "Am I a 'Negative' or a 'Positive' Arab?" *Israel Horizons* 24, no. 6 (June–July 1976): 12.

141. Yosef Waschitz, "The Plight of the Bedouin," *New Outlook* 18, no. 7 (October–November 1975): 63.

142. Shimoni, *The Arabs of the Land of Israel*, p. 213.

143. Oded, "Bedouin Lands Threatened by Takeover," p. 45.

144. Ibid., pp. 47–48.

145. For details of these schemes and various controversies surrounding the issue of compensation to Bedouin, see Waschitz, "The Plight of the Bedouin," pp. 63–64; *Zoo Haderech*, August 11, 1976; Ori Stendel, *Israeli Arabs: Trends and Developments*, pp. 36–39 (Hebrew).

146. Gidon Karsel, "Kiryat-Jureish: Dynamics of the Urbanization of an Israeli-Arab Community" (Ph.D. dissertation, Tel Aviv University, 1972) (Hebrew).

6. Cooptation as a Component of Control: The Capture of Arab Elites

1. Subhi Abu-Ghosh, "The Politics of an Arab Village in Israel" (Ph.D. dissertation, Princeton University, 1965), p. 11.

2. Henry Rosenfeld, "The Contradictions between Property, Kinship and Power, as Reflected in the Marriage System of an Arab Village," in J. G. Peristiany, ed., *Contributions to Mediterranean Sociology*, p. 248.

3. For an excellent description of British use of the same techniques regarding Bedouin sheiks and their tribesmen, see Emanual Marx, *Bedouin of the Negev*, p. 34. On the role of the Mukhtar in Palestine, see Gabriel Baer, "The Economic and Social Position of the Village Mukhtar in Palestine," paper presented at International Conference on the Palestinians and the Middle East Conflict, University of Haifa, April 5–8, 1976.

4. For an extended discussion of the political culture of Syria and Palestine in the 19th century, see Moshe Maoz, *Ottoman Reform in Syria and Palestine, 1840–1861: The Impact of the Tanzimat on Politics and Society.*

5. In southern Italy, for example, as described by Edward Banfield, traditional society was composed of large numbers of nuclear families. Given this form of social organization, cooptation would necessitate the capture of large numbers of household heads. Moreover, the political returns per coopted individual would be very small and terror, random searches and interrogations, or other forms of intimidation would suggest themselves as reasonable alternative strategies. In traditional Somali society, where cultural commitments to open, participatory political processes are strong and where clan groups, though large, are democratically organized, cooptation as a strategy of control failed miserably. Since there were no real "chiefs," it did not matter how handsomely the colonial authorities tried to pay off individuals who seemed to be chiefs (see Edward C. Banfield, *The Moral Basis of a Backward Society,* and I. M. Lewis, *Pastoral Democracy*).

6. Attempts by Rustum Bastuni, a one-time Mapam member of Knesset, to propagate an ideology which substitutes "Israeliness" rather than "Arabness" as the core identity of non-Jews in Israel were vigorously opposed by the regime. In 1966 Bastuni emigrated to the United States.

   Amnon Linn, at present a Likud member of Knesset, was director of the Arab Department of the Labor Party during the 1960's. He has at regular intervals proposed that the cooptation of Israeli Arabs be institutionalized by means of an Israeli-Arab ideology and a national party. He has often coupled this proposal with suggestions that Arabs be conscripted into the army and that a "strong hand" be used against those Arabs who fail to commit themselves actively to the support of the regime. Linn's ideas have assumed greater importance since the Likud election victory in May 1977 and are considered more extensively in the final chapter.

   For Bastuni's ideas and the response of government Arabists (including Amnon Linn), see A. Ben-Ami, "Israeli Jews and Israeli Arabs: A Symposium," *Jewish Frontier* 33, no. 9 (November 1966): 15–24. See also Chapter 4.

7. Abu-Ghosh, "The Politics of an Arab Village in Israel," pp. 108–109.

8. G. Shamir, "The Establishment of the 'Military Government'

over the Arab Population during the War of Independence" (seminar paper, Tel Aviv University, 1973) (Hebrew); Larry Collins and Dominique Lapierre, *O Jerusalem*, pp. 207–208.

9. Yosef Waschitz, "Changes in the Life of Israeli Arabs," *Hamizrah Hechadash* 1, no. 4 (July 1950): 263 (Hebrew).

10. Shlomo Avineri, "Political Representation of the Arab Minority," *Beterem* 11, no. 5 (March 1, 1953): 32 (Hebrew).

11. Personal interview with Zvi Alpeleg, Tel Aviv, April 24, 1974.

12. Concerning the government's official "neutrality" regarding the intergenerational conflict in the Arab sector, see Yehezkel Shammash, *Minority Groups in Israel*, Office of the Adviser to the Prime Minister on Arab Affairs, p. 42. See also the remarks of Shmuel Toledano as quoted by Eli Ayal in "How Young Israeli Arabs See Their Future," *Atlas* 20, no. 4 (April 1971): 27.

13. Henry Rosenfeld, "Change, Barriers to Change, and Contradictions in the Arab Village Family," *American Anthropologist* 70, no. 4 (August 1968): 732.

14. Henry Rosenfeld, "Processes of Change and Factors of Conservation in the Rural Arab Family in Israel," *Hamizrah Hechadash* 19, no. 3 (1969): 216 (Hebrew).

15. Abu-Ghosh, "The Politics of an Arab Village in Israel," p. 21.

16. Ibid., p. 126.

17. H. Baruch, "Facing the 180,000: How the Military Government Rules," *Ner* 10, nos. 3–4 (December 1958–January 1959): 51. See also Ibrahim Musa Ibrahim, "The Last Letter," *Ner* 9, nos. 5–7 (February–April 1958): 48–50.

18. Abu-Ghosh, "The Politics of an Arab Village," pp. 126–127; Don Peretz, *Israel and the Palestine Arabs*, pp. 51–52; Waschitz, "Changes in the Life of Israeli Arabs," p. 259.

19. Personal interview with residents of the Arab village of Baka el-Gharbiyey (Little Triangle), April 20, 1974. See also Eli Ayal, "How Young Israeli Arabs see Their Future," p. 26; Abu-Ghosh, "The Politics of an Arab Village," pp. 126–127.

20. Deborah Dror, "In the Shadow of the Military Government," reprinted from *al-Hamishmar* in *Ner* 14, nos. 10–12 (June–August 1963): xviii–xix.

21. Personal interview with Eliezer Beeri, Jerusalem, May 6, 1974. See Gerda Luft, "Military Government and Travel Permits," *Jerusalem Post*, January 12, 1956; Abner Cohen, *Arab Border Villages in Israel*, p. 60.

22. Cohen, *Arab Border Villages in Israel*, p. 67.

23. Dror, "In the Shadow of the Military Government," pp. xxiii–xxiv. For a description of a variety of techniques used by the Mil-

itary Government to exert pressure on politically uncooperative Arabs, see Rustum Bastuni, "Whither the Arab Minority?" *Ner* 7, nos. 10–11 (June–July 1956): 15–16. See also Walter Schwarz, *The Arabs in Israel*, pp. 83–87.

24. Personal interview with Shimon Landman, Jerusalem, February 25, 1974.

25. Personal interview with Mahmoud Meari, Jerusalem, March 1974. See also, for example, the account of local elections in several Arab villages in the Galilee in the *Jerusalem Post*, May 26, 1976.

26. Personal interview with Abraham Oved, Nazareth, March 4, 1974.

27. Ministry of the Interior, *Elections to Local Authorities in the Arab Sector: 1969*, and *Elections for Eight Local Authorities in the Arab Sector: 1971, 1972* (both Hebrew). See also Attalah Mansour, in *Haaretz*, April 22, 1966.

    Although other parties, notably the National Religious Party, have established connections with hamulas in various villages, before 1977 they did not challenge the dominant position of the Labor Party in the Arab sector. It is unclear whether the Likud victory in the 1977 Knesset election will alter this pattern in any substantial way. While many hamula leaders made strenuous efforts to contact Likud Arabists after the election results were announced, it is also true that in the Histadrut elections held the following month the Labor Party list won a substantial majority in the Arab sector.

28. Personal interview with Violet Khouri, Kfar Yasif, March 7, 1974.

29. Personal interviews with residents of Baka el-Gharbiyeh, April 19, 1974; personal interview with Emanuel Kopelovitz, Jerusalem, May 29, 1974. See Micah Nino, "The Situation of Minorities and of Christian Communities under Israeli Jurisdiction," *International Problems* 11, nos. 3–4 (December 1972): 1–17.

30. Khalil Nakhleh, "Shifting Patterns of Conflict in Selected Arab Villages in Israel," (Ph.D. dissertation, Indiana University, 1973), pp. 187–188; Jalal Abu-Tama, "The Arabs in Israel and the Elections to Local Authorities" (seminar paper, Bar Ilan University, 1972), p. 43 (Hebrew).

31. Waschitz, "Changes in the Life of Israeli Arabs," p. 259; personal interview with Shimon Landman, Jerusalem, February 25, 1974.

32. Ron Linberg, "The Penetration of a Minorities Village by the National Parties," *Medinah Vemimshal* 1, no. 1 (Summer 1971): 131–132, 140–142 (Hebrew); Moshe Shokeid, "Strategy and

Change in the Arab Vote: Observations in a Mixed Town," in Asher Arian, ed., *The Elections: 1973*, pp. 145–166.

33. Shokeid, "Strategy and Change in the Arab Vote," pp. 145–166.

34. "The Druse Community's Angry Young Men," *Ner* 13, nos. 11–12 (July–August 1962):xxv.

35. Ori Stendel, *The Minorities in Israel*, p. 43.

36. Abu-Ghosh, "The Politics of an Arab Village," pp. 136–138; Aharon Layish, "The Muslim Waqf in Israel," *Asian and African Studies* 1 (1965):58.

37. Abu-Ghosh, "The Politics of an Arab Village," p. 61; personal interview with Violet Khouri, Kfar Yasif, March 7, 1974. Government branches in the Arab sector are, for all practical purposes, those offices wherein Arabs are eligible for employment. Very few Arabs are employed in government offices which serve the Jewish sector.

38. Marx, *Bedouin of the Negev*, pp. 40–45.

39. The term "Arabistim," as used in the Israeli press, refers to those officials who administer government policy in the Arab sector. The connotation is that these men speak Arabic, know the "Arab mentality," and have had long experience in the security services in connection with Arab affairs (see, for example, *Maariv*, April 1, 1976).

40. Arab lists have also been entered in Knesset elections affiliated to the General Zionist Party, Rafi, the National Religious Party, and the Likud, but none of their candidates has ever been elected. In the 1977 election, however, three Druse were elected to the Knesset: one on the Likud list, and two others on the list of the Democratic Movement for Change, a centrist group formed mainly by disgruntled Labor Party technocrats.

41. See Jacob Landau, *The Arabs in Israel*, pp. 195–198.

42. Ibid., p. 38.

43. Personal interview with David Zechariah, Tel Aviv, January 29, 1974. See Daniel Bloch in *Davar*, August 23, 1968; Landau, *The Arabs in Israel*, Appendix F, pp. 243–245.

44. Landau, *The Arabs in Israel*, p. 139.

45. Ibid., p. 166.

46. In 1959 Salah Khnefes and Massad Qasis were dropped from the affiliated lists. In 1973 De'ib Obeid and Elias Nakhle were similarly dismissed. In both cases these men attempted to run for reelection without the backing of the Labor Party, and in both cases they failed.

47. This holds true for the small Circassian community as well and,

to a lesser degree, for the various Christian sects. For example, in contrast to the government's large-scale confiscation of the assets of the Moslem Waqf (see Chapter 5), Christian religious trusts were soon returned to the control of Church authorities. See Ministry of Religious Affairs, *Christian News from Israel*, no. 1 (August 1949): 8, and subsequent issues, passim. Concerning special dispensations granted the Greek Catholic Church and its one-time leader in Israel, Archbishop George Hakim, see Landau, *The Arabs in Israel*, pp. 203–204.

48. Ministry of the Interior, *Arab Local Councils in Israel*, no. 13 (November 1960): 16–19. The average total budget for all Arab local councils during this period was I£ 152,000.

49. Personal interview with Sasoon Rashdi, Acre, April 1, 1974.

50. A. Harel et al., *Conclusions of the Committee Concerning the Activities of the Histadrut in the Arab Sector*, p. 37, (Hebrew). The efforts of the government to channel industry into Druse villages is noted by Stendel in *The Minorities in Israel*, p. 44.

51. For comment on Israel's "house" Druse, see Alfred Friendly, *Israel's Oriental Immigrants and Druzes* (Minority Rights Group Report No. 12), p. 28. See also in this regard Schwarz, *The Arabs in Israel*, Chapter 12, "Model Arabs," pp. 148–156; and an interview with members of a model Druse family, in *Maariv*, January 28, 1977. Concerning a government decision to staff the Office of the Adviser to the Prime Minister on Arab Affairs with members of the Druse community, see *Davar*, April 27, 1972. In 1977 Attassi and another Druse, Shafiq Assad, were elected to the Knesset on the list of the centrist Democratic Movement for Change.

52. The hegemony of hamula elders is particularly well entrenched in small, isolated Arab villages. In the larger villages and in Arab towns the processes mentioned in this section are progressing much more rapidly.

53. It is not uncommon, for example, to read in the Israeli press of Arab women in Israel killed by their fathers and brothers for dishonoring the family (see, for example, *Jerusalem Post*, March 31, 1974; April 22, 1974).

54. See Yochanan Peres, "Modernization and Nationalism in the Identity of the Israeli Arab," *Middle East Journal* 24, no. 4 (Autumn 1970): 479–492; Ehud Yaari, "Dahaf Survey of Israeli Arabs," *Davar*, September 22, 1968; Eliahu Guttman, Haim Klaff, and Shulamith Levi, *The Histadrut and Its Activities in the Arab Sector*, Appendix, pp. 5, 7, 26–28, 38 (Hebrew); and Em-

manuel Yalan et al., *The Modernization of Traditional Agricultural Villages: Minority Villages in Israel*, pp. 29, 32.

55. Concerning changing patterns of social and economic relations within Israeli Arab kinship groups, see Stendel, *The Minorities in Israel*, pp. 100–106, 111–115; "Arab Intellectuals on Israel," *New Outlook* 5, no. 8 (October 1962): 8–9; and Henry Rosenfeld, "Wage Labor and Status in an Arab Village," *New Outlook* 6, no. 1 (January 1963): 4–9.

56. For an official evaluation of the process of the "changing of the guard," see Shammash, *Minority Groups in Israel*, pp. 41–42.

57. For a particularly instructive article in this regard, see Linberg, "The Penetration of a Minorities Village by the National Parties," pp. 136ff.

58. Histadrut Arab Department, *The Histadrut's Arab Members*, 1969, p. 3. See also Stendel, *The Minorities in Israel*, Chapter 1, "The Histadrut as a Factor of Change in the Arab Sector," pp. 149–169.

59. Histadrut Arab Department, *The Histadrut's Arab Members*, pp. 23–24; Harry M. Rosen, *The Arabs and Jews in Israel: The Reality, the Dilemma, the Promise*, pp. 46–50. As noted, the Information Center or Information Center—Arab Branch serves as liaison between the Shin Bet (secret security service) and the Office of the Adviser to the Prime Minister on Arab Affairs.

60. Histadrut Arab Department, *The Histadrut's Arab Members*, p. 4.

61. Ibid., p. 40.

62. Ibid., p. 41.

63. Ibid., p. 43 (emphasis added). As indicated above, Zeidan Attassi (Attasheh) subsequently was appointed as the first Arab in the Israeli foreign service and in 1977 was elected to the Knesset.

64. Stendel, *The Minorities in Israel*, p. 166.

65. Harel et al., *Conclusions of the Committee Concerning Activities of the Histadrut in the Arab Sector*, pp. 29–33.

66. Personal interview with Yosef Ginat, Jerusalem, May 13, 1974. From an analytical standpoint, "integration" can be understood as a process according to which social groups and their representatives acquire and/or are awarded proportionate shares of control over economic and political resources. "Cooptation," as used in this study, refers to the use of personal rewards to out-group representatives in return for their implicit or explicit cooperation in *preventing* the transfer of political or economic power (see Chapter 3, note 33). As reflected in the findings of the Rekhess

study, the operational definition of "integration" used by government officials in connection with the Arab minority is the hiring of more educated Arabs by various branches of the civil service and the Histadrut, mainly in those branches which deal directly with the mundane affairs of Arab citizens. These efforts are considered advisable as a means of eliminating the frustrations of jobless Arab intellectuals, of encouraging in them a positive attitude toward the regime, and of enlisting their political assistance. Such programs thus far have not had and have not been intended to have the effect of placing Arabs in decision-making positions. Of course, *when* "cooptation" becomes "integration" is an important empirical problem. Much depends on the political and economic environment within which the process takes place.

67. Shammash, *Israel's Arabs—1976*, p. 51.
68. Eli Rekhess, *A Survey of Israeli-Arab Graduates from Institutions of Higher Learning in Israel (1967–1971)*, p. 2.
69. Ibid., quoted from "Summary, Conclusions, and Recommendations," p. 28.
70. During an interview with an official in the Histadrut's Arab Department, I asked about the application for Labor Party membership submitted some eight months previously by a young Arab well known for his popularity among educated Arabs in the Little Triangle. In response to my question the official took from his desk a thick sheaf of applications for party membership which he had been asked to comment on. Concerning the application of the individual in question: "I just haven't had time to look at it" (personal interview with Nawaf Masalha, Tel Aviv, April 24, 1974). Out of a total of three thousand delegates to a Labor Party nominating convention in 1977, ninety-five were Arabs.
71. Personal interview with Abraham Oved, Nazareth, March 4, 1974.
72. Personal interview with Yechiel Harari, Givat Haviva, January, 1974; information based on the preliminary results of a survey of the results of local council elections in the Arab sector conducted by Harari in 1973.
73. Ministry of the Interior, *Elections for Eight Local Authorities in the Arab Sector: 1971–1972*, pp. 2–3. For a summary of much of the data included in the Interior's studies of Arab local council elections, see Yechiel Harari, *The Arabs in Israel: Facts and Figures*, p. 38–39; and, by the same author, *The Arabs in Israel—1976*, pp. 25–30.
74. *New Outlook* 4, no. 1 (October 1959): 54. See also Abu-Ghosh,

"The Politics of an Arab Village," p. 107, concerning the "role of local leaders as unofficial security agents."

75. *Ner* 21, nos. 1–2 (November–December 1960): 10; *Jerusalem Post*, August 30, 1960.

76. Personal interview with Shmuel Porath, Jerusalem, March 28, 1974. Concerning the network of informers in Arab villages, see Schwarz, *The Arabs in Israel*, p. 87; and S. Ginat in *Yamim ve Laylot, Maariv* supplement, May 21, 1976, p. 27.

77. Personal interview, March 29, 1974. The treasurer was an ex-officio member of the fund-raising committee.

78. Ellen Geffner, "Attitudes of Arab Editorialists in Israel, 1948–67: An Analysis of AL-ITTIHAD, AL-MIRSAD, and AL-YAWM" (Ph.D. dissertation, University of Michigan, 1973), pp. 70–73, 84–86.

79. Translated from *Bisaraha*, the campaign newspaper of the affiliated Arab lists (1969), by Subhi Abu-Ghosh, "The Election Campaign in the Arab Sector," in Alan Arian, ed., *The Elections in Israel—1969*, pp. 247–248. See also Geffner, "Attitudes of Arab Editorialists," pp. 19–20, 76–78.

80. Geffner, "Attitudes of Arab Editorialists," pp. 108–111. For a more recent instance, see *Jerusalem Post*, March 25, 1976.

81. *Jerusalem Post*, November 21, 1963.

82. See Shmuel Segev, in *Maariv*, November 27, 1969.

83. *Jerusalem Post*, November 23, 1969. See also for references to condemnation from Moslem Waqf trustees, Arab school principals, and Labor Party–affiliated members of Knesset of Israeli Arab participation in guerrilla activities.

84. *Jerusalem Post*, March 21, 1976.

85. *Jerusalem Post*, March 24, 1976; March 26, 1976; *Haaretz*, March 26, 1976.

86. *Yediot Acharonot*, March 17, 1976.

87. *Maariv*, April 1, 1976.

88. Personal interview with Zvi Alpeleg, Tel Aviv, April 24, 1974.

89. Harari, *The Arabs in Israel—1976*, pp. 28, 30.

90. Calculated from detailed election statistics published in Harel et al., *The Conclusions of the Committee Concerning the Activities of the Histadrut in the Arab Sector*, appendix. On the relative success of Rakah in large as opposed to small villages and towns, see Harari, *The Arabs in Israel: Facts and Figures*, pp. 33a–34, 42; Landau, *The Arabs in Israel*, pp. 121, 127, 133, 147.

91. Personal interview with Yoram Katz, Haifa, March 31, 1974.

92. Personal interview with Eliyahu Ronen, Acre, April 1, 1974.

93. Personal interview with Morris Zilke, Jerusalem, March 28, 1974.

94. Personal interview with Kemal Kassem, Haifa, April 3, 1974.

95. Ibid.; personal interview with Amr Nasser al-Din, Haifa, April 3, 1974. See Yaacov Ardon, "Young Druse Charge Discrimination," *Jerusalem Post*, February 8, 1971; *Haaretz*, February 8, 1971. Soon after the demise of this group it was announced that another of its leaders was to become the first non-Jew to serve in the Office of the Adviser to the Prime Minister on Arab Affairs.

96. Personal interview with Kemal Kassem, Haifa, April 3, 1974. The character of the ties which bound Kassem to the Labor Party is clearly reflected by his decision, several days after the defeat of the Labor Party in May 1977, to desert it and offer his services as a spokesman in the Arab sector to the new Likud government (*Maariv*, June 9, 1977).

97. Personal interview with Morris Zilke, Jerusalem, March 28, 1974.

98. Personal notes of the author taken while attending the conference on Coexistence on the Campus, Ramat Gan, May 3–4, 1974.

99. "Labor Party" here refers to "Mapai" in 1949, 1951, 1955, 1959, and 1961; the "Labor Alignment" in 1965; and the expanded alignment or "Maarach" in 1969, 1973, and 1977. The Communist Party has been Labor's most serious competition in the battle for Arab votes. In recent elections its performance in the Arab sector has dramatically improved. In 1973, 37 percent of Arab voters voted communist; it was by far the party's best showing. In 1977 Rakah participated for electoral purposes in a Democratic Front for Peace and Equality which included some noncommunist Arab mayors along with noncommunist radical Jewish groups. The Front received 49 percent of the votes cast by Israeli Arabs, but only three of the five mandates in the Knesset won by the Front went to Rakah.

100. The figures for Arab support as a percentage of total Labor Party strength range from a high of 15.8 percent in 1951 to a low of 8.0 percent in 1969. The majority of these voters, in every election, were garnered by Arab affiliated lists. Although in 1977 Arab lists affiliated to the Labor Party gained only enough votes to elect one Arab member to the Knesset, the strongest of these lists came very close to electing a second member. Because of its affiliation with this list the Labor Party was able to transfer these "extra" votes to its list, thereby electing another of its Jewish candidates to Parliament (*Maariv*, May 22, 1977).

101. See Amos Eilon, "Arab Moods on the Eve of the Elections," *Jewish Frontier* 18, no. 7 (July 1951): 22–29; Leonard J. Fein, *Politics in Israel*, pp. 225–228.

102. Concerning the political role played by the Military Administration as an instrument of the Labor Party in the Arab sector, see Subhi Abu-Ghosh, "The Politics of an Arab Village," p. 106; Dror, "In the Shadow of the Military Government" pp. xviii–xix; Zeev Schiff, "The Pros and Cons of the Military Government," *New Outlook* 5, no. 3 (March–April 1962): 67–69; Yigal Allon, *A Curtain of Sand*, pp. 326–329.

103. For examples of the opposition of right-wing Jewish parties to the Military Administration, see *Jerusalem Post*, July 20, 1955; December 9, 1958; January 14, 1962; November 21, 1963.

104. The percentage of Arab votes gleaned by the National Religious Party is as follows: 1949—0.6 percent; 1951—0.7 percent; 1955—1.5 percent; 1959—3.5 percent; 1961—3.7 percent; 1965—5.3 percent; 1969—8.5 percent; 1973—8.2 percent; 1977—4.6 percent. The decline in the party's Arab vote in 1977 is almost certainly due to the extremely unfavorable publicity which it received as a result of the publication of the Koenig memorandum (see Chapter 3). Israel Koenig, the Ministry of the Interior High Commissioner for the Northern region, is a member of the NRP. Analysts of the election results expressed amazement at the party's ability to perform as well as it did in the Arab sector in 1977 in the aftermath of the memorandum's publication (Ehud Yaari, "Contradictory Trends among Arabs," *Davar*, June 3, 1977, translated in *Israleft*, no. 108 [June 15, 1977]).

105. It is the division of labor which explains this very large number of votes received in 1973 by Hamad Abu Rabiah, a Negev Bedouin sheik, in Galilean and Little Triangle villages. For information on Labor Party tactical considerations in forming different affiliated lists from election to election, see Landau, *The Arabs in Israel*, Appendix F, pp. 237–248.

106. Personal interview with a voting inspector from the Galilean village of Rama, Jerusalem, February 17, 1974; personal interviews with residents of Sakhnin, March 1–3, 1974; personal interview with resident of Kfar Kana, Nazareth, March 4, 1974; personal interviews with residents of Kfar Yasif, March 7, 1974. For details concerning tactics used by traditional elites and Labor Party apparatchiks to deliver the Arab vote for the Labor Party, see Eilon, "Arab Moods on the Eve of the Elections," pp. 22–25; Yosef Waschitz, "Arabs in Israeli Politics," *New Outlook*, 5, no.

3 (March–April, 1962): 34–38; Abu-Ghosh, "The Politics of an Arab Village," pp. 63–69, 106–107; Cohen, *Arab Border Villages in Israel,* pp. 128; 154–172; Abu-Ghosh, "The Election Campaign in the Arab Sector," in Arian, ed., *The Elections in Israel—1969,* pp. 239–252. For an especially detailed study concerning the methods used by the Labor Party, Herut, the National Religious Party, and others to harness rival hamula leaders for political advantage, see Linberg, "The Penetration of a Minority Village by the National Parties," pp. 129–143.

107. Personal interview with Emile Tuma, Haifa, April 3, 1974. See *Jerusalem Post,* March 20, 1974; March 27, 1974; April 4, 1974, for references to the stuffing of ballot boxes in Bedouin areas.

108. See, for example, Ecumenical Theological Research Fraternity in Israel, *Christians in Israel and the Yom Kippur War,* pp. 2, 17, 28, 37, 38, 50–52; Howard Blake, "We Are Israelis Too," *Hadassah Magazine,* December 1973, pp. 16–17; Donald Rossing, "Israel's Minorities Contribute to the War Effort," *Christian News from Israel* 24, nos. 2–3 (December 1973): 86.

109. *Divrei Haknesset,* March 29, 1978, pp. 2329–2330.

110. For examples of the use of coopted Arabs for propaganda purposes, see Horacio Elizalde, "Impressions of a Visitor from the Argentine," *Christian News from Israel* 5, nos. 3–4 (February 1955): 29–30; Alexander Ramati, *Israel Today,* pp. 150–151; "Nazareth Mayor: Arabs in U.S. Want Peace," *Christian News from Israel* 18, nos. 3–4 (December 1967): 7–9; 19, nos. 3–4 (December, 1968): 9; Shefi Advertising, ed., *Arab-Jewish Association to Promote Fraternity and Peace; Maariv,* December 5, 1969; Alfred Friendly, *Israel's Oriental Immigrants and Druzes;* Ruth Gruber, *Israel Today: Land of Many Nations,* pp. 175–177; Saumyendranath Tagore, *Israeli Chiaroscuro,* pp. 63–66; George Mikes, *Coat of Many Colors: Israel,* pp. 137–140.

Significantly, when President Carter arrived in Israel from Egypt during the peace negotiations of March 1979, he was greeted at Ben-Gurion Airport by an Israeli honor guard. As noted by Walter Cronkite, the guard commander who escorted President Carter as he reviewed the troops was a Druse major in the Israeli army.

111. P. Cohen, "Minority Soldiers Help in Guarding the Negev," *Ner* 11, no. 12 (September–October 1960): 15–16. More recently the minorities regiment has been asssigned to patrol the border with Lebanon and has been used to combat guerrilla infiltration into the Galilee.

For examples of the use of the border police to control rioting and demonstrations in Arab villages, see *Jerusalem Post*, March 31, 1976; May 11, 1976; *Maariv*, May 31, 1976. Druse army veterans are employed in relatively large numbers in the national police force, assigned for the most part to predominantly Arab districts. In one Druse village it was reported in late 1975 that three-fourths of the workingmen were employed by one branch or another of the security services (*New Outlook* 18, no. 7 [October–November 1975]: 79). See also Israeli Ministry of Foreign Affairs, *The Arabs in Israel*, p. 26.

7. Control as a System and the Future of Jewish-Arab Relations

1. Ernest Stock, *From Conflict to Understanding*, p. 56. See also *Jerusalem Post*, March 30, 1967.

2. *Laws of the State of Israel* 15 (1960/1961): 101; 26 (1971/1972): 184. See also Efraim Orni, *Forms of Settlement*, p. 111.

3. See *Laws of the State of Israel* 26 (1971/1972): 186, 188–189, 195–196.

4. For a list of exact administrative definitions, see *Statistical Abstract of Israel* 28 (1977): 17, "Introduction to the Tables."

5. Concerning the impact of the 1972 property tax law on the Arab sector, see *Davar*, July 20, 1976; *Zoo Haderech*, August 31, 1977; November 23, 1977.

6. In June 1977 seven Arab educators resigned from what was the third aborted commission appointed since 1972 to conduct a reform of the Arabic curriculum. For an interview with those who resigned, see *Zoo Haderech*, September 7, 1977.

7. Personal interview with Aga Schwartz, Jerusalem, March 11, 1974; personal interview with Dan Tichon, Jerusalem, March 18, 1974. See the remarks of Mahmoud Arhein during a symposium on "Israel's Arabs after 1973," *New Outlook* 18, no. 7 (October–November 1975): 78.

8. Rakah's percentage of the Arab vote in the last four Knesset and Histadrut elections has been as shown in Table 9.

9. See "Riad Comes Home," a short story by Attalah Mansour, translated by Aubrey Hodes, *New Outlook* 5, no. 3 (March–April 1962): 89–90. See also Mustapha Ghanaim, "Arab Village Youth," *New Outlook* 18, no. 7 (October–November 1975): 54–57.

10. See Danny Rubinstein, "The Area is Open to Rakah Activists," *Davar*, March 31, 1974.

Table 9. Percentage of the Arab Vote for Rakah

Year	Knesset	Histadrut
1965	23.6	20.0
1969	29.6	31.4
1973	37.0	26.9
1977[a]	49.4	32.0

[a]Figures for 1977 refer to Arab votes cast for the Democratic Front for Peace and Equality.

11. For discussion of literature on the Palestinian self-identification of Israeli Arabs, see John E. Hofman and Benjamin Beit Hallahmi, "The Palestinian Identity and Israel's Arabs," *Peace Research* 9, no. 1 (January 1977): 13–21.

12. See *Israleft*, no. 106 (May 15, 1977): 2.

13. The minority is customarily referred to by Rakah spokesmen as "the Arab population of Israel" (*haoochlusivah ha-Aravit b'Yisrael*). It is clear, however, that Rakah leaders, who have always opposed the Arab minority's parochial fragmentation, understand the importance of its emerging Palestinian consciousness. On May Day 1976, Taufik Ziad, Rakah's mayor of Nazareth, declared: "From now on there will be no communities and religious groups but only a single Arab minority, part of the Palestinian nation." Ziad's speech sparked an enthusiastic response from the crowd (*Jerusalem Post*, May 2, 1976; *Zoo Haderech*, May 3, 1976).

   For a discussion of the ideological formulas used by Emil Tuma, Rakah's leading Arab ideologue, see "Rakah on PLO, Zionism . . . ," translated from *Davar*, November 30, 1976, in *Israleft* no. 96 (December 15, 1976).

14. A sensitive problem for Rakah is conscription of Arabs into the army. In principle Rakah does not oppose conscription on an equal basis with Jews. This is consonant with the demand for equal rights for all Israelis. Rakah's current position on the issue seems to be that no Israeli should be drafted into an "occupation army." See remarks of Taufik Ziad, *Maariv*, September 23, 1976.

15. Ori Stendel, *The Minorities in Israel*, p. 129; personal interview with David Zechariah, Tel Aviv, January 29, 1974.

16. In 1977 the Democratic Front received 80,100 votes in the Knesset election; only 8,400 of these were cast by Jews (Ehud Yaari, "Contradictory Trends among Arabs," *Davar*, June 3, 1977, translated in *Israleft*, no. 108 [June 15, 1977]).

17. For information on veteran Arab communists in Israel, see Stendel, *The Minorities in Israel,* pp. 125–129; Jacob Landau, *The Arabs in Israel,* p. 88.

18. Rakah's formation of the Democratic Front for Peace and Equality, involving an electoral alliance with disgruntled Arab mayors and various small Jewish dissident groups, alienated radical Arab intellectuals. With no alternative repository for protest votes, the Jerusalem Arab student organization and various "Sons of the Village" groups called for an Arab boycott of the elections. There is little doubt that their efforts in this regard deprived the Democratic Front of a sixth seat in the Knesset.

19. It can be assumed, however, that the mixed Arab-Jewish composition of Rakah's leadership also presents opportunities for infiltration and surveillance by government security agents that would not be available in a purely Arab party.

20. As one of many examples: In May 1976, the Israel–Soviet Union Friendship Movement held a rally at the Red Army Forest in Jerusalem commemorating the Allied victory over Nazi Germany. A Soviet delegation which had come to Israel specifically for the occasion participated in the rally. The head of the Soviet delegation, in answer to a newsman's question concerning Soviet-Israeli relations, responded that the exchange of such a delegation "will contribute to the creation of an atmosphere which can bring about normalization." Also appearing at the rally were Mordechai Avi-Shaul, president of the Israel–Soviet Union Friendship Movement, and Taufik Ziad, mayor of Nazareth (*Davar,* May 9, 1976). See also the text of a speech by Alexander Aksionov, chairman of the Soviet delegation to Rakah's eighteenth party congress, in *Zoo Haderech,* December 22, 1976.

21. Israeli officials also stress their desire, out of concern for the future immigration of Soviet Jews to Israel, not to alienate the Soviets by banning the Communist Party (personal interview with David Zechariah, Tel Aviv, January 29, 1974).

22. Personal interviews with David Zechariah, Tel Aviv, January 29, 1974; with Ibrahim Bayadsi, Baka el-Gharbiyeh, April 20, 1974; and with Suleiman Mohammed Salim, Deir Hana, March 1, 1974. See Aliza Auerbach, "Ibni the Doctor," *Jerusalem Post Weekly,* January 20, 1976; *Zoo Haderech,* April 22, 1976, p. 5; Yair Kutler's interview with Rakah MK Tawfiq Tubi, reprinted in *SWASIA,* May 21, 1976, p. 7.

23. Renewed regularly by the Knesset, the Defense Regulations are still in effect. Under the terms of these laws most Rakah activists have been barred from entering the occupied territories, others

have been, and are, confined to their places of residence, and all are subject to preventive arrest and administrative detention (see *Zoo Haderech*, September 10, 1975; August 16, 1975; March 31, 1976).

24. The traditional slogan used to designate Zionism's goal of establishing an unassailable Jewish majority in the Galilee is Yehud ha-Galil (to Judaize the Galilee). However, because of the rhetorical inconvenience of this stress upon Judaization, Labor government spokesmen tended to substitute other phrases—notably Lichloos ha-Galil (to populate the Galilee) and Liftoach ha-Galil (to develop the Galilee). Nevertheless, the crucial concern remains making and keeping the Galilee Jewish. See, inter alia, Yosef Galili in *Zoo Haderech*, January 8, 1975; Yehuda Arieli, "Judaising the Galilee—Plans and Reality," *Haaretz*, February 29, 1976; Israel Harel, "The 'Dead Land' Comes to Life in Opposition to the Development of the Galilee," *Maariv*, October 17, 1975; Yosef Goell, "Collision Course in Galilee," *Jerusalem Post Weekly*, March 6, 1976.

25. Altogether seven Arabs were killed by the army and the border police on Land Day. Two of the deaths occurred in the Little Triangle. For differing accounts as to whether the security forces or the villages were responsible for the violence, see *Jerusalem Post*, March 31, 1976; *Haaretz*, March 31, 1976; *Zoo Haderech*, April 7, 1976; April 12, 1976.

26. Concerning the success or failure of the general strike and impact of Land Day outside of Israel, see Jewish Telegraphic Agency, *Daily News Summary*, March 31, 1976; *Haaretz*, March 31, 1976; *Jerusalem Post Weekly*, April 6, 1976; *Zoo Haderech*, March 31, 1976; *New York Times*, March 31, 1976; April 1, 1976, April 4, 1976. For a thorough analysis of the events leading up to Land Day, the positions taken by various Arab groups, and the impact of the events on the consciousness of the Arab population, see Eli Rekhess, *Arabs in Israel and the Land Expropriations in the Galilee: Background, Events and Implications* (Hebrew).

27. *Haaretz*, May 2, 1976; *Zoo Haderech*, May 3, 1976. The bloodshed on Land Day made a deep impact on the Arab community. Rakah refrained from calling another general strike in 1977 and 1978, but a commemorative rally held in the Galilee village of Sakhnin on March 30, 1978, drew an overwhelmingly Arab crowd, variously reported at five thousand to twenty thousand people (*Zoo Haderech*, April 5, 1978).

28. See Yosef Goell, "Talking with Arabs," *Jerusalem Post Weekly*,

January 13, 1976; Yehuda Litani, "Stop Rakah in Nazareth," *Haaretz*, October 27, 1975; Yitzhak White, in *Yediot Acharonot*, December 7, 1975, and December 9, 1975.

29. See Attalah Mansour, "Radical Opposition to the Druze Leadership," reprinted from *Haaretz*, April 23, 1976, in *SWASIA*, May 28, 1976, pp. 7–8. In 1977 the Druse Initiative Committee had branches in twelve of the eighteen villages with substantial Druse populations (*Zoo Haderech*, December 7, 1977). Concerning resistance to the draft among young Druse since 1976, see *Jerusalem Post*, November 1, 1977; *Zoo Haderech*, July 26, 1976; July 19, 1978; August 2, 1978.

30. See *Haaretz*, October 23, 1977.

31. See *Jerusalem Post*, June 9, 1976; *Jerusalem Post* editorials, May 23, 1976, and March 21, 1976; *Israleft*, no. 83 (May 1, 1976): 8; Ori Stendel, in *Haaretz*, March 31, 1976.

32. See *Zoo Haderech*, January 18, 1978, for Rakah's side of this argument. See *The Attack on the Arab Students Committee*, a report by the Arab Students Committee at the Hebrew University in Jerusalem, 1978, for the radical student side.

For a particularly strong attack on Rakah as an "obstacle to the struggles of the Arab Palestinian people," see the text of a leaflet distributed by a group of Arab students at the Hebrew University ("The Conscience of the Conquered Land: To Comrades of the Palestinian Path," translated in *Israleft*, no. 143 [February 15, 1979]). Six Arab students were confined to their villages by the army as a result of this leaflet, which expressed strong support for the "confrontationist" front in the Arab world. The leaflet was signed "Progressive National Movement."

33. For the text of a leaflet published jointly by Ibn el-Bilad and the Haifa and Jerusalem Arab Students Committees (attacking the Sadat peace initiative and the Begin Home Rule proposal for the West Bank), see *The Attack on the Arab Students Committee*, appendix. For some details concerning Ibn el-Bilad's activities in Um el-Fahm, see Avshalom Ginat, "Movement for Return of Confiscated Arab Lands," *al-Hamishmar*, translated in *Israleft*, no. 131 (August 1, 1978).

34. *Statistical Abstract of Israel* 28 (1977): 63–64, 42.

35. *Jerusalem Post*, March 10, 1978. These projections, it should be emphasized, exclude Arabs living in the territories occupied by Israel in 1967. An Arab population inside Israel of 1,086,000 is predicted for 1995. It should also be noted that the Jewish migration balance into Israel dipped to six hundred in 1976.

36. *Statistical Abstract of Israel* 28 (1977): 26, 32.

37. See *Jerusalem Post*, February 8, 1978, for data on Arab savings deposits.

38. It has been argued that one reason for anti-Rakah feeling among Arab students in Jerusalem is the party's financial inability to send young Arabs who are not Rakah activists or the children of party members to the East bloc for training (Attalah Mansour, "Radicalization in the Arab Street," *Haaretz*, March 9, 1978).

39. See the editorial in *al-Ittihad*, April 1, 1977. See also *Zoo Haderech*, May 9, 1978, for the text of an interview with Meir Vilner, general secretary of Rakah.

40. Indeed, because two of the Democratic Front's Knesset seats are held by noncommunists, Rakah itself suffered a net loss of one seat.

41. *Summary of World Broadcasts*, BBC, ME/5757/A/8, March 7, 1978.

42. *Maariv*, June 7, 1976.

43. *Jerusalem Post*, editorial, June 9, 1976.

44. *Haaretz*, June 8, 1976.

45. *Jerusalem Post Weekly*, April 6, 1976.

46. Mattityahu Peled, "The Cure for Nazareth," *New Outlook* 19, no. 1 (January 1976): 36–37.

47. Ori Stendel, "Rakah Tries to Seize a Decisive Position in the Arab Street," *Haaretz*, January 31, 1976. See also extracts from a confidential report submitted to the secretary general of the Labor Party by the director of its Arab Department, reprinted in *Israleft*, no. 90 (September 15, 1976).

48. For detailed information concerning Koenig and his policies in the Arab sector, see Kassem Zeid, "To Live in Israel with Respect: Arab Sector Reactions to Koenig's Report," reprinted from *al-Hamishmar* in *SWASIA* 3, no. 48 (December 3, 1976).

49. For an English translation of the text of the Koenig memorandum see *SWASIA* 3, no. 41 (October 15, 1976).

50. See the texts of interviews with Moshe Sharon in the *Jerusalem Post Weekly*, April 4, 1978; January 23, 1979. See also Mansour, "Radicalization in the Arab Street"; *Haaretz*, October 21, 1977.

51. For translations of several articles from the Hebrew press concerning this incident, see *Israleft*, no. 117 (November 30, 1977): 4–6.

52. For examples of housing demolitions in Arab localities carried out in the context of the agriculture minister's campaign, see *Zoo Haderech*, June 29, 1977; July 6, 1977; October 19, 1977; November 16, 1977; December 21, 1977; July 26, 1978.
    The Green Patrol is a special police unit attached to the Minis-

try of Agriculture. Concerning its tactics against the Bedouin, see *Jerusalem Post*, June 6, 1978; *Zoo Haderech*, May 24, 1978; May 31, 1978; June 14, 1978.

    For the text of Arik Sharon's remarks, see *Jerusalem Post*, August 8, 1977.

53. For specific comparisons of the approaches of Shmuel Toledano and Amnon Linn to the Arab problem, see Attalah Mansour, "Amnon Linn and the Arabs," *Haaretz*, February 17, 1967; Yosef Goell, "Bankrupt Policy," *Jerusalem Post Magazine*, March 2, 1979, pp. 6–7.

54. *Davar*, April 16, 1976; *Jerusalem Post*, June 8, 1976.

55. Personal interview with Amnon Linn, June 4, 1974, Jerusalem. The influence of Linn's ideas was apparent in the expulsion of six Arab students from the Hebrew University in January 1979, and in statements made by Foreign Minister Moshe Dayan threatening Arab supporters of the PLO with deportation (see *New York Times*, January 24, 1979; January 27, 1979).

56. For Amnon Linn's position on the return of Arab villagers to Ikrit and Biram, see *Jerusalem Post*, February 28, 1978. For first-hand accounts of "police riots" in Baka el-Gharbiyeh and Jatt on March 30, 1977, see *Zoo Haderech*, April 6, 1978; April 19, 1978. For criticism of these police and border patrol operations, see *Jerusalem Post*, April 8, 1977; editorial, April 13, 1977. According to Benyamin Gur-Aryeh, who was appointed acting adviser to the prime minister on Arab affairs following Toledano's resignation in February 1977, the actions in these villages showed that the government had learned its lesson since Land Day 1978—the lesson being that *overwhelming* security forces must be present when quelling Arab demonstrations (personal interview with Benyamin Gur-Aryeh, August 25, 1977, Jerusalem).

    For a description of the general escalation in the use of coercion and political harassment under the Likud government, see a speech delivered before the Knesset by MK Toufik Toubi, reprinted in *Zoo Haderech*, April 19, 1978. For details concerning specific incidents in Tamra, see *Zoo Haderech*, August 24, 1977; in Majd-el-Krum, see *Zoo Haderech*, September 7, 1977; in Julis, see *Zoo Haderech*, November 2, 1977; in Shfaram, see *Zoo Haderech*, January 4, 1978; in Taibe, see *Zoo Haderech*, March 1, 1978; and in Jatt, see *Zoo Haderech*, May 3, 1978; August 30, 1978.

57. *Haaretz*, March 6, 1978. Concerning Linn's attitude toward Moshe Sharon, see Mansour, "Radicalization."

58. *Haaretz*, March 6, 1978.

59. For example, in 1974 one prominent "young generation" Arab, Mahmoud Abassi, was known as an ally of Uri Thon, a Labor Party Arabist who had been Yigal Allon's favorite for the job of Arab Affairs adviser. Yusuf Khamis, assistant director of the Histadrut's Arab Department, was known for his close ties with Yaacov Cohen, the director of that department. Shmuel Toledano was known to favor Kamal Kassem as a candidate for leadership of the young generation of Israeli Druse, while other government Arabists were known to lean toward others, such as Salman Falah (information from interviews with these men or their deputies).

    For information concerning quarrels that erupted between rival Arab "key men" over choice appointments made by the Histadrut in 1978, see *Zoo Haderech*, July 19, 1978.

60. Harel et al., *Conclusions of the Committee Concerning the Activities of the Histadrut in the Arab Sector*, pp. 14–15, 26–29, 31–33, 39.

61. Ibid., p. 29.

62. *Maariv*, June 23, 1977.

63. Letter to author from Reuven Katsab, deputy director, Arab Department of the Histadrut, dated August 2, 1978, Tel Aviv.

64. Interview with Shmuel Toledano by Doron Rosenblum, in *Haaretz* (supplement), January 28, 1977.

65. Ibid.

66. Personal interview with Amnon Linn, June 4, 1974, Jerusalem.

67. See for example the editorial in the *Israel Economist* 32, nos. 4–5 (April–May 1976): 8.

68. Goell, "Bankrupt Policy," p. 7.

69. See Abba Eban, "A New Look at Partition," *Jerusalem Post Weekly*, June 29, 1976; Boaz Evron, "The Burden of the Territories," *Yediot Acharonot,* May 14, 1976, reprinted in *SWASIA*, June 25, 1976: 3–4.

70. *Maariv*, July 8, 1976. Some have speculated that following the establishment of a Palestinian state, significant numbers of Israeli Arabs would emigrate to the West Bank. But given the difficulties which the new Palestinian regime would face in its efforts to assimilate tens or hundreds of thousands of refugees from Lebanon, Syria, Jordan and the Gaza Strip, given the resentment among many Palestinians against Israeli Arabs for their relatively high standard of living and their "cooperation" with the Israeli regime, and given the deep attachment of Israeli Arabs to their

own localities, a voluntary transfer of population of any substantial size would be very unlikely. On the contrary, most individuals in Palestinian refugee camps who favor the establishment of a separate, nonbelligerent Palestinian state express their support for the idea on the condition that Palestinian refugees in the West Bank be given a choice of compensation or return to their former areas of residence inside Israel.

71. In this regard see Moshe Maoz, director of the Afro-Asian Studies Center at the Hebrew University in Jerusalem, "The 'Moderation' of the PLO and Israeli Policies," *Maariv*, December 12, 1975.

72. For examples of such advice, see Moshe Keren, "Have we an Arab Policy?" reprinted in *Ner* 5, no. 5 (February 1954): 32–33; Amnon Rubinstein, "Arabs of Israel: A Realistic Approach," *Kalkala VeHevra*, no. 1 (June 1966): 29–31 (Hebrew); *Haaretz*, October 16, 1967; Eli Elad, "The Tired Arabists," *Haaretz*, January 30, 1970; Zev Schiff, "Lack of Coordination among Agencies," *Haaretz*, April 23, 1976; *Jerusalem Post*, June 2, 1977.

73. Concerning the electoral failure of Shelli and the Civil Rights Movement in the Arab sector in the 1977 Knesset election, see *Davar*, June 3, 1977.

74. For a convenient statement of the reforms advocated by Mapam, see Latif Dori, "Mapam on Israeli Arabs," *New Outlook* 19, no. 5 (July–August, 1976): 51–52. Concerning Moked's attempts to combine Zionist ideology with support for a pluralist Israel, see *Israleft*, no. 87 (July 1, 1976): 6–8.

Glossary

aliyah: Jewish immigration to Palestine/Israel.

Balfour Declaration: proclamation of the British government in 1917 in support of the establishment of a "Jewish national home" in Palestine.

Divrei Haknesset: proceedings of the Knesset.

dunam: about one quarter of an acre.

Eretz Yisrael: the Land of Israel.

habaayah haAravit: the Arab problem; specifically the Arab minority problem in Israel.

Haganah: underground Jewish army established by the Labor Zionist Movement during the British mandate in Palestine.

hamula: patrilineal Arab kinship group, usually comprised of a number of extended families; hamulas may have from forty to four hundred (or even more) members.

Hashomer Hatzair: left-wing Zionist settlement movement associated with Mapam.

Herut: right-wing Zionist party headed by Menachem Begin.

Histadrut: General Federation of Workers of the Land of Israel, a federation of trade unions.

Ibn el-Bilad: Sons of the Village; local groups of young Arab radicals.

Ihud: a small but articulate group of Jews active on the fringe of the Zionist movement in the prestate period (and up to 1965) who favored binationalism and a policy of concession toward the Arabs. Publisher of *Ner*.

kibbutz: collectivist Jewish settlement; mainly agricultural.

kibbutz galluiot: in-gathering of the exiles; a Zionist slogan.

Knesset: parliament of Israel.

Likud: coalition of right-wing Zionist political parties headed by Menachem Begin.

Little Triangle: a strip of land along Israel's "narrow waist" ceded to Israel in 1949 as part of its armistice agreement with Jordan. See Map 2.

Maki: the original Israel Communist Party. It retained the name after the party schism of 1965. What was left of Maki joined with left-wing Zionists to form Moked. *See also* Rakah.

Mapai: Israel Workers' Party; combined with other parties to form the Israel Labor Party in 1968.

Mapam: a small left-wing Labor Zionist party with the base of its support among its affiliated kibbutzim. Both before and after 1948 Mapam has shown particular interest in Zionism's relations with the Arabs. Since 1969 the party has been formally aligned with the Labor Party. Publisher of *New Outlook*.

Memshal Tzvai: Military Administration, or Military Government; ruled in most Arab areas of Israel from 1948 to 1966.

mohar: bride price; sum of money and/or property paid by groom's family in an Arab village for the bride.

Moked: a combination of several socialist-Zionist splinter groups on the extreme left wing of the Zionist political spectrum in Israel which elected one member to the Knesset in 1973. As "Shelli" in 1977 it elected two members to the Knesset.

moshav: cooperative Jewish settlement; mainly agricultural.

moshav shitufi: a form of Jewish settlement which combines the collectivist production techniques of the kibbutz with individual homesteads; mainly agricultural.

Mukhtar: traditional term for headman or leading notable in an Arab village.

Nebi Shueib: religious festival of the Druse.

Ner: an Arabic-Hebrew-English journal published by Ihud from 1950 to 1964.

nifkadim nochachim: present absentees; internal refugees; Arab residents of Israel who are classified as absentees.

protectzia: colloquial expression for "pull," or informal influence in Israeli society.

qadi (Arabic): a religious judge, either Moslem or Druse.

Rafi: a breakaway faction from the Labor Party, led by David Ben-Gurion, Moshe Dayan, and Shimon Peres, which entered a separate list in the Knesset elections of 1965.

Rakah: the New Israel Communist Party; split from Maki in 1965.

Sayigh: a reservation for Bedouin in the northeastern Negev.

Shelli: *See* Moked.

Sochnut: the Jewish Agency.

tnuot: political movements.

Tzahal: Hebrew acronym for the Israel Defense Forces (the Israeli armed forces).

ulpanim: intensive Hebrew language programs.
Waqf: religious endowment (Arabic).
wasta: connection; a go-between.
Yehud ha-Galil: Judaization of the Galilee; a Zionist slogan.
Yishuv: term used to refer to the Jewish population of Palestine/Israel.

Bibliography

Books

Adam, Heribert. *Modernizing Racial Domination*. Berkeley: University of California Press, 1971.

Allon, Yigal. *A Curtain of Sand*. Israel: Hakibbutz Hameuchad, 1959. (Hebrew)

American Zionist Youth Foundation. *See* Research Monographs, Reprints, and Unpublished Papers.

Arian, Asher, ed. *The Elections in Israel: 1969*. Jerusalem: Jerusalem Academic Press, 1972.

———. *The Elections in Israel: 1973*. Jerusalem: Jerusalem Academic Press, 1975.

Aron, Y., and S. Molcho. *See* Government Publications and Documents—Israel.

Avnery, Uri. *Israel without Zionists*. New York: MacMillan and Co., 1968.

Banfield, Edward C. *The Moral Basis of a Backward Society*. Chicago: The Free Press, 1958.

Ben-Gurion, David. *Israel: A Personal History*. Tel Aviv: Sabra Books, 1972.

Ben-Porath, Yoram. *The Arab Labor Force in Israel*. Jerusalem: Central Press, 1966.

Berger, L., ed. *See* Official Publications of Nongovernmental Organizations—Jewish Agency.

Burg, Yosef. *See* Government Publications and Documents—Israel.

Cockcroft, James D., et al., eds. *Dependence and Underdevelopment*. Garden City: Anchor Books, 1972.

Cohen, Abner. *Arab Border Villages in Israel: A Study of Continuity and Change in Social Organization*. Manchester: Manchester University Press, 1965.

Cohen, Aharon. *Israel and the Arab World*. New York: Funk and

Wagnalls, 1970. Hebrew edition, Merhavia: Kibbutz Hartzi, 1964.

Cohen, Erik. *See* Research Monographs, Reprints, and Unpublished Papers.

Collins, Larry, and Dominique Lapierre. *O Jerusalem.* New York: Simon and Schuster, 1972.

Curtis, Michael, and Mordechai Chertoff, eds. *Israel: Social Structure and Change.* New Brunswick, N.J.: Transaction Books, 1973.

Davis, Uri, and Norton Mezvinsky, eds. *Documents from Israel, 1967–1973.* London: Ithaca Press, 1975.

Deshen, Shlomo A. *Immigrant Voters in Israel.* Manchester: Manchester University Press, 1970.

Eban, Aubrey S. (Abba). *See* Government Publications and Documents—Israel.

El-Asmar, Fouzi. *To Be an Arab in Israel.* London: Frances Pinter, 1975.

Eliav, Arie Lova. *Land of the Hart: Israelis, Arabs, the Territories, and a Vision of the Future.* Philadelphia: Jewish Publication Society of America, 1974.

Elon, Amos. *Israelis: Founders and Sons.* New York: Holt, Rinehart and Winston, 1971.

Emerson, Rupert. *From Empire to Nation.* Boston: Beacon Press, 1960.

Enloe, Cynthia. *Ethnic Conflict and Political Development.* Boston: Little, Brown and Co., 1973.

Fein, Leonard J. *Politics in Israel.* Boston: Little, Brown and Co., 1967.

Finkle, Jason L., and Richard W. Gable, eds. *Political Development and Social Change.* New York: John Wiley and Sons, 1971.

Friendly, Alfred. *See* Research Monographs, Reprints, and Unpublished Papers.

Gabbay, Rony E. *A Political Study of the Arab-Jewish Conflict.* Geneva: Libraire E. Droz, 1959.

Ghilan, Maxim. *How Israel Lost Its Soul.* Harmondsworth: Penguin, 1975.

Granott, Abraham. *Agrarian Reform and the Record of Israel.* London: Eyre and Spottiswoode, 1956.

Gruber, Ruth. *Israel Today: Land of Many Nations.* New York: Hill and Wang, 1958.

Gutman, Eliahu, et al. *See* Research Monographs, Reprints, and Unpublished Papers.

Hadawi, Sami. *See* Official Publications of Nongovernmental Organizations—Arab Information Center.

Halpern, Ben. *The Idea of the Jewish State.* Cambridge, Mass.: Harvard University Press, 1961.

Hammond, Paul Y., and Sidney S. Alexander. *Political Dynamics in the Middle East.* New York: American Elsevier, 1972.

Harari, Yechiel. *See* Research Monographs, Reprints, and Unpublished Papers.

Harel, A., et al. *See* Official Publications of Nongovernmental Organizations—Histadrut.

Hattis, Susan Lee. *The Bi-National Idea in Palestine during Mandatory Times.* Israel: Shikmona Publishing Company, 1970.

Hechter, Michael. *Internal Colonialism: The Celtic Fringe in British National Development, 1536–1966.* Berkeley: University of California Press, 1975.

Herzl, Theodor. *Alteneuland.* New York: Bloch Publishing Co., 1960.

———. *The Complete Diaries of Theodor Herzl.* Edited by Raphael Patai. New York: Herzl Press and Thomas Yoseloff, 1960.

Hindus, Maurice. *In Search of a Future: Persia, Egypt, Iraq, and Palestine.* Garden City, N.J.: Doubleday and Co., 1949.

Huntington, Samuel P. *Political Order in Changing Societies.* New Haven: Yale University Press, 1970.

Immigration and Settlement. Israel Pocket Library Series. Jerusalem: Keter Publishing House, 1974.

Jiryis, Sabri. *The Arabs of Israel.* Beirut: Institute for Palestine Studies, 1969.

Kahane, Reuven, and Simcha Kopstein, eds. *Israeli Society, 1967–1973.* Jerusalem: Keter Publishing House, 1974. (Hebrew and English)

Kuper, Leo, and M. G. Smith, eds. *Pluralism in Africa.* Berkeley: University of California Press, 1971.

Landau, Jacob M. *The Arabs in Israel.* London: Oxford University Press, 1969.

Lehrman, Hal. *Israel: The Beginning and Tomorrow.* New York: William Sloane Assocs., 1951.

Lerner, Abba, and Haim Ben-Shahar. *The Economics of Efficiency and Growth: Lessons from Israel and the West Bank.* Cambridge, Mass.: Ballinger Publishing Co., 1975.

Lewis, I. M. *Pastoral Democracy.* London: Oxford University Press, 1961.

Lijphart, Arend. *The Politics of Accommodation.* Berkeley: University of California Press, 1968.

Loftus, P. J. *See* Government Publications and Documents—Great Britain.

MacDonald, James G. *My Mission in Israel, 1948–1951*. New York: Simon and Schuster, 1951.

Manners, Robert A., ed. *Process and Pattern in Culture*. Chicago: Aldine Publishing Co., 1964.

Maoz, Moshe. *Ottoman Reform in Syria and Palestine, 1840–1861: The Impact of the Tanzimat on Politics and Society*. London: Clarendon, 1968.

Marx, Emanuel. *Bedouin of the Negev*. Manchester: Manchester University Press, 1967.

Mikes, George. *Coat of Many Colors: Israel*. Boston: Gambit, 1969.

Myrdal, Gunnar. *Economic Theory and Underdeveloped Regions*. New York: Harper and Row, 1957.

Nathan, Robert R., Oscar Gass, and Daniel Creamer. *Palestine: Problem and Promise*. Washington, D.C.: Public Affairs Press, 1946.

Nino, Micah. *See* Research Monographs, Reprints, and Unpublished Papers.

Nordlinger, Eric A. *Conflict Regulation in Divided Societies*. Cambridge, Mass.: Harvard University, 1972.

Orni, Efraim. *Agrarian Reform and Social Progress in Israel*. Jerusalem: Ahva Cooperative Press, 1972.

———. *Forms of Settlement*. Jerusalem: Ahva Cooperative Press, 1976.

Oxaal, Ivar, et al., eds. *Beyond the Sociology of Development*. London: Routledge and Kegan Paul, 1975.

Peretz, Don. *Israel and the Palestine Arabs*. Washington, D.C.: Middle East Institute, 1958.

Peristiany, J. G., ed. *Contributions to Mediterranean Sociology: Acts of the Mediterranean Sociological Conference, July 1963*. Paris and the Hague: Mouton, 1968.

Prittie, Terence. *Israel's Miracle in the Desert*. New York: Frederick Praeger, 1967.

Quandt, William, Fuad Jabber, and Ann Mosely Lesch. *The Politics of Palestinian Nationalism*. Berkeley: University of California Press, 1973.

Rabushka, Alvin, and Kenneth A. Shepsle. *Politics in Plural Societies: A Theory of Democratic Instability*. Columbus, Ohio: Merrill Publishing Co., 1972.

Ramati, Alexander. *Israel Today*. London: Eyre and Spottiswoode, 1962.

Rekhess, Eli. *See* Research Monographs, Reprints, and Unpublished Papers.

Religious Life and Communities. Israel Pocket Library Series. Jerusalem: Keter Publishing House, 1974.

Rosen, Harry M. *The Arabs and Jews in Israel: The Reality, the Dilemma, the Promise.* Jerusalem: Keter Press, 1970.

Rosenfeld, Henry. *They Were Peasants.* Israel: Hakibbutz Hameuchad, 1964. (Hebrew)

Schwarz, Walter. *The Arabs in Israel.* London: Faber and Faber, 1959.

Selznick, Phillip. *TVA and the Grass Roots.* New York: Harper and Row, 1966.

Sereni, Enzo, and R. E. Ashery, eds. *Jews and Arabs in Palestine.* New York: Hechalutz Press, 1936.

Shammash, Yehezkel. *See* Government Publications and Documents—Israel.

Sharef, Zeev. *See* Government Publications and Documents—Israel.

Shefi Advertising, ed. *See* Official Publications of Nongovernmental Organizations—Arab-Jewish Association to Promote Fraternity and Peace.

Shimoni, Jacob. *Arabs of the Land of Israel.* Human Relations Area Files, 1947.

Smooha, Sammy. *Israel: Pluralism and Conflict.* Berkeley: University of California Press, 1978.

Society. Israel Pocket Library Series. Jerusalem: Keter Publishing House, 1974.

Stein, Leonard. *The Balfour Declaration.* New York: Simon and Schuster, 1961.

Stendel, Ori. *The Minorities in Israel.* Jerusalem: Israel Economist, 1973.

———. *See also* Research Monographs, Reprints and Unpublished Papers; Government Publications and Documents—Israel.

Stock, Ernest. *From Conflict to Understanding.* New York: Institute of Human Relations Press, 1968.

———. *See also* Research Monographs, Reprints, and Unpublished Papers.

Szerzewski, Robert. *Essays on the Structure of the Jewish Economy in Palestine and Israel.* Jerusalem: Israel Universities Press, 1968.

Tachau, Frank, ed. *Political Elites and Political Development in the Middle East.* New York: John Wiley and Sons, 1975.

Tagore, Saumyendranath. *Israeli Chiaroscuro.* Calcutta: Sri Supriya Sarkan, 1965.

Toledano, Shmuel. *See* Official Publications of Nongovernmental Organizations—Labor Zionist Movement.

Waschitz, Yosef. *The Arabs of the Land of Israel.* Merhavia: Sifriat Hapoalim, 1947. (Hebrew)

Weigert, Gideon. *See* Government Publications and Documents—Israel.

348   *Bibliography*

Weitz, Raanan, and Avshalom Rokah. *Agricultural Development: Planning and Implementation.* Dordrecht, Holland: D. Reidel Publishing Co., 1968.

Yalan, Emmanuel, et al. *The Modernization of Traditional Agricultural Villages: Minority Villages in Israel.* Settlement Study Center Publications on Problems of Regional Development, no. 11. Rehovot: Keter Press, 1972.

Zarhi, Shaul, and A. Achiezra. *See* Research Monographs, Reprints and Unpublished Papers.

Zureik, Elia. *Palestinians in Israel: A Study in Internal Colonialism.* London: Routledge and Kegan Paul, 1979.

Articles (English)

Abu-Ghosh, Subhi. "The Election Campaign in the Arab Sector." In Alan Arian, ed., *The Elections in Israel—1969* (Israel: Jerusalem Academic Press, 1972), pp. 239–252.

Al-Atawna, Musa. "What the Bedouin Want." *New Outlook* 3, no. 9 (September 1960): 15–18.

Aloni, Shulamit. "Discrimination against Arab Settlements." Reprinted from *Yediot Acharonot* in *SWASIA*, November 14, 1975.

Ardon, Yaacov. "Young Druse Charge Discrimination." *Jerusalem Post*, February 8, 1971, p. 7.

Arhein, Mahmoud. "Israel's Arabs after 1973." *New Outlook* 18, no. 7 (October–November 1975): 78–79.

Auerbach, Aliza. "Ibni the Doctor." *Jerusalem Post Weekly*, January 20, 1976.

Ayal, Eli. "How Young Israeli Arabs See Their Future." *Atlas* 20, no. 4 (April 1971): 26–27.

Baruch, H. "Facing the 180,000: How the Military Government Rules." Translated and reprinted from *Davar*, August 8, 1958, in *Ner* 10, nos. 3–4 (December 1958–January 1959): 37–51.

Bayadsi, Mahmud. "The Arab Local Authorities: Achievements and Problems." *New Outlook* 18, no. 7 (October–November 1975): 58–61.

Ben-Ami, A. "Israeli Jews and Israeli Arabs: A Symposium." *Jewish Frontier* 33, no. 9 (November 1966): 15–24.

Ben-Meir, Gad. "Arab Water Supply Cooperatives." *Ner* 13, nos. 1–2 (September–October 1961): xii–xiv.

———. "The Development of Arab Cooperation in Israel." *New Outlook* 5, no. 7 (July 1961): 31–36.

Ben Moshe, Eliezer. "Does Arab Youth Have a Future in Israel?" *Ner* 15, no. 4–5 (December 1964–January 1965): 21–27.

————. "The Tragedy of Kfar Bir'am." *Ner* 12, nos. 1–2 (November–December 1960): xviii–xxi.

Blake, Howard. "We Are Israelis Too." *Hadassah Magazine* (December 1973): 16–17.

Chinitz, Zelig S. "The Meaning of the Reconstitution of the Jewish Agency." *Dispersion and Unity* (Winter 1970): 97–103.

Cohen, P. "Minority Soldiers Help in Guarding the Negev." *Ner* 11, no. 12 (September–October 1960): 15–16.

Connor, Walker. "Nation-Building or Nation-Destroying." *World Politics* 24, no. 3 (April 1972): 319–355.

Daalder, Hans. "The Consociational Democracy Theme." *World Politics* 26, no. 4 (July 1974): 604–621.

Dalal, Elias. "Arab Education in Israel." Reprinted in *Ner* 9, nos. 1–2 (October–November 1957): 41–44.

Dayan, Moshe. "Israel's Border Problems." *Foreign Affairs* 33, no. 2 (January 1955): 250–267.

————. "Minister Dayan Answers New Outlook." *New Outlook*, no. 3. (March–April 1964): 85–88.

Dori, Latif. "Mapam on Israeli Arabs." *New Outlook* 19, no. 5 (July–August 1976): 51–52.

Dror, Deborah. "In the Shadow of the Military Government." Reprinted from *al-Hamishmar* in *Ner* 14, nos. 10–12 (June–August 1963): xviii–xix.

Eban, Abba. "A New Look at Partition." *Jerusalem Post Weekly*, June 29, 1976.

Eilon, Amos. "Arab Moods on the Eve of the Elections." *Jewish Frontier* 18, no. 7 (July 1951): 22–29.

Elizalde, Horacio. "Impressions of a Visitor from the Argentine." *Christian News from Israel* 5, nos. 3–4 (February 1955).

Epstein, Edwin M. "The Social and Economic Role of Hevrat Ovdim in Israel, 1923–1973: An American Perspective." *Annals of Public and Cooperative Economy* 45, no. 2: 119–146.

Esman, Milton J. "The Management of Communal Conflict." *Public Policy* 21, no. 1 (Winter 1973): 49–78.

Evron, Boaz. "The Burden of the Territories." Reprinted in *SWASIA*, June 25, 1976, pp. 3–4.

Fahoum, Walid. "A Socialist Perspective on the Arab-Israeli Conflict." *Student World* 62, no. 11 (First Quarter 1969): 93–95.

Flapan, Simcha. "Israel's Arabs after October 1973." *New Outlook* 18, no. 7 (October–November 1975): 75–76.

————. "The Minister Admits He Has No Plan." *New Outlook* 7, no. 3 (March–April 1964): 88–90.

——. "Planning Arab Agriculture." *New Outlook* 6, no. 9 (November–December 1963): 65–73.

——. "Planning for the Arab Village." *New Outlook* 6, no. 8 (October 1963): 23–31.

Friedler, Yaacov. "Arab Villagers and Minister on Give-and-Take Projects." Reprinted from the *Jerusalem Post* in *Ner* 8, nos. 10–12 (July–September 1957): 46.

Geertz, Clifford. "The Integrative Revolution: Primordial Sentiments and Civil Politics in the New States." In Jason L. Finkle and Richard W. Gable, eds., *Political Development and Social Change*, pp. 655–669. New York: John Wiley and Sons, 1971.

Ghanaim, Mustaphe. "Arab Village Youth." *New Outlook* 18, no. 7 (October–November 1975): 54–57.

Ginat, Avshalom. "Movement for Return of Confiscated Arab Lands." From *al-Hamishmar*, translated in *Israleft*, no. 131 (August 1, 1978).

Goell, Yosef. "Bankrupt Policy." *The Jerusalem Post Magazine*, March 2, 1979, pp. 6–7.

——. "Collision Course in Galilee." *Jerusalem Post Weekly*, March 6, 1976.

——. "Talking with Arabs." *Jerusalem Post Weekly*, January 13, 1976.

Gottheil, Fred M. "On the Economic Development of the Arab Region in Israel." In Michael Curtis and Mordechai Chertoff, eds., *Israel: Social Structure and Change*, pp. 237–248. New Brunswick, N.J.: Transaction Books, 1973.

Guilboa, Yehoshua. "Envious Arab Boys." *Ner* 9, nos. 1–2 (October–November 1957): 39–41.

Gutmann, Emanuel. "Israel: A Study in Political Finance." *Journal of Politics* 25, no. 4 (November 1963): 703–717.

Hofman, John E., and Benjamin Beit Hallahmi. "The Palestinian Identity and Israel's Arabs." *Peace Research* 9, no. 1 (January 1977): 13–21.

Hurwitz, David. "Agrarian Problem of the Fellahein." In Enzo Sereni and R. E. Ashery, eds., *Jews and Arabs in Palestine*, pp. 3–74. New York: Hechalutz Press, 1936.

Jiryis, Sabri. "Recent Knesset Legislation and the Arabs in Israel." *Journal of Palestine Studies* 1, no. 1 (Autumn 1971).

Kanann, Jamal. "Symposium: Israel's Arabs after October 1973." *New Outlook* 18, no. 7 (October–November 1975): 79–80.

Kassis, Massad. "Outcry in the Knesset." *Ner* 4, no. 11 (July 1953): 45–47.

Katznelson, Ira. "Comparative Studies of Race and Ethnicity." *Comparative Politics* 5, no. 1 (October 1972): 135–154.

Keren, Moshe. "Have We an Arab Policy?" Translated and reprinted in *Ner* 5, no. 5 (February 1954): 32–33.

Kimche, Jon. "Nazareth—Political Cameo of Jewish-Arab Relations." *Palestine Post*, August 3, 1948.

Kislev, Ran. "Land Expropriations: History of Oppression." *New Outlook* 19, no. 6 (September–October 1976): 23–32.

Koenig, Israel. "Koenig Memorandum." Translated from *al-Hamishmar* in *SWASIA* 3, no. 41 (October 15, 1976): 1–8.

Koussa, Elias N. "Israel and the Arab People." *Ner* 4, no. 1 (October 1952): 21–24.

———. "Memorandum of the Proposed Expropriation of Arab Agricultural Lands." *Ner* 4, nos. 7–8 (April 1953): 43–47.

———. "Memorandum on Properties Belonging to Arabs Living in Israel." *Ner* 2 (January 8, 1951): 22–24; 2 (July 13, 1951): 26–28.

"The Kubersky Committee Report on Illegal Construction and Takeover of Land in the Minorities Sector" (excerpts). *Middle East Review* 9, no. 2 (Winter 1976/1977): 30.

Landau, Jacob M. "A Note on the Leadership of Israeli Arabs." Reprinted from *Il Politico* (University of Pavia, Milan), 27, no. 3 (1962): 625–632.

Layish, Aharon. "The Muslim Waqf In Israel." In *Asian and African Studies* 1 (1965): 49–79.

Lehrman, Hal. "Arabs in Israel: Pages from a Correspondent's Notebook." *Commentary* 8, no. 12 (December 1949): 523–533.

Lijphart, Arend. "Consociational Democracy." *World Politics* 21, no. 2 (January 1969): 207–225.

Livne (Liebenstein), Eliezer. "Israeli Democracy and the Arabs." *New Outlook* 3, no. 7 (June 1960): 45–48.

Lustick, Ian. "Stability in Deeply Divided Societies: Consociationalism vs. Control." *World Politics* 31, no. 3 (April 1979) 325–344.

Makhoul, Naim. "The Arab Village in Israel." *Ner* 9, nos. 8–9 (May–June 1958): 47–50.

Mansour, Attalah. "Arab Intellectuals Not Integrated." *New Outlook* 7, no. 3 (June 1964): 26–31.

———. "Arab Land: Sale or Requisition?" *New Outlook* 7, no. 3 (March–April 1964): 82–84.

———. "Radical Opposition to the Druze Leadership." Reprinted from *Haaretz*, April 23, 1976, in *SWASIA*, May 28, 1976, pp. 7–8.

———. "Riad Comes Home." Translated by Aubrey Hobes in *New Outlook* 5, no. 3 (March–April 1962): 88–90.

Marmorstein, Emile. "Rashid Hussein: Portrait of an Angry Young Arab." *Middle Eastern Studies* 1, no. 1 (January 1964): 3–20.

Melson, Robert, and Harold Wolpe. "Modernization and the Politics of Communalism: A Theoretical Perspective." *American Political Science Review* 64 (December 1970): 1112–1130.

Menachem, K. "The Affair of Abasiye [Ghabasiyeh] Village." Reprinted from *Davar* in *Ner* 1, no. 3 (March 1950).

Moreh, Shmuel. "Arabic Literature in Israel." *Middle Eastern Studies* 3, no. 3 (April 1967): 283–294.

N., Abu. "The Arabs and the Knesset Elections." *Ner* 10, nos. 5–7 (February–April 1959): 31–52.

Nakhleh, Emile A. "Wells of Bitterness: A Survey of Israeli-Arab Political Poetry." *The Arab World* 16, no. 2 (February 1970): 30–36.

Nobel, Robert. "Industry's Impact on the Kibbutz." In *Israel Year Book, 1978*, pp. 251–253. Tel Aviv: Jepheth Printing Press, 1977.

Oded, Yitzhak. "Bedouin Lands Threatened by Takeover." *New Outlook* 7, no. 9 (November–December 1964): 45–52.

———. "Israel's Arab Villagers Are Being Driven from Their Land." *Ner* 13, nos. 11–12 (July–August 1962): i–v.

———. "Land Losses among Israel's Arab Villagers." *New Outlook* 7, no. 7 (September 1964): 10–25.

Peled, Mattityahu. "The Cure for Nazareth." *New Outlook* 19, no. 1 (January 1976): 36–37.

Peres, Yochanan. "Ethnic Relations in Israel." *American Journal of Sociology* 76, no. 6 (May 1971): 1021–1047.

———. "Modernization and Nationalism in the Identity of the Israeli Arab." *Middle East Journal* 24, no. 4 (Autumn 1970): 479–492.

Peres, Yochanan, and Nira Yuval-Davis. "Some Observations on the National Identity of the Israeli Arabs." *Human Relations* 22, no. 3 (June 1969): 219–233.

Peretz, Don. "Problems of Arab Refugee Compensation." *Middle East Journal* 8, no. 4 (Autumn 1954): 403–416.

Pike, James A. "A Good Word for Israel." *New Outlook* 6, no. 3 (March–April 1963): 25.

Remba, Oded. "Income Inequality in Israel: Ethnic Aspects." In Michael Curtis and Mordechai Chertoff, eds., *Israel: Social Structure and Change*, New Brunswick, N.J.: Transaction Books, 1973.

Rosenfeld, Henry. "Change, Barriers to Change, and Contradictions in the Arab Village Family." *American Anthropologist* 70, no. 4 (August 1968): 732–752.

———. "From Peasantry to Wage Labor and Residual Peasantry: The

Transformation of an Arab Village." In Robert A. Manners, ed., *Process and Pattern in Culture*. Chicago: Aldine Publishing Co., 1964.

―――. "Wage Labor and Status in an Arab Village." *New Outlook* 6, no. 1 (January 1963): 5–9.

Rossing, Donald. "Israel's Minorities Contribute to the War Effort." *Christian News from Israel* 24, nos. 2–3 (December 1973).

Rothchild, Donald. "Ethnicity and Conflict Resolution." *World Politics* 22, no. 4 (July 1970): 597–616.

Rubinstein, Danny. "Reform in Educational Objectives for the Arab Sector." *New Outlook* 19, no. 2 (February–March 1976): 70–71.

Safran, Nadav. "Israel's Internal Politics and Foreign Policy." In Paul Y. Hammond and Sidney S. Alexander, eds., *Political Dynamics in the Middle East*, pp. 155–185. New York: American Elsevier Publishing Co., 1972.

Schiff, Zeev. "The Pros and Cons of the Military Government." *New Outlook* 5, no. 3 (March–April 1962): 64–71.

Shamir, Shimon. "Changes in Village Leadership." *New Outlook* 5, no. 3 (March–April 1962): 93–112.

Shemesh, Ezekiel. "Israel's Arabs—1975." *New Outlook* 18, no 7 (October–November 1975): 24–30.

Shereshevsky, S. "Against the Agricultural Lands Consolidation Law." *Ner* 12, nos. 5–6 (March–April 1961): i–v.

Shokeid, Moshe. "Strategy and Change in the Arab Vote: Observations in a Mixed Town." In Asher Arian, ed., *Elections in Israel—1973*, pp. 145–166. Jerusalem: Jerusalem Academic Press, 1975.

Sirhan, Mohammed. "Is There a Solution to the Problem of the Israeli Arabs?" *Student World* 62, no. 1 (First Quarter 1969): 81–82.

Smith, Terence. "Israeli Arabs in Galilee Area Assail Government Plan to Acquire Land and Resettle Jews." *New York Times*, November 7, 1975, p. 4.

Smooha, Sammy, and John Hofman. "Some Problems of Arab-Jewish Coexistence." *Middle East Review* 9, no. 2 (Winter 1976/1977): 5–14.

Teller, Judd L. "Israel Faces Its Arab Minority." *Commentary* 12, no. 12 (December 1951): 551–557.

Verba, Sidney. "Some Dilemmas in Comparative Research." *World Politics* 20, no. 1 (October 1967): 111–127.

Waschitz, Yosef. "Arabs in Israeli Politics." *New Outlook* 5, no. 3 (March–April 1962): 33–42.

―――. "Commuters and Entrepreneurs." *New Outlook* 18, no. 7 (October–November 1975): 45–53.

———. "The Plight of the Bedouin." *New Outlook* 18, no. 7 (October–November 1975): 62–66.

Watad, Mohammed. "Co-existence." *New Outlook* 13, no. 7 (September–October 1970): 68–73.

Weiner, Myron. "The Macedonian Syndrome: An Historical Model of International Relations and Political Development." *World Politics* 23, no. 4 (July 1971): 665–683.

Weisman, Joshua. "The Land Law, 1969: A Critical Analysis." *Israel Law Review* 5, no. 3 (July 1970): 379—456.

Williamson, J. G. "Regional Inequality and the Process of National Development: A Description of the Patterns." *Economic Development and Cultural Change* 13 (1965): 3–45.

Yaari, Ehud. "Contradictory Trends among Arabs." *Davar*, June 3, 1977. Translated in *Israleft*, no. 108 (June 15, 1977).

Yahia, Mustafa. "Reflections on the National Identity of the Arabs in Israel." *Student World* 62, no. 1 (First Quarter 1969): 71–77.

Zayad, Kassem. "Am I a 'Positive' or a 'Negative' Arab?" *Israel Horizons* 24, no. 6 (June–July 1976): 9–12.

Zeid, Kassem. "To Live in Israel with Respect: Arab Sector Reactions to Koenig's Report." Reprinted from *al-Hamishmar* in *SWASIA* 3, no. 48 (December 3, 1976): 5, 7.

Zubi, Abdul Magid. "A Plan for Arab Agriculture." *New Outlook* 1, no. 3 (September 1957): 10–16.

Zureik, Elia T. "Transformation of Class Structure among the Arabs in Israel: From Peasantry to Proletariat." *Journal of Palestine Studies* 6, no. 1 (1976): 39–66.

Articles (Hebrew)

Arieli, Yehuda. "Judaising the Galilee—Plans and Reality." *Haaretz*, February 29, 1976.

Assaf, Michael. "The Arab Refugees and the State of Israel." In *Palestine Yearbook and Israel Annual, 1948–1949* 4 (August–September 1948): 234.

———. "The Evil Story of the Military Administration." *Beterem* 11 (May 1953): 8–9.

———. "The Integration of the Arabs in Israel." *Hamizrah Hechadash* 1, no. 1 (October 1949).

Aviel, Yaacov. "The Military Government." *Haaretz*, December 31, 1954.

———. "The Uprooted and the Abandoned." *Haaretz*, January 7, 1955.

Avineri, Shlomo. "Political Representation of the Arab Minority." *Beterem* 11, no. 5 (March 1, 1953).

Bastuni, Rustum. "The Arab Minority—to Where?" *Ner* 7, nos. 10–11 (June–July 1956).

Ben Shemesh, Simon. "Toward a Second Land Reform." *Karka* (Land), nos. 6–7 (Autumn–Winter 1973/1974): 73–79.

Bloch, Daniel. "Expected Adjustments in the Partisan Map." *Davar*, March 10, 1975.

Elad, Eli. "The Tired Arabists." *Haaretz*, January 30, 1970.

Elon, Amos. "Land-Acquisition: The Tragedy of Ghabisiye and Israeli Justice." *Haaretz*, October 19, 1951.

Harel, Israel. "The 'Dead Land' Comes to Life in Opposition to the Development of the Galilee." *Maariv*, October 17, 1975.

Ibrahim, Ibrahim Musa. "The Last Letter." *Ner* 9, nos. 5–7 (February–April 1958): 48–50.

Keren, Moshe. "Have We an Arab Policy?" *Haaretz*, January 1, 1955.

———. "In a Vicious Circle." *Haaretz*, December 29, 1954.

Layish, Aharon. "The Muslim Waqf in Israel." *Hamizrah Hechadash* 15, nos. 1–2 (1965).

Lazar, David. "Not Almogi, not Dulzin." *Maariv*, November 21, 1975.

Linberg, Ron. "The Penetration of a Minorities Village by the National Parties." *Medinah Vemimshal* 1, no. 1 (Summer 1971).

Liskovsky, Abraham. "The Present Absentees in Israel." *Hamizrah Hechadash* 10, no. 3 (1960).

Litani, Yehuda. "Stop Rakah in Nazareth." *Haaretz*, October 27, 1975.

Mansour, Attalah. "Amnon Linn and the Arabs." *Haaretz*, February 17, 1967.

———. "Radicalization in the Arab Street." *Haaretz*, March 9, 1978.

———. "A Wall of Strangeness between Nazareth and Upper Nazareth." *Haaretz*, July 14, 1975.

Maoz, Moshe. "The 'Moderation' of the PLO and Israeli Policies." *Maariv*, December 12, 1975.

Peled, Mattityahu. "The Arab Minority in Israel." *Maariv*, August 1, 1975. Reprinted in *SWASIA*, September 19, 1975.

Peres, Shimon. "The Military Government Is the Product of the War Regime." *Davar*, January 26, 1962.

Peres, Yochanan, Avishai Erlich, and Nira Yuval-Davis. "The National Education of Arab Youth in Israel: A Comparison of Courses of Studies." *Megamot* 16, no. 1 (October 1968): 26–36.

Rosenfeld, Henry. "Processes of Change and Factors of Conservation in the Rural Arab Family in Israel." *Hamizrah Hechadash*, 19, no. 3 (1969).

Rotem, Avraham. "The Leasing of Cemeteries, the Throwing of Grenades." *Maariv*, November 21, 1975.

Rubinstein, Amnon. "Arabs of Israel: A Realistic Approach." *Kalkala VeHevra*, no. 1 (June 1966): 29–31.

Rubinstein, Danny. "The Area Is Open to Rakah Activists." *Davar*, March 31, 1974.

Schiff, Zeev. "If I Were an Arab." *Haaretz*, April 4, 1961.

———. "Lack of Coordination among Agencies." *Haaretz*, April 23, 1976.

———. "The Problem of the Arab Minority and Its Relationship to the State." *Temurot*, nos. 1–2 (November 1960): 9–11.

Shidlovsky, Binyamin. "Changes in the Development of the Arab Village in Israel." *Hamizrah Hechadash* 15, nos. 1–2 (1965): 25–37.

Shimoni, Yaacov. "The Arabs of the Land of Israel: Pride and Catastrophe." *Molad* 3, no. 15 (June 1949): 150–156.

Spiegel, Gideon. "We Did Not Come in Order to Be Absorbed by the Inhabitants of This Area." *Ramzor* (March 1967).

Stendel, Ori. "Rakah Tries to Seize a Decisive Position in the Arab Street." *Haaretz*, January 31, 1976.

Waschitz, Yosef. "Changes in the Life of Israel's Arabs." *Hamizrah Hechadash* 1, no. 4 (July 1950): 257–264.

Yaari, Ehud. "Dahaf Survey of Israeli Arabs." *Davar*, September 22, 1968.

Yinnon, Avraham. "Some Central Themes of the Literature of Israeli Arabs." *Hamizrah Hechadash*, 15, no. 1 (1965): 57–84.

Dissertations

Abu-Ghosh, Subhi. "The Politics of an Arab Village in Israel." Princeton University, Department of Political Science, 1965.

Bitan-Buttenwieser, Arie. "Changes in Settlement and Land Use in Eastern Lower Galilee from the Beginning of the 19th Century until the Present Day." Hebrew University, 1969. (Hebrew)

Geffner, Ellen Joyce Kubersky. "Attitudes of Arab Editorialists in Israel, 1948–67: An Analysis of AL-ITTIHAD, AL-MIRSAD, and AL-YAWM." University of Michigan, Department of Near Eastern Language and Literature, 1973.

Geraisy, Sami Farah. "Arab Village Youth in Jewish Urban Centers: A Study of Youth from Um el Fahm Working in Tel Aviv Metropolitan Area." Brandeis University, Department of Sociology, 1971.

Karsel, Gidon. "Kiryat-Jureish: Dynamics of the Urbanization of an Israeli-Arab Community." Tel Aviv University, Department of Anthropology, 1972. (Hebrew)

Nakhleh, Khalil. "Shifting Patterns of Conflict in Selected Arab Villages in Israel." Indiana University, Department of Anthropology, 1973.

Robins, Edward Alan. "Pluralism in Israel: Relations between Arabs and Jews." Tulane University, Department of Anthropology, 1972.

Smooha, Sammy. "Pluralism: A Study of Intergroup Relations in Israel." University of California, Los Angeles, Department of Sociology, 1973.

Sussman, Zvi. "The Policy of the Histadrut with Regard to Wage Differentials: A Study of the Impact of Egalitarian Ideology and Arab Labour on Jewish Wages in Palestine." Hebrew University, 1969.

Research Monographs, Reprints, and Unpublished Papers

Abu-Tama, Jalal. "The Arabs in Israel and the Elections to Local Authorities." Seminar Paper, Bar-Ilan University, Department of Political Science, 1972. (Hebrew)

American Zionist Youth Foundation. *Zionism: Israel—Vision and Realization.* New York: Background Papers, 1970.

Baer, Gabriel. "The Economic and Social Position of the Village Mukhtar in Palestine." Paper presented at International Conference on the Palestinians and the Middle East Conflict, University of Haifa, April 5–8, 1976.

Cohen, Erik. *Integration vs. Separation in the Planning of a Mixed Jewish-Arab City in Israel.* Jerusalem: Levi Eshkol Institute for Economic, Social, and Political Research, 1973.

Friendly, Alfred. *Israel's Oriental Immigrants and Druzes.* Minority Rights Group Report, no. 12. London: Expedite Multi Print Ltd., 1972.

Gutman, Eliahu, Haim Klaf, and Shulamith Levi. *The Histadrut and Its Activities in the Arab Sector: Research on the Status, Opinions and Behavior of Arab Villagers in Israel.* Jerusalem: Israel Institute for Applied Social Research, 1971. (Hebrew)

Harari, Yechiel, ed. *The Arabs in Israel: Facts and Figures.* Arab and Afro-Asian Monograph Series, no. 4. Givat Haviva: Center for Arab and Afro-Asian Studies, 1974.

———. *The Arabs in Israel—1974.* Givat Haviva: Center for Arab and Afro-Asian Studies, 1974. (Hebrew)

————. *The Arabs in Israel—1976.* Givat Haviva: Center for Arab and Afro-Asian Studies, 1976. (Hebrew)

————. *Arabs in Israel in Numbers, 1971.* Arab and Afro-Asian Monograph Series, no. 10. Givat Haviva: Center for Arab and Afro-Asian Studies, July 1972. (Hebrew)

Nino, Micah. *The Situation of Minorities and of Christian Communities under Israeli Jurisdiction.* Reprinted from *International Problems* (Journal of the Israeli Institute for the Study of International Affairs) 11, nos. 3–4 (December 1972).

Rekhess, Eli. *Arabs in Israel and the Land Expropriations in the Galilee: Background, Events, and Implications.* Shiloah Institute for Middle Eastern and African Studies Series, no. 53. Tel Aviv: 1977. (Hebrew)

————. *A Survey of Israeli-Arab Graduates from Institutions of Higher Learning in Israel (1961–1971).* Shiloah Institute for Middle Eastern and African Studies Series. Jerusalem: American Jewish Committee, 1974.

Shamir, G. "The Establishment of the 'Military Government' over the Arab Population during the War of Independence." Seminar paper, Tel Aviv University, Department of History, 1973. (Hebrew)

Smooha, Sammy. "Control of Minorities in Israel and Northern Ireland." Paper presented at the Ninth World Congress of Sociology in Uppsala, August 1978.

Stendel, Ori. *The Arab Minority in Israel.* Reprinted from *Israel Yearbook on Human Rights*, vol. 1. Tel Aviv University, Faculty of Law, 1971.

Stock, Ernest. *The Reconstitution of the Jewish Agency: A Political Analysis.* Reprinted from *American Jewish Yearbook*, vol. 73 (1972).

Zarhi, Shaul, and A. Achiezra. *The Economic Conditions of the Arab Minority in Israel.* Arab and Afro-Asian Monograph Series, no. 1. Givat Haviva: Center for Arab and Afro-Asian Studies, 1963.

Government Publications and Documents

GREAT BRITAIN

Loftus, P. J. *National Income of Palestine, 1944.* Palestine: Government Printer, no. 5 of 1946.

Palestine Royal Commission Report. London: H. M. Stationery Office, Command Paper 5479, 1937.

ISRAEL

Aron, Y., and S. Molcho. *Trends in Agriculture in Two Arab Villages (1948–1970).* Ministry of Agriculture, 1971.

Burg, Yosef. *The Activities of the Ministry of the Interior: Report by the Minister of the Interior for the Fiscal Year 1973/1974.* Ministry of the Interior, 1973.

Central Bureau of Statistics. *Labor Force Survey.* (Annual)

———. *Statistical Abstract of Israel.* (Annual)

Comptroller's Report, no. 22, 1972. (Hebrew)

Eban, Aubrey S. (Abba). *Israel: The Case for Admission to the United Nations.* An address delivered before the Ad Hoc Political Committee of the United Nations, May 5, 1949.

Israel Government Year Book. (Annual)

Israel Information Center, Jerusalem. "Basic Principles of the Government's Programme." Information Briefing 24, 1974.

———. *Facts about Israel.* 1978.

———. "Minorities in Israel." Information Briefing 9, 1973.

———. *The New Plan for the Development of the Galilee,* no. 51. January 1976. (Hebrew)

Israel Office of Information, New York. *The Arabs in Israel.* 1952, 1955.

Laws of the State of Israel: Authorized Translation from the Hebrew.

Ministry of Finance. *Israel: Investors Manual.* Jerusalem, 1973, 1974, 1975.

Ministry of Foreign Affairs. *The Arabs in Israel.* 1958, 1961.

———. *Review of the Hebrew Press.* Press and Information Division, November 1948–March 1949.

Ministry of Information. *Facts about Israel.* 1974, 1975.

———. *Minorities in Israel.* 1973.

Ministry of the Interior. *Arab Local Councils in Israel.* (Annual until 1967)

———. *Elections for Eight Local Authorities in the Arab Sector: 1971, 1972.* June 1972. (Hebrew)

———. *Elections to Local Authorities in the Arab Sector—1969.* Local Government Division, Minorities Department. Jerusalem, 1969.

Ministry of Labor. *Atlas of Israel.* Amsterdam: Jerusalem and Elsevier Publishing Co., 1970.

Ministry of Religious Affairs. *Christian News from Israel.* (Monthly)

Proceedings of the Knesset (Divrei Haknesset). (Hebrew)

Shammash, Yehezkel. *Minority Groups in Israel.* Jerusalem: Office of the Adviser to the Prime Minister on Arab Affairs, 1970.

Sharef, Zeev. *On the Activities of the Ministry of Housing: Report to the Knesset by the Minister of Housing.* Jerusalem: Ministry of Housing, June 28, 1971. (Hebrew)

Stendel, Ori. *Israeli Arabs: Trends and Developments.* Jerusalem: Ministry of Education and Culture, n.d. (approx. 1975). (Hebrew)

Weigert, Gideon. *The Arabs of Israel.* Ministry of Foreign Affairs, n.d.

Official Publications of Nongovernmental Organizations

ARAB INFORMATION CENTER

Hadawi, Sami. *Israel and the Arab Minority.* Information Paper No. 7. New York: July 1959.

ARAB-JEWISH ASSOCIATION TO PROMOTE FRATERNITY AND PEACE

Shefi Advertising, ed. *Arab-Jewish Association to Promote Fraternity and Peace.* Haifa, 1966.

ECUMENICAL THEOLOGICAL RESEARCH FRATERNITY IN ISRAEL

Christians in Israel and the Yom Kippur War. Jerusalem, 1974.

HISTADRUT

Harel, A., et al. *The Conclusions of the Committee Concerning the Activities of the Histadrut in the Arab Sector.* Tel Aviv: Vaad Hapoel, October 1976. (Hebrew)

Histadrut Agricultural Center. *The Agricultural Histadrut and Its Activities* (Report of the Agricultural Center to the Twelfth Committee). Tel Aviv, 1974. (Hebrew)

Histadrut Arab Department. *The Histadrut's Arab Members.* Tel Aviv, 1969.

JEWISH AGENCY

Berger, L., ed. *Immigration and Israel's Survival.* Tel Aviv: Office for Economic and Social Research, 1975. (Annual)

The Executive of the Jewish Agency. *Memo, Re: Jewish Agency Investments in Companies.* Jerusalem, April 1972. (Mimeographed)

The Jewish Agency for Israel. *25 Years of Partnership, 1948–1973.* Jerusalem: Carta, 1973.

The Jewish Agency for Israel, Finance Department. *Proposed Budget for the Year 1973/1974*. Jerusalem, January 1973.
The Jewish Case: Before the Anglo-American Committee of Inquiry on Palestine as Presented by the Jewish Agency for Palestine. Jerusalem, 1947.

JEWISH NATIONAL FUND

The Blue Box That Keeps Israel Green. New York: JNF, 1978.
Jewish National Fund Yearbook. New York, 1976.

LABOR ZIONIST MOVEMENT

Toledano, Shmuel. *The Israeli Arabs—Achievements and Perplexities*. Tel Aviv, 1974.

UNITED NATIONS

————. *Assistance to Palestine Refugees*. Interim Report of the Director of the UNRWA for Palestinian Refugees in the Near East. GA OR 5th Session, Supplement No. 19. New York, 1951.
————. *Progress Report of the United Nations Mediator on Palestine*. GA OR 3rd Session, Supplement No. 11 (A/648), 1948.
United Nations Conciliation Commission for Palestine. *General Progress Report and Supplementary Report, December 11, 1949—October 23, 1950*. GA OR 5th Session, Supplement No. 19.
United Nations Special Committee on Palestine (UNSCOP). *Report to the General Assembly*. 1947.

Reference Books, Newspapers, and News Digests

REFERENCE BOOKS

American Jewish Year Book. Philadelphia: Jewish Publication Society of America. (Annual)
Encyclopaedia Judaica. Jerusalem: Keter Publishing House, 1974.
Palestine Yearbook and Israel Annual, vols. 1–4. Washington, D.C.: Zionist Organization of America, 1945–1949.
Who's Who in Israel. Tel Aviv: Bronfman and Cohen, Publishers. (Annual)

NEWSPAPERS

Al-Hamishmar. Official organ of Mapam; daily.

Al-Ittihad. Official Arabic language organ of Rakah; daily.

Davar. Official organ of the Histadrut; daily.

Jerusalem Post. Semi-official English language daily; previously the *Palestine Post.*

Jerusalem Post Weekly. Overseas edition of the *Jerusalem Post.*

Maariv. Mass circulation; daily.

Yediot Acharonot. Mass circulation; daily.

Zoo Haderech. Official organ of the New Israel Communist Party, Rakah; published twice weekly.

NEWS DIGESTS

Israleft: Biweekly News Service. Jerusalem.

Jewish Telegraphic Agency: Daily News Digest and Weekly Summary. New York.

Summary of World Broadcasts: The Middle East and Africa. Reading, England: British Broadcasting Corporation.

SWASIA. Washington, D.C.

Identification of Interviewees

Abu-Tama, Jalal. Arab youth leader and chairman (1976) of the local council of Baka el-Gharbiyeh (a large Arab village in the Little Triangle).

Abu-Nasr. Prominent Nazareth businessman.

Alpeleg, Zvi. Military governor in various regions, including the Little Triangle from 1948 to 1956.

Bayadsi, Ibrahim. Communist member of Baka el-Gharbiyeh's local council (1974).

Bayadsi, Mahmoud. Mayor of Baka el-Gharbiyeh (1974).

Beeri, Eliezer. Director of the Arab Department of the Ministry of Labor in the early 1950's.

Cohen, Yaacov. Director of the Histadrut Arab Department.

Dror. Official of the Israel Land Administration.

Efron, Yitzhak. Official of the Jewish National Fund.

Feinstein, Akiva. Director of the Arab Department of the Ministry of Housing.

Flapan, Simcha. Editor of *New Outlook*; director of Mapam's Arab Department from 1954 to 1965.

Ginat, Yosef. Deputy to the adviser to the prime minister on Arab affairs.

Harari, Yechiel. Researcher at the Givat Haviva Institute for Arab and Afro-Asian Studies.

Kahan, Adam. Official spokesman of the Finance Department of the Jewish Agency.

Karkabi, Z. Communist Party organizer and member of Rakah's Central Committee.

Kassem, Kemal. Assistant adviser to the Minister of Industry and Commerce for the development of industry in the Arab sector.

Katz, Yoram. Representative of the adviser to the prime minister on Arab affairs for the northern region.

Khamis, Yusuf. Deputy director of the Histadrut Arab Department.

Khouri, Violet. Formerly chairman of the local council of Kfar Yasif (a large Arab village in western Galilee).

Kopelovitz, Emanuel. Senior official in the Arab Department of the Ministry of Education and Culture.

Landman, Shimon. Director of the Arab Department of the Ministry of the Interior.

Lichtman, Yosef. Coordinator of the Board of Directors of the Land Settlement Department of the Jewish Agency.

Linn, Amnon. Likud member of Knesset, formerly Director of Mapai's Arab Department.

Mansour, Attalah. Prominent Arab journalist who writes mainly for *Haaretz*.

Masalha, Nawaf. Director for Arab Youth in the Arab Department of the Histadrut.

Meari, Mahmoud. A native of Sakhnin (a large Arab village in central Galilee) and a researcher at the Israel Institute for Applied Social Research.

Nasser el-Din, Amr. Druse political activist; when interviewed he was directing the Labor Party's Arab Department in Haifa. In 1977 he was elected to the Knesset on the Likud slate.

Oved, Abraham. Director of the Labor Party's Arab Branch, eastern Galilee.

Palmon, Yehoshua. Israel's first adviser to the prime minister on Arab affairs.

Porath, Shmuel. Director of the Information Center—Arab Branch.

Rashdi, Sasoon. District officer for western Galilee in the Arab Department of the Ministry of the Interior.

Ronen, Eliyahu. Director of Labor Party's Arab Branch, western Galilee.

Salim, Suleiman Mohammed. Communist Party organizer in the central Galilean Arab village of Deir Hana.

Schwartz, Aga. Director of the Arab Department of the (now defunct) Ministry of Development.

Thon, Uri. Long-time adviser on Arab affairs to Yigal Allon in the latter's capacity as deputy prime minister and as minister of education and culture. When interviewed Mr. Thon was serving as director of the Arab Department of the Ministry of Education.

Tichon, Dan. Official in the Ministry of Commerce and Industry with experience in the Arab sector.

Tuma, Emile. Editor of *al-Ittihad*, Rakah's Arabic newspaper.

Verben, Yoshua. Military governor of the Ashkelon area in 1950, the Negev from 1951 to 1953, the Little Triangle from 1953 to 1956, and the Galilee from 1956 to 1962.

Zechariah, David. Chief of the Labor Party's Arab Department; in charge of the party's campaign in the Arab sector in 1973.

Zilke, Morris. Official in the Youth and Hechalutz Department of the Jewish Agency, with experience in the Arab Department of the Ministry of Education and in other agencies responsible for Arab affairs.

Index